INDEX

TO

UNITED STATES CENSUS *of* GEORGIA

FOR

1820

Dedicated
With
Love and Appreciation
to
Lilla Mills Hawes

INDEX

TO

UNITED STATES CENSUS *of* GEORGIA

FOR

1820

Compiled Under the Auspices of

THE GEORGIA HISTORICAL SOCIETY

SECOND EDITION

With Additions and Corrections

By Mrs. Eugene A. Stanley

CLEARFIELD

First Edition
Savannah, 1963

Second Edition
with Additions and Corrections in the Text
By Mrs. Eugene A. Stanley
Genealogical Publishing Company
Baltimore, 1969

Library of Congress Catalog Card Number 79-90052

Reprinted for
Clearfield Company, Inc. by
Genealogical Publishing Co., Inc.
Baltimore, Maryland
1989, 1995, 2000

International Standard Book Number: 0-8063-0156-2

Made in the United States of America

INDEX TO THE 1820 UNITED STATES CENSUS OF GEORGIA

Foreword.

Even though Georgia was not the scene of major fighting in the War of 1812, the state suffered a grievous loss when the British burned Washington in 1814. Among the papers that were lost in the destruction of public buildings were the first three Federal censuses of Georgia—1790, 1800, and 1810. The 1820 Census, therefore, is the earliest extant for the state. Except for some tax records in the counties, which are incomplete, this is the earliest list of Georgia citizens.

Georgia is the only one of the original 13 states that has not yet had a census printed. This publication, therefore, will fill a long-felt need and the Georgia Historical Society takes pride in presenting it. It is not a complete copy of the census but an index to it, giving names of heads of families, followed by county of residence. If one wants to know the number of persons in a family and the age groups, they can be found by referring to the original schedule for that county. A brief outline of the formation of the 1820 counties and a map are included in this publication. For detailed information on all the counties, see *Georgia's Official Register, 1959-1960* (Atlanta, 1961) (or earlier editions) compiled by Mary Givens Bryan, Director, Department of Archives and History.

This index was made from microfilm copies of the original records in Washing, with the exception of Morgan County, which was copied from the original. It is arranged alphabetically by surnames, with given names also in alphabetical order. Titles such as Capt., Dr., Mrs., etc., have been disregarded in alphabetizing. Abbreviations of given names have been spelled out when there is no doubt, as William for Wm. In cases of doubt, the abbreviations remain. Jos. and Jas. were often indistinguishable. Mc is alphabetized as though spelled Mac. Phonetic spelling was often used so the reader must check all possible spellings of surnames. If there was more than one person of identical name in the same county, that name is followed by a numeral; e. g., Bailey, John (2) indicates two of the same name in the same county.

Some county schedules are so faded, poorly written, or torn that they are particularly hard to decipher. These are Chatham, Laurens, Pulaski, Hancock, Richmond, and Wilkes. Some names had to be omitted because of illegibility.

The work of indexing the 1820 Census for publication was done by a committee headed by Mrs. Eugene Anderson Stanley; sub-chairmen were Mrs. Olaf Otto and Mrs. Thomas Clark Johnson. Other members of the committee were Mrs. Earle F. Bidez, Miss Miriam Brown, the late Mrs. Margaret Davis Cate, Mrs. John L. DeGroen, Mrs. Fred C. Hack, Mrs. H. V. Hayden, Mrs. Bernard A. Lazard, Mrs. Raymond V. Malecki, Mrs. Antoinette J. Matthews of Atlanta, Mrs. Ralph B. Miller, Mrs. Robert P. Miller, Mrs. Walter A. Norton, and Mrs. J. B. Smith. The committee is greatly indebted to Mary Givens Bryan for her cooperation and advice, and to John E. Ladson, Jr. for making the publication possible.

Lilla Mills Hawes
Director Georgia Historical Society

From H. C. Carey and I. Lea, a complete historical, chronological and
geographical American Atlas.
(Philadelphia, 1823) in Georgia Historical Society Collection.

GEORGIA COUNTIES IN 1820

Name	Date Formed	Parent County	County Seat
Appling	1818	Creek cessions	Baxley
Baldwin	1803	Creek cessions	Milledgeville
Bryan	1793	Chatham	Pembroke
Bulloch	1796	Bryan & Screven	Statesboro
Burke	1777	Creek cession (as Parish St. George)	Waynesboro
Camden	1777	Creek cession (as parishes: St. Thomas & St. Mary)	Woodbine
Chatham	1777	Creek cession (St. Philip & Christ Church Parishes)	Savannah
Clarke	1801	Jackson	Athens
Columbia	1790	Richmond	Appling
Early	1818	Creek cession	Blakely
Effingham	1777	Creek cession (as Parishes St. Philip & St. Matthew)	Springfield
Elbert	1790	Wilkes	Elberton
Emanuel	1812	Bulloch & Montgomery	Swainsboro
Franklin	1784	Cherokee cession *1820 census lost*	Carnesville
Glynn	1777	Creek cession (Parishes: St. David & St. Patrick)	Brunswick
Greene	1786	Washington	Greensboro
Gwinnett	1818	Cherokee and Creek cessions	Lawrenceville
Habersham	1818	Cherokee cessions	Clarkesville
Hall	1818	Cherokee cessions	Gainesville
Hancock	1793	Greene & Washington	Sparta
Irwin	1818	Creek cessions	Ocilla
Jackson	1796	Franklin	Jefferson
Jasper	1807	Baldwin	Monticello
Jefferson	1796	Burke & Warren	Louisville
Jones	1807	Baldwin	Gray
Laurens	1807	Wilkinson	Dublin
Liberty	1777	Creek cession (Par. St. John, St. Andrew, St. James)	Hinesville
Lincoln	1796	Wilkes	Lincolnton
McIntosh	1793	Liberty	Darien
Madison	1811	Clarke, Elbert, Franklin, Jackson, Oglethorpe	Danielsville
Montgomery	1793	Washington	Mount Vernon
Morgan	1807	Baldwin	Madison
Oglethorpe	1793	Wilkes	Lexington
Pulaski	1808	Laurens	Hawkinsvile
Putnam	1807	Baldwin	Eatonton
Rabun	1819	Cherokee cession *1820 Census lost*	Clayton
Richmond	1777	Creek cession (St. Pauls Parish)	Augusta
Screven	1793	Burke & Effingham	Sylvania
Tattnall	1801	Montgomery	Reidsville
Telfair	1807	Wilkinson	McRae
Twiggs	1809	Wilkinson *1820 census lost*	Jeffersonville
Walton	1818	Creek cession	Monroe
Warren	1793	Columbia, Hancock, Richmond, Wilkes	Warrenton
Washington	1784	Creek cession	Sandersville
Wayne	1803	Creek cession	Jesup
Wilkes	1777	Cherokee & Creek cessions	Washington
Wilkinson	1806	Creek cessions	Irwinton

Abbreviations in the original census are:

R. S.—presumablely Revolutionary Soldier   col.—colored
Jr., junr.—Junior   E., est.—Estate
Sr., senr.—Senior   M. C.—presumably Man or Color
Col.—Colonel   W. C.—presumably Woman of Color

Abbreviations added by the committee are:
    ind.—indecipherable, indistinct
    (?)—uncertain

ALPHABETICAL LIST OF NAMES

Arrangement: Surname, Given Name (County of Residence)

A

Abbett, Joseph (Jones)
  Josiah H. T. (Jones)
Abbitt, William (Warren)
Abbot, Barton (Gwinnett)
  Bennett (Appling)
  E. (Jasper)
  Eli (Habersham)
  George (Glynn)
  George (Jasper)
  James O. (Burke)
  Joel (Wilkes)
  John (Chatham)
  Thomas (Washington)
  William (Gwinnett)
  William W. (Laurens)
  Z. (Richmond)
Aberercrombie, Anderson
          (Hancock)
Abercrombie, Charles (Hancock)
  Edmund (Hancock)
  James (2) (Hall)
  John (Hall)
  John (Hancock)
  Leonard (Putnam)
  Martin (Hancock)
  Wyley (Putnam)
Aberheart, Jacob (Hall)
  John (Hall)
Abny, Hezekiah (Jackson)
Abraham, J. (Richmond)
Abrahams, Isaac (Glynn)
Abrcombie, James (Walton)
Achord, John, Sr. (Washington)
  John (Washington)
  Lewis (Chatham)
Acock, Rederick (Walton)
Acols, Zelph (Washington)
Acre, Mrs. Elizabeth (Greene)
  John (Greene)
Acridge, William (Jefferson)
Adair, Farmer (Morgan)
  Hiram (Morgan)
  James (Putnam)
  John F. (Morgan)
  Joseph A. (Jackson)
  Robert S. (Gwinnett)
  Walter (Habersham)
  William (Morgan)
Adams, (torn) (Gwinnett)
  (ind.) (Jackson)
  Abner (Washington)
  Arthur (Columbia)
  Baker (Pulaski)
  Benjamin (Laurens)
  Benjamin (Warren)
  Dancy, Jr. (Columbia)

Dancy, Sr. (Columbia)
David (Jasper)
David (Warren)
David E. (Chatham)
David I. (Emanuel)
Edward (2) (Jackson)
Farly (Columbia)
Gillisen (Walton)
Hanner (Walton)
Henry (Warren)
Henry, Jr. (Warren)
Hezekiah D. (Clarke)
Hopewell (Washington)
James (Elbert)
James B. (Elbert)
James M. (Morgan)
Jesse (Jackson)
John (Chatham)
John (Clarke)
John (Gwinnett)
John (Jackson)
John (Jones)
John (Walton)
John (Warren)
Jonathan (Putnam)
Joseph (Wilkes)
Kinchen (Columbia)
M. (Jasper)
Martin (Elbert)
Matthias (Montgomery)
Miles (Jefferson)
Milly (Jackson)
Nancy (Clarke)
Nancy (Morgan)
Noah (Burke)
Rheubon (Walton)
Richard (Habersham)
Richard (Hall)
Richard (Wilkes)
Richard (M. C.) (Wilkes)
Richard C. (Elbert)
Robert (Hancock)
S. & D. E. (Chatham)
Samuel (Elbert)
Susana (Jackson)
Thomas (Chatham)
Thomas (Elbert)
Thomas (Jackson)
Thomas (Pulaski)
Thomas F. (Elbert)
William (Chatham)
William (Clarke)
William (Columbia)
William (Elbert)
William (Gwinnett)
William (Jackson)
William A. (Morgan)

William E. (Putnam)
Williby (Appling)
Adamson, Greenberry (Morgan)
  William C. (Morgan)
Adare, Bozeman (Madison)
  Whitmill H. (Madison)
  William (Madison)
Adcock, Edmund (2) (Morgan)
  John (Putnam)
  John E. (Morgan)
Addams, Alexander (Wilkinson)
  David (2) (Wilkinson)
  Sarah, Jr. (Wilkinson)
  Sarah, Sr. (Wilkinson)
Addison, Christopher (Gwinnett)
  Mark (Liberty)
Aden, William (Jones)
Aderson, Joseph (Bulloch)
Adkins, Aron (Warren)
  James (Greene)
  John (Greene)
  John (Warren)
  Joseph (Washington)
  Sophia (Wilkinson)
Adkinson, Benjamin (Laurens)
  J. (ind.) (Laurens)
  James (Laurens)
  Lucy (Jones)
  Mary (Oglethorpe)
  Ranson (Emanuel)
Adley, Henry (Warren)
Adolph, Henry (Jones)
Adridge, William (Baldwin)
Aera, Sterling (2) (Warren)
Aerey, Williams (Warren)
Agnew, John (Gwinnett)
Agy, Humphrey, Jr. (Wilkes)
  Humphrey, Sr. (Wilkes)
Aidmore, Nazareth
          (Montgomery)
Aiken, F. (Chatham)
  Thomas (Morgan)
Aikin, Mrs. (Chatham)
  Bartlett (Morgan)
  James (2) (Morgan)
  John (Morgan)
  Jon (Morgan)
Aikins, William (Morgan)
Aken, Peter (Madison)
  Thomas (Elbert)
Akers, Mary (Greene)
Akien, James (Walton)
Akin, Benjamon (Putnam)
  Elizabeth (Clarke)
  James S. (Clarke)
  William (Clarke)
  William (Putnam)

(1)

Akins, Francis (Bulloch)
Hill (Walton)
James (Jackson)
James (Warren)
Lewis (Bulloch)
Nancy (Greene)
Robert (Wilkes)
Samuel (Camden)
Thomas (Jackson)
William (Warren)
Winifred (Warren)
Akridge, Ezekiel (Clarke)
Greenbery (Montgomery)
John (Washington)
Levi (Jackson)
Alawine, (?) David (Jasper)
Alberson, William (Hall)
Albert, John (Wilkes)
William (Laurens)
William (Wilkes)
Albright, Joseph (Madison)
William (Madison)
Albriton, Enock (Wilkinson)
John T. (Wilkinson)
Albritton, Asa (Washington)
Elijah (Washington)
Elizabeth (Hancock)
Henry (Laurens)
James (Columbia)
Mrs. Martha (Columbia)
Mathew (Bulloch)
Matthew (Burke)
Peter (Washington)
Thomas (Bryan)
Zacheriah (Washington)
Alday, Benjamin (Wilkinson)
Alderman, David (Bulloch)
Samuel (Bulloch)
Thomas (Screven)
William (Bulloch)
Aldridge, Aaron (Warren)
Nathan (Morgan)
Richard (Wilkes)
Thomas B. (Baldwin)
Aleherson, Benjamin (Wilkes)
Aleran, John (Baldwin)
Ales, Willie (Baldwin)
Alexander, Adam (2) (Jasper)
Allen (Elbert)
Arthur (Habersham)
Asa (Jones)
Asa C. (Warren)
Benjamin (Tattnall)
David (Jefferson)
Edmond (Elbert)
George (Elbert)
George (Jasper)
Hugh (Jefferson)
Isaac (Habersham)
James (Bryan)

James (Columbia)
James (Madison)
James W. (Early)
John (Bryan)
John (Clarke)
John (Elbert)
John H. (Jefferson)
Joseph (Wilkes)
Mary (Elbert)
Matthew (Habersham)
Mordica (Elbert)
Moses (Warren)
Nancy (Elbert)
Nathanael G. (Greene)
Peter (Elbert)
Thomas (Morgan)
Traver (Wilkes)
Uriah (Putnam)
Mrs. W. (Liberty)
William (Elbert)
William (Greene)
William (Hall)
Alexander, William (Putnam)
William (Washington)
Willis (Elbert)
Alford, Assoneth (Hancock)
Benom (Walton)
Bias (Jefferson)
Britton (Walton)
Colton (Greene)
Halcut (Morgan)
Haywood (Burke)
Henry (Putnam)
I. (Jasper)
Jacob (2) (Hancock)
Jason (Jefferson)
Julius, Sr. (Greene)
Ladwick (Greene)
Lodwink (Clarke)
Olven (Hancock)
Owen (Hancock)
William (Chatham)
William, Jr. (Hancock)
William, Sr. (Hancock)
Wyly (Hancock)
Zadoc (Morgan)
Alfred, Goodedge (Jones)
Job (Jones)
Alfriend, Edward D. (Greene)
Algor, Nahum (Chatham)
Algood, John (Elbert)
John Y. (Elbert)
Alice, Robert G. (Wilkes)
Allan, James (Burke)
Allber, (?) Peter (Chatham)
Allcock. Mary (Tattnall)
Siddy (Washington)
Allday, John P. (Burke)
Josiah (Burke)
Nancy (Burke)
Peter (Burke)

Allen, (ind.) (2) (Laurens)
A. M. (Burke)
Alexander (Morgan)
Andrew (Warren)
Mrs. Ann (Greene)
Ann (Richmond)
Benjamin (Jones)
Benjamin (Warren)
Berry (Putnam)
Beverly ·(Elbert)
Beverly (Jackson)
Boler (Jones)
Bowsen (Irwin)
Cason (Laurens)
Charles (Burke)
Charles (Hancock)
Charles (2) (Morgan)
Charles (Washington)
Churchil (Putnam)
Clement (Greene)
Clocy (Putnam)
Cuzzy (Baldwin)
David (Morgan)
David (Wilkinson)
Dennis (Jasper)
Drury (Greene)
Edmond (Elbert)
Elijah Johnson (Warren)
Elizabeth C. (Columbia)
Elizabeth J. (Morgan)
Ephraim (Elbert)
Frances T. (Columbia)
G. (Richmond)
George (Hancock)
George W. (Clarke)
Gideon (Warren)
Harris (Baldwin)
Henry (Oglethorpe)
Herry (Irwin)
Howard (Oglethorpe)
Hugh (Burke)
Ira (Hancock)
James (Burke)
James (Gwinnett)
James (Habersham)
James (Hancock)
James (Pulaski)
James (Putnam)
Jeremiah (Walton)
Jesse (Putnam)
Job (Warren)
John (Baldwin)
John (Bulloch)
John (Burke)
John (Gwinnett)
John (Jones)
John R. (Greene)
John T. (Columbia)
John W. (Elbert)
Jordin (Putnam)

(2)

Allen, Joseph (Elbert)
Joseph (Jefferson)
Mary (Morgan)
Milly (Jones)
Nat. B. (Madison)
Nate (Morgan)
Nathaniel (Greene)
Phillip (Clarke)
Polly (Jones)
Reuben (Jones)
Reuben (2) (Morgan)
Richard (2) (Jones)
Richard (Richmond)
Robert (2) (Burke)
Robert (Greene)
Robert (Richmond)
Robert T. (Columbia)
Samuel (Elbert)
Samuel (Warren)
Sarah (Burke)
Sarah (Hancock)
Sherrard (Pulaski)
Singleton (Elbert)
Stephen (Oglethorpe)
Susan (Washington)
Tanney (Madison)
Thomas (Burke)
Thomas (Elbert)
W. (Richmond)
Welcome (Richmond)
William (2) (Elbert)
William (Greene)
William (Jackson)
William (Jasper)
William (2) (Jones)
William (Morgan)
William (Pulaski)
William (2) (Putnam)
William F. (Putnam)
Woodson (Clarke)
Young (Jefferson)
Young D. (Greene)
Alley, Jas. (Baldwin)
Alleygood, Hillery (Laurens)
Alford, William (Putnam)
Allfred, Patin (Jones)
Allgood, Edward (Elbert)
Peter (Elbert)
Samuel (Elbert)
William, Jr. (Elbert)
William, Sr. (Elbert)
Allin, David (Irwin)
Dennis (Irwin)
Isaac (Irwin)
James (Irwin)
John (Camden)
William (Oglethorpe)
Allinder, Thomas (Emanuel)
Allington, Rice (Richmond)
Allison, Alexander (Habersham)
Christiana (Oglethorpe)

David (Habersham)
Elias (Wilkes)
Jared E. (Wilkes)
John (Morgan)
John (Wilkes)
Rebecca (Wilkes)
Allman, John (Burke)
William (Burke)
Allmand, John (Madison)
Allowine, Elijah (Jasper)
Allred, Aaron (Hall)
Elias (Hall)
Allum, Nancy (Baldwin)
Allums, Edmond (Putnam)
John (2) (Putnam)
William (Putnam)
Almon, Isaac (Elbert)
John (Elbert)
Thomas (Elbert)
Usery (Elbert)
Almy, Mrs. (Chatham)
Alredd, John (Hall)
Alridge, Henry (Hall)
Alsabrook, (ind.) (Jones)
Alsabrooks, Amos (Jones)
Asa (Jones)
James (Jones)
Landon (Jones)
Alsinette, Andrew (Telfair)
Alsobrook, Claburn (Tattnall)
Alston, Gulley (Elbert)
James (Montgomery)
John (Elbert)
John D. (Montgomery)
Robert W. (Hancock)
William H. (Elbert)
Alsworthy, James (Hancock)
Altimus, (?) Gorman (Chatham)
Altman, Frances (Wayne)
James (Wayne)
Alwarter, Elihu (Camden)
Ambers, Warren (Jasper)
Amberson, Matthew (Morgan)
Ambross, David (Effingham)
Amerson, Britian (Hancock)
Ames, B. (Richmond)
Thomas (Oglethorpe)
Amey, John (Greene)
Amilt (?), Peter (Screven)
Amison, Abram (Washington)
Cullin (Washington)
Eli (Washington)
Jessee (Washington)
Josiah (Washington)
Warren (Washington)
William (2) Washington
Ammons, Elizabeth (Wayne)
Jacob (Wilkes)
John (Wayne)
Sterling (Morgan)
Uriah E. (Morgan)

Amons, Jonathon (Morgan)
Amos, George (Hancock)
James (Jones)
Mrs. Lenna (Hancock)
Mauldon (Jones)
William (Warren)
Amoson, Nathan (Warren)
Anann, Asa (Elbert)
Jeremiah (Elbert)
Anciaux, Lydia (Bulloch)
Anderson (ind.), (Pulaski)
Abija (Baldwin)
Amos (Tattnall)
Ann (Clarke)
Augustus H. (Burke)
Brice (Tattnall)
Carolus (Burke)
Charles (Walton)
David (Emanuel)
David (Gwinnett)
David (Jasper)
Dover (Habersham)
Eleazor (Jefferson)
Elijah (Jefferson)
Elijah (Putnam)
Elisha (2) (Burke)
Elisha Jr. (Burke)
George (2) (Chatham)
George (Elbert)
Gilbert (Wilkes)
Hardy (Emanuel)
Hezekiah (Screven)
Henry (Irwin)
I. L. (Jasper)
J. L. (Richmond)
Jacob (Madison)
James (Burke)
James (Effingham)
James (2) (Elbert)
James (Greene)
James (Jefferson)
James (Madison)
James (Screven)
James (Washington)
James (2) (Wilkes)
John (Bulloch)
John (Elbert)
John (Habersham)
John (Richmond)
John (Tattnall)
John (Wilkes)
John B. (Warren)
John C. (Putnam)
John S. (Madison)
Joseph (Emanuel)
Joseph (Screven)
Lavina (Jefferson)
Lewis (Tattnall)
Mary (Glynn)
Mary (Laurens)
Mourning (Putnam)

Anderson, Nancy (Wilkes)
Reuben (Habersham)
Robert (Washington)
Salley (Madison)
Shadrach (Washington)
Stephen (Morgan)
Susannah (Jefferson)
Terrel (Madison)
Thomas (Greene)
Thomas (2) (Wilkes)
Thos. W. (Chatham)
Uriah (Emanuel)
Vinson (Tattnall)
Wm. (Baldwin)
Wm. (2) (Burke)
William (Greene)
William (Gwinnett)
William (Jackson)
William (Liberty)
William (Morgan)
William (Wilkes)
William R. (Jackson)
Andrew, Benjamin (2) (Elbert)
Burly (Elbert)
John (Oglethorpe)
Samuel L. (Jefferson)
Andrews, Adams (Greene)
Allen (Warren)
David (2) (Putnam)
Green (Hancock)
Harvy (Burke)
J. P. (Richmond)
James (Richmond)
John (Burke)
John (Hancock)
John (Jones)
John (Screven)
Joseph (Burke)
Joseph (Liberty)
Mark (Hancock)
Mark (Oglethorpe)
Mary (Warren)
Mary (Wilkes)
Micajah (Liberty)
Nancy (Hancock)
Nancy (Oglethorpe)
Nancy (Warren)
Olven (Gwinnett)
R. (Richmond)
Richard (Warren)
Robert (Hancock)
William (Gwinnett)
William (Oglethorpe)
William, Jr. (Oglethorpe)
William (Screven)
William (Warren)
William (Wilkes)
Wyatt (Oglethorpe)
Angel, Martin (Chatham)
Angle, John (Walton)
Anglen, John (Putnam)

William (Putnam)
Anglin, David (Morgan)
Henry (2) (Jackson)
James (Jackson)
John (Clarke)
John (Oglethorpe)
Peter (2) (Jackson)
Thomas (Oglethorpe)
William, Jr. (Putnam)
Anow, John (Walton)
Ansley, Mrs. (Chatham)
Abel (Warren)
Amy (Lincoln)
Gilbert (Jones)
J. (Richmond)
James (Warren)
Jesse (Warren)
John (Warren)
Joseph (Warren)
Samuel (Warren)
Thomas (Warren)
William (Warren)
Anthony, Ansalm (Morgan)
Bowling (Wilkes)
Emanuel (Liberty)
Isaac (Wilkes)
James (Jones)
Mark (Lincoln)
Micajah (Elbert)
Micajah (Lincoln)
Middleton (Oglethorpe)
Antoine, Mrs. (Chatham)
Antony, Josh. (Jasper)
Appleby, James (Jackson)
William (Jackson)
Applewhite, Robert (Morgan)
William (Oglethorpe)
Appling, Mrs. Elinor (Columbia)
Joel (Wilkes)
Otho H. (Clarke)
Mrs. Rebecca (Columbia)
Walter A. (Columbia)
William (Clarke)
Archer, Alexander (Burke)
Frederick (Hancock)
Hugh (Chatham)
J. N. (Tattnall)
Thomas (Tattnall)
William (Hancock)
Archey, James (Screven)
Ard, Easter (Pulaski)
John (Pulaski)
Neal (Pulaski)
Ardis, John (Putnam)
Arey, John (Jones)
Argo, Nimrod (Putnam)
Arington, Ezekiel (Jefferson)
Henry (Jefferson)
James (Jefferson)
John (2) (Jefferson)
Rebecca (Jefferson)

Samuel (Morgan)
Silas (Jefferson)
Armand, J. F. (?) (Chatham)
John (Chatham)
Armer, Robert (Hall)
Armestead, John (Greene)
Armor, Andrew (Jackson)
William (Jackson)
Armour, Mrs. (Chatham)
John (Greene)
Robert (Wilkes)
William (Greene)
Armstrong, Alexander,
(Washington)
Alexander, Sr. (Washington)
Edward (Washington)
Hugh (Warren)
James (Greene)
James (Hall)
James (Warren)
James (Washington)
James (Wilkes)
Jessee (Washington)
John (Pulaski)
Ludwall (Pulaski)
Samuel (Hall)
Wiley (Baldwin)
William (Glynn)
William (Jasper)
Arnet, John (Telfair)
John (Wilkes)
Samuel (Wilkes)
Arnett, Robert (Screven)
William (Screven)
William (Wilkes)
Arnette, Timothy (Screven)
Arnold, (ind.) (Montgomery)
Allen (Wilkes)
Ambrose (Washington)
Berry (Oglethorpe)
C. (Richmond)
C. W. (Richmond)
Charles (Oglethorpe)
Davis (Elbert)
Fielding (Morgan)
George (Montgomery)
James (Elbert)
James (Morgan)
James (Washington)
James (Wilkes)
John (2) (Hancock)
John (Oglethorpe)
Jonathan (Richmond)
Joseph (Oglethorpe)
Moses (Wilkes)
Priscilla (Wilkes)
Reason (Hancock)
S. W. (Chatham)
Stephen (Jackson)
Stephen (Oglethorpe)
Stephen (Wilkes)

(4)

Arnold, Thomas (Washington)
William (Chatham)
William (Clarke)
William (Hancock)
William, Sr. (Hancock)
William, Sr. (Oglethorpe)
William (Putnam)
William (Telfair)
William (2) (Washington)
William P. (Madison)
William W. (Oglethorpe)
Wiot (Burke)
Arnsdorff, John (?)
(Effingham)
Solomon (Effingham)
Arnstoff, Christian (Effingham)
Aron, John (Jones)
Arrant, Cornelius (Lincoln)
John (Lincoln)
Nimrod (Lincoln)
Peter (Lincoln)
Peter, Jr. (Lincoln)
William, Jr., (Lincoln)
William, Sr. (Lincoln)
Arrenton, Isaac (Washington)
Arrington, Catharin (Gwinnett)
Charles (Morgan)
Isham (Morgan)
James (Jefferson)
Arthur, Barnabas (Oglethorpe)
Barney (Habersham)
Caleb (Clarke)
Lewis (Habersham)
Louis (Jackson)
Mathew (Habersham)
Mathews, Sr. (Habersham)
William (Hall)
Asbury, Henry (Greene)
Jesse (Putnam)
Richard (Greene)
Asby, Thomas (Jones)
Ashterry, Jonathan (Burke)
Ashe, George (Chatham)
Ashely, Jessey (Wilkinson)
Asher, John (Putnam)
Robert (Putnam)
Ashfield, Frederick (Putnam)
Johnson (Putnam)
Ashley, Grantham (Telfair)
John (Hancock)
John (Putnam)
John (Telfair)
John (Wilkinson)
Lodawick (Telfair)
Nathaniel (Telfair)
Robert (Lincoln)
Thomas (Lincoln)
William (Lincoln)
William (Telfair)
Ashly, Robert (Wilkes)
William (Wilkes)

Ashmore, John (Liberty)
John (Wilkes)
Joseph (Liberty)
Peter (Lincoln)
Prate (?) (Jasper)
William (Jasper)
Ashworth, Elisha (Elbert)
John (Elbert)
Askew, (ind.), (2) (Laurens)
Mrs. (Richmond)
Henry (Wilkinson)
James (2) (Hancock)
John (2) (Hancock)
John (Jasper)
Joshua (Morgan)
Thomas (Chatham)
William (Hancock)
William (Jasper)
Askin, James (Putnam)
Josiah (Putnam)
Asolin, Thomas (Jones)
Aspingall, George (Richmond)
Aspinwall, Elijah (Chatham)
Asten, William L. (Greene)
Astin, Robert (Greene)
Atchinson, Charles (Warren)
Atcheson, J. A. (Jasper)
Atchison, John (Warren)
Atha, Mahala (Columbia)
Warren J. (Columbia)
Atkerson, Isaih (Chatham)
Atkins, Ica (Pulaski)
Joseph C. (Greene)
Lewis (Walton)
Robert (2) (Walton)
Thomas (Baldwin)
Atkinson, Abner (Hancock)
Alexander (Camden)
Ann (Camden)
Armstead (Greene)
Arthur C. (Clarke)
Burrel (Camden)
Cornelius (Jackson)
D. (Richmond)
Elbert (Hancock)
Francis (Pulaski)
Hiram (Pulaski)
James (Greene)
Lazarus (Greene)
Lemuel (Oglethorpe)
Lewis (Hancock)
Mary (Camden)
Nathan (Greene)
Robert R. (Burke)
Sarah (Burke)
Shadrack (Pulaski)
Thomas (Appling)
Thomas (Morgan)
Thomas (Pulaski)
William (Madison)
Attaway, David (Burke)

Elijah (Burke)
Harly (Burke)
James (Wilkinson)
Jesse (Burke)
Jesse, Sr. (Burke)
Joseph (Burke)
Joseph, Jr. (Burke)
Thomas (Warren)
Atwater, Elihu (Camden)
Atwell, Crecy (Richmond)
James (Richmond)
Atwood, Berry (Gwinnett)
Audinot, P. (Chatham)
Augley (ind.), (Pulaski)
Augur, Rebecca (Glynn)
Ausbon, John (Elbert)
Plesant (Elbert)
Aush, Jenerett (col.)
(McIntosh)
Austen, Fielder (Oglethorpe)
Joseph (Liberty)
Mary (Warren)
Austin, Charles (Walton)
Elizabeth (Liberty)
Ethelred (Walton)
Harris (Burke)
Herman (Habersham)
Isaac (Walton)
Jesse (Gwinnett)
John (Walton)
Nancy (Habersham)
Rachel (Habersham)
Sarah (McIntosh)
Walter (Greene)
William (2) (Jones)
Autrey, Absolem (Greene)
Alexander (Morgan)
Isaac (Morgan)
Jacob (Greene)
Jacob, Sr. (Greene)
John (Greene)
Runnels (Greene)
Autry, Isaac (Walton)
M. (Richmond)
Awtry, Jacob (Walton)
Avant, Ransom (Washington)
Avent, Isaiah (Washington)
Avent (?), William (Wilkinson)
Avera, Alexander (Warren)
John (Washington)
Patience (Washington)
Sally (Washington)
Samuel (Washington)
Sanders (Washington)
Thomas (Warren)
Averell, Thomas (Richmond)
Averet, Alexander (Richmond)
J. (Richmond)
Averett, Archer (Hancock)
Benjamin (Hancock)
Drury (Hancock)

Averitt, David (Putnam)
Avery, Archer (Columbia)
  Asa (Columbia)
  Jacob (Hall)
  John (Columbia)
  Moor (Wilkinson)
  William C. (Columbia)
Avrea, Arter (Putnam)
  Bradley (Putnam)
  Ingram (Putnam)
  John (Putnam)
  Needham (Putnam)
  Samuel (Putnam)
  William H. (Putnam)
  Zelphy (Putnam)
Avrey, Charles (Walton)
Awbrey, Thomas (Morgan)
  William (Morgan)
Awbry, Benjamin (Morgan)
  Hannah (Morgan)
Awtry, John (Walton)
Axom, Samuel I. (Liberty)
Aycock, Benjamin (Wilkinson)
  Burwell (Oglethorpe)
  Elias (Laurens)
  Joel (Oglethorpe)
  Jonathan (Oglethorpe)
  Presley (Wilkes)
  Richard (Oglethorpe)
  Seaborn (Wilkes)
  Zacriah (Oglethorpe)
Ayers, Abraham (Baldwin)
  William (Baldwin) *see below*
Ayres, Abram (Lincoln)
  Dread (Columbia)
  Jesse (Habersham)
  John (Columbia)
  John D. (Lincoln)
  Moses (Habersham)
  Thomas (Columbia)
  Thomas (Lincoln)
  Thomas G. (Hall)

B

Baar, David (Elbert)
Baas, Rebecca (Effingham)
Babb, William (Gwinnett)
  William (Baldwin)
Baber, William (Wilkes)
Bachelor, Archibald (Putnam)
  Jesse (Putnam)
Bachelott, Joseph (Camden)
Bachlot, Mrs. (Chatham)
Backus, John (Morgan)
  Thomas (Morgan)
Backler, Eugene (Chatham)
  John (Chatham)
Backley, Aaron (Tattnall)
  Jonathan (Effingham)
Bacon, Eugene (Liberty)
  J. B. (Tattnall)

Bagley, Benjamin (Appling)

John (Liberty)
John P. (Columbia)
Jonathan (Liberty)
Joseph (Liberty)
Lucy (Richmond)
Lydda (Jones)
Martha (Liberty)
Nathaniel (Tattnall)
Thomas (Liberty)
Thomas, Sr. (Liberty)
Thomas (Richmond)
Thomas W. (Liberty)
Thomas W. (Greene)
William H. (Jackson)
Baddy (?), Nathan (Jones)
Badger, Leven (Putnam)
Baduly, John (Burke)
Bagan, John (Jasper)
Bagby, James (Hancock)
  John (Walton)
  Joseph (Jackson)
Baget, Brury (Jones)
Bagger, David (McIntosh)
Bagget, Josiah (Emanuel)
  Andrew, (Jackson)
  Ervin (Walton)
  Wilie (Greene)
Baggitt, Uziel (Walton)
Baggot, Elias (Columbia)
  Jesse (Columbia)
Baggs, James (Chatham)
Bagley, Christopher (Effingham)
  Dorsan (Jones)
  Henry (Greene)
  Robert (Columbia)
  Thomas (Columbia)
  Thomas (Jones)
  William (Hancock)
  William (Richmond)
Bagly, Shadwick (Emanuel)
Bags, Ester C. (McIntosh)
Bagwell, Crawford (Gwinnett)
  Frederick (Gwinnett)
Bailey (ind.), (Camden)
  (ind.), (Chatham)
  Aaron (Chatham)
  Alexander (Warren)
  Azariah (Morgan)
  Caleb (Walton)
  Charity (Jones)
  David (Washington)
  Elias (Burke)
  Elizabeth (Morgan)
  Francis (Morgan)
  Green (Putnam)
  Henry (Oglethorpe)
  Henry I. (Oglethorpe)
  Isaac (Warren)
  Isham (Morgan)
  Jacob (Oglethorpe)
  James (2) (Burke)

James (3) (Oglethorpe)
James (Washington)
James (2) (Warren)
John (2) (Morgan)
John (2) (Washington)
John (Wilkes)
John A. (Clarke)
Jonathon (Oglethorpe)
Joseph (Walton)
Julian (Morgan)
Matthew (Warren)
Moses (Madison)
Nathaniel (Wilkes)
Ralph (Jackson)
Richmond (Jones)
Russell (Wilkes)
Samuel (Jackson)
Sally (Morgan)
Sarah (Jefferson)
Simon (Putnam)
Thomas (Jefferson)
Thomas (Warren)
William (Elbert)
William (Morgan)
Capt. Wm. (Oglethorpe)
William (Washington)
Zachariah (Warren)
Baillie, George (Chatham)
Baily, Francis (Jackson)
  John (Jackson)
  John, Sr. (Hancock)
  Mary (Baldwin)
  William (Jackson)
Bain, Robert (Morgan)
  William (McIntosh)
Bairfield, James (Jefferson)
  Jessey (Wilkinson)
Baisden, Ann B. (McIntosh)
  Joseph (Liberty)
Baites, John (Elbert)
Baker, Abner (Greene)
  Amos (Elbert)
  Archibald (Burke)
  Austin (Warren)
  Benjamin (Gwinnett)
  Bernard W. (Morgan)
  Blake (Washington)
  Calvin (Chatham)
  Charles (Wilkinson)
  Charlotte (Habersham)
  Christopher Sr. (Gwinnett)
  Dancy (Jasper)
  Edward B. (McIntosh)
  Edwin (Warren)
  Elijah (Elbert)
  Elijah (Liberty)
  Elizabeth (Richmond)
  Greene (Gwinnett)
  Henry (Hall)
  Hinley (Jasper)
  Honor (Gwinnett)

Baker, James (Bulloch)
James & Thos. (Liberty)
James S. (R. S.) (Liberty)
Jane (McIntosh)
Jeremiah (Liberty)
Jeremiah, Jr. (Montgomery)
Jeremiah, Sr. (Montgomery)
Jesse (Jasper)
Joel (Habersham)
John (Jones)
John (Washington)
John G. (Liberty)
Jonathon (Greene)
Jonathon (Lincoln)
Jonathon (Warren)
Jordon (Laurens)
Jordon (Walton)
Joseph (Jasper)
Josh (Jasper)
Joshua (Walton)
Martha (Warren)
Nancy (McIntosh)
Nicholas (Laurens)
Peyton (Warren)
Polly (Gwinnett)
Richard F. (Liberty)
Samuel (2) (Morgan)
Estate of Thomas (Liberty)
William (Gwinnett)
William (Jones)
William (Liberty)
William (Warren)
Wm. Quarterman (Liberty)
William W. (Liberty)
Willis P. (Wilkinson)
Balayon (?), Michel (Chatham)
Balderee, Isaac (Tattnall)
Baldwin (ind.), (2) (Chatham)
Catherine (Oglethorpe)
Charles (Greene)
David (Jones)
Demaras (Oglethorpe)
Henry (Greene)
John (Jasper)
John (Wilkinson)
Lewis (Greene)
Owen (Columbia)
Robert (Jones)
Samuel (Greene)
William (Jones)
Samuel (Oglethorpe)
William W. (Oglethorpe)
Balentine, John (Pulaski)
Bales, Liddy (Wilkinson)
Baley, (torn) (Laurens)
Anne (Camden)
Burrell (Irwin)
Charles (Jasper)
Henry (Wilkinson)
John, est. of (McIntosh)
N. (Jasper)

Samuel N. (Elbert)
Stephen (Jasper)
Thomas S. (Oglethorpe)
William (Oglethorpe)
William (Richmond)
Balkcom, Alexander (Jones)
Ichabod (Jones)
Sarah (Jones)
Ball (ind.), (Jones)
Anson (Wilkinson)
Caswell (Pulaski)
Elizabeth (Greene)
Isaiah (Morgan)
J. (Wilkes)
James (Richmond)
Jesse (Oglethorpe)
Joel (Morgan)
John (Clarke)
John (Habersham)
Larkin (Telfair)
Rebecca (Morgan)
Salley (Warren)
Thomas (Richmond)
William (Baldwin)
William (Clarke)
Ballard (torn), (Laurens)
Benjamin (Morgan)
Charles (Pulaski)
Edward (Burke)
Elijah (Greene)
J. (Richmond)
James (Hall)
James (Jones)
James (Wilkinson)
Jesse (Elbert)
Jesse G. (Madison)
John (Morgan)
John B. (McIntosh)
Joshua (Gwinnett)
Mary (Oglethorpe)
Phillip (Putnam)
Ransome (Putnam)
Reddick (Burke)
Taplen (Jones)
Telathy (Warren)
Winnifred (Washington)
Ballane, Elias (Pulaski)
Ballenger, David (Elbert)
John, Jr. (Elbert)
John, Sr. (Elbert)
Ballias, John William
(Chatham)
Ballinger, William (Elbert)
Balthrip (?), James (Jefferson)
Baly, William (Gwinnett)
William (Jasper)
Bandreme (?), Isiah
(Oglethorpe)
Bandy, James (Morgan)
John (McIntosh)
Lewis (Morgan)

Samuel (Chatham)
Banes, Labon (Telfair)
Banister, Alexander (Pulaski)
Garret (Hall)
Bank, Henry P. (Oglethorpe)
Banks, Anne (Jones)
Anny (Walton)
David (Chatham)
David (Lincoln)
Drury (Warren)
Eaten (Jasper)
Edmon (Jasper)
Eli (Putnam)
George (Warren)
James (Oglethorpe)
James, Sr. (2) (Elbert)
James A. (Elbert)
James J. (Elbert)
John (Jasper)
John, Sr. (Elbert)
John A. (Lincoln)
John H. (Elbert)
Joseph (Warren)
Josiah (Jasper)
Ralph (Elbert)
Richard (Oglethorpe)
Simeon (Emanuel)
Solomon (Putnam)
Thomas N. (Baldwin)
William (Elbert)
William (Wilkes)
Willis (Elbert)
Bankston, Abner (Jasper)
Elijah (Walton)
J. L. (Jasper)
James L. (Jasper)
Louvanie (Wilkes)
Sarah (Gwinnett)
William (Gwinnett)
Banon, James (Jones)
Samuel (Jones)
Banorefield, James (Appling)
Baptist, Betsy (Chatham)
Emilia (Chatham)
Polly (Chatham)
Barbee, James (Wilkinson)
Barbaree, Edward (Columbia)
Barber, Aaron (Clarke)
Asa (Washington)
Charles (Glynn)
Cornelius (Wayne)
Cunnely (Glynn)
Frederick (Washington)
George (Oglethorpe)
George, Sr. (Oglethorpe)
Isaac (Bryan)
Israel (Camden)
Jessie (Oglethorpe)
John (Bulloch)
John (2) (Jones)
Joseph (Jones)

(7)

Barber, Mathew (Oglethorpe)
Moses (Clarke)
N. (Jasper)
Rees (Clarke)
Robert (Clarke)
Thomas (Jefferson)
Samuel (Bryan)
Samuel (Jasper)
Samuel (Jefferson)
William (Clarke)
William (Liberty)
William (McIntosh)
William (Oglethorpe)
William (Screven)
William (Washington)
William (Wayne)
Barbin, David (Oglethorpe)
John (Oglethorpe)
Sarah (Oglethorpe)
Barclay, A. (Chatham)
Anthony (Chatham)
Bard (?), O. (Appling)
Barden, William (Columbia)
Bardin (ind.), (Pulaski)
Bardon, John S. (Columbia)
Bare, John (Jones)
Barefield, James (Morgan)
James (Warren)
Ward (Jasper)
William (Morgan)
Barer, Seth (Wilkes)
Barey, Jesse (Oglethorpe)
Barfield, Collin (Burke)
John (2) (Jones)
Sampson (Jones)
Solomon (Hancock)
Vincent (Burke)
William (Burke)
Barfoot, Miles (Pulaski)
William (Pulaski)
Barganer, William (Jefferson)
Barganes, Margaret (Jones)
Barganier, William (Jones)
Barge, Richmond (Washington)
Barker, B. Edmund (Baldwin)
Daniel (Camden)
Edward (Putnam)
Elijah (Pulaski)
Ephrem (Hall)
Holan (Burke)
Isham (Jackson)
Jesse (Gwinnett)
John (Putnam)
John (Wilkes)
Joseph (Putnam)
Louis (Jackson)
Louis, Jr. (Jackson)
Robert (Elbert)
Sussannah (Greene)
William (Greene)
William (Putnam)

William (Wilkinson)
Barkley, John (Morgan)
William (2) (Morgan)
Barksdale, Daniel (Hancock)
Higgerson (Lincoln)
Jeffry (Hancock)
Nathaniel (Putnam)
Nicholas (Wilkes)
Samuel (Warren)
Steth (Wilkes)
William (Hancock)
William (Putnam)
William (Warren)
Barkwell, J. W. (Oglethorpe)
Major (Oglethorpe)
Mary (Oglethorpe)
Barley, Bates (Burke)
Barlone, Edith (Washington)
Henry (Washington)
Barlow, (torn) (Laurens)
Elisha (Laurens)
John (Laurens)
Larkin (Wilkes)
Philip (Hall)
Barnadore, Nancy (Washington)
Barnam, William (Pulaski)
William, Jr., Pulaski)
Barnard, Edward (Chatham)
James (Chatham)
James (Tattnall)
John (Baldwin)
John W. (Chatham)
L. (Chatham)
Mary E. (Chatham)
Timothy (Chatham)
Barneck, John (Washington)
Barnes, Mrs. (Chatham)
Absalom (Morgan)
Amos (Wilkinson)
B. L. (Hancock)
Benjamin (Jasper)
Benjamin (2) (Hancock)
Charles (Early)
Corden (Screven)
Dempsy (Burke)
Edward (Putnam)
Elizabeth (Hancock)
Enos (Jasper)
George (Hancock)
James (Hancock)
James (Jones)
James (Putnam)
James B. (Lincoln)
James P. (Lincoln)
Jesse (Hancock)
Jethro (Jasper)
John (Madison)
John (Morgan)
John (Washington)
Joseph (Hancock)
Josiah (Jasper)

Lemmon (Hancock)
Louis (Richmond)
Mary (Putnam)
P. A. (Jasper)
Philip (Lincoln)
Pricilla (Elbert)
Thomas (Hancock)
Thomas (Wilkes)
William (Jones)
William (Washington)
Barnet, John (Gwinnett)
Jonathon (Gwinnett)
Barnett, Mrs. Avy (Greene)
Benj. G. (Oglethorpe)
Claborn (Putnam)
Eliza (Jackson)
George (Morgan)
James (Morgan)
Jeremiah (Elbert)
Joel (Oglethorpe)
John (Gwinnett)
John (Putnam)
John (Washington)
Leonard (Greene)
Lewis (Wilkes)
Mile J. (Morgan)
Nathan (Oglethorpe)
Nathaniel (Elbert)
Richard (Lincoln)
Robart (Wilkinson)
Samuel (Jackson)
Samuel (Wilkes)
Sarah (Washington)
William (Columbia)
William (Greene)
William (Wilkes)
William C. (Putnam)
William H. (Putnam)
Zadoc (2) (Morgan)
Barney, Eliza (2) (Jones)
J. S. (Richmond)
Barnhart, Brice (Greene)
George (Greene)
George, Sr. (Greene)
John (Greene)
Rachel (Putnam)
Barnhill, Robert (Gwinnett)
Barnwell, Alexander (Greene)
David (Hall)
George (Hall)
John (2) (Hall)
Robert, Jr. (Hall)
Robert, Sr. (Hall)
William (Hall)
Baron, David (Elbert)
Samuel (Burke)
Thomas (Elbert)
William (Burke)
Barr, Elizabeth (Jefferson)
James (Jackson)
Nathan D. (Burke)

(8)

Barr, Robert O. (Hall)
Samuel M. (Jefferson)
Barrantine, Jacob (Baldwin)
John (Wilkinson)
Barrat, Nancy (Richmond)
Barren, Thomas (Morgan)
Thomas C. (Jackson)
Barret, John (Hall)
Robert (Wilkes)
Barrett, David (Oglethorpe)
Elizabeth (Morgan)
James (Putnam)
Jeremiah (Walton)
Ninian (Morgan)
Richard (Morgan)
Robert (Morgan)
William (Gwinnett)
William (Putnam)
Barrie, Cullen (Bulloch)
Barrington, Isaac (Jefferson)
Barron, Miss (Chatham)
Barnabas (Jackson)
Barney (2) (Washington)
Hyram (Wilkinson)
Jacob (Jones)
James (Jackson)
James (Jasper)
James (Washington)
John (Jasper)
John (Jones)
Leonard (Lincoln)
Millie (Jones)
Samuel (Warren)
Thomas (Jasper)
William (Jasper)
William (Jones)
William (Pulaski)
William (Washington)
Barrott, Sally (Walton)
Barrow, Henry (Baldwin)
Jacob (Baldwin)
James (Baldwin)
James (Morgan)
James (Telfair)
Barrow (?), John (Clarke)
Barrow, Martha (Burke)
Michael (Warren)
Richard (Warren) see below
Thomas (Putnam)
Warren (Putnam)
William (2) (Jefferson)
William (Putnam)
Barry, William (Wilkes)
Barset, John (Walton)
Bartard, William (Jones)
Barthlemess, John (Chatham)
Bartlett, Abner (Jasper)
Allin (Putnam)
Cosam E. (Chatham)
John (Hancock)
Sterling (Hancock)

Bartlette, Lucinda (Washington)
Bartley, Joseph S. (Putnam)
Barton, D. (Richmond)
David (Hall)
Henry (Hall)
Holly (Hall)
James (Warren)
John (Morgan)
Nancy (Richmond)
Polley (Morgan)
Presley (Morgan)
William (Morgan)
William C. (Chatham)
Willis (Lincoln)
Bartow, Doctor (Chatham)
Bartram, James (Jasper)
Barwick, Benjamin
(Washington)
Nathaniel (Emanuel)
William (Washington)
Baset, Eli (Appling)
Bashelote, John (Camden)
Bashler, Charles (Bryan)
Baskins, James S. (Wilkinson)
William (Gwinnett)
Bass. Bryan (Burke)
Burwell (Hancock)
Christopher (Oglethorpe)
Edin (Putnam)
Edmund (Hancock)
Edward (Jones)
Elizabeth (Greene)
Elizabeth (Jasper)
Ephraim (Burke)
Eseau (Montgomery)
Ezekiel (Montgomery)
George (Jefferson)
Henry (Clarke)
Jesse (Burke)
John H. (Putnam)
Larkin (Hancock)
Persom (Warren)
Reddick (Warren)
Richard (Morgan)
Stirling (Baldwin)
Zadock (Warren)
Basset (?), Ezekiel (Clarke)
Bassett, Stephens (Jones)
Bassitt, Thomas (McIntosh)
Bastion, William (Columbia)
Batchelder, Cornelius
(Wilkinson)
Batchelor, Alex (Jackson)
Eli (Jackson)
John (Jackson)
William (Putnam)
Batefield, Sharlate (Jones)
Batelle, Washington (Morgan)
Bateman, Bryant (Washington)
Clabourn (Washington)
David (Washington)

James (Baldwin)
John (Washington)
William (Washington)
Bates, Anderson (Wilkes)
Daniel (Lincoln)
David (Oglethorpe)
Fleming (Warren)
Horis T. (Putnam)
James (2) (Greene)
James M. (Warren)
Jesse (Elbert)
Job W. (Wilkes)
John (Burke)
John (Hall)
John (Wilkes)
John A. (Greene)
Julius (Hall)
Mary (Wilkinson)
Mathia (Gwinnett)
Wilson (Warren)
Batey, Henery (Jefferson)
James (Laurens)
Batson, Dennis (Hancock)
Battey, Sheldon (Jefferson)
William (Jefferson)
Battle, (ind.) (Laurens)
Collier (Hancock)
Elisha (2) (Hancock)
Isaac (Hancock)
Jesse (2) (Hancock)
Jesse B. (Hancock)
John R. (Warren)
John W. (Greene)
Lazarus (Morgan)
Reuben T. (Hancock)
Rhode (Warren)
Thomas (Warren)
William S. (Warren)
Batts, Nathan (Jefferson)
Batty, John (Jones)
Baugh, John A. (Greene)
Josiah (Jackson)
Mary Ann (Greene)
Peter (Putnam)
Richard (Hancock)
William (Putnam)
Baughan, Edward (Clark)
John (Oglethorpe)
Joseph (Oglethorpe)
Bauson, Joseph J. (McIntosh)
Bawley, John (Camden)
Bawls, Amelia (Oglethorpe)
Henry (Oglethorpe)
Baxley, Aaron (Jasper)
Caleb (Burke)
Henrietta (Gwinnett)
William (Appling)
William (Walton)
Baxter, Charles (Burke)
Daniel (Jasper)
Eli H. (Hancock)

Bassett, Eli (Appling)   (9)

Baxter, Elizabeth (Hancock)
   Israel (Tattnall)
   James (Madison)
   John (Greene)
   John (Tattnall)
   Stephen (Tattnall)
Bayless, Thomas A. (Columbia)
Bayley, Moore (Jasper)
Bayliss, Isham (Columbia)
Bayly, Asa (Emanuel)
Bayne, Abraham (2) (Jones)
   Alexander (Jones)
   John (Jones)
   John R. (Jones)
   William (Jones)
Baynes, Heyward (Jasper)
Bays, Mary (Greene)
Bazemore, Auford (Screven)
   Reddick (Jones)
   Thomas (Jones)
Bazor, William Sr. (Hancock)
Beadle, William (Oglethorpe)
Beal, Francis (Jackson)
   George (Jackson)
   H., Jr. (Richmond)
   James (Richmond)
   Joseph (Jackson)
   Matilda G. (Jefferson)
   N. (Richmond)
   Nathaniel (Burke)
   Nathaniel (Jefferson)
   Walter (Jackson)
   William (Effingham)
   William (2) (Jackson)
   William M. (Wilkinson)
Beale, Francis (Warren)
   Mathew (Putnam)
Beall, Alexander E. (Columbia)
   Alphans (Wilkinson)
   Andrews (Columbia)
   Augustus (Columbia)
   Bradley (Warren)
   Harrison (Warren)
   Hezekiah (Columbia)
   Jeremiah (Warren)
   John (Columbia)
   Mary (Warren)
   Nathan (Warren)
   Robert (Warren)
   Robert A. (Warren)
   Samuel (Warren)
   Samuel (Wilkinson)
   Thomas (Columbia)
   William P. (Columbia)
Beals, Joshua (Screven)
Bealy, Hugh (Madison)
Beam, Darcas (Gwinnett)
   Mary (Gwinnett)
Beaman, Ralph (Chatham)
Bean, John (Jasper)
Beard, Benjamin W. (Morgan)

   Edmund (Morgan)
   James (Jones)
   James (2) (Wilkes)
   John (Madison)
   John (Screven)
   Kesiah (Jones)
   Mary (Jones)
   Mathew (Jones)
   Robert (Elbert)
   William (Wilkes)
Bearden, Richard (Hall)
   Wiley (Jasper)
   William (Hall)
Beardin, Aquilla (Putnam)
   John H. (Putnam)
   Thomas (Putnam)
   William (Putnam)
Beardon, Ansel (Hall)
   Jacob (Hall)
   Richard (Hall)
   Robin (Hall)
Beasley, Berry (Jones)
   Charles (Putnam)
   David (Jones)
   Elijah (Emanuel)
   Elijah (Irwin)
   Hiram (Clarke)
   Isiah (Bulloch)
   Jacob (Tattnall)
   James (2) (Clarke)
   James (Walton)
   Jarrel (Jasper)
   John (Bulloch)
   John (Gwinnett)
   John (Oglethorpe)
   John (Washington)
   Nancy (Morgan)
   Robert (Jones)
   Royland (Wilkes)
   Stephen (Putnam)
   Thomas, Sr. (Bulloch)
   William (Emanuel)
   William (Gwinnett)
   William (Morgan)
   William (Oglethorpe)
   William M. (Gwinnett)
Beasly, John (Columbia)
   Jonathan (Bryan)
   Richard (Clarke)
   Robert (Jasper)
   Thomas (Bulloch)
   William (Baldwin)
   William (Bulloch)
Beason, John F. (Gwinnett)
Beatman, Theophilus
          (Washington)
Beatty, Alexander (Chatham)
   James (2) (Jefferson)
   Robert (Jefferson)
Beaty, George (Habersham)
   James (Burke)

   James (Oglethorpe)
Beauchamp, John W. (Gwinnett)
   William (Gwinnett)
Beauford, John (Gwinnett)
Beaulard, J. (Chatham)
Beavey, William (Clarke)
Beavers, James (Jasper)
Bech, William (Wilkinson)
Beck, Catherine Ann (Glynn)
   Francis (Wilkinson)
   James (Morgan)
   Jesse (2) (Morgan)
   John (Elbert)
   John (Morgan)
   John B. (Burke)
   Robert (Elbert)
   Samuel (Screven)
   William A. (Elbert)
Beckam, Laban (Baldwin)
Beckham, Anney (Wilkinson)
   I. Z. (Liberty)
   James (Jones)
   Solomon (Jones)
   Benjamin (Putnam)
Beckom, Abel (Washington)
   Daniel (Washington)
   John (Washington)
   John S. (Greene)
   Sherwood (Greene)
   William (Greene)
   William (Jefferson)
Beckton, Samuel S. (Jefferson)
Beckum, Simon (Glynn)
   Thomas (Glynn)
Beckworth, Sion (Putnam)
   Willis (Warren)
Beddingfield, Hardy (Greene)
Bedford, William (Putnam)
Bedgood, John (Washington)
   John Sr. (Washington)
   Matthew (Burke)
   Richard (Washington)
   Samuel (Washington)
Bedingfield, Martha (Burke)
Bedsel, Godfrey (Jefferson)
Bee, William (Richmond)
Beeks, John (Walton)
Beevers, Joseph (Jasper)
Beeves, William (Morgan)
Beezly, Abraham (Jefferson)
Beggs, James (Jefferson)
   John (Jefferson)
Beght, William (Jasper)
Beil, Charles (Richmond)
Beland, Benjamin (Jones)
   James (Jasper)
   William (Jones)
Belch, John Sr. (Jasper)
Belcher, Abner (Burke)
   Ann (Chatham)
   John (Putnam)

Belcher, Daniel (Screven)
Mary (Burke)
Mournin (Burke)
Samuel (Morgan)
Wiley (Burke)
William (Laurens)
William (2) (Morgan)
Belding, Nelson S. (Hancock)
Belflower, Wiilliam
(Wilkinson)
Belk, James (Wilkes)
Bell, (ind.) (Laurens)
Alexander A. (Columbia)
Ann (Richmond)
Archibald (Burke)
Arthur (Burke)
Bailey (Jones)
Bartholmew (Wilkes)
Bazel (Wilkinson)
Benjamin (Burke)
Daniel (Tattnall)
Elisha (Burke)
Elizabeth (Elbert)
Elizabeth (Wilkinson)
Elias (Oglethorpe)
George (Walton) see below
Green (Burke)
Henry (Burke) see below
Henry (Camden)
Henry (Greene)
James (Burke)
James (Elbert)
James (Jackson)
James (2) (Morgan)
Bell, James (Putnam)
James (Richmond)
Jarrett (Greene)
John (Burke)
John (Liberty)
John (Lincoln)
John (Oglethorpe)
Jordan (Burke)
Joseph (Early)
Joseph (Elbert)
Joseph (Putnam)
Joseph (Wilkes) see below
Joshua (Wilkes)
Martha (Burke)
Mayfield (Elbert)
Nathaniel (Camden)
Nathaniel (McIntosh)
Olive (Washington)
Paul (McIntosh)
Polly (Jackson)
Richard (Burke)
Riddick (Wilkinson)
Russel G. Putnam)
Samuel (Oglethorpe)
Tandy (Baldwin)
Thadeus (Morgan)
Thomas (Burke)

Benefield, James (Appling)

Thomas, Sr. (Elbert)
Thomas (Greene)
Thomas (Habersham)
Thomas (Madison)
Tobort (Wilkinson)
Walter (Hall)
William (Burke)
William (Elbert)
William (Walton)
Bellabe, Morgan (Morgan)
Samuel (Morgan)
Bellah, John (Morgan)
Samuel (Jasper)
Bellany, Alexander (Jasper)
Belle, Loyd (Wilkes)
Bellinger, Mr. (Chatham)
Bellingly, James (Jasper)
Bellings, Adam (Pulaski)
Belsal (?), Elija (Richmond)
Belt, Lloyd (Jefferson)
Beman, Nathan S. S. (Hancock)
Bemming, Pain L. (Wilkinson)
Bence, William (Morgan)
Bender, Booker (Laurens)
John (Jasper)
Benedict, E. P. (Chatham)
Benham, Lyman (Morgan)
Benia, Mr. (Chatham)
Bening, Thomas (Columbia)
Bennefield, Collord (Columbia)
Needham (Jefferson)
Bennet, Aron (Emanuel)
Elizabeth (Wilkes)
Emanuel (Emanuel)
Peter (Wilkes)
Ranson (Gwinnett)
Reuben (Wilkes)
Richard (2) (Appling)
William (Appling)
Winston (Walton)
Bennett, Alexander (Jones)
Alexander (Oglethorpe)
Edmond (Walton)
Eliza (Jones)
Green (Hall)
Henry (Hall)
Isreal (Hall)
James (Bulloch)
James R. (Morgan)
Jeremiah (Jones)
Jerry (Washington)
Joel (Hall)
John (Bryan)
John (Bulloch)
John (Jackson)
John (Jones)
Joseph (Jones)
Luke (Wilkinson)
Mary Ann F. (Jones)
Matthew (Liberty)
Micajah (Jackson)

(11) Bennett, Henry (Appling)

Mitchel (Jackson)
Nancy (Irwin)
Nancy M. (Walton)
Sanders (Jones)
Stephen (Jackson)
Taply (Jackson)
William (Bryan)
William (Gwinnett)
William (Jackson)
William, Sr. (Jackson)
William (Washington)
Benning, Pleasant A.
(Columbia)
Bennotte, Jacob (Lincoln)
Bennyfield, Lewis (Jones)
Benom, Drury (Warren)
Benris, John (Emanuel)
Benson, Aaron (Putnam)
Collier (Hancock)
Eli (Putnam)
Enoch (Gwinnett)
John (Lincoln)
John (Putnam)
Levi (Morgan)
Levi (Putnam)
Reuben (Gwinnett)
Robert (Morgan)
William (Putnam)
William (Wilkes)
Willis (Wilkinson)
Bentley, Aly (Wilkes)
Isaac (Walton)
James (Wilkes)
Jeny (Washington)
Jesse (Walton)
John (Lincoln)
John (Washington)
John (Wilkes)
John T. (Walton)
Joseph (Walton)
Sam (Elbert)
Bently, Mrs. (Chatham)
William (Oglethorpe)
Benton, A. (Jasper)
Ann (Jasper)
Isom (Bryan)
James (Jackson)
James (Wilkinson)
Jeremiah (Jasper)
Jesse (Jasper)
John (Jones)
John (Warren)
Jonathan (Jasper)
Martha (Pulaski)
Nathan (Columbia)
Nelson (Columbia)
Resen (Jackson)
Stephen (Jackson)
William B. (Richmond)
Beran, John (Wilkes)
Berdet, Samuel B. (Jones)

Bergen, Mathew (2) (Jones)
Bergeron, Abigail (Burke)
    Elijah (Burke)
    Elizabeth (Burke)
Bergman, John E. (Effingham)
Berlingson, Jessey (Wilkinson)
Berman, Lewis R. (Lincoln)
Bernard, William (Morgan)
Bernardy, P. (Glynn)
Bernier, Bijotte (Chatham)
Berrian, J. McP. (Chatham)
Berrien, R. M. (?) (Chatham)
    Thomas M. (Washington)
    Wilimina S. E.
        (Jefferson)
Berrough, Phillip (Jasper)
Berry, Benjamin (Columbia)
    Bradley (Oglethorpe)
    Charles (Oglethorpe)
    D. (Richmond)
    David (Jones)
    Edmund (Morgan)
    Elijah (Elbert)
    Mrs. Frances (Greene)
    Hosa (Wilkinson)
    James (Chatham)
    James (Gwinnett)
    James (Jones)
    James (Putnam)
    Jesse (Habersham)
    Jesse (Putnam)
    Jilson (Warren)
    John (Gwinnett)
    John, Sr. (Gwinnett) *see below*
    John, Sr. (Hancock)
    John D. (Oglethorpe)
    John J. (2) (Hancock)
    Lewis T. (Morgan)
    Robert (Jones)
    Samuel (Wilkinson)
    Simon (Gwinnett)
    Susannah (Oglethorpe)
    Thalifery L. (Oglethorpe)
    Thomas (Warren)
    Thomas D. (Putnam)
    William (Camden)
    William (Warren)
    William (Wilkes)
Berryhill, Alexandria (Tattnall)
    James (Jefferson)
    James (Washington)
    John (Jefferson)
    Samuel (Tattnall)
    Sarah (Jefferson)
Berryman, Charles (Madison)
    John (Madison)
Berton, Mather (?) (Jackson)
Bertram, A. (Richmond)
Besom, John (Chatham)
Best, Absalem (Screven)
    Daniel (Lincoln)

    George (Screven)
    Jacob (Screven)
    Thomas (Lincoln)
    William (Lincoln)
Beston, William, Jr. (Columbia)
Betcher, Obadiah (Jasper)
Bethune, Daniel (Greene)
    John (Greene)
    Laughlin (Greene)
Bets, Elisha (Walton)
Betsil, William (Washington)
Bettenbock, John (Effingham)
    Mary (Effingham)
    Matthew (Effingham)
Betton, Solomon (Baldwin)
Betts, A. (Jasper)
    James (Jasper)
    Jonathan (Jackson)
    Joseph (Jasper)
    William (Columbia)
Bevan, John (Lincoln)
    Joseph V. (Effingham)
Bevel, Randle (Columbia)
    Zacheriah (Putnam)
Bevell, Thomas (Elbert)
Beverage, James (Wilkes)
Beverly, Abner (Jones)
    Anthony (Elbert)
    John (Jones)
    William (Tattnall)
Bevers, Johnson (Madison)
Bevill, Granvil (Screven)
    Dilley (Screven)
    Robert (Screven)
Bezly, John (Jefferson)
Bibb, Benjamin (Elbert)
    Joseph W. (Elbert)
Bichton, Micagey (Screven)
Bickell, John (Effingham)
    William (Effingham)
Bickers, John (Wilkinson)
Bickerstaff, R. (Jasper)
Bicolau, B. (Glynn)
Biddell, Isaac (Greene)
Biddle, John (Jones)
    Micajah (Greene)
Biffle, John (Hall)
Bigelow, A. B. (Richmond)
Biggers, Jonathan (Greene)
Biggs, Mary (Warren)
Bigham, Jane (Jefferson)
    John (Jefferson)
    Joshua (Washington)
    Samuel (Jefferson)
Bignion, Joseph (Richmond)
Bigs, Sarah (Wilkes)
Bigsby, Joseph (Camden)
Bihl (?), Gotlieb (Chatham)
Bilbo, James (Chatham)
Bilbro, Thomas (Greene)
Biles, William (Telfair)

Billings, Sarah (Columbia)
Billingslea, Cyrus (Morgan)
    Francis (Wilkes)
    James (2) (Jones)
    John (Wilkes)
    Thomas (Wilkes)
Bills, Lucy (Glynn)
Billups, James est. of
    (Oglethorpe)
    Joseph (Clarke)
Billops, Robert R. (Walton)
Binion, David (Jones)
    Job (Gwinnett)
    John (Columbia)
    William (Columbia)
Binson(?), Thomas (Wilkinson)
Birch, Benjamin (Laurens)
    James (?) Hancock
    Richd C. (Hancock)
Bird, Alex (Bryan)
    Allen (Hancock)
    Andrew (Bryan)
    Buford (Wilkes)
    David (Pulaski)
    Ebenezer (Warren)
    George (Morgan)
    Henry (Bulloch)
    Jacob (Effingham)
    James (Hancock)
    James (Wilkes)
    Jese (Telfair)
    Joel (Emanuel)
    John (Emanuel)
    John (Greene)
    John (Pulaski)
    John W. (Richmond)
    Judy (Putnam)
    Margaret (Wilkes)
    Phillip (Wilkes)
    Pui (Putnam)
    Sarah (Bryan)
    Susan (Putnam)
    Thompson (Baldwin)
    Wiley (Emanuel)
    William (Bulloch)
    William, Sr. (Effingham)
    William (Greene)
    William (2) (Putnam)
    Wilson (Warren)
    Young (Wilkes)
Birdet, James (Wilkes)
Birdit, Peggy (Wilkes)
Birdite, John (Wilkes)
Birdsong, Benjamin (Jasper)
    Freeman (Oglethorpe)
    Isaac (Hancock)
    James (Putnam)
    John (3) (Oglethorpe)
    John W. (Putnam)
    Joseph (Morgan)
Biscoe, William (Putnam)

Bexley, William (Appling) (12)

Bishon, Susannah (Chatham)
Bishop, Asa (Greene)
D. (Jasper)
David (Morgan)
Elizabeth (Jackson)
Elizabeth (Greene)
Elliott (Pulaski)
Ephraim (Putnam)
George (Appling)
Gulder (Morgan)
James B. (Richmond)
John (Hall)
John (Putnam)
John (Warren)
Joseph (Hall)
Littleberry (Warren)
Pernal (Morgan)
Philip (Jasper)
Rhoda (Habersham)
S. (Richmond)
Samuel (Washington)
Stephen (Greene)
Thomas D. (Jackson)
Bivens, Stephens (Jones)
William (Wilkinson)
Bivins, Benjamin (Baldwin)
James (Baldwin)
John (Baldwin)
Milly (Baldwin)
Robert (Madison)
Rolen (Baldwin)
Sarah (Baldwin)
Shadrak (Baldwin)
Thomas (Baldwin)
William (Baldwin)
William (2) (Putnam)
Wilson (Warren)
Black, Absalem (Putnam)
Archibald (Baldwin)
David (Hall)
Edward (Wilkes)
Garvin (Hall)
J. A. (Richmond)
James (2) (Hall)
James (Jasper)
John (Habersham)
John (Hall)
John (Putnam)
John (Warren)
John H. (Jackson)
Loyal (Hancock)
Peter (Hancock)
Richardson (Putnam)
Robert (Hall)
Robert (Jefferson)
Robert (Walton)
Samuel (Morgan)
Thomas (Morgan)
William (Habersham)
William (Screven)
Blackborn, John (Lincoln)

Blackburn, Daniel J. (Bulloch)
David (Screven)
Elijah (Wilkes)
John (Screven)
John (Wilkinson)
N. (Wilkes)
Stephen (Screven)
Thomas (2) (Wilkes)
Blackly, Eliza (Washington)
Blackman, J. P. (Tattnall)
James (Screven)
John (Oglethorpe)
William (Tattnall)
Blackshear, (ind.) (Laurens)
Edward (Pulaski)
Joseph (Laurens)
Blackson, D. (Richmond)
Blackson (?), James
(Richmond)
Blackstock, Daniel (Hall)
James (2) (Hall)
Richard (Hall)
William (Hall)
Blackston, John, Jr. (Warren)
John, Sr. (Warren)
A. (Richmond)
Francis (Jasper)
Blackwell, Banks (Elbert)
Dunston (Elbert)
Hardy (Elbert)
Jodiah (Hall)
Joseph (Elbert)
Nancy (Hall)
Parker (Elbert)
Ralph (Elbert)
Sally C. (Elbert)
Samuel (Columbia)
Sarah (Bryan)
William (Hall)
Blackwood, F. (Jasper)
Francis (Jasper)
Blair, Andrew (Walton)
George (Hancock)
George (Washington)
James, Jr. (Habersham)
James, Sr. (Habersham)
James (Walton)
Jemina (Columbia)
Mary (Chatham)
Nancy (Hancock)
Richard (Hancock)
Thomas (Habersham)
Thomas (Hall)
Thomas (Washington)
Blake, Benjamin (Oglethorpe)
Henry (Oglethorpe)
John (Hall)
Lemuel (Oglethorpe)
William (Gwinnett)
William (Hall)

Blakely, Aquilla (Jones)
Blakemoore, Thomas (Clarke)
Blakey, Churchill (Wilkes)
Jesse (Putnam)
Levi (Putnam)
William (Jones)
Blaky, John (Hancock)
Blalock, Allen (Gwinnett)
Alsey (Jones)
David (Lincoln)
E. M. (Telfair)
Gipson (Lincoln)
Hardin (Gwinnett)
James (Jones)
John (Gwinnett)
John (2) (Lincoln)
William (Jones)
James (Jones)
Blanchard, F. (Chatham)
James (Columbia)
Jeremiah (Columbia)
Blanckard, Sarah (Columbia)
Uriah (Columbia)
Bland, Elisha (Washington)
William (Bulloch)
William (Wilkinson)
Blandford, Clarke (Warren)
Blanford, William (Camden)
Blank, Arthur (Telfair)
Blankenship, James (Jones)
John (Clarke)
Blanks, James (Jackson)
William (Greene)
Blanton, Alex (Bulloch)
Benjamin (Oglethorpe)
Blassingame, James (Morgan)
Blausingim, Phillip (Greene)
Blaylock, Edmund (Putnam)
Giles (Hall)
Micajor (Wilkinson)
Solomon (Putnam)
William (Putnam)
Bledsoe, Benjamin (Warren)
James (Greene)
Jesse (Putnam)
John (Oglethorpe)
Joseph (Oglethorpe)
Margaret (Morgan)
Miller (Oglethorpe)
Peachy (Morgan)
Richard (Jones)
Robert (Putnam)
Bleosit, Elisha (Walton)
Blessett, Stephen (Jasper)
Blitch, Benjamin (Effingham)
Spear (Effingham)
Willis (Effingham)
Blocker, Jacob (Tattnall)
Blogg, Mrs. (Chatham)
Blois, James G. (Chatham)

Bloodsox, Mrs. (Richmond)
Bloodworth, John (Walton)
   Junius (Walton)
   Thomas (Morgan)
   William (2) (Morgan)
Blount, Isaac (2) (Morgan)
   Isaac (Pulaski)
   James (Burke)
   Luke (Glynn)
   Philip (Washington)
   Richard A. (Washington)
   S. W. (Burke)
   Sarah (Washington)
   Thomas (Jones)
   William (Jones)
   William H. (Warren)
Blow, Benjamin (Hancock)
   Micajah (Jones)
Bludworth, Henry (Wilkinson)
   John W. (Wilkinson)
   Samuel (Wilkinson)
Blue, Daniel (Glynn)
Bluitt (?), Zilph (Pulaski)
Blunt, Edmond (Putnam)
   George (Camden)
   Henry (Putnam)
   James (Jones)
   John (Jasper)
   Joseph (Columbia)
   Major (Putnam)
   Richard (Jones)
   Thomas (Jones)
Boatright, Benjamin (Wayne)
   Chesley (Wayne)
   Daniel (Elbert)
   George (Washington)
   James (Wilkes)
   Margaret (Emanuel)
   Reubin (Emanuel)
   William (Lincoln)
Bober, Thomas J. (Wilkes)
Bobo, Benjamin (Elbert)
   Burrel (Elbert)
Boclair, P. F. (Richmond)
Boen, Mathew (Walton)
Bogan, Elizabeth (Richmond)
Bogdan, Shadrick (Gwinnett)
Boggers, Jeremiah (Morgan)
   Silas (Morgan)
Boggins, Thomas (Hall)
Boggs, Aaron (Clarke)
   Ezekiel (Wilkinson)
   George (Wilkinson)
   James (Jackson)
   James (Putnam)
   James (Wilkinson)
   Jeremiah (Putnam)
   John (Warren)
   Joseph (Jackson)
   Joseph (Putnam)
   Viletta (Jackson)

Bogue, John (Camden)
Bogus, Ezze (Oglethorpe)
Bohannon, Alexander (Lincoln)
   Buddy (Morgan)
   Duncan (Wayne)
   Henry (Laurens)
   John (Liberty)
   Joseph (Wilkinson)
   K. (Jasper)
   William (Montgomery)
Boice, Elsy (Jackson)
   John (Jackson)
   Thomas (Jones)
Boid, Samuel (Irwin)
Boil, Kitty (Putnam)
Boils, Charles (Montgomery)
Bolan, Smith (Morgan)
Boldeman, J. D. (Chatham)
Boles, Christopher (Lincoln)
   James (Jones)
   John (Jones)
   John (Putnam)
   William (Lincoln)
Bolin, John (Hall)
   John (Putnam)
   Mary (Putnam)
   Shubal (Hall)
   William (Pulaski)
Boling, R. (Richmond)
Boll, William (Early)
Boller, Job F. (Chatham)
Bolling, John (Hall)
   John (Oglethorpe)
   William (Habersham)
Bolos, Amos (Lincoln)
Bolton, Archy (Washington)
   D. (Richmond)
   Elizabeth (Wilkes)
   James (Burke)
   John (Chatham)
   Manoh (Oglethorpe)
   Matthew (Columbia)
   Robert (Columbia)
   Rubin (Screven)
   Sarah (col.) (McIntosh)
   Thomas (Wilkes)
   Thomas C. (Columbia)
Boman, Ezekiel (Gwinnett)
   Gilbert (2) (Gwinnett)
   Henry D. (Hancock)
   Isham (Gwinnett)
   John (Morgan)
   Richard (Lincoln)
   Thomas (Gwinnett)
   Thomas (Morgan)
Bond, Ann (Bryan)
   Ann (Chatham)
   Chappel (Pulaski)
   Edward (Wilkes)
   Elizabeth (Elbert)
   Evin (Madison)

   Gabriel (Madison)
   James (Richmond)
   Joel (Oglethorpe)
   Lewis (Wilkinson)
   Mark (Lincoln)
   Micajah (Columbia)
   Nathan (Elbert)
   Nelson (Elbert)
   Samuel M. (Chatham)
   William (Elbert)
   William (Jones)
Bonds, James (Hall)
   James (Gwinnett)
   Luke (Jones)
   Richard (Walton)
   Robert (Early)
   Robert P. (Hall)
   Samuel (2) (Jones)
   Vardy (Walton)
Bone, Bishop (Wilkes)
   James (Madison)
   John (Madison)
   John (Wilkes)
   Matthew (Madison)
   William, Jr. (Madison)
   William, Sr. (Madison)
   William (Richmond)
Bonell, John (Camden)
Boneon (?), William (Putnam)
Boner, William H. (Greene)
Bones, I. (Richmond)
   John (Richmond)
Boney, Joshua (Warren)
Bonfeulet, J. P. (Chatham)
Bonner, Allen (Clarke)
   Hamilton (Hancock)
   James (Jones)
   Jonathan (Jasper)
   Joseph (Jones)
   Pleasant (Hancock)
   Robert (Warren)
   Thomas (2) (Morgan)
   Thomas M. (Putnam)
   Smith (Gwinnett)
   Uriah (Jones)
   William (Jones)
   Willie (Clarke)
   Willis (Walton)
   Zodac (Clarke)
Booker, John (Wilkes)
   Richardson (Wilkes)
   William (Greene)
   William (Wilkes)
   William M. (Wilkes)
Booler, Allen (Greene)
   Jessie (Greene)
   Sally (Greene)
Booles, Jackson (Greene)
   John Sr. (Greene)
   Thomas (Greene)
   William (Greene)

Boon, Benjamin (Morgan)
    Daniel (Wilkinson)
    Jacob (Wilkinson)
    Jesse (Greene)
    Joshua (Morgan)
    Kenchen (Hancock)
    Lewis (Hancock)
    Martha (Jefferson)
    Martha (Madison)
    Ratliff (Wilkinson)
    Sion (Morgan)
    Thomas (M. C.) (Wilkes)
Boone, James (Jasper)
Boorfield, William (Jasper)
Booth, Benj. H. (Clarke)
    Edward (Warren)
    Gabriel (Elbert)
    John (Clarke)
    Robert (Greene)
    Stephen (Lincoln)
    Thomas (Clarke)
Boothe, Andrew (Baldwin)
    Bevely (Greene)
    David S. (Elbert)
    Edward (Liberty)
    Elizabeth (Elbert)
    Elizabeth (Jones)
    John (Elbert)
    Melton (Baldwin)
    Nancy (Elbert)
    Prudence (Elbert)
    Richard (Jones)
    Robert (Elbert)
    Zachariah (2) (Jones)
Booty, Sarah (Warren)
Borden, Stephen (Jackson)
Borders, John (Jackson)
Bordess, John (Jones)
Boreing, David (Jackson)
    Isaac (2) (Jackson)
    John (Jackson)
    Robert (Jackson)
Boren, William (Wilkes)
Borland, Abraham (Baldwin)
    John (Hancock)
    William (Baldwin)
Born, Bennett (Richmond)
    Fariby B. (Richmond)
    Samuel (Gwinnett)
Borquin, Bened (?) (Chatham)
Borrum, Benjamin (Madison)
Borum, Benjamin (Wilkes)
    Nathaniel (Oglethorpe)
    Thomas (Wilkes)
Bosby, William (Jefferson)
Boseman, David (Jones)
Bosher, George W. (Putnam)
Bosley, George (Hall)
Bosman, Thomas (Wilkinson)
Bostick, Ann (Baldwin)
    Hillary (Jefferson)

J. (Richmond)
Jacob, (Overseer for)
            (Burke)
Jane (Lincoln)
John (Jefferson)
John G. (Jefferson)
Joshua S. (Baldwin)
Littlebury, Sr. (Jefferson)
Nathan (Jefferson)
R., (Overseer for) (Burke)
Thomas (Burke)
Tilman (Hancock)
Boston, Jacob (Jackson)
    James (Screven)
    Mathew (Jackson)
Bostwick, John (Jefferson)
    John (Morgan)
    Littleberry (Greene)
    Littleberry, Jr. (Jefferson)
    Littleberry (Morgan)
    Nancy (Morgan)
    Wade (Lincoln)
Boswell, B. (Chatham)
    Charles (Wilkes)
    H. (Richmond)
    James (Richmond)
    John (Wilkes)
    Josias (Putnam)
    Levi (Putnam)
    Sarah (Wilkes)
    Thomas (Jones)
    William (Jasper)
    William (2) (Putnam)
    Williamson (Putnam)
Bosworth, Britton (Columbia)
    Jacob (Jackson)
    Phillip (Clarke)
Bothwell, Ebenezer (Jefferson)
    James J. (Burke)
    John W. (Jefferson)
    Samuel (Jefferson)
Boting, Henry (Clarke)
Bottoms, Robert (Putnam)
Bott, James (Walton)
Botts, Elizabeth (Gwinnett)
Bouche, O. (Chatham)
Bouleneau, Mrs. John B.
           (Richmond)
Boulton, Samuel (Jones)
Boundridge, Jesse (Hancock)
Bourke, Jane (2) (Chatham)
    Joshua (Chatham)
Bourkes, Edward (Burke)
Bourn, George (Oglethorpe)
Bourquin, Benedict (Chatham)
    D. F. (Chatham)
Bouten, John (Jefferson)
Bowden, Dangerfield (Greene)
    James (Jasper)
    Jesse (Jasper)
    Joshua (Putnam)

Mary (Oglethorpe)
William (Greene)
William (Oglethorpe)
Bowdin, James (Putnam)
    John (Putnam)
    Travis (Putnam)
    William (Putnam)
    Willis (Putnam)
Bowdon, Luban (Jasper)
Bowdre, Edmond (Columbia)
    Polly (Columbia)
    Thomas (Columbia)
Bowen, Charles (Jones)
    Christopher (Oglethorpe)
    David (Richmond)
    Dickson (Wilkes)
    Edward (Jones)
    Elijah (Tattnall)
    Herod (Washington)
    Horatio G. (Elbert)
    Jane (Clarke)
    Levi (Tattnall)
    Malechi (Washington)
    Mark (Bulloch)
    Martha (Jones)
    Meredith (Habersham)
Bowen (?), Munford (Lincoln)
Bowen, Owen J. (Jackson)
    Rawly (Jackson)
    Samuel (Wilkes)
    Steve (Tattnall)
    Thomas (Habersham)
    Thomas (Jackson)
    William (Appling)
    William (Elbert)
    William (Jackson)
Bower, Dennand (Baldwin)
    Elam G. (Jones)
    Elisha (Bulloch)
    Jesse (Jones)
Bowers, Benjamin (Baldwin)
    George (Habersham)
    Isaac (Jackson)
    William (Elbert)
Bowes, Isaac (Jones)
Bowing, Elizabeth (Wilkinson)
    John (Wilkinson)
    Sparkman (Wilkinson)
Bowlding, John (Jasper)
Bowles, Elizabeth (Hall)
    Henry (Putnam)
    Isaac (Warren)
    Isiah (Jones)
    Nathan (Jackson)
    William (Warren)
Bowling, Simon (Jefferson)
    Thornbury (Oglethorpe)
Bowls, William (Jackson)
Bowman, (ind.) (Effingham
    Drewry M. (Clarke)
    Zuhariah (Elbert)

Branham, Michael (Habersham)
Susan (Washington)
Branin, Jonathon (Morgan)
Brannan, Isham (Morgan)
Brannen, Alex (Bulloch)
Ralph (Screven)
Solomon (Bulloch)
Thomas (Bulloch)
Thomas (Early)
Thomas (Screven)
William (Bulloch)
Brannon, James (Richmond)
John (Richmond)
Ugan (?) (Richmond)
Brannum, John (Walton)
Russell (Walton)
William C. (Warren)
Bransford, John (Jasper)
Branson, J. (Richmond)
Brantley, (torn) (Laurens)
Abba (Washington)
Aron (Washington)
Benjamin (Hancock)
Benjamin (Warren)
Danby (Oglethorpe)
Edward (Washington)
Green (Washington)
Harris (Washington)
James (2) (Hancock)
James (Jones)
James (Washington)
Jepthah (Warren)
Jerry (Laurens)
John (Chatham)
John (Emanuel)
John (Jones)
John (Washington)
Joseph (2) (Chatham)
Joseph (Emanuel)
Joshua (Walton)
Lewis (Morgan)
Malekiah (Putnam)
Patsy (Washington)
Philip (Warren)
Rebecca (Warren)
Spencer (2) (Washington)
Thomas (Hancock)
Thomas (Washington)
William T. (Richmond)
Zacheriah (Washington)
Brantly, James (Columbia)
Mary (Burke)
Branzley, Joseph (Jones)
Brasell, Arthur (Wilkinson)
Mary (Wilkinson)
Braselton, Edward (Jackson)
Brash, W. L. (Liberty)
Brasiel, Robert (Camden)
Brassil, Jesse (Wilkes)
Nathan (Wilkes)
Braswell, Kindred (Emanuel)

Robert (Laurens)
Samuel (2) (Clarke)
Bratcher, Elijah (Hall)
Brawner, Henry (Elbert)
Henry P. (Elbert)
James M. (Elbert)
Joel (Elbert)
John (Elbert)
Joseph (Elbert)
Bray, Ann (Screven)
Banister (Lincoln)
Benjamin (Washington)
David (Elbert)
Elizabeth (Jones)
George (Putnam)
John (Putnam)
John (Elbert)
Joseph (Washington)
Peter (Hancock)
Peter (Washington)
Richard (Warren)
Brazel, Byrd (Hancock)
Mansfield (Hancock)
Brazell, (torn) (Laurens)
(ind.) (Laurens)
Briton (Jones)
William (Jones)
Brazelton, Jacob, Jr. (Jackson)
Jacob, Sr. (Jackson)
Braziel, Bn (Ben?) (Jackson)
Elijah Lincoln
Martha (Jackson)
Brazil Bang. (Jones)
James (Jones)
Brazwell, Valentine (Madison)
Brazzel, Elizabeth (Jefferson)
Brazzelton, Green (Hall)
Rueben (Hall)
Breadlove, Samuel (Putnam)
Brean, (ind.) (Elbert)
Moses (Hancock)
Bredlove, John (Hancock)
William W. (Hancock)
William (Hancock)
Breed, Nathan, Jr. (Warren)
William (Warren)
Breedlove, Nathan (Jones)
Richard F. (Putnam)
Sally (Hancock)
Bressie, William (Baldwin)
Brett. Esther (Jefferson)
Henry (Laurens)
Brewer, Ambrose (Wilkes)
Arthur (Telfair)
Asa (Pulaski)
Barrett (Putnam)
Benruss (Liberty)
Drury (Morgan)
E. W. (Jasper)
Elizabeth (Elbert)
George (Putnam)

Henley (Clarke)
Henry (Baldwin)
James (Liberty)
Joel (Wilkinson)
John (Morgan)
Joseph (Clarke)
Mary (Effingham)
Mary (Putnam)
Martha (Morgan)
Pierson (Pulaski)
Robert (Tattnall)
Roland (Putnam)
Samuel (Wilkinson)
Simond (Wilkinson)
Susan (Jasper)
Valuntine (Putnam)
William (Oglethorpe)
William B. (Elbert)
Brewner, William (Wilkinson)
Brewster, John (2) (Morgan)
Sheriff (Morgan)
Brewstle, Peter (Chatham)
Brewton, Nathan (Tattnall)
Brey, Elijah (Bulloch)
Bri - -(?), Benjamon (Putnam)
Brian, Mary (Glynn)
Briant, Benjamin (Hall)
Hugh (Jackson)
Peter (Hall)
Philomon (Appling)
Samuel (Jackson)
Stephens (Hall)
William (Jackson)
William L. (Jackson)
Brice, Brinkley (Morgan)
Brickell, Lucinda (Chatham)
Brickley, Hiram (Morgan)
Bridge, Abil A. (Montgomery)
Jeremiah (Baldwin)
Bridger, Blake (Washington)
Martha (Chatham)
William (Washington)
William F. (Washington)
Bridgers, G. R. (Richmond)
Bridges, Aaron (Jackson)
Berry I. (Oglethorpe)
J. T. (Jasper)
Jacob (Oglethorpe)
James (Oglethorpe)
John (Morgan)
Jonathan (Jones)
Joseph (Washington)
Joshua (Jackson)
Killes C. (Oglethorpe)
Mary (Oglethorpe)
Solomon (Gwinnett)
Solomon (Oglethorpe)
Thomas (Greene)
Thomas (Putnam)
Wiley (Gwinnett)
Bridwall, Moses (Wilkes)

(17)

Brigdon, William (Screven)
Briges, J. W. (Richmond)
Briggs, Burwell (Jones)
    Eleanor (Jones)
    R. I. (?) (Richmond)
Brigham, E. (Camden)
    John (Burke)
Bright, Absalom (Burke)
    Levi (Washington)
    Samuel (Habersham)
    Samuel (Oglethorpe)
    Sarah (Habersham)
Brigwell, Wilson (Laurens)
Briley, Charlotte(Chatham)
Brimberry, John (Hancock)
Bringhurst, John (Putnam)
Brinkley, Abraham (Warren)
    Eli (Washington)
    Richard (Putnam)
    William (Hancock)
Brinson, Adam (2) (Screven)
    Cypron (Burke)
    Daniel (Tattnall)
    David (Jefferson)
    David (Screven)
    Isaac (Jefferson)
    Jason (Telfair)
    John (Burke)
    John, Jr. (Burke)
    John (Hancock)
    Mary (Burke)
    Mathew (Lincoln)
    Moses (Jefferson)
    Shepherd (Burke)
    Stephen (Burke)
    Thomas (Burke)
Brisco, John (Oglethorpe)
Briscoe, Catherine (Columbia)
    George (Hancock)
Briston, Chesley (Greene)
Britonham, Joseph (Warren)
Britt, David J. (Morgan)
    Edward (Clarke)
    Ephriam (Hall)
    Hugh, Jr. (Madison)
    Hugh, Sr. (Madison)
    James (Washington)
    Jessee (Washington)
    John (Washington)
    John I. (Jasper)
    Obed (Baldwin)
Britton, G. B. (Richmond)
Brittten, George (Oglethorpe)
    Henry (Oglethorpe)
    John (Jasper)
    Sanford (Jasper)
    Stephen (Chatham)
Broach, George (Oglethorpe)
    William H. (Greene)
Broadhus, James (Richmond)
Broadnax, Henry P. (Putnam)

John (Putnam)
John H. (Putnam)
Broadus, Thomas (Jasper)
Broadwater, Josiah (Richmond)
Brock, Benjamin (Chatham)
    Daniel (Wilkinson)
    Harden (Emanuel)
    Henry (Habersham)
    James (Habersham)
    John (Habersham)
    John (Pulaski)
    John, Sr. (Pulaski)
    John (Washington)
    Thomas (Habersham)
    Waddy (Walton)
    William (Pulaski)
Brockington, Danel (Camden)
    Daniel (Camden)
Brockman, John (Early)
    John (Oglethorpe)
    Moses (Oglethorpe)
Brodnax, Edward B. (Hancock)
    John T. (Baldwin)
    R. E. (Burke)
    Robert B. (Hancock)
    William (Hancock)
Brogdon, David (Hall)
    George (Gwinnett)
Bronson, Zenos (Oglethorpe)
Brook, Gilbert (Oglethorpe)
    Jabes (Morgan)
    John (Morgan)
    John L. (Oglethorpe)
    Robert (Greene)
    Samuel (Oglethorpe)
Brooker, John (Greene)
    Joseph (Emanuel)
Brooking, Edward B. (Hancock)
    William (Hancock)
Brookins, Benjamin
            (Washington)
    Charles V. (Washington)
    Nancy (Washington)
    Samuel (Burke)
    Theoph (Laurens)
Brooks, Mrs. (Chatham)
    Abijah (Morgan)
    Abraham (Wilkes)
    Amos (Jackson)
    Balam (Warren)
    Biving (Walton)
    Catherine (Warren)
    Caty (Walton)
    Charles (Jones)
    Charles (Warren)
    Christopher (Wilkes)
    E. (Jasper)
    Edward (Jones)
    Elizabeth (Jasper)
    Hana (Jackson)
    Isaac (Warren)

Isham (Jones)
Isham (Putnam)
Jacob R. (Gwinnett)
James (Columbia)
James (2) (Putnam)
James (Washington)
Job (Jackson)
John (Camden)
John (Hall)
John (Jones)
John (Madison)
John (Morgan)
John (2) (Putnam)
John (Walton)
John (Warren)
John (Wilkinson)
Jonathan (Putnam)
Jordan (Jones)
Joseph (Jasper)
Joseph (Warren)
Jourdan (Wilkinson)
Littlejohn (Oglethorpe)
M. (Jasper)
Magner (Jackson)
Maney (Wilkinson)
Meags (Jasper)
Middleton (Jackson)
Moses (Jasper)
Nancy (Warren)
P. L. W. (Hall)
Paschal (Gwinnett)
Philop H. (Jones)
Polly (Greene)
Preston (Wilkes)
Robert, Jr. (Jones)
Robert, Sr. (Jones)
Capt. Robert (Wilkinson)
Robert, Jr. (Wilkinson)
Robert, Sr. (Wilkinson)
Samuel (2) (Jones)
Samuel (Wilkes)
Samuel, Sr. (Wilkes)
Sarah (Washington)
Thomas (Jackson)
Thomas (Jasper)
Toby (Chatham)
William (Greene)
William (Jones)
William (Morgan)
William (Wilkes)
William H. (Jones)
William T. (Jones)
Wilson (Oglethorpe)
Broom, Adam (Warren)
    David (Liberty)
    David (Warren)
    Ishmel (Warren)
    John (Clarke)
    Rufus (Warren)
    Solomon (Warren)
    Major (Chatham)

Broose, Benjamin H.
    (Wilkinson)
Brorton, John (Telfair)
    William (Telfair)
Broughton, A. (Jasper)
    Charles (Jasper)
    Elijah (Chatham)
    John (Liberty)
    John H. (Greene)
    Daniel (Liberty)
    William (Chatham)
    William (Morgan)
Brovell, Lewis (Camden)
Brown, (ind.) Pulaski)
    Mrs. (Chatham)
    Aaron (Elbert)
    Abraham (Elbert)
    Abraham (Jones)
    Absalem (Wilkinson)
    Agnes (Chatham)
    Alexander (Oglethorpe)
    Alfred H. (Jasper)
    Ambrose (Morgan)
    Amelia (Richmond)
    Anderson (Putnam)
    Andrew (Chatham)
    Andrew (Elbert)
    Andrew (Morgan)
    Andrew (Wilkinson)
    Archable M. (Oglethorpe)
    Aaron (Walton)
    Asa (Jefferson)
    Austin (Richmond)
    B. (Jasper)
    Benjamin (Burke)
    Benjamin (Elbert)
    Benjamin (Greene)
    Benjamin (Jasper)
    Benjamin (Madison)
    Benjamin (2) (Morgan)
    Brinkley (Pulaski)
    Brittan (Emanuel)
    Burrel (Burke)
    Burrel J. (Jefferson)
    Burton (Wilkes)
    Burwell (Hancock)
    Charles (Burke)
    Charles (Jones)
    Charles M. (Oglethorpe)
    Christopher (Morgan)
    Collins (Lincoln)
    Daniel (Jasper)
    Daniel (Laurens)
    Daniel (Screven)
    David (Camden)
    David (Jefferson)
    David (Oglethorpe)
    Drewcilla (Baldwin)
    Edards (Baldwin)
    Edward (Elbert)
    Edy (Camden)

    Elijah (Jefferson)
    Elisha (Jones)
    Elizabeth (Jones)
    Elizabeth (McIntosh)
    Elizabeth (Wilkes)
    Enoch G. (Putnam)
    Ephraim (Gwinnett)
    Ephraim (Hall)
    Epps (Hancock)
    Ezekil (Camden)
    Ezekial (Lincoln)
    Ezekiel (Greene)
    Ezekiel (Madison)
    Fanning (Gwinnett)
    Frederick (Columbia)
    George (Hancock)
    George R. (Jefferson)
    Godfrey (Wilkinson)
    Henry (Baldwin)
    Henry (Emanuel)
    Henry (Jefferson)
    Henry (Morgan)
    Henry (Putnam)
    Henry (Warren)
    Hezekiah (Washington)
    Hiram (Wilkes)
    Hollinger (Baldwin)
    Horatio (Elbert)
    Hubbard (Putnam)
    Hugh (Camden)
    Isaac (Gwinnett)
    Isaac (2) (Oglethorpe)
    Isabella (Jasper)
    Mrs. J. (Richmond)
    J. G. W. (Jasper)
    Jacob (Lincoln)
    James (Burke)
    James (Clarke)
    James (Greene)
    James (Gwinnett)
    James (2) (Habersham)
    James (Jasper)
    James (Pulaski)
    James (Putnam)
    James (Richmond)
    James (Wilkinson)
    James (Wilkes)
    James B. (Burke)
    James B. (Putnam)
    James L. (Elbert)
    James N. (Elbert)
    James W. (Oglethorpe)
    Jeptha (Hall)
    Jesse (Bulloch)
    Jesse (Elbert)
    Jesse (Emanuel)
    Jesse (Warren)
    Jessee D. (Washington)
    Jesse S. (Hancock)
    Joel (Wilkinson)
    John (2) (Baldwin)

    John (Elbert)
    John (Greene)
    John (Gwinnett)
    John (Habersham)
    John (2) (Hall)
    John (Hancock)
    John (2) (Jasper)
    John (2) (Jones)
    John (Liberty)
    John (Morgan)
    John (Pulaski)
    John (Walton)
    John (Washington)
    John (Wilkinson)
    John H. (Jones)
    John S. (Baldwin)
    John U. (Baldwin)
    Jonathon (Wilkinson)
    Joseph (Gwinnett)
    Joseph (Hall)
    Joseph (Hancock)
    Joseph (Pulaski)
    Josiah (Gwinnett)
    Keshah (Oglethorpe)
    Larkin (Hall)
    Lewis (Madison)
    Lewis S. (Wilkes)
    Mrs. Lizza (Greene)
    Louis (Hancock)
    Lucy (Chatham)
    Lovet (Laurens)
    Mark (Baldwin)
    Mark M. (Wilkinson)
    Martin H. (Jefferson)
    Mary (Chatham)
    Mary (Jefferson)
    Mary (Bulloch)
    Maryanne (Wayne)
    Meredith (Habersham)
    Mildred (Baldwin)
    Morgan (Washington)
    Nancy (Columbia)
    Nelson (Elbert)
    P. H. (Richmond)
    Pattrick (Madison)
    Philip (Telfair)
    R. (Camden)
    Reuben (Elbert)
    Rewben (Greene)
    Richard (Burke)
    Richard (Habersham)
    Richard (Jefferson)
    Richard (Pulaski)
    Robert (Clarke)
    Robert (Habersham)
    Robert (Lincoln)
    Robert (Putnam)
    Rockmon (Putnam)
    Roda (Wilkinson)
    Sally (Habersham)
    Samuel (Clarke)

(19)

Brown, Samuel (Emanuel)
Samuel (Jefferson)
Samuel (Morgan)
Samuel (Putnam)
Samuel (Washington)
Sarah (Camden)
Sarah (Putnam)
Sarah (Wilkinson)
Simon (Baldwin)
Stark (Walton)
Thomas (Gwinnett)
Thomas (2) (Morgan)
Thomas B. (Oglethorpe)
Thomas R. (Oglethorpe)
Turner (Washington)
Uriah (Baldwin)
Valentine (Wilkes)
W. H. (Chatham)
Walter (Hancock)
Wiley (Gwinnett)
William (Baldwin)
William Jr. (Bulloch)
William (2) (Burke)
William (Camden)
William (Columbia)
William (2) (Elbert)
William (Hancock)
William (Irwin)
William (2) (Jasper)
William (4) (Jones)
William (Madison)
William (McIntosh)
William (Morgan)
William (2) (Pulaski)
William (3) (Putnam)
William (2) (Washington)
William, Sr. (Wilkinson)
William (Wilkes)
William F. (Hancock)
William H. (Morgan)
William P. (Baldwin)
William T. (Jones)
William W. (Wilkinson)
Wyatt (Elbert)
Zealous (Jones)
Browne, Hiram (Elbert)
Brownfield, John (Jasper)
Robert (Jasper)
Browning, Daniel (Montgomery)
Edward (Morgan)
Eli B. (Jefferson)
George (Montgomery)
Isabella (Morgan)
James (Montgomery)
John (Clarke)
John (Hancock)
Margaret (Clarke)
Nathan (Greene)
Radford (Montgomery)
Sol (Jackson)
Stephen (Wayne)

Browny, Marget (Jackson)
Broxton, John (Burke)
Silas (Burke)
Thomas (Burke)
Bruce, Aziel (Greene)
Elizabeth (Wilkes)
James (Greene)
James (Habersham)
John (Clarke)
John (Greene)
Nancy (Burke)
Ward (Greene)
Bruckner, Daniel (Wilkes)
Bruen, E. (Richmond)
Timothy (Baldwin)
Brumbalo, Edward (Gwinnett)
Isaac (Gwinnett)
Brumbler, James (Laurens)
Brumfield, James (Putnam)
Brummett, James (Wilkes)
Brunson, Daniel (Lincoln)
Brunt, Nancy (Grene)
Bruster, Sheriff (Walton)
Hugh (Walton)
Bruton, John (Early)
Brux, Augustus (Richmond)
Bryan (?), Doctor (Chatham)
Mrs. (Chatham)
Bryan, Alexander (Richmond)
Ann (Chatham)
B. (Richmond)
Brinson (Hancock)
Clement (Montgomery)
David (Pulaski)
Dolly (Chatham)
Edward (Pulaski)
Elisha (Habersham)
Frederick (Wayne)
Hannah (Chatham)
Isaac (Columbia)
J. est. of (Chatham)
Jacob (Burke)
Jacob (Chatham)
James (Pulaski)
James (Walton)
James H. (Burke)
Jesse (Pulaski)
Jesse (Walton)
John (Elbert)
John (Habersham)
John (Pulaski)
John (Screven)
John (Walton)
John K. (Montgomery)
Joseph (Hancock)
Joseph B. (Pulaski)
Laury (Clarke)
Lewis (Burke)
M. (Chatham)
Mary (Pulaski)
Moses (Burke)

Moses (Elbert)
Moses (Pulaski)
Needham (Burke)
Patrick I. (Chatham)
Reading D. (Burke)
Samuel (Walton)
Stephen (Pulaski)
Susan (McIntosh)
T. (Jasper)
Thomas (Elbert)
Wiley (Putnam)
William (Burke)
William (Pulaski)
William (Richmond)
Wilis (Pulaski)
Bryant, (ind.) (Wilkes)
Austin (Morgan)
Benjamin (Warren)
Benjamin (Wilkes)
Daniel (Screven)
David (Washington)
Elias (Wilkes)
Elizabeth (Morgan)
Isaac (Putnam)
J. (Richmond)
James (Camden)
James (Putnam)
James (Screven)
James, Jr. (Screven)
Jane (Screven)
Jarrell (Jasper)
Jason (Washington)
John (Jasper)
John (Madison)
John (Oglethorpe)
John (2) (Putnam)
John (Screven)
John (Wilkes)
John T. E. (Jones)
Jesse (Greene)
Jesse (Putnam)
Langly (Camden)
Little (Warren)
Mary (Putnam)
Nathan (Wilkes)
Pennie (Camden)
Pleasant (Clarke)
Robert (Putnam)
Sam (Screven)
Sarah (Putnam)
Solomon (Screven)
William (Lincoln)
William (Morgan)
William (2) (Oglethorpe)
William (Putnam)
Brynan, William (Madison)
Bryne, John (Chatham)
Bualien (?) James (Oglethorpe)
Buchan, John (Pulaski)
Buchanan, John (Jones)
Buchannon, John (Jasper)

(20)

Buchanon, George (Jasper)
James (Jasper)
John (Putnam)
Patrick (Madison)
Buchner, Henry M. (Hancock)
Buchsten, James (Pulaski)
Buck, Charles (Columbia)
William (Washington)
Buckanan, J. B. (Jasper)
W. B. (Jasper)
Bucker, John T. (Jasper)
W. (Jasper)
Buckhalter, Cuyler (Greene)
Buckham, Benjamin (Baldwin)
Buckhannon, John D. (Greene)
Buckhanon, Thomas (Wilkinson)
Buckles, Peter (Wilkinson)
Buckley, Bartlet (Burke)
Benjamin (Burke)
William B. (Chatham)
Buckner, Avrea (Putnam)
Benjamin (Jones)
Benjamon (Putnam)
Daniel (Putnam)
Hiram (Putnam)
John (Putnam)
Lester (Jones)
Lucy (Putnam)
Mary (Putnam)
Millie (Jones)
Parham (Putnam)
Richman (Putnam)
Bucks, John (Hall)
Buffet, Mrs. (Chatham)
Buffington, Ezekiel (Hall)
Jacob (Jackson)
Jonathan (Hall)
Joseph (Elbert)
Oburn (Hall)
Samuel (Baldwin)
William (Hall)
Bufort, John (Screven)
Bug, Archabald (Bulloch)
Neill (Screven)
William A. (Richmond)
Buge, Henry (Glynn)
Bugg, Anselem (Richmond)
E. (Richmond)
Edmond (Columbia)
Peter T. (Richmond)
Sarah A. (Columbia)
Samuel (Richmond)
Shackal (Richmond)
William (Oglethorpe)
Buie, (Archibald (Tattnall)
Betsey (Washington)
John (Tattnall)
Malcolm (Tattnall)
Buis, John (Jasper)
Noah (Jones)
Buisyou (?). Silas (Richmond)

Bujos, James (Jasper)
Bulger, John (Washington)
Bull, Edmund (Warren)
Fred (?) (Chatham)
Martha (Columbia)
Robert (Jasper)
William (Wilkes)
Bullard, Amos (Burke)
Henry (Burke)
James (Jasper)
John (Jones)
Lydia (Washington)
Robert (Wilkinson)
T. (Jasper)
Thomas (Elbert)
Thomas (Jasper)
William (Jones)
Buller, Bushaby (Jones)
Bullin, John (McIntosh)
Bullis, John (Elbert)
Bulloch, Alexander (Madison)
G. (Richmond)
Hardy (Oglethorpe)
James S. (Chatham)
John J. (Chatham)
Bullock, A. S. (Chatham)
Carter (Washington)
James (Wilkinson)
James (Columbia)
Margaret (Walton)
Mil - - (Chatham)
S. (2) (Jasper)
William B. (Chatham)
Wyatt (Oglethorpe)
Bunce, Joseph (Richmond)
William I. (Richmond)
Bunch, Austen (Greene)
Bunche, Mrs. (Chatham)
Bungy, John (Jones)
Bunkley, Breten (Camden)
James (Warren)
Jesse (Warren)
John (Greene)
John (Liberty)
Joshua (Greene)
Thomas (Camden)
Bunn, Moses (Burke)
Bunting, Leving (Tattnall)
Buntz, C. F. (Bulloch)
Simon (Effingham)
Burbage, George (Columbia)
Burch, Allen (Gwinnett)
Charles (Laurens)
E. (Richmond)
Edward (Wilkinson)
Gerrard (Wilkinson)
James (Richmond)
Jasper (Oglethorpe)
Jesse (Burke)
John (Baldwin)
John (Richmond)

John (Wilkes)
Reb (Richmond)
Sb (sic) (Burke)
William S. (Elbert)
Burchshiner, Mathew
(Effingham)
Burd, Aaron (?) (Appling)
Burden, Archibald (Elbert)
F. (Chatham)
Henry (Elbert)
Henry (Jones)
James (Elbert)
Mary F. (Jones)
William (Elbert)
Burdot, Mary (Chatham)
Burford, Leonard (Jones)
Philip W. (Oglethorpe)
Thomas (Jackson)
Thomas B. (Greene)
William (Greene)
Burgamy, Drury (Washington)
Nathaniel (Wilkes)
William (Washington)
Burgan, David (Jackson)
Burganey, William (Warren)
Burge, (ind.) Jr. (Laurens)
Abel (Washington)
Rebecca (Jones)
Wiley (Morgan)
Burger, Jonthon (Greene)
Burges, Elijah (Walton)
James (Jackson)
Burgess, John (Gwinnett)
John M. (Jackson)
Josiah (Jasper)
Moses (McIntosh)
Samuel (Baldwin)
Burgis, Mary (Gwinnett)
Burk, Charles (Greene)
John (Bulloch)
Joseph (Wilkes)
R. (Richmond)
Rebbeccah (Bulloch)
Theoplulus (Greene)
William T. (Jones)
Burke, Ed. (Telfair)
Matthew (Burke)
Thomas (Burke)
Burkes, Robert (Jackson)
Burket, John (Telfair)
Burkhalter, Isaac (Pulaski)
Jacob (Warren)
Jeremiah (Warren)
John (Warren)
Michael (Jones)
William (Warren)
Burks, Elisha (Madison)
William (Jasper)
William (Madison)
Burnam, Thomas (Pulaski)
Burnapp, Ela (Putnam)

Burnell, Anthony (Burke)
Jean (Jackson)
Burnes, F. J. (Burke)
Feriby (Burke)
Burnett, Dannul (Irwin)
Isaac (Jones)
James (Irwin)
Jeremiah (Clarke)
John, Jr. (Glynn)
John, Sr. (Glynn)
Sanders (Jefferson)
Thomas (Irwin)
Burney, (ind.) (Washington)
Arthur (Glynn)
Arthur (Wilkinson)
Elizabeth (Washington)
Harris (Washington)
John (Morgan)
Randle (Morgan)
William (Glynn)
Willis (Washington)
Burnley, Henry (Warren)
Richmond (Warren)
Samuel (McIntosh)
Stephen W. (Warren)
Burns, David M. (Jackson)
Jack (M. C.) (Columbia)
Jacob (Walton)
James (Wilkinson)
John (Screven)
Jonas (Screven)
Michael (Jasper)
Robert (Hall)
Ruth (Morgan)
Samuel (Jackson)
Samuel L. (Wilkes)
Thomas H. (Ecreven)
William (2) (Elbert)
William (Jackson)
Burnseds, William (Bulloch)
Burnside, Elinor (Columbia)
Thomas H. (Screven)
Burnsides, John (Bulloch)
Burrell, Anthony (Emanuel)
Burres, Taylor (Jasper)
Burreson, William (Telfair)
Burrett, Elijah H. (Columbia)
Burridge, James (Columbia)
Burrough, G. G. (Richmond)
J. (Jasper)
Burroughs, Benjamin (Chatham)
James (Columbia)
Burrow, Philip (Jones)
Burson, Brooks (Jackson)
Elisha (Jackson)
Isaac (Jackson)
Joseph (Jackson)
Nancy (Warren)
Burt, Christopher (Tattnall)
James (Putnam)
Richard (Putnam)

Robert (Jones)
William (Putnam)
Zacheus (Putnam)
Burton, Ann (Richmond)
Bathshaba (Elbert)
Benjamin (Burke)
Benjamin (Chatham)
Bins (Elbert)
Blackman (Elbert)
Charles (Burke)
E. (Wilkes)
J. S. (Richmond)
Jacob (Madison)
James M. (Clarke)
John (Jackson)
John (Putnam)
John (Richmond)
Leroy (Elbert)
Richard (Elbert)
Robert (Effingham)
Robert (Liberty)
Samuel (Lincoln)
Tabitha (Elbert)
Thomas (2) (Elbert)
Thomas W. (Hancock)
William (Burke)
Burwell, Hezekiah (Habersham)
Margot (Wilkes)
Busbey, B. A. (Liberty)
John (Camden)
Buse, John (Walton)
Bush, (ind.) (3) (Laurens)
Andrew (2) (Warren)
David (Habersham)
David (Jones)
David F. Burke)
Gideon (Laurens)
James (Early)
John (Emanuel)
John (Hall)
James (Pulaski)
James (Warren)
John B. (Pulaski)
Joseph (Burke)
Levi (Burke)
Levi (Washington)
Moses E. (Laurens)
Nathan (Wilkinson)
Thomas (Warren)
William (Early)
Zachariah (Early)
Bushel (John)
Bussey, Benjamin (Morgan)
David (Putnam)
James (Putnam)
Nathan (Putnam)
Bussy, Barkley (Lincoln)
Duncan (Lincoln)
Ma (ind.) (Lincoln)
Nathan (Lincoln)
Thomas (Lincoln)

Bustin, Christopher (Putnam)
John, Sr. (Putnam)
William (Putnam)
Bustle, Isaac (Washington)
John (Washington)
Nancy (Washington)
Priscilla (Washington)
Solomon (Washington)
Butcher, Thomas (Washington)
Butler, Curry (Morgan)
Daniel (Elbert)
David (Wilkes)
Edward (Morgan)
Elizabeth (Wilkes)
Fanny (Hancock)
G. W. (Richmond)
George (Madison)
Haley (Elbert)
James (Bryan)
James (Elbert)
James (Walton)
Jessey (Bryan)
Joel (Madison)
Joel (Wilkinson)
John (Bryan)
John (Elbert)
John (Morgan)
John (Walton)
John G. (Chatham)
John W. (Wilkes)
Keziah (Clarke)
Larkin (Jackson)
Louise (Chatham)
Martha (Walton)
Martha (Wilkinson)
Mary (Morgan)
Maxwell (Irwin)
Miner (McIntosh)
Morris (Putnam)
N. H. (for H. Wood & Self)
(Liberty)
Nathan (Elbert)
Officer (Bryan)
Patrick (Elbert)
Pearce (McIntosh)
Peter E. (Elbert)
Pierce (Glynn)
Prudence (Hall)
Samuel (Jones)
Shem (Liberty)
Stephen (Screven)
William (Washington)
William (Wilkinson)
Zacheus (Putnam)
Butlers, S. & J. (Liberty)
Butridge, Ivy (Hancock)
Butt, Eldridge (Morgan)
Jeremiah (Warren)
John (Habersham)
John (Warren)
Moses (Columbia)

Butt, Noah (Jones)
Butter, Damsey (Jones)
Butterworth, Stephen (Hall)
Button, Joseph (Screven)
Buttrell, Thomas (Warren)
Butts, Aziah (Hancock)
   David (Laurens)
   Edmond (2) (Hancock)
   Elizabeth (Putnam)
   Frederick (Jones)
   Henry (Putnam)
   James, Jr. (Hancock)
   James, Sr. (Hancock)
   James (Jones)
   Jesse G. (Hancock)
   John (Jefferson)
   John H. (Putnam)
   Martha (Hancock)
   Sally (Putnam)
   Simmons (Hancock)
   Thomas C. (2) (Hancock)
   William R. (Putnam)
Buxton, Benjamin (Burke)
   William (Burke)
Buzos, Coswell (Jasper)
Byacorn, Thomas (Jasper)
Byat, William (Jones)
Byford, Auquiller (Madison)
Byhim (?), Sarah (Oglethorpe)
Bynaum, John (Columbia)
Byne, Elijah (Burke)
   Enoch (Burke)
   George (Burke)
   Henry (Burke)
   John (Burke)
   Lewis (Burke)
   Richard (Burke)
   Thomas (Burke)
   William (Burke)
Byng, Judah (Chatham)
Bynum, James (Jones)
   Reuben (Pulaski)
   Sugar (Pulaski)
   William (Washington)
Byrd, E. (Richmond)
   H. (Richmond)
   Harmon (Burke)
   Henry (Richmond)
   Hiram (Jasper)
   James (Wilkinson)
   John (Burke)
   John (Elbert)
   John (2) (Hall)
   Nathan (Burke)
   Philip (Hall)
   Rebecca (Wilkinson)
   Samuel (Burke)
   Thomas (Hall)
Byriand, William (Putnam)
Byrom, Cynthia (Jasper)
   Isabel (Warren)

John (2) (Jasper)
William (Warren)

C

Cabbe, John (Oglethorpe)
Cabell, Robert J. (Clarke)
Cabiness, George (Jones)
   Henry B. (Jones)
   John (Jones)
   Sally (Jones)
   William (Jones)
Caboness, Henry (Elbert)
Cabus, John (Chatham)
Cade, James (Wilkes)
   Robert (2) (Wilkes)
Caddenhead, Alexander (Jones)
   Isham (Jones)
   James (2) (Jones)
Cadenhead, Edmond (Jones)
Cadenhead, Edmond (Jones)
   James (Hancock)
   John (Early)
   William (Jones)
Cagle, George (Clarke)
   George (Habersham)
   Henry (Jones)
   Honor (Habersham)
   Jacob (Habersham)
   John (Habersham)
   William (Habersham)
Cagler, David (Walton)
Cahoon, Esther (Jackson)
Cain, Elisha (Pulaski)
   John (Hancock)
   Joseph (Hall)
   Josiah (Wilkes)
   Mage (Hall)
   Nancy (Hall)
   Nathaniel (Washington)
Cair, William (Wilkinson)
Caisy, Robert (Jackson)
Calahan, Edward S. (Clarke)
   Jacob (Wilkes)
   Joshua (Clarke)
   William (Clarke)
Calaway, David (Wilkes)
   Edward (Wilkes)
   Elijah M. (Jones)
   Elisha H. (Jones)
   Ely (Wilkes)
   Enoch (Wilkes)
   Isaac (Wilkes)
   Job (Wilkes)
   John C. (Baldwin)
   John M. (Wilkes)
   Jonathan (Jones)
   Joseph (Wilkes)
   Joseph M. (Wilkes)
   Joshua (Jones)
   Leven (Baldwin)

   Luke J. (Wilkes)
   Noah (Wilkes)
   Parker (Wilkes)
   Winifred (Wilkes)
Calbert, Thomas (Elbert)
Calder, Henry, Jr. (McIntosh)
   James (McIntosh)
   John, Sr. (McIntosh)
Caldwell, Alexander (Clarke)
   Curtis (Gwinnett)
   D. (Jasper)
   David (Habersham)
   Ed'd (Jasper)
   J. (Richmond)
   James (Clarke)
   James (Gwinnett)
   John (Gwinnett)
   John (McIntosh)
   M. (Jasper)
   Mary (Burke)
   Mathew (Jones)
   Rosetta (McIntosh)
   Sarah (Lincoln)
   Simon (Jefferson)
   William (Clarke)
Calhoun, (ind.) (2) (Laurens)
   Levi (Burke)
Calhoun, Abram C. (Laurens)
   Elbert (Baldwin)
   James (2) (Jones)
   John (Clarke)
   John (Jones)
   Josiah (Jones)
   Patrick (Jones)
   Samuel (Jones)
   Wiliam (Gwinnett)
   William (Jefferson)
Caliham, David (Lincoln)
Callaham, Bryant (Emanuel)
Callahan, Martha (Chatham)
   William (Oglethorpe)
Callaway, David (Irwin)
   Elijah H. (Emanuel)
   Gehu (Baldwin)
   Isaac (Madison)
   Jesse (Wilkes)
   Jethrop (Wilkes)
   John (Wilkes)
   Joshua (Wilkes)
   Mary (Wilkes)
   Seaborn (Wilkes)
   Susannah (Wilkes)
   William (Oglethorpe)
Callender, Jane (Liberty)
Calley, Devenport (Putnam)
Callifer, Edward (Putnam)
   Henry (Putnam)
Callihan, James (Jackson)
   John (Jackson)
Calloway, James (Jasper)
   John (Putnam)

Caloway, P. (Jasper)
W. W. (Jasper)
Calquhon, Ainguis
(Montgomery)
Calvert, Nichlace (Oglethorpe)
Phillip P. (Oglethorpe)
Calvery, Thomas (Oglethorpe)
Calvin, Charles W. (Hancock)
Cambell, B. (Richmond)
John (Appling)
William (Oglethorpe)
Camel, John (Jasper)
Levi (Richmond)
Cameron, Allen (Lincoln)
Allen (Tattnall)
Cammel, John (Jackson)
N. (Jackson)
Camp, Abner (Gwinnett)
Abner (Hall)
Andrew (Gwinnett)
Burrell (Walton)
Edmund (Clarke)
Gerrard (Warren)
Hosea (2) (Jackson)
James (Gwinnett)
John (Gwinnett)
John, Sr. (Gwinnett)
John (Walton)
Joseph (Walton)
Mary (Jackson)
Nathan (Jackson)
Orsamus (Jackson)
Robert B. (Gwinnett)
Samuel (Warren)
Shadrack (Warren)
Sherwood (Walton)
Solomon (Gwinnett)
Susannah (Hall)
Thomas (Walton)
William (Jackson)
Campbell, Alexander (Telfair)
Andrew (Greene)
Archibald (Jefferson)
Archibald (Telfair)
Burrel (Washington)
Catlett (Morgan)
Charter (Morgan)
Daniel (Appling)
Duncan (Telfair)
Duncan G. (Wilkes)
Elisha (Jefferson)
Elizabeth (Warren)
George (Morgan)
Griffen (Morgan)
I. (Jasper)
James (Elbert)
James (Greene)
James (Morgan)
James A. (Wilkes)
Jessee (Liberty)
John (Greene)
John (Appling)

John (Jones)
John (Walton)
Joseph (Wilkes)
Matthew (Morgan)
Peter (Morgan)
Robert (Chatham)
Robert C. (Morgan)
Thomas (Clarke)
Waller L. (Wilkes)
William (Chatham)
William (Gwinnett)
William (Jones)
William (Madison)
Campel, John (Camden)
Camper, James (Jasper)
Campfield, E. (Richmond)
Camron, Abrm (Jackson)
Camson, Allen, Jr. (Lincoln)
Canachand, Mary B.
(Montgomery)
Canada, Caleb (Putnam)
Canady, David (Hall)
John (Bryan)
John (Gwinnett)
John, Jr. (Hall)
John, Sr. (Hall)
Marion (McIntosh)
Stephen (Bryan)
Candle, William (Washington)
Candler, Henry (Jones)
Mark (Columbia)
William (Jones)
Candy, Prince (Chatham)
Cane, Dennis (Richmond)
James (Columbia)
John (Columbia)
Polly (Richmond)
William (Richmond)
Canidy, Alexander (Jones)
Canidy (?), Gustavus
(Richmond)
Cannady, Edmond (Emanuel)
Henry (Emanuel)
John (Emanuel)
Samuel (Emanuel)
Solomon (Emanuel)
Cannaford, John (Jones)
Cannamon, John (Gwinnett)
Cannefax, Elijah B. (Walton)
Canniman, David (Gwinnett)
Cannon, Dempsy (Bulloch)
Edward (Greene)
Elisha (Washington)
George P. (Putnam)
Henry (McIntosh)
Henry (Walton)
Jesse (Pulaski)
John (Bryan)
John (Chatham)
John (Putnam)
Joshua (Greene)

Mathew (Pulaski)
Miles (Wilkinson)
Nathaniel (Wilkinson)
Reddic (Bulloch)
Richard (Washington)
Samuel (Jones)
Spires (Jefferson)
Spyvy (?) (Hancock)
Thomas (Bulloch)
W. W. (Jasper)
William (Washington)
Willy, Jr. (Wilkinson)
Cannyfax, Benjamin (Morgan)
Canon, Elizabeth (Jones)
Cantelou, Lewis C. (Richmond)
P. L. Richmond)
Canter, Richard D.
(Washington)
Cantrel, Thomas (Hall)
Cantroll, P. (Chatham)
Canuel, Mrs. (Chatham)
Capehart, John (Walton)
Capeheart, John (Jones)
Capel, Sterling (Jones)
Capers, Mary (Chatham)
William (Chatham)
Capps, Turany (Effingham)
Caps, Mariah (Glynn)
Car, A. (Richmond)
Richard (Putnam)
Rody (Richmond)
Carathen, James (Gwinnett)
Caraway, (ind.) (Early)
Alexander (Lincoln)
John (Lincoln)
William (Lincoln)
William, Sr. (Lincoln)
Card, Abraham (Jones)
Cardell, E. (Chatham)
Carden, David (Jasper)
James (Jasper)
William (Jasper)
Cardin, Leonard (Morgan)
Millen (Pulaski)
Cardwell, John (Oglethorpe)
Simon (Madison)
Careker, Jacob (Laurens)
Carethers, James (Oglethorpe)
Robert (Oglethorpe)
Carey, James (Chatham)
Lucy (Clarke)
Cargell, Charles (Jasper)
William (Jasper)
Cargil, John N. (Gwinnett)
Thomas (Gwinnett)
Cargill, Charles (Jasper)
James (Jasper)
John (Jasper)
John R. (Jasper)
Thomas (Jasper)
Carhron, Mary (Richmond)

(24)

Carkcourn, Samuel (Oglethorpe)
Carleton, Archd (Greene)
   Henry (Clarke)
   Henry (Warren)
   James (Greene)
   James R. (Greene)
   Larkin (Greene)
Carlile, Jesse (Telfair)
   Mary (Columbia)
   William (Telfair)
Carlisle, Benjamin (Columbia)
   Edmund (Morgan)
   Edward (Lincoln)
   Hosea (Jackson)
   John (Jackson)
   Robert (Hall)
   Robert (Morgan)
   Susanna (Washington)
   William (Wilkinson)
Carlton, Leonard (Jones)
   Stephen (Elbert)
Carmen, Celia (Hancock)
Carmichael, James (Washington)
   John (Richmond)
   Joseph (Morgan)
   Joseph W. (Columbia)
   William (Clarke)
Carmikel, John (Telfair)
Carmmel, Alexander (Warren)
Carmyie, Peter (Camden)
Carnday (?), Sarah (Richmond)
Carne (?), Mary Hancock)
Carner, Mathew (Oglethorpe)
Carnes, James (Hall)
   John (Habersham)
   John (Richmond)
   Peter (Richmond)
   Thomas P. (Clarke)
Carnochar (?), John (Chatham)
Carns, Edmon (Hall)
   Joseph (Hall)
   Peter (Hall)
   Thomas (Hall)
Caro, Benjamin (Warren)
Caron, John (Wilkes)
Carothers, William (Oglethorpe)
Carpenter, Absalom (Elbert)
   Bailey, Jr. (Burke)
   Bailey, Sr. (Burke)
   Charles W. (Chatham)
   John (Burke)
   John (Hancock)
   John (Lincoln)
   Jonathon (Hall)
   Joshua (Elbert)
   Josiah (Tattnall)
   Thomas (Warren)
Carpey, Zecheriah (Tattnall)
Carr, Allen (Pulaski)

   Benajmin (Clarke)
   David (Elbert)
   Henry (Early)
   Hugh (Hall)
   Hugh (Pulaski)
   James (Hall)
   John (Elbert)
   John B. (Chatham)
   Nancy (Greene)
   Robin (Hancock)
   Samuel (Elbert)
   Thomas, Jr. (Columbia)
   William (Chatham)
   William (Hall)
   William (Warren)
   William A. (Clarke)
Carrel, John (Richmond)
Carrell, Benjamin (Gwinnett)
   Delana (Warren)
   James H. (Gwinnett)
   Jesse W. (Morgan)
   Mary (Elbert)
   Peter (Gwinnett)
   Thomas (Gwinnett)
Carrill, Leonard (Jasper)
Carrington, Daniel (Wilkes)
   Henson (Madison)
   John (Oglethorpe)
   Jonathan W. (Jones)
   Timothy (Madison)
Carrinton, John (Baldwin)
Carrol, Abner (Jackson)
   Ann (Columbia)
   Harvell H. (Greene)
   Jesse (Wilkes)
   John (Warren)
   John W. (Burke)
   Jonathan (McIntosh)
   Mitchell (Columbia)
   Polly (Hall)
   Roween (Jefferson)
   Thomas (Wilkinson)
   William (Columbia)
   William (Hancock)
Carroll, Briton (Warren)
   David Jasper)
   Isaac (Montgomery)
   James (Columbia)
   Sarah (Hall)
Carruth, Adam (Madison)
   James (Madison)
   Robert (Madison)
Carruthers, Anderson (Jones)
   John (Pulaski)
   Joseph (Chatham)
   Robert (Jones)
   Thomas (Jones)
   William (Madison)
Carry, Thomas (Putnam)
Carsan, John (Appling)
Carsey, Aggy (Wilkes)

Carson Mrs. (Chatham)
   Adam (Jones)
   James (Pulaski)
   John (Jones)
   Ranson (Wayne)
Carstarphin, O. D. (Putnam)
   Thomas C. (Putnam)
Carswell, Alexander (Burke)
   Alexander (Telfair)
   Elizabeth (Burke)
   Matthew (Burke)
   Mathew (Wilkinson)
Carter, (ind.) (Laurens)
   Abram (Hancock)
   Alexander (Burke)
   Allen (Warren)
   Armsted (Oglethorpe)
   Benjamin D. (Walton)
   Benoney (Oglethorpe)
   Cader (Greene)
   Cally (Jackson)
   Charles (2) (Oglethorpe)
   Charles R. (2) (Wilkes)
   Christopher A. (Clarke)
   D. (Jasper)
   Daniel (Warren)
   David (Appling)
   David (Washington)
   Edward (Oglethorpe)
   Elisha (Oglethorpe)
   Elizabeth (Elbert)
   Elizabeth (Oglethorpe)
   Elizabeth (Warren)
   Elmore (Emanuel)
   Ezekiel (Washington)
   Favis (Baldwin)
   Francis (Walton)
   George (Elbert)
   George (Jasper)
   George (Putnam)
   George (Tattnall)
   Giles (Washington)
   Harwick (Hancock)
   Henry (Warren)
   Isaac (Appling)
   Isaac (2) (Hancock)
   Isaac (Jasper)
   Jacob (2) (Appling)
   Jacob (Liberty)
   James (Elbert)
   James (Emanuel)
   James (2) (Hancock)
   James (2) (Warren)
   James, Sr. (Warren)
   James (Wilkes)
   Jane (Appling)
   Jared (Hancock)
   Jesse (Oglethorpe)
   Jesse (Warren)
   John (Camden)
   John (Chatham)

Carter, John (Elbert)
John (Habersham)
John (Gwinnett)
John (Oglethorpe)
John (2) (Richmond)
John A. (Jasper)
John A. (Oglethorpe)
Jonathan (Putnam)
Joseph (Greene)
Joseph (Jasper)
Josiah (Appling)
Josiah (McIntosh)
Josiah (Warren)
Kindred (Hancock)
Moore (Warren)
Moses (Chatham)
Nancy (Warren)
Nathan (Morgan)
Nicholas (Chatham)
Pall (Oglethorpe)
Peesley (Habersham)
Phebe (Liberty)
Rebeccah (Jackson)
Richard (Jasper)
Robart (Oglethorpe)
Robert (Habersham)
Robert D. (Hall)
Robert M. (Elbert)
Samuel (Wilkinson)
Sherling (Wilkes)
Silas (Washington)
Silas, Sr. (Washington)
Silverster (Female) (Jones)
Thomas (Early)
Thomas (Habersham)
Thomas (Hancock)
Thomas (3) (Oglethorpe)
Thomas, Jr. (Oglethorpe)
Thomas (Putnam)
Thomas P. (Elbert)
Thomas S. (Elbert)
Tillman (Habersham) John
W. (Richmond) (Appling)
Wiley (Chatham)
Wiley (Oglethorpe)
William (Appling)
Wiliam (Chatham)
William (Hancock)
William (2) (Oglethorpe)
William R. (Elbert)
Carterson, R. (Richmond)
Carthan, (ind.) (Laurens)
Cartier, P. (Chatham)
Cartledge, Edmond (Columbia)
James (Columbia)
John (2) (Columbia)
Carttidge (?), Samuel
(Madison)
Cartwright, Jonas (Greene)
Martha (Greene)
Carty, S. (ind.) (Oglethorpe)

Sarah (Clarke)
Caruthers, Nancy (Burke)
Samuel (Gwinnett)
William (Burke)
Carver, Elijah (2) (Appling)
Jese (Appling)
Sampson (Appling)
Thomas (Hall)
William (Montgomery)
Cary, Edward (Baldwin)
Elphasen (Warren)
George (Columbia)
John (Laurens)
Robert (Jones)
Casar, Celea (Chatham)
Casey, Elisha (Walton)
Henry (Morgan)
Hiram (Walton)
Mary (Richmond)
P. H. (Richmond)
Cash, Dawson (Columbia)
I. H. (Richmond)
James (Jackson)
Jesse (Elbert)
John (Elbert)
John (Jackson)
Moses (Elbert)
Nelson (Habersham)
Patrick (Jackson)
Reuben (Elbert)
Cashin, Mary (Richmond)
Cason, (torn) (Laurens)
Connon, Tattnall)
Dennis (Tattnall)
Eli (Appling)
Elisha (Oglethorpe)
Eliza (Lincoln)
Frederick (Appling)
Gabriel (Tattnall)
Henry (Washington)
Hillary (Screven)
John (Elbert)
Paeples (Lincoln)
Seth (Lincoln)
William (Warren)
William (Washington)
Williby (Bryan)
Willis (Bryan)
Casselberry, Web. (Baldwin)
Cassels, Sarah (Liberty)
William H. Liberty)
Cassey, Philip (Greene)
Cassidy, Hugh (Chatham)
Castleberry, (ind.) (Gwinnett)
Claborn (Hall)
David (Gwinnett)
E. (Jasper)
Elisha (Hancock)
Ephraim (Putnam)
James (Gwinnett)
James (Wilkinson)

Jeremiah (Putnam)
Mark (Hall)
Mary (Warren)
Odin (Hall)
Peter (Warren)
Robert (Wilkinson)
Sarah (Hancock)
Thomas (Gwinnett)
Thomas (Jasper)
William (Jasper)
Castlebery, Henry (Telfair)
Castles, Absalom (Morgan)
Henry (Morgan)
Castleton, James (Washington)
William (Washington)
Castorten, Thomas (Oglethorpe)
Caswell, Allison (Chatham)
Isham (Putnam)
James (Tattnall)
Lewis (Chatham)
M. M. (Liberty)
Nathen (Putnam)
Catcherson, James (Oglethorpe)
Catchings, Benjamin (Putnam)
Leamir (Putnam)
William (Putnam)
Cater, Benjamin F. (Glynn)
Cates, Charles (Walton)
James (Burke)
John (Burke)
John (Jackson)
John (Walton)
Catlepp, Benjamin (Elbert)
Catlet, Polly (Burke)
Cato, Francis (Washington)
Green (Hancock)
Jinny (Burke)
William (Montgomery)
William (Wilkes)
Catoe, George (Wilkinson)
Cauley, Resin (Jefferson)
William (Jefferson)
Cauly(?), Alford (Jefferson)
Rowland (Jefferson)
Causey, Ezekial (Jefferson)
John (Jefferson)
Philip (Burke)
Caussin, Lewis (Chatham)
Caustin, Hester (Burke)
Cave, Mary (2) (Jones)
Caven, Alexander (Hall)
William (Hall)
Cavenah, Edward (Putnam)
Cavender, Clemouth (Hall)
George (2) (Walton)
Joseph (Gwinnett)
William (Emanuel)
Caver (?), Catherine (Lincoln)
Caver, Jacob (Lincoln)
Cavern, Forgy (Jackson)
Cawby, Willis (Columbia)

{ 26 }

Cawley, George (Laurens)
  Joel (Morgan)
  M. (Laurens)
  Robert (Wilkinson)
  William (Wilkinson)
  Zachariah (Morgan)
Cawthorn, James (Morgan)
  Thomas (Morgan)
Cay, Wiliam (Baldwin)
Cayton, John D. (Jones)
Cazy, John (Hall)
Cearlin, Elizabeth (Elbert)
Cellers, Alford (Jefferson)
  William (Jefferson)
  William C. (Jefferson)
Cercy, Duncan (Telfair)
Cessna, Robert (Morgan)
  Robert Baker (Morgan)
Cessums, Patrick (Burke)
Cha(ind.), Charles (Chatham)
Chadbourn, (ind.) (Effingham)
Chadrias, Mrs. (Chatham)
Chaffin, Isham (Wilkes)
  Lemuel (Morgan)
  Leonard (Wilkes)
Chafin, Joshua (Jasper)
  Robert (Jasper)
  W. (Jasper)
Chafue(?), John (Jasper)
Chainey, Thomas (Morgan)
Chains, William (Jones)
Chair, Amos (Wilkes)
Chairs (?), Benjamin (Pulaski)
Chaistian(?), Joseph (Hancock)
Chalker, Hodges (Warren)
  Nathaniel (Warren)
  Samuel (Warren)
Chamber, William (Habersham)
Chamberlain, Washington
       (Gwinnett)
Chambers, David (Montgomery)
  Dicy (Warren)
  Edwin (Putnam)
  Harden (Hancock)
  Henry (Effingham)
  Isaac (Habersham)
  John (Jefferson)
  John (Hall)
  Joseph (Jones)
  Peter (Washington)
  Thomas (Elbert)
  William (Elbert)
  William (Hall)
  William (Putnam)
Chamblee, William (Hall)
Chambles, Henry (Warren)
Chambless, Ephraim (Bulloch)
  Jesse (Jones)
  John (Baldwin)
  John (Jones)
  Littleton (Jones)

  Samuel (Washington)
  William (Jones)
  Zachariah (Baldwin)
Chambliss, Christopher
       (Warren)
  Jetha (Warren)
Chambour, William (Wilkinson)
Champain, Charles L.
       (McIntosh)
Champeon, Abner (Putnam)
  Henry (Putnam)
  James (Putnam)
Champion, (torn) (Laurens)
  Eleas (Hancock)
  Eli (Hancock)
  Henry (Hancock)
  John (Jefferson)
  John (Warren)
  Littleberry (Jones)
  Murphy (Warren)
Chance, Henry (Burke)
  James (Jefferson)
  Jesse (Burke)
  Joseph (Burke)
  Reuben (Burke)
  Simpson (Jefferson)
  Stephen (Burke)
  William (Burke)
Chancely, William (Washington)
Chancy, Finey (Appling)
  John (Jones)
  Thomas (Chatham)
Chandler, Abraham (Gwinnett)
  Baily (Jackson)
  George (Burke)
  Joseph (Walton)
  John (Walton)
  John, Sr. (Walton)
  Lewis (Oglethorpe)
  Mary (Elbert)
  Mary (Wilkinson)
  Parker (Jackson)
  Robert (Jackson)
  Solomon (Jackson)
  Tabitha (Jackson)
  William C. (Oglethorpe)
Chandor (?), Isaac (Jackson)
Chaney, Hugh (Camden)
  James (Montgomery)
  Jeremiah (McIntosh)
  John (Montgomery)
  John (2) (Wilkes)
  Quilla (Morgan)
Channel, Harman (Putnam)
  Thomas (Hancock)
Channell, Michel (Greene)
Channet (?) Mr. (Chatham)
Chapel, John A. (Camden)
  Thomas B. (Elbert)
Chapman, Abner (Jasper)
  Ambros (Baldwin)

  Asa (Warren)
  Benjamin (Wilkes)
  Debera S. (Baldwin)
  Francis I. (Liberty)
  Isaih (Baldwin)
  Irsael (Burke)
  John (Putnam)
  John D. Baldwin)
  Joseph (Elbert)
  M. A. (Chatham)
  Nathan (Wilkes)
  Randle (Greene)
  Robert (Warren)
  Samond (Samuel) (Jones)
  Samuel (Jackson)
  Sanford (Jones)
  Thomas (Wilkes)
  William (Wilkinson)
Chappel, Benjamin (Putnam)
Chappell, Jessie (Greene)
  John (Greene)
  John (Hancock)
  John (Jones)
Chapple, Abraham (Walton)
  Allen (Greene)
  Obadiah (Walton)
Chapps, James (2) (Jones)
Charles, Ray (Wilkes)
Charlton, Arthur M. (Wilkes)
  John (Effingham)
  John K. M. (Wilkes)
  Robert (Chatham)
  Samuel (Screven)
  Thomas M. (Chatham)
Chase, George (McIntosh)
Chason, John (Emanuel)
  William (Jones)
Chastain, John (Pulaski)
Chasteen, John (Hall)
Chastien, Blas (Washington)
  Peter (Washington)
  Raney (Washington)
Chatfield, George (Morgan)
  John (Jasper)
Chatham, George (Putnam)
  Josiah (Wilkes)
Chatman, Frances (Jones)
  Naban (Jasper)
Chatteen, Benjamin
       (Habersham)
Chattier, Plaied L. (McIntosh)
Chavers, Margaret (Chatham)
Cheatain, Thomas (Greene)
Cheatham, Ann (Jefferson)
  Anthony R. (Jefferson)
  Charles (Jefferson)
  Isham (2) (Oglethorpe)
  Josiah (Oglethorpe)
  Obadiah P. (Jefferson)
Cheaves, Grief (Morgan)

(27)

Cheek, Burgess (Elbert)
   James (Morgan)
   John (Madison)
   Thomas (Habersham)
   William, Jr. (Elbert)
   William, Sr. (Elbert)
Cheely, John (Hancock)
   Thomas (Hancock)
Cheeves, Abner (Washington)
Chenault, John (Columbia)
Chenning, Mary (Putnam)
Cherry, George (Pulaski)
   Samuel (Pulaski)
Cheser, John (Tattnall)
Cheshire, Turpen (Baldwin)
Chesser, widow (Morgan)
Chessher, Thomas (Liberty)
Chester, Absolam (Washington)
Chevrier, Doctor (Chatham)
Chew, John (Greene)
Chewning, David (Greene)
Chick, Anderson (Madison)
   James (Madison)
Chieves, James (Putnam)
   Sarah (Putnam)
Childam, Josua (Jones)
Childers, Duglas (Gwinnett)
   Gilford (Lincoln)
   Holman (Elbert)
   John (Elbert)
   John (Jackson)
   N. (Hancock)
   Nathan (Wilkinson)
   Richard (Washington)
   Thomas (Elbert)
   William (Hancock)
   Wiley (Elbert)
Childress, John (Lincoln)
Childs, James (Jones)
   John, Sr. (Jones)
   Jon. W. (Jones)
   Martha (Washington)
Chiles, Daniel (Wilkinson)
   Elizabeth (Wilkinson)
   John E. (Jones)
   John (Elbert)
   John (Jones)
   Jonathon (Gwinnett)
   Matthew (Jones)
Chilly, William (Chatham)
Chislom, John (Elbert)
Chisolm, A. R. (McIntosh)
   Andrew (Walton)
   George W. (Morgan)
   Sily (Jefferson)
   Thomas (Morgan)
Chissin, John (Screven)
Chitchens, Joseph (Greene)
Chitwood, Daniel, Sr.
        (Habersham)
Chivers, (ind.) (Wilkes)

James (Wilkes)
Joel (Early)
Larkin (Early)
Nancy (Washington)
Robert (Wilkes)
Choice, Tuley (Hancock)
Chosher, Penson O. (Wilkes)
Chrenshaw, William H.
        (Baldwin)
Christar, Absalom (Jackson)
Christian, Charles (Baldwin)
   Charles W. (Elbert)
   Edward L. (Madison)
   Elijah (Elbert)
   Elizabeth (Madison)
   Isaac (Elbert)
   James (Elbert)
   John (Elbert)
   Reuben (Elbert)
   Robert B. (Elbert)
   Rufus (Elbert)
   Simon (Madison)
   Turner (Elbert)
   William (Hall)
   William B. (Elbert)
   William P. (Elbert)
Christians, Presley (Elbert)
Christin, Gabriel (Oglethorpe)
Christmas, Mrs. M. A. (Greene)
Christo, Robert (Chatham)
   Victoire (Chatham)
Christopher, Cory (Morgan)
   David (Greene)
   David (Oglethorpe)
   John (Oglethorpe)
   Rebecca (Liberty)
   William (Oglethorpe)
Christy, Nathan (Jefferson)
   Patrick (Chatham)
Chritendon, Lemuel (Putnam)
Church, Alonzo (Clarke)
   Benjamin (Habersham)
   Constantine (Wilkes)
   Samuel (Camden)
   Timothy (Habersham)
Churchill, James (Richmond)
   William (Richmond)
Chyher (?), Esther (Clarke)
Cimbrough, Leonard (Baldwin)
Cissac, John M. (Putnam)
Clack, John (Walton)
Clackley, Pacole (Jasper)
Clagg, David (Burke)
Clancy, Elliott (Habersham)
Clandon, Frank (Jones)
Clanton, Littlebury (Columbia)
Clardy, Abram (Jackson)
Clark, Abigail (McIntosh)
   Amelia (Warren)
   Andrew (Chatham)
   Angel (McIntosh)

C. W. (Richmond)
Christiana (Bryan)
Christopher (Burke)
Christopher (Elbert)
D. (Richmond)
Daniel (Wilkinson)
David (Elbert)
David (Habersham)
David (Jones)
Drewrey (Wilkinson)
Edward, Sr. (Elbert)
Eli (Jones)
Elizabeth (Montgomery)
Francis (Richmond)
G. (Richmond)
George (Jasper)
Gibson (Telfair)
Henry (Montgomery)
Hoseah W. (Columbia)
J. (Richmond)
J. M. (Richmond)
J. R. (Jasper)
James (Elbert)
James (Greene)
James, Jr. (Greene)
James W. (Wilkinson
Jeremiah (Putnam)
John (Baldwin)
John (Camden)
John (Gwinnett)
John (Hancock)
John (Laurens)
John (Lincoln)
John (Richmond)
John H. (Putnam)
John M. (Putnam)
Johnson (Greene)
Joshua (Elbert)
Joshua B. (Jones)
Larkin (Elbert)
Larkin (Morgan)
Mark D. (Lincoln)
Nancy (Habersham)
Nathan (Montgomery)
Nathaniel (Greene)
Nathaniel (Richmond)
Oliver (Putnam)
Rebecca (Elbert)
Richard (Jasper)
Robert (Elbert)
S. W. G. (Laurens)
Samuel (Jasper)
Samuel (McIntosh)
Samuel (Morgan)
Samuel (Wilkinson)
Susasanah (Chatham)
Thomas (Montgomery)
Thomas (Putnam)
Thomas (Walton)
William (Clark)
William (Hall)

Clark, William (Hancock)
William (Jones)
William (Putnam)
William (Walton)
William B. (Baldwin)
Williamson (Elbert)
Clarke, Archibald (Camden)
Asa (Chatham)
Mrs. C. (Chatham)
Charles (2) (Burke)
David (Washington)
George (Camden)
J. (Camden)
James (McIntosh)
Jesse (Wilkes)
John (Burke)
John (Chatham)
John (Jackson)
Fanny (Burke)
Sammie (Camden)
Samuel (Jefferson)
Thomas (Camden)
Thomas (Jefferson)
William (2) (Jefferson)
William P. (Chatham)
Clarny (?), Barbara M. (Burke)
Clary, David (Jackson)
Rody (Appling)
Claton, Robert (Jasper)
Clay, Augusta (Columbia)
Charles (Columbia)
Eve (Wilkinson) *Eve*
James (Richmond)
Jesse (Columbia)
Jesse (Jasper)
Maryan (Morgan)
Perce (Wilkinson)
Pierce (Washington)
Richard (Jasper)
Robert (Wilkinson)
Samuel (Jasper)
Thomas (Jasper)
Wiliam (Washington)
Claybourne, James (Hancock)
Clayton, Augustin S. (Clarke)
Elizabeth (Putnam)
Geo. R. (Baldwin)
James (2) (Hancock)
James, Sr. (Hancock)
Nelson (Pulaski)
Stephen (Hall)
Thomas (2) (Hancock)
Clealand, G. (Richmond)
Cleary, John (Bryan)
Cleatin, Middleton (Gwinnett)
Cleaton, (ind.) (Gwinnett)
Henrietta (Gwinnett)
William (Gwinnett)
Cleghorn, George (Columbia)
James (Hall)
John (Madison)

William (Madison)
Clelard, John (Chatham)
Moses (Chatham)
Clemant, James (Wilkes)
Clemens, Henry (Wilkes)
Clement, Jacob (Telfair)
John (Hall)
Joseph (Laurens)
Clements, Andrew (Gwinnett)
Anna (Putnam)
Austin (Morgan)
Charles (Gwinnett)
Charles (Madison)
David (Putnam)
Eleanor (Madison)
Ellice (Greene)
Gabriel (Madison)
Henry (Wilkes)
Isaac (Wilkes)
Jacob (Burke)
Jacob (Putnam)
James (Gwinnett)
James (Jefferson)
Jeptha (Putnam)
Lucy (Oglethorpe)
Mary (Jefferson)
Mary (Putnam)
Mary A. (Burke)
Michael (Wayne)
Payton (Greene)
Peyton (2) (Putnam)
Samuel (Jefferson)
Stephen (Baldwin)
William (Jefferson)
William (Gwinnett)
William T. (Greene)
Clemments, Joseph
(Montgomery)
Sam (Wayne)
William (Wayne)
Clementz, Thomas (Jefferson)
Clemmons, Thomas (Jones)
Thomas (Richmond)
Clemon, Jesse (Oglethorpe)
Clemons, Joseph (Pulaski)
William (Jones)
Clemmonts, Moses (Wilkinson)
Clemonts, Philip (Putnam)
Cleton, Richard (Clarke)
Cleveland, Benjamin
(Habersham)
I. J. (Jasper)
Jeremiah (Habersham)
John (Elbert)
John (Habersham)
Reuben (Elbert)
Cleves, John (2) (Morgan)
Cley, Sebowrn (Greene)
Cliat, Jesse (Lincoln)
Cliatt, Isom (Richmond)
Thomas (Warren)

Clift, William (Morgan)
Zacriah (Oglethorpe)
Clifton, Aaron (Clarke)
Archibald (Liberty)
Curtis (Greene)
Daniel (Jones)
Elizabeth (Screven
Henry (Bulloch)
John (Emanuel)
Liven (Putnam)
Thomas (Screven)
Cliffton, Ezekiel (Tattnall)
William (Tattnall)
William (Clarke)
Clinch, Edward (Pulaski)
Cline, Henry (Baldwin)
Jonathan (Chatham)
Clock, George W. (Walton)
Clopton, Allford (Putnam)
James B. (Putnam)
Miller (Putnam)
Thomas (Putnam)
Cloud Elizabeth (Early)
Ezekeal (Putnam)
Joel, Sr. (Warren)
John (Early)
Reuben (Baldwin)
Clover, Wiley (Hall)
Clowder, Wiley C. (Oglethorpe)
Clower, George (Putnam)
Jane (Morgan)
Jesse (Morgan)
Morgan (Jasper)
Peter (Jones)
Thomas (Baldwin)
Club, Colin (Camden)
James (Camden)
James A. (Camden)
William (Camden)
Clyatt, Samuel (Tattnall)
Coal, Mark (Early)
Coalman, John (Bryan)
Coalson, Joseph B. (Pulaski)
Sanders (Pulaski)
Coates, Martha (Chatham)
Coats, Calvin (Wilkes)
Henry (Putnam)
James (Morgan)
John (Wilkes)
Lemuel (Hall)
Lesly (Wilkes)
Nathaniel (Putnam)
Robert (Laurens)
Thomas (Laurens)
Thomas G. (Laurens)
Cobb, Benjamin (Baldwin)
Briton (Burke)
Bryant (Telfair)
Curtis (Emanuel)
Daniel (Baldwin)
Edward (Pulaski)

Horatio (Tattnall)
Jacob (Baldwin)
Jacob (Hancock)
James (Wilkinson)
John (Wilkes)
John A. (Jefferson)
Levy (Hancock)
Lewis (Tattnall)
Mary (Elbert)
Nathaniel (Putnam)
Thomas (Columbia)
Thomas W. (Oglethorpe)
Thomas W. (Greene)
Wiley (Wilkinson)
William (Hall)
William A. (Hancock)
Willis (Columbia)
Cobbin, John (Washington)
Cobbs, Samuel B. (Morgan)
Cobhm, William (McIntosh)
Cochran, Elisha (Morgan)
   Felix (Columbia)
   Hugh (Effingham)
   John (Columbia)
   William (Morgan)
Cochrum, Banister (Morgan)
   Matthew (Morgan)
Cock, John (Burke)
   Richard (Jasper)
Cockburn, George (Hall)
Cocker, Thomas (Richmond)
Cockerun, James (Gwinnett)
Cockram, Archibald (Hall)
   Charles (Hall)
   James (Jackson)
   Robert (Hall)
Cockran, Alford (Wilkes)
   Marten (Jasper)
Cockrum, Cheadle (Gwinnett)
Cocks, Aaron B. (Wilkinson)
Cocroft, Henry (Warren)
Codding, Elisha (Chatham)
Cody, Barnett (Warren)
   David, Jr. (Warren)
   David, Sr. (Warren)
   Edmund (Warren)
   Elizabeth (Warren)
   James (Warren)
   James, Sr. (Warren)
   Jesse (Jackson)
   John (Warren)
   Michael (Warren)
Coffee, John (Telfair)
   John (Wilkes)
Coffer, Thomas B. (Wilkes)
Coffman, A. (Jasper)
Cofield, John (Pulaski)
   John (Washington)
   Willis (Putnam)
Cogburn, Cyprus (Washington)
   James C. (Putnam)

Moses H. (Clarke)
Coggin, William (Walton)
   Zilphy (Walton)
Coggins, Alex (Hall)
   Joshua (Morgan)
Cohen, Isaac (Chatham)
   Maria (Chatham)
Coher, Anderson (Wilkinson)
Cohn, Joseph M. (Burke)
Cohoon, Adam (2) (Washington)
   Alan (Washington)
   James (Washington)
   Sarah (Washington)
Cohran, John (Wilkes)
   Joseph (Wilkes)
Cohron, Cornelius (Wilkes)
Cohroon, Elizabeth (Hancock)
Coil, Gideon M. (Burke)
   John (Hall)
   Robert (Hall)
Coker, Abraham (Elbert)
   Alsey (Elbert)
Coker and Butler (Jasper)
   Elisha (Putnam)
   Francis, Jr. (Telfair)
   Francis, Sr. (Telfair)
   Jacob (Elbert)
   James (Walton)
   Jonth C. (Jackson)
   Malacia (Elbert)
   Pleasant (Walton)
   Robert (Walton)
   Sollomon (Walton)
   Thomas (Jackson)
   William (Washington)
Colbart, Elizabeth (Wilkes)
Colbert, Frederick G. (Greene)
   James (Jasper)
   John (2) (Hancock)
   John G. (Morgan)
   Jonathan (Baldwin)
   Larken (Oglethorpe)
   Richmond (Hancock)
   Susannah (Elbert)
   William (Elbert)
Colby, Jonathon (Wilkes)
   John (Greene)
Colclough, William (Greene)
Colding, Thomas (Screven)
Coldwell, Charles Y. (Putnam)
   Margaret (Morgan)
   Peter (Morgan)
Cole, Benjamin (Washington)
   Bud (Screven)
   Duke (Greene)
   Eliza (Richmond)
   George M. (Warren)
   Grovey (Putnam)
   John (Chatham)
   John (Glynn)
   John (Habersham)

John (Jefferson)
Reuben (Jones)
Robert (2) (Jasper)
Samuel (Lincoln)
Sarah (Columbia)
Simeon (Glynn)
Thomas (Pulaski)
William (Greene)
William (Screven)
Coleman, (torn) (2) (Laurens)
   (ind.) (Gwinnett)
   Abner (Gwinnett)
   Allen W. (Greene)
   Archibald (Morgan)
   Charles (Burke)
   David (Putnam)
   Elisha (Burke)
   Elisha (Wilkes)
   Elizabeth (Greene)
   Fanny (Greene)
   Harriet (Columbia)
   Isham (Washington)
   Jacob (Emanuel)
   Jesse (Burke)
   Jesse (Greene) John
   John (Elbert) (Appling)
   John (Greene)
   John (2) (Jefferson)
   John (Morgan)
   John (Pulaski)
   John (Wilkes)
   Jonathon (Emanuel)
   L. (Richmond) Moses
   Philip (Gwinnett) (Appling
   (torn) R. (Laurens)
   Robert (Laurens)
   Robert (Washington)
   Samuel (Walton)
   Sarah (Baldwin)
   Thomas (Hancock)
   Thomas (Morgan)
   Thompson (Wilkes)
   William (Jefferson)
   William (Tattnal)
   Willis (Baldwin)
Colement (?), G. L. (Richmond)
Coleson, Abraham (Elbert)
   James (Elbert)
Colevert, John (Putnam)
Coley, Gabriel (Hall)
Colhan, Henry (Jones)
Colhoon, Ephraim (Putnam)
Colier, John (Jasper)
   Richard (Baldwin)
Colins, G. (Richmond)
   J. (Richmond)
   John (Richmond)
Collada, William (Elbert)
Collant, Wilson (Jasper)
Collar (?), Matthews (Lincoln)
Collars, Benajab (Lincoln)

Matthews, Jr. (Lincoln)
Elijah (Lincoln)
Collatt, John (Elbert)
Coller, David (Jefferson)
William (Oglethorpe)
Colley, Anderson (Oglethorpe)
Edward (Madison)
James (Habersham)
James (Oglethorpe)
John ,Greene)
John (Madison)
Nelson (Jasper)
Sarah (Madison)
Zachariah (Madison)
Colliar, Benjamin (Oglethorpe)
Collier, Mrs. C. C. (Greene)
Cuthburth (Oglethorpe)
Henden (Oglethorpe)
Henry (Greene)
Isaac (Oglethorpe)
James (Greene)
James (Laurens)
Martha (Columbia)
Meredith (Gwinnett)
Meril (Gwinnett)
Robert (Jasper)
Robert W. (Wilkes)
Thomas (Greene)
Vines (Oglethorpe)
Colliers, William (Oglethorpe)
Collins, Alfred (Lincoln)
Andrew (Jackson)
Benj. I. D. (Hancock)
Benj. M. (Hancock)
Cornelius (Columbia)
Crees (Washington)
Dennis (Baldwin)
Eleanor (Tattnall)
George (Chatham)
George (Hancock)
Gibson (Wilkes)
Hardy (Tattnall)
Henderson (Baldwin)
Henry (Jackson)
Henry (Oglethorpe)
James (Bulloch)
James (2) (Columbia)
James (Hall)
James (Irwin)
James (Jackson)
James (Wilkinson)
Jesse (Tattnall)
Joab (Tattnall)
John (Burke)
John (Columbia)
John, Jr. (Columbia)
John (Hall)
John (Madison)
John (McIntosh)
John (Washington)
John M. (Chatham)

Jonus (Oglethorpe)
Joseph (Baldwin)
Joseph (Gwinnett)
Joseph (Morgan)
Joseph (Tattnall)
Joseph, Jr. (Tattnall)
Joseph, Sr. (Tattnall)
Josiah (Tattnall)
Joshua (Washington)
Levin (Burke)
Lewis (Washington)
Littleton (Columbia)
Major (Jefferson)
Margaret (McIntosh)
Moses (Wilkes)
Peter H. (Columbia)
Robert (Hancock)
Seaborn (Columbia)
Thomas (Washington)
Thomas (Wilkinson)
Timothy (Wilkes)
Washington (Wilkes)
William (Chatham)
William (Hancock)
William (Morgan)
William (Washington)
William (Wilkinson)
Willis (Oglethorpe)
Willis (Walton)
Wilson (Wilkinson)
Wyatt (Wilkes)
Zacka (Jackson)
Collinsworth, John (Morgan)
Collon, Solomon (Hall)
Collum, Sarah (Oglethorpe)
Colly, Francis (Wilkes)
Colly, Lewis (Walton)
Sarah (Wilkes)
Colquet, Thomas (Greene)
Colquit, James (2) (Oglethorpe)
John (Oglethorpe)
Robert (Oglethorpe)
Colquitt, Lucy (Greene)
Nancy S. (Hancock)
Nancy T. (Hancock)
William (Oglethorpe)
Colson, B. M. (Tattnall)
Dennis (Screven)
Colson (?) George (Lincoln)
Colson, Hope (Screven)
Jacob (Lincoln)
Henry (Bulloch)
Mathew (Screven)
Paul B. (Screven)
William (Camden)
Colt, John (Greene)
Colvard, John S. (Elbert)
Colvend, William (Columbia)
Colvin, John (Washington)
Colwell, Glenn (Oglethorpe)
James (Greene)

John (Greene)
Joshua (Greene)
Samual (Greene)
Samuel (Laurens)
William (Greene)
William (Hancock)
William (Oglethorpe)
Colyer, Wyatt (Hancock)
Combs, B. (Jasper)
Enoch (Wilkes)
John (Camden)
John (Wilkes)
Milly (Wilkes)
Nathaniel (Jasper)
Phillip (2) (Wilkes)
Phillip, Jr. (Wilkes)
Sterling (Jackson)
Thomas (Wilkes)
William (Jackson)
Comens, David (Washington)
Eli (Washington)
Robert (Washington)
William (Washington)
Comer, Anderson (Jones)
Archa. (Bulloch)
Hugh M. (Jones)
James (Jones)
Joseph F. (Hall)
Commander, Samuel
(Richmond)
Compton, John W. (Jasper)
Pleasant (Oglethorpe)
Con (?), David (Baldwin)
Con, Zilphy (Baldwin)
Conant, Airs (Clarke)
Conden, John (Oglethorpe)
Condon, Caleb (Putnam)
Cone, Aaron (Bulloch)
Archelaus (Washington)
Bazil (Baldwin)
Ezekiel (Greene)
James (Baldwin)
James (Washington)
John (Jones)
John (Washington)
Joseph (Camden)
Levi (Washington)
Lewis (Washington)
Martha (Camden)
Mary (Washington)
Southertam (Jones)
William (Bulloch)
William (Greene)
Coner, Henry (Morgan)
Coney, Jeremiah (Laurens)
Joel (Laurens)
Conger, Simeon (Gwinnett)
Congo, Eli (Jasper)
Conky, David, M. M. (Jefferson)
Conn, William (Jones)
Connel, Daniel (Jefferson)

Connel, Jesse (Jefferson)
  Thomas (Jefferson)
Connell, Daniel (Greene)
  John (Jasper)
  Needy G. (Hancock)
  Penelope (Hancock)
  Thomas (Greene)
  William (Jasper)
Connelly, Charles (Clarke)
  John (Screven)
Connels, Hannah (Jasper)
Conner, Benjamin (Putnam)
  Creasy, Sr. (Screven)
  Edward (Clarke)
  Edward (Emanuel)
  Elijah (Warren)
  Frederick (Putnam)
  James (Putnam)
  James, Sr. (Screven)
  James (Tattnall)
  James G. (Montgomery)
  Jesse (Jasper)
  John (Burke)
  John (Clarke)
  John (Lincoln)
  John (Tattnall)
  John (Walton)
  Lewis (Screven)
  Mary (Burke)
  Micajah (Lincoln)
  Thomas (Clarke)
  William (Tattnall)
  Willis (Tattnall)
  Wilson (Montgomery)
  Wilson (Tattnall)
Connerat, Fanny (?) (Chatham)
Conners, Ross (Greene)
  Thomas (Screven)
Connie, Henry (Jackson)
Connifax, Benjamin (Walton)
Connor, Edward (Glynn)
  Nancy (Burke)
  Wilson (Jasper)
Connolley, Philoman,
            (Wilkinson)
Conoway, Curtis (Putnam)
  William (Putnam)
Conray, (Conrsey) John (Jones)
Constontin, B. (Chatham)
Conway, Henry (Warren)
Conyer, Daniel (Screven)
Conyers, Isaac (Screven)
  Henry (Washington)
  John (Screven)
  Rachel (Washington)
  William (Washington)
Coody, Lewis (Burke)
Cook, A. (Richmond)
  Abraham (Elbert)
  Abraham (Washington)
  Abram (Burke)

Alan (Washington)
Amos (Bryan)
Ast (Jones)
Augusta (Jasper)
Augustus (Jasper)
Benjamin (Elbert)
Benjamin (Hancock)
Benjamin (Putnam)
Benjamin (Washington)
Burwell (Jackson)
Caleb (Morgan)
Charles (Elbert)
Deborah (Washington)
Domingo (Chatham)
Edward (Jones)
Elizabeth (Jackson)
Fenton (Elbert)
Frances (Morgan)
Frederick (Irwin)
George (Elbert)
Gilphen (female) (Jones)
Harbard (Jefferson)
Henry (Effingham)
Isaac (Baldwin)
Issachai (Elbert)
James (Burke)
James (Effingham)
James (2) (Jefferson)
James (Jones)
James (Washington)
James C. (Morgan)
James W. (Hall)
Jeremiah (Richmond)
John (Elbert)
John (Gwinnett)
John (2) (Jefferson)
John (Morgan)
John (Pulaski)
John (2) (Washington)
John B. (Elbert)
John F. (Elbert)
John R. (Telfair)
Joseph (Baldwin)
Joseph (Greene)
Joshua (Elbert)
Joshua (Greene)
Julius (Putnam)
M. (ind.) (Richmond)
Mary (Elbert)
Mike (Washington)
Nancy (Jackson)
Nathan (Hancock)
Nathan (2) (Washington)
Nathaniel (Elbert)
Philip (Putnam)
R. W. (Richmond)
Samuel (Elbert)
Samuel (Jones)
Samuel (Putnam)
Savary (Washington)
Shem (Putnam)

Smith (Elbert)
Thomas (Elbert)
Thomas (Hall)
Thomas (Morgan)
William (Baldwin)
William (Bulloch)
William (Jasper)
William (Putnam)
William (Telfair)
William B. (Walton)
Zadock (Clarke)
Cooke, Adam (Chatham)
  Jeremiah (Putnam)
Cooksam, Jacob (Hall)
Cooksey, Caleb (Jefferson)
  Hezihiah, Sr. (Warren)
  John (Pulaski)
  John W. (Wilkes)
  Thomas W. (Wilkes)
Cooky, (Cooley) Walter Stephen
            (Jones)
Cooley, Turner (Pulaski)
Cooms, John S. (Richmond)
Cooney, James (Habersham)
Cooper, A. (Camden)
  Allies (wid.) (Wayne)
  Abner (?) (Greene)
  Arthur (Clarke)
  Augustin (Wilkes)
  Benjamin (Hall)
  Benjamin (Wilkinson)
  Beverly (2) (Hancock)
  David (Columbia)
  Davis (Baldwin)
  Drewry (Morgan)
  Elizabeth (Emanuel)
  Ephraim (Chatham)
  George (Montgomery)
  George (Pulaski)
  Gideon (Wilkes)
  Henry (Putnam)
  Howell (Jasper)
  Isaac (Wilkinson)
  James (Glynn)
  James (Greene)
  James (Jasper)
  James (Madison)
  James (Putnam)
  James A. (Columbia)
  James W. (Putnam)
  Jesse (Liberty)
  Jeremiah (Putnam)
  Joel (Columbia)
  John (Chatham)
  John (Hancock)
  John (Putnam)
  John, Sr. (Wilkes)
  John B. (Laurens)
  John M. (Richmond)
  John W. (Wilkes)
  Jonathon (Madison)

Cooper, Joseph (Burke)
  Joseph (Pulaski)
  Joseph, Jr. (Putnam)
  Josiah (Jones)
  Martha (Putnam)
  Micajah (Putnam)
  Mittloie (Putnam)
  Newton (Putnam)
  Philip (Putnam)
  Richard (Tattnall)
  Robert (Jasper)
  Samuel (2) (Putnam)
  Savian or Lavian (Baldwin)
  Thomas (Baldwin)
  Thomas (2) (Hancock)
  Thomas (Oglethorpe)
  Umphra (Jones)
  Vining (Madison)
  William (Laurens)
  William (Putnam)
  William J. (Warren)
  Woliby (Wayne)
  Capt. (Chatham)
Coots, John (Jasper)
Cope, Adam (Chatham)
  Brinkley (Elbert)
  George D. (Chatham)
  George L. (Chatham)
  John (McIntosh)
  Lewis (Madison)
  Maparipa (?) (Madison)
  Selah (Elbert)
Copeland, Benjamin (Greene)
  Colson (Greene)
  Elisha (Pulaski)
  Henry C. (Columbia)
  James (Gwinnett)
  Jesse (Liberty)
  John (Putnam)
  Masse M. (Jefferson)
  Nancy (Greene)
  Richard (Morgan)
  Robert (Montgomery)
  William (Morgan)
Copelin, John (Jasper)
  Isaac (Baldwin)
  Thomas (Gwinnett)
  William (Gwinnett)
Copeland, Colson (Greene)
  Elisha (Gwinnett)
  William (Greene)
Coplin, Gilbert (Wilkinson)
Coppage, Lewis (Wilkinson)
  William (Wilkes)
Coppee, Edward (Chatham)
Coguehon, F. B. (Richmond)
Coram, Thomas (Warren) .
  William (Warren)
Corbett, Grove (Washington)
  Richard (Jefferson)
Corbin, John (Richmond)

Leonard (M. C.) (Wilkes)
Cordel, Elnathan (Habersham)
Cordell, Benjamin (Habersham)
  Isham (Habersham)
Corden, John (Jasper)
Corder, Benjamin (Warren)
Cordery, (torn) (Gwinnett)
Cordry, Jonathon (Washington)
Corey (?), Thomas (Appling)
Corker, James (Liberty)
  Stephen (Burke)
Corlee, James (Gwinnett)
  Martha (Gwinnett)
  William, Jr. (Gwinnett)
  William, Sr. (Gwinnett)
Corley, Carter (Gwinnett)
  Jeremiah (Jones)
  Jonathon (Walton)
  Nancy (Jones)
  Robert (Putnam)
  Tubal (Putnam)
  Zachariah (Morgan)
Cormick, John (Richmond)
Cormikle, Richard (Oglethorpe)
Cornaham, William (McIntosh)
Cornelison, William (Wilkes)
Cornet. Eli (Burke)
Cornine, Richard (Putnam)
Cornwall, Daniel (Pulaski)
Cornwell, E. Jr. (Jasper)
  E. Sr. (Jasper)
Coro, Solomon (Washington)
Corrant, Jeremiah (Jasper)
Carrell, Sally (Greene)
Correy (?), Joseph (Chatham)
Corry, James (Greene)
Cortin, Thomas (Jasper)
Cory, Alexander (Morgan)
  John (Baldwin)
Cosby, Hickerson (Columbia)
  Nancy (Wilkes)
  Wingfield (Warren)
Coskes (?), John (Appling)
Cosly, Michael (Jackson)
Cosser, Joel B. (Wilkes)
Cossey, James (Wayne)
Costin, Francis (Jefferson)
Costly, Elizabeth (Morgan)
  Perce (Morgan)
Cotney, Francis (Walton)
  James (Walton)
Cotter, John V. (Hall)
Cottle, John J. (Jefferson)
  Josiah (Jones)
Cotton, Elijah (Jones)
  George (Warren)
  J. (Richmond)
  John (Jones)
  John (Putnam)
  Joseph (Gwinnett)
  Peter (Jackson)

Pleasant (Burke)
S. W. (Richmond)
Weaver (Wilkes)
Joseph (Columbia)
Smith (Putnam)
Susan (Columbia)
Syrus (Jones)
William (Jones)
William G. (Putnam)
Cottineau, Made. (Chatham)
Couch, James (Camden)
  John (Elbert)
  John (Putnam)
Couden, D. (Jasper)
Couey, Joseph (Gwinnett)
Couling, J. G. (Richmond)
Coulson, John (Burke)
  William (Burke)
Coulter, William (Jones)
Countes, C. L. (Camden)
  Harmon (Camden)
  J. K. (Camden)
  John (Camden)
Couper, J. Hamilton (Glynn)
  John (Glynn)
Coursey, Absalom (Jones)
  Daniel (Elbert)
  William (Jones)
Courtney, Ann (Chatham)
Courvoisie, Frances (Chatham)
Cousens, John (Richmond)
Cousins, Green (Baldwin)
Coursey, Alfred (Washington)
Coutch, Druery (Jasper)
  John (Jasper)
  William (Jasper)
Couttean, Charles (Burke)
Covennah, Charles (Burke)
  Sb(sic) (Burke)
Coville(?), Elisa (Screven)
Covington, John (Washington)
  Levin (Jefferson)
  Rubal(?) (Lincoln)
  William (Lincoln)
Cowan, Edward (Jackson)
  George (Jackson)
  Isaac (Gwinnett)
  James (Jackson)
  James (Jasper)
  Prudence (Jackson)
  William A. (Jones)
Coward, Abram (Emanuel)
  Elias (Wilkinson)
  John (Appling)
  John (Tattnall)
  Thomas (Wilkes)
Cowart, Hugh (Jefferson)
  James R. (Bulloch)
  John (Jefferson)
  Nathaniel (Emanuel)
  Stephen (Jefferson)

Cowart, William (Jefferson)
Zachariah (Burke)
Zachry (Screven)
Cowdon, Joseph (Jackson)
Cowen, John (Putnam)
William (Hall)
Cower, Lucy (Jones)
Cowles, Asbury (Putnam)
Thomas F. (Putnam)
Samuel (Greene)
Cowset, Ann (Putnam)
Cox, (torn) (Gwinnett)
Aaron (Burke)
Aaron (Washington)
Absalom (Jasper)
Agustus (Camden)
Asa (Putnam)
Betsy (Washington)
Caren (Putnam)
Chappel (Putnam)
Cury (2) (Jones)
Darius (Washington)
Edward (Oglethorpe)
Elizabeth (Morgan)
Ephraim (Jones)
Ichabod (Jones)
James (Jefferson)
James (Morgan)
James (2) (Washington)
Jepha (Madison)
Jesse (Burke)
Jesse (Jasper)
Jesse (Jones)
John (Gwinnett)
John (2) (Hall)
John (Jefferson)
John (Pulaski)
John R. (Richmond)
Joseph (Jones)
Joshua (Hall)
Milly (Burke)
Moses (Burke)
Moses (2) (Jones)
Moses (Washington)
Odum M. (Jackson)
Peggy (Burke)
Priestly (Jasper)
Rachel (Jefferson)
Richard (Habersham)
Robert (Oglethorpe)
Sam (Bulloch)
Samuel H. (Appling)
Stephen (Morgan)
Thomas (Gwinnett)
Thomas I. (Oglethorpe)
William (Burke)
William (Columbia)
William (Hall)
William (Morgan)
William (Putnam)
William (Wilkes)

William C. (Wilkes)
Williamson (Washington)
Zach'y. (Jasper)
Coxwell, Benjamin (Warren)
Mitchell (Warren)
Cozeast, Hubbard (Putnam)
Crab, Asa (Putnam)
Benjamin (Lincoln)
Robert (Washington)
Samuel (Putnam)
Crabb, Enoch (Jasper)
Samuel (Columbia)
Crabtree, John (Baldwin)
Craft, Anderson (Elbert)
Benjamin (Pulaski)
Daniel (2) (Clarke)
Edward (Clarke)
Garrett (Clarke)
Hugh (Baldwin)
Jesse (Burke)
John (Elbert)
Pleasant (Lincoln)
Raven (2) (Early)
William (Elbert)
Craig, Mrs. (Chatham)
Andrew (Jasper)
Charlotte (Chatham)
William (Camden)
William (Clarke)
Crain, George (Jasper)
Joshua R. (Wilkes)
Spencer, Jr. (Jasper)
Spencer, Sr. (Jasper)
Crainman, Mary (Warren)
Cramer, Samuel (Oglethorpe)
Solomon (Effingham)
Crane, Benj. (McIntosh)
Ezekiel (Putnam)
John (Burke)
John (Chatham)
Levi (Burke)
Moses (Burke)
Phillip (Richmond)
Theophelus (Putnam)
Thomas (Greene)
Cranford, James (Putnam)
Jesse (Putnam)
Mc & D. McDowell
(Jasper)
Cranson, John (Jasper)
Cranston, J. W. (Jasper)
Crapps, P. (ind.) (Chatham)
Cratin, John (Wilkes)
Cravey, David (Telfair)
Henry (Montgomery)
Cravy. Joshua (Bulloch)
Crawford, (ind.) (Warren)
Alexander (Hall)
Mrs. Alia S. (Columbia)
Ann (Laurens)
Arthur (Hall)

Augustus (Columbia)
B. (Jasper)
C. (Richmond)
Caliborn (Morgan)
Charles (Habersham)
Cynthia (Pulaski)
David (Greene)
David (Morgan)
David (Oglethorpe)
E. G. (Jasper)
Elijah (Gwinnett)
Elisha (Habersham)
Elizabeth (Jones)
George (Morgan)
Hardy (Jasper)
Hardy (Morgan)
Henry (Oglethorpe)
Hinton (Greene)
J. (Chatham)
James (Gwinnett)
James (Hancock)
James (McIntosh)
Jesse (Jasper)
John (Laurens)
John, Sr. (Lincoln)
John (Screven)
Joseph (Oglethorpe)
Lewey (Elbert)
Nathan (Columbia)
Rachel (Columbia)
Rawly (2) (Jackson)
Robert (Columbia)
Robart (Oglethorpe)
Samuel (Jasper)
Simeon (Columbia)
Thomas (Chatham)
Thomas (Greene)
Thomas (Washington)
Tod (Columbia)
William (Chatham)
William (Elbert)
William (Greene)
William (Jasper)
William (Lincoln)
William H. (Oglethorpe)
William W. (Jackson)
Crawley, Abraham (Oglethorpe)
Archable (Oglethorpe)
Charles (Morgan)
James (Jasper)
James (Oglethorpe)
Robert (Morgan)
Cray. Benjamin G.
(Montgomery)
Spott (McIntosh)
Crayton, John (Jackson)
T. (Richmond)
Creach, Charles (Laurens)
David (Laurens)
Creadle, George (Oglethorpe)
Creaf, Isaac (Greene)

Crean, Patrick (Camden)
Creel, George (Jackson)
  John (Jasper)
  Mary (Effingham)
  William (Jasper)
Cremart(?), Mrs. (Chatham)
Cremer, Henry (Lincoln)
Crenshaw, Benjamin (Warren)
  Jarrell (Jasper)
  Paschal (Warren)
  Patsey (Wilkes)
  Precious or Patience (?)
    (Wilkes)
Creswell, Salley (Wilkinson)
Crew, Anna (Chatham)
  Elbert (Burke)
  Elisha (Washington)
  Henry (Burke)
Crewer, Robert (Jasper)
Crews, Alexander (Camden)
  George (Greene)
  Isaac (Camden)
  James (Chatham)
  James (Wilkes)
  Joseph (Camden)
  Joseph (Tattnall)
  Micajah(?) (Camden)
  Peter (Walton)
  Roger (Camden)
  Stevens (Camden)
Crewse(?), Jessee (Wilkes)
  John (Wilkes)
  William (Wilkes)
Cribb, (ind.) (Bulloch)
Cribs, Elijah (Appling)
Criddelle, Abigale (Greene)
  Henry (Greene)
  Jesse (Greene)
  William (Greene)
  William, Sr. (Greene)
Cridelle(?), Gray (Greene)
Cridenton, Pryor (Madison)
Crimer, Jane (Chatham)
Crisop, Jared (Hancock)
Crisler, Joseph (Elbert)
Cristler, Julius (Elbert)
Criswale, John (Richmond)
Critenton, Elijah (Elbert)
  Juda (Elbert)
Crittendon, Robert C. (Baldwin)
Croan, Zilphay M. (Burke)
Crocket, David M. (Morgan)
  Floyd (Burke)
  Joseph (Gwinnett)
  Joseph (Jasper)
Crockett, David (Jones)
  Samuel (Jasper)
Crofford, Thomas (Wilkinson)
  Williamson (Wilkinson)
Crofton, G. H. (Jasper)
  Joseph (Columbia)

  Mathew (Washington)
Cromwell, Olliver (Greene)
Crook, John (2) (Oglethorpe)
  Lewis (Oglethorpe)
  Valentine (Oglethorpe)
Crooks, Robert (Washington)
  T. (Richmond)
Croose, Jeremiah (Jefferson)
Crop, G. (Jasper)
Crosby, Aaron (Bulloch)
  Areal (Wilkes)
  Bailess (Wilkes)
  Elizabeth (Columbia)
  Henry (Screven)
  Hezekiah (Chatham)
  Nancy (Columbia)
  John (Columbia)
  Thomas (Bulloch)
  Thomas (Camden)
  Thomas (Columbia)
  Polly (Walton)
Cross, Christian (Bryan)
  David (Hall)
  Edward (Washington)
  Fetherston (Greene)
  Isaac (Burke)
  John (Laurens)
  Joseph (Hall)
  Stephen (Burke)
  Thomas (Habersham)
  William (Burke)
Crossly, Isabella (Jefferson)
Crosson, John (Lincoln)
  Lewis (Lincoln)
Crosway, Lemuel (Jones)
Crouch, George (Putnam)
Crow, Amos (Clarke)
  Elisha (Jasper)
  Isaac (Clarke)
  Isaac (Putnam)
  Jacob (Hall)
  James (Habersham)
  James (Jackson)
  Levi (Hall)
  Lewis (Hall)
  Stephen (Clarke)
  Thomas S. (Baldwin)
Crowder, Frederick (Putnam)
  Frederick L. (Putnam)
  James (2) (Hancock)
  James H. (Putnam)
  John M. (Baldwin)
  Nancy (2) (Hancock)
Crowe, Aaron (Clarke)
Crowell, Henry (Washington)
  J. A. (Richmond)
Crows, Arthur (Jones)
Croxton, James (Clarke)
Crozier, John (Lincoln)
  Nancy (Burke)
  Thomas (Burke)

Cruce, John (Burke)
Cruis, Robert (Richmond)
Crum, Benjamin (Telfair)
  David (Camden)
  James H. (Telfair)
Crumbley, Anthony
  (Washington)
  Anthony, Jr. (Washington)
  George (Washington)
  John (Wilkinson)
Crumbs, Abraham (Bryan)
Crumer, David (Baldwin)
Crump, Aggy (Elbert)
  Robert (Elbert)
  Samuel (Columbia)
Cruse, Martin (Oglethorpe)
  Richard (Jackson)
Crutchfield, (ind.) (Pulaski)
  John (Wilkinson)
  John W. (Oglethorpe)
  Lydia (Pulaski)
  Robert (Greene)
  Stapleton (Jones)
  Thomas (Wilkinson)
Cryer, George (Morgan)
Cubbage, John (Bryan)
Cubberson, Robert (Jasper)
Cubbidge, John, Jr. (Bryan)
Cue(?), Anthony (Hancock)
Cugge, Robert (Baldwin)
Culberson, Celia (Gwinnett)
  David B. (Greene)
  G. S. (Laurens)
  James (Greene)
  John S. (Laurens)
  Robert (Jasper)
Culbertson, Isaac (Morgan)
  William P. (Madison)
Culbreath, Anguish (Madison)
  James (2) (Columbia)
  John, Sr. (Columbia)
  John (Greene)
  Nancy (Columbia)
  Thomas (Columbia)
  Thomas (Richmond)
  William (Columbia)
  William L. (Columbia)
Cullin, Charles (Telfair)
Cullins, Frederick (Washington)
Culp, Peter (Jones)
  Elizabeth (Jones)
Culpeper, Charles (Wilkinson)
  Elijah (Laurens)
  Joel (Laurens)
  Robert (Columbia)
Culpepper, (torn) (2) (Laurens)
  Allenson (Jackson)
  Benjamin (Warren)
  Cath (Laurens)
  Daniel (Jones)
  Dickenson (Warren)

(35)

Culpepper, Joel (Jones)
Joseph (Warren)
L. (Jasper)
Mariner (Warren)
Nancy (Jackson)
Nathan (Warren)
Sally (Warren)
Simeon(?) (Jackson)
Thomas (Jackson)
William (Jones)
William (Warren)
Culpepper, Malakiah (Morgan)
Joseph (Wilkinson)
Sampson (Wilkinson)
Culver, Augustus (Hancock)
George (Hancock)
James (Hancock)
Joseph (Hancock)
Joshua (Hancock)
Nathan (2) (Hancock)
Warren D. (Hancock)
Culverhouse, Charles (Wilkes)
Cloe (Hancock)
Culwell, Mathew (Jones)
Cuming, F (or T) C. (Chatham)
Cumming, Elijah (Greene)
Francis (Greene)
Gray (Warren)
John (Jefferson)
Joseph (Chatham)
Luther (Richmond)
Thomas (Oglethorpe)
Cummings, Eli (Putnam)
Gideon (Putnam)
James (Putnam)
Samuel (Putnam)
Thomas (Richmond)
Cunard, John (Jasper)
Cunningham, A. (Richmond)
A. (Jackson)
And (Jackson)
Drury (Wilkes)
Franklin (Elbert)
George (Jasper)
H or K (?) (2) (Chatham)
J. (Richmond)
James (Jackson)
James (Oglethorpe)
James T. (Jackson)
John (Elbert)
John (Morgan)
John (Putnam)
Robert (Jones)
Samuel (Baldwin)
Thomas (Greene)
Thomas (Richmond)
William (Elbert)
William (Jackson)
William (Madison)
Cunpagn(?), Mrs. (Chatham)
Cunup, Ailsey (Morgan)

Cunzen, J. M. (Richmond)
Cupp, Henry (Gwinnett)
John (Gwinnett)
William (Gwinnett)
Curbow, Henry (Gwinnett)
Curby, Moses (Emanuel)
Cureton, Henry (Madison)
Mrs. W. W. (Richmond)
William (Pulaski)
Curington, Edward (Putnam)
Curkpatrick, D. (Richmond)
Curl, Kinchen (Jones)
Matthew (Emanuel)
Wilson (Washington)
Curlee, Jesse (Morgan)
Curles, George (Chatham)
Curley, James (Chatham)
Curran, John (Chatham)
Currey, Whitmel (Wilkinson)
Currie, John (Liberty)
Curry, Benjamin (Washington)
Cary (Baldwin)
Duncan (Telfair)
Grace (Montgomery)
Curry(?), Hugh (Montgomery)
Curry, Isaiah (Wilkes)
Jacob (Habersham)
Jacob (Wilkinson)
James (Lincoln)
Jane (Greene)
John (Effingham)
John (2) (Washington)
John, Jr. (Washington)
John H. (Baldwin)
Joseph (Tattnall)
Leroy (Wilkes)
Malcolm (Oglethorpe)
Margaret (Washington)
Nathaniel (Lincoln)
Nicholas (Washington)
Curry(?), Peter (Wilkes)
Curry, Robert (Chatham)
Samuel (Early)
Samuel (Lincoln)
Solzy (Washington)
Thomas (Lincoln)
Thomas, Sr. (Lincoln)
William (Effingham)
William (Greene)
William (Lincoln)
William (Telfair)
Curtis, Henry (Gwinnett)
Hezekiah (Greene)
Robert (Greene)
Curton, John (Hancock)
Reason (Hancock)
Robert (Hancock)
William (Hancock)
Curviller(?), A. (Chatham)
Cury, Jesse (Jasper)
Curyie, Lewis (Richmond)

Cushing, Isaac T. (Baldwin)
James (Baldwin)
Cushman, Hlagues (Bryan)
Isiah (Chatham)
Cust, James (Richmond)
Custard, Jesse (Putnam)
Cuthbert, Alfred slaves of
(Liberty)
Lucy (Chatham)
Hannah (Chatham)
John A. (Putnam)
Cuthwell, Joshua (Telfair)
Cutliff, Abraham (Putnam)
John (Putnam)
Cutts, Creey (Washington)
Elisha (Washington)
Joseph (Washington)
Major (Pulaski)
Cuwalt(?), Allen (Jones)
Cuyler, J. (Chatham)
Jermiah (Effingham)

D

Dabey, John (Jasper)
Dabney, A. (Jasper)
Tyre G. (Morgan)
Dacres, Thomas (Jasper)
Dadson, A. (Jasper)
Daggett, Garson (Jasper)
Mark (Walton)
Dagnal, John (Columbia)
Dailey, John (Elbert)
John M. (Putnam)
Joseph (Richmond)
Daismorky, Edmond (Jones)
Dale, J. (Richmond)
Daley, Beville L. (Chatham)
Dallas, Thomas (Lincoln)
Dalrympel, James (Oglethorpe)
William (Oglethorpe)
Dalton, Bailey (Putnam)
John (Clarke)
Olive (Putnam)
Thomas (Richmond)
Daly, Daniel (Screven)
John (Effingham)
Dame, George (Emanuel)
John (Jones)
Damorell, Eli (Putnam)
Dampier, John (Tattnall)
William (Tattnall)
Dampyear, James (Screven)
Damron, Charles (Jackson)
Dan, Waters (Columbia)
William S. (Columbia)
Dance, Mathew (Putnam)
Dancy, Francis (Wilkinson)
Danel, Isaac (Jasper)
Danell, William (Jones)
Danely, Andrew (Warren)

Danesby, Thomas (Putnam)
Danfort, J. (2) (Richmond)
    J. R. (Richmond)
    Oliver (Hancock)
    William (Habersham)
Daniby, Arthur Baldwin)
Daniel, (torn) (Laurens)
    (ind.) (Montgomery)
    Aaron (Columbia)
    Aaron (Tattnall)
    Abraham (Liberty)
    Abraham (Telfair)
    Allen (Madison)
    Amos (Washington)
    Annis M. (Burke)
    Appellus (Liberty)
    Cunningham (Wilkes)
    David (Oglethorpe)
    David (Putnam)
    Denton (Putnam)
    Eline W. (Putnam)
    Elizabeth (Pulaski)
    Enoch (Liberty)
    Ephraim (Walton)
    Ezekiel Jr. (Washington)
    Ezekiel, Sr. (Washington)
    Francis (Washington)
    Frederick (Jones)
    Hannah (Greene)
    Isaac (Tattnall)
    Isaac (Walton)
    James (Columbia)
    James (Elbert)
    James (Greene)
    James (Hancock)
    James (Jones)
    James (Laurens)
    James (Morgan)
    James (Oglethorpe)
    James (Putnam)
    James K. (Greene)
    James L. (Hancock)
    Jesse (Liberty)
    John (Chatham)
    John (Elbert)
    John (Hancock)
    John, Jr. (Liberty)
    John, Sr. (Liberty)
    John (2) (Morgan)
    John (Pulaski)
    John (Washington)
    John W. (Wilkes)
    Jonas (Washington)
    Joseph (Burke)
    Joseph (Putnam)
    Joseph (Warren)
    Joseph (Washington)
    Kenneth (Washington)
    Littleton (Washington)
    Louis (Putnam)
    Martha (Burke)

    Mary (Burke)
    Mary (Greene)
    Mathew (Pulaski)
    Moses (Washington)
    Pendexter (Walton)
    Peter (Washington)
    Polly (Greene)
    Robert C. (Burke)
    Rufus (Washington)
    Russel I. (Madison)
    Samuel (Greene)
    Sophia (Putnam)
    Stephen (Richmond)
    Stephen (Washington)
    Stith (Putnam)
    Thomas (2) (Jasper)
    Thomas (Pulaski)
    Thomas (Washington)
    Thomas (Wilkes)
    William (Emanuel)
    William (Greene)
    William (Laurens)
    William (Putnam)
Daniell, James (Clarke)
    Jeremiah (Clarke)
    Jesse (Baldwin)
    Josiah (Clarke)
    William (Clarke)
Danielly, Andrew (Hancock)
    Arthur (Hancock)
Danil, Hobson (Jasper)
    Moses (Jasper)
Danislly, Arthur (Hancock)
Dannel, William (Wilkinson)
Dannely, Daniel (Columbia)
Danner, David (Wilkes)
Danniel, Ezekiel (Walton)
    Richard (Walton)
Dansetty, Frances (Putnam)
Dantignac, John (Richmond)
Darby, Armstead (Washington)
    Jacob (Laurens)
    James (Baldwin)
    James (Putnam)
    Jerimiah (Columbia)
    John (Jefferson)
    Richard (Lincoln)
    Richard (Morgan)
Darden, Abner (Warren)
    Burch (Oglethorpe)
    B. H. (Jasper)
    David (Warren)
    Elisha (Warren)
    George (Jasper)
    George (Wilkes)
    Jethro (2) (Warren)
    Lemuel (Wilkes)
    Micajah (Warren)
    Moses (Warren)
    Nancy (Warren)
    Stephen (Morgan)

    William (Warren)
    Willis (Warren)
    Zachariah (2) (Warren)
Darean, (ind.) (Wilkes)
Darke, Thomas (Jones)
Darley(?), James (Jefferson)
    Thomas (Jefferson)
Darmek (?), M. (Richmond)
Darnal, Benjamin (Morgan)
    John (Hancock)
Darnald, Jeremiah (Morgan)
Darnell, David (Morgan)
    Henry (Baldwin)
    Joseph (Greene)
    William (Morgan)
    Zachariah (Greene)
Darricott, Garland (Wilkes)
Darsey, (torn) (2) (Laurens)
    Benjamin (Laurens)
    George (Columbia)
    James (Laurens)
    James (Liberty)
    Joel (Jefferson)
    John (Burke)
    Joseph (Columbia)
    William (Liberty)
Dart, Ann (Glynn)
Dasgus, Jane (Richmond)
Dasher, Benjamin (Effingham)
    Christian (Effingham)
    Christian H. (Effingham)
    Elizabeth (Effingham)
    Joshua (Tattnall)
    Martin (Effingham)
    Solomon (Effingham)
Datwry(?), Charles N.
        (Camden)
Daugerty, Thomas (Walton)
Daugherty, Danny (Appling)
    Rebecca (Clarke)
Daughtry, Bryant (Emanuel)
    Jacob (Emanuel)
    Lemuel (Emanuel)
    Mary (Wilkinson)
Davant, Mrs. (Chatham)
Davenport, Francis (Oglethorpe)
    J. M. (Richmond)
    Jack S. (Warren)
    James (Clarke)
    Joel (Wilkinson)
    John (Putnam)
    Josiah (Chatham)
    Smith (Jasper)
    William (Morgan)
Daves, Joel (Washington)
    Thomas (Jasper)
Davey, Joseph (Jones)
David, Frederick (Wilkinson)
    Isaac (Madison)
    Jacob W. (Elbert)
    Joseph (Columbia)

Morsett (Madison)
Peter (Elbert)
Peter (Madison)
William (Madison)
Davidson, Asa (Warren)
E. (Jasper)
Elisha (Habersham)
Frederic (Habersham)
H. (Jackson)
James (Jones)
James (Wilkinson)
John (Chatham)
John (Jasper)
John (Jones)
John (Warren)
John (Wilkinson)
Joseph, Jr. (Wilkinson)
Nancy (2) (Jones)
Talbot (Jones)
Thomas (Jasper)
William (Warren)
Davies, William W. (Burke)
Davis, Mrs. (2) (Chatham)
Aaron (Wilkinson)
Abraham (Columbia)
Abner (Jones)
Allen (Greene)
Allen J. (Jones)
Amos (Bulloch)
Ann (Bryan)
Ann (Chatham)
Ann (Richmond)
Archibald (Putnam)
Aron (Richmond)
Arthur (Montgomery)
Arthur (Morgan)
Baldwin (Washington)
Benjamin (Jasper)
Benjamin (Oglethorpe)
Benjamin (Wayne)
Briton (Elbert)
Catherine (Richmond)
Celia (Burke)
Champen (Oglethorpe)
Charles (Wilkes)
Clementins (Columbia)
Cullen (Hall)
Daniel (Hall)
Daniel, Sr. (Montgomery)
David (Camden)
David (Greene)
David, Jr. (Montgomery)
David (Oglethorpe)
Demey (Tattnall)
Deoclesian (Washington)
Dolphin (Warren)
Drury (Morgan)
E. (Richmond)
Edmund (Washington)
Elias (Gwinnett)
Elijah (Washington)

Eliza (2) (Hancock)
Elizabeth (Bulloch)
Elizabeth (Jefferson)
Elizabeth (Warren)
Elizabeth (Wilkinson)
Elizabeth B. (Wilkes)
Elnathan (Burke)
Erby (Appling)
Evan (Columbia)
Francis (Warren)
Gazaway (Columbia)
George (Hall)
George B. (Jasper)
George C. (Jasper)
Goodrum (Washington)
Goodrum, Sr. (Washington)
Grant (Morgan)
Harias (Pulaski)
Henry (Habersham)
Henry (Wilkinson)
Hickman (Jasper)
Hustes (Tattnall)
Ichabod (Jones)
Isabella (Morgan)
Isom (Oglethorpe)
Jacob (Telfair)
James (2) (Hall)
James (Jasper)
James (Jefferson)
James (Jones)
James (Madison)
James (McIntosh)
James (Putnam)
James (Walton)
James (Wilkinson)
James G. (Wilkinson)
Jane (Greene)
Jeremiah (Emanuel)
Jeremiah (Morgan)
Jeremiah (Warren)
Jesse (Early)
John (Baldwin)
John (Chatham)
John, Sr. (Columbia)
John (2) (Elbert)
John (Habersham)
John (Jones)
John (3) (Morgan)
John (Tattnall)
John (Telfair)
John (Walton)
John (Warren)
John (Washington)
John (Wilkinson)
John G. (Columbia)
Jonothon (Habersham)
Jonathon (Wilkes)
Joseph (Bulloch)
Joseph (Columbia)
Joseph (Jackson)
Joseph (Screven)

Joseph (Wilkinson)
Joshua (Warren)
Joshua (Wilkes)
Josiah (McIntosh)
Levy, Jr. (Effingham)
Levy, Sr. (Effingham)
Lewis (Effingham)
Lewis (Washington)
Lewis, Sr. (Washington)
Lewis L. (Wilkes)
Littleberry (Warren)
Mark (Columbia)
Mary (Richmond)
Mary E. (Hancock)
Mathew (Jasper)
Micajah E (Pulaski)
Micajah (Wilkes)
Moses (Oglethorpe)
Moses (Warren)
Nancy (Elbert)
Nancy, Sr. (Elbert)
Nathaniel (Columbia)
Penny (Tattnall)
Peter (Jones)
Pleasant (Elbert)
Pleasant (Wilkinson)
Price (Warren)
Randolph (Oglethorpe)
Ransom (Lincoln)
Reuben (Columbia)
Reuben (Jones)
Richard (Bulloch)
Richard (Elbert)
Richard (Jefferson)
Richard (Telfair)
Richard R. (Pulaski)
Richard W. (Washington)
Robbin (Burke)
Sally (Washington)
Samuel (Bulloch)
Samuel (2) (Burke)
Samuel (Hancock)
Samuel (Wilkes)
Sarah (Burke)
Sarah (Greene)
Sarah (Wilkinson)
Seburn (Oglethorpe)
Sian (Appling)
Simeon (Burke)
Stafford (Montgomery)
Susannah (Jones)
Terry (Elbert)
Thomas (Baldwin)
Thomas (Elbert)
Thomas (Hancock)
Thomas (Jones)
Thomas (Morgan)
Thomas (Oglethorpe)
Thomas (Putnam)
Thomas (Warren)

Thomas (Wilkes)
Thomas (Wilkinson)
Thomas W. (Burke)
Toliver (Baldwin)
Vincen (Washington)
Vincent (Warren)
Capt. W. P. (Chatham)
Watkins (Warren)
William (Bryan)
William (Bulloch)
William (Burke)
William (Chatham)
William (Columbia)
William (Elbert)
William (Greene)
William (Jefferson)
William (2) (Jones)
William (Montgomery)
William (Morgan)
William (Screven)
William (Warren)
William (3) (Wilkes)
William (Wilkinson)
William C. (Elbert)
William E. (Hall)
William G. (Chatham)
William (Oglethorpe)
Zachariah (Appling)
Zadoc (Jones)
Davison, Joseph (Laurens)
Davy, Randle (Columbia)
Dawkins, Francis (Washington)
G. (Jasper)
George (Jasper)
Mary (Putnam)
Michael (Pulaski)
Dawsey, Daniel (Jasper)
Jarrart (Wilkes)
Thomas (Morgan)
Dawson, Briton (Burke)
George, Jr. (Greene)
George, Sr. (Greene)
Gibson (Putnam)
John (Morgan)
Kenchen (Pulaski)
Lemuel (Putnam)
Reuben (Greene)
Robert (Wilkes)
Thomas (Greene)
William C. (Greene)
Day, Elizabeth (Greene)
Elizabeth (Walton)
John (Columbia)
Jonathan (Morgan)
Joseph (col.) (Columbia)
Joseph (Emanuel)
Joseph (Jones)
Lewis (Jones)
Nathaniel (Wilkes)
Robert (Walton)
Stephen (Columbia)

William (Columbia)
William (Walton)
Zachariah (Gwinnett)
Deadwyler, Joseph (Elbert)
Martin (2) (Elbert)
Deakle, George (Emanuel)
John L. (Emanuel)
John L. Sr. (Emanuel)
Thomas (Emanuel)
William L. (Emanuel)
Deal, Ezediel (Burke)
I. (Emanuel)
William (Habersham)
Dean, (ind.) (Laurens)
Archibald (Habersham)
Burkett (Morgan)
Charles (Elbert)
Frederick (Elbert)
Frederick (Morgan)
Gedion (Liberty)
Henry (Walton)
Jane (Baldwin)
Joel (Washington)
John (Hall)
John (Jones)
Mary (McIntosh)
Micajah (Telfair)
Rachael (Washington)
Robert (Jasper)
Shadrack (Hall)
Thomas (Jasper)
Thomas (Morgan)
William (Jackson)
Wilie (Early)
Dearing, A. F. (Jasper)
Asa (Wilkes)
Elijah (Wilkes)
Robert (Wilkes)
William (Wilkes)
Dearman, William P.
(Richmond)
Deas, John (Baldwin)
Mary (Pulaski)
Deason, Absolom (Washington)
Denny (Lincoln)
Sheppard (Washington)
Thomas (Wilkinson)
Deaton, Joseph (Hall)
William (Hall)
Debeaux, Peter (Chatham)
Debenpart, Martin S.
(Oglethorpe)
William (Oglethorpe)
Deboro, Mary (Early)
Deborse, Elisha (Jones)
Debose, Lunis (Camden)
Debross(?), James (Chatham)
Debus, Nancy (Appling)
De Champs, Mrs. (Chatham)
Decker, Allen (Elbert)
Robert (Richmond)

Deel, Lewis (Jefferson)
Deen, Jinny (Pulaski)
Silas M. (Pulaski) Smith
Thomas (Madison) (Appling)
Deene, Smith (Appling)
Deerbold, Se (Jones)
Deering, John B. (Wilkes)
Reuben (Wilkes)
Dees, Benjamin (Pulaski)
Boling (Jackson)
Bryant (Jefferson)
James (Tattnall)
Joel (Wilkinson)
John (Tattnall)
Jordon (Pulaski)
M. M. (Tattnall)
William (Tattnall)
Defoor, John (Gwinnett)
Deforset, L. G. (Putnam)
Degarnett, Elias (Putnam)
Degraffenreid, Boswell(?) B.
(Clarke)
Dejernett, Nancy (Putnam)
Delagall, Thomas D. (McIntosh)
Delaigle, N. (Richmond)
Delais, (ind.) (Chatham)
Delamar, Thomas (Richmond)
Delaney, Lewis (Pulaski)
Delegal Edward (McIntosh)
Delisli, Ann A. (McIntosh)
Delk, David (Liberty)
David (Walton)
David (Wilkinson)
Elisha (Wilkinson)
Jacob (Morgan)
Joseph (Wilkinson)
Samuel (Tattnall)
Thomas (2) (Walton)
Dellamar, Fanney (Pulaski)
Deloach, Hardy (Liberty)
Deloche, Jeppok (Jones)
Delong, James A. (Jones)
Delotch, Abraham (Tattnall)
Elisabeth (Tattnall)
Sarah (Tattnall)
William (Bulloch)
Delporl(?), Elizabeth (Jackson)
James (Jackson)
Delratch(?), John (Clarke)
DeLyon, Abram, Sr. (Chatham)
Demere, Mrs. (Chatham)
Raymond (Glynn)
Raymond, Jr (McIntosh)
Raymond, Sr. (McIntosh)
Raymond P. (Bryan)
Demortt, Margaret (Camden)
Demott, John (Camden)
Dempsey, Henson (Gwinnett)
Jesse (Gwinnett)
Lazarus (Gwinnett)
Levi (Gwinnett)

(39)

Denard, John (Elbert)
Denby, John (Hancock)
Dengler, Henry (Jasper)
John (Jasper)
Denham, Arthur (Hall)
Charles (Putnam)
Nathaniel (Putnam)
Denison, Samuel (McIntosh)
Denkins, James E. (Richmond)
Denmark, Allen (Bulloch)
Malachi (Bulloch)
Thomas (Bulloch)
William (Warren)
Dennan, Hanover (Putnam)
Dennard, John (Madison)
Denney, Edward (Madison)
Dennis, Abejah (Putnam)
Allen (Lincoln)
Catharin (Hancock)
Daniel (Hancock)
Daniel (Warren)
Eleanor (Putnam)
Gethro (Wilkinson)
Isaac, Jr. (Jones)
Isaac, Sr. (Jones)
Jacob (Columbia)
Jesse (Lincoln)
Jessey (Wilkinson)
John (Chatham)
John, Jr. (2) (Hancock)
John (Jones)
Josiah (Morgan)
Mary (Jones)
Mathias (Putnam)
Peter (Putnam)
Richmond (Warren)
Samuel (Hall)
Samuel (Lincoln)
Simeon (Putnam)
William (Hancock)
William, Sr. (Lincoln)
William (Putnam)
Dennison, Mary (Wayne)
Denny, David (Elbert)
Edward (Elbert)
Robert (Elbert)
Robert (Richmond)
Samuel (2) (Jefferson)
Thomas (Elbert)
Yearly (Jasper)
Denrus, Johnson (Putnam)
William (Putnam)
Densler(?), Frederick
(Chatham)
Henry (Baldwin)
Denson, Calley (Putnam)
John E. (Hancock)
Joseph W. (Pulaski)
William (Putnam)
Dent, Allison (Morgan)
Charles (McIntosh)

Elkanah (Jasper)
George W. (Columbia)
J. (Richmond)
John (Hall)
John T. (Wilkes)
Lossen (Wilkes)
Nancy (Jones)
Nathaniel (Hancock)
Richard (Oglethorpe)
Thomas (Putnam)
Thomas (Telfair)
Walter (Putnam)
Walter C. (Putnam)
Denton, Aron (Warren)
James (Oglethorpe)
John (Hancock)
John T. (Wilkes)
Depriest, James A. (Elbert)
Deprist, Elizabeth (Elbert)
Depue, John (Hall)
Dericot, William (Greene)
Derren, Joseph (Jones)
Derrifield, William (Hall)
Derry, Maria (Effingham)
Derumple, Isaac (Hall)
Desan, Michael (Jasper)
Zach (Jasper)
Deshazo, William K .(Putnam)
Deshion, Timothy (Habersham)
Deshron, Isaac (Habersham)
Waitman (Habersham)
William (Habersham)
Desmor, John (Jones)
Desnal, Bath (Pulaski)
David (Pulaski)
Dissaux, Jeptha V. (Hancock)
Desson, Elijah (Jasper)
Devan, Partrick S. (Walton)
Devane, Benjamin (Bulloch)
Devann, Francis (Bulloch)
Devaux, Catherine (Chatham)
Devenport, Henry (Greene)
Deverause, Samuel M.
(Hancock)
Deveraux, Samuel M. (Hancock)
Devers, George (Habersham)
DeVillers, Petit (Chatham)
Devine, John (Putnam)
William H. (Putnam)
Dewberry, Henry (Warren)
Irby (Warren)
James (Warren)
Mary (Warren)
Thomas (Jasper)
Dewit, Robert (Irwin)
Dewitt, Charles (Glynn)
Dewsenberry, Susan (Columbia)
Dexter, B. W. (McIntosh)
DeYumpert, Alsey (Washington)
Diah, Marcijah(?) (Oglethorpe)
Dial, Martin (Walton)

Mary (Madison)
Diamond, James (Gwinnett)
Nancy (Telfair)
Dias, George (Wilkinson)
Thomas (Wilkinson)
Dice, Solomon (Elbert)
Dick, John (Tattnall)
Dickarson, Zurchariah (Elbert)
Dickason, John (Elbert)
Robert (Elbert)
Dicken, Elizabeth (Jones)
James (Morgan)
Dickens, Elijah (Warren)
John (Warren)
Robert (Warren)
Dickenson, C. (Richmond)
James (Clarke)
Joel (Hancock)
Dickerson, John (Hancock)
John (Walton)
William (Chatham)
William (Wilkes)
Dickeson, Henry (Hancock)
Dickey, Joseph (Screven)
Owen (Putnam)
Patrick (Putnam)
Robert (Putnam)
Samuel (Putnam)
Dickin, Jeremiah (Morgan)
Richard (Clarke)
Dickins, John (Oglethorpe)
Thomas (Clarke)
William (Clarke)
Dickinson, Charles
(Washington)
D. F. (Richmond)
George (Habersham)
John (Habersham)
Joseph (Habersham)
Mary (Hall)
Dickison, John (Pulaski)
Dickray(?), Hezekiah (Screven)
Dicks, Charles (Liberty)
David Est. of (Liberty)
Dickson, David (Elbert)
Enoch (Jones)
H. (Richmond)
James (Chatham)
James (Hall)
James (Hancock)
Jeremiah (Wilkinson)
John (Emanuel)
John (Jones)
Micajah (Wilkinson)
Michael (Hall)
Michael (Screven)
Robert (Greene)
Robert (Wilkinson)
Sampson (Wilkinson)
Thomas (Laurens)
Dicky, Andrew (Jones)

(40)

Dickey, John (Elbert)
Didwilder, C. (Jasper)
DieMass, John (Jones)
Diffy, Nancy (Hall)
Dikings, Frederick (Tattnall)
Dilard, James (Elbert)
Dildy, Seth (Jackson)
Dile, Jacob (Richmond)
    John (Early)
Dilie, Jacob (Early)
Dill, John (Bulloch)
    Philip (Lincoln)
Dillard, Arthur (Jones)
    Edmond (Washington)
    Elizabeth (Burke)
    George W. (Greene)
    Isaac (Burke)
    John (Chatham)
    John (Jones)
    Martha (Oglethorpe)
    Mary (Washington)
    Nathan (Washington)
    Owen (Emanuel)
    Philip (Burke)
    Reuben (Oglethorpe)
    Sampson (Emanuel)
    Sarah (Chatham)
    Theophilus (Jefferson)
    Thomas (Jones)
    William (Burke)
Dillon, Michael (Chatham)
    Robert (Chatham)
    Robert (Richmond)
    Thomas (2) Jasper)
    Tolliver (Burke)
    W. C. (Richmond)
Dilworth, Catherine (Morgan)
Dillworth, J. C. (Camden)
Dimond, A. (Richmond)
Dingler, Nancy (Morgan)
Dingley, W. (Jasper)
Dinkins, Horrace (Baldwin)
Dinsmore, David (Habersham)
DisCloe, Joseph (Camden)
Disdor, Thomas (Jasper)
Dishong, Charles (Camden)
Dishron, Jesse (Habersham)
Dismuke, William H. (Clarke)
Dismukes, Finney (Putnam)
    James (2) (Putnam)
    John F. (Putnam)
    Rhuebin (Richmond)
    William (2) (Jones)
Disy(?), Henry (Appling)
Divenport, Stephen (Burke)
Divine, William (Chatham)
Dix, John (Oglethorpe)
Dixon, Aaron (Early)
    Alla (Washington)
    Bryan (Putnam)
    Davis (Gwinnett)

Guin (Warren)
Henry (Putnam)
Hickman (Putnam)
Hickman (Warren)
James (Screven)
John (Hancock)
Joseph (Hancock)
Mary (Chatham)
Nathan (Putnam)
Nicholas (Putnam)
Rebecca (Columbia)
Robert (Burke)
Robert (Elbert)
Robert (Hancock)
Robert (Putnam)
Robert (Telfair)
Robert L. (Screven)
Mrs. Tamur (Clarke)
Tilman (Washington)
Thomas, Jr. (Hancock)
Thomas (2) (Hancock)
Thomas (2) (Morgan)
William (Hall)
William (Hancock)
William (Madison)
William H. (Gwinnett)
Winsor (Screven)
D'Lyon, Levi S. (Chatham)
Dobb, Jesse (Hall)
Dobbins, Bruce (Chatham)
    James (Hall)
    John M. (Clarke)
    Moses W. (Clarke)
    William (Hall)
Dobbs, Auslin (Gwinnett)
    David (Elbert)
    Jesse (Gwinnett)
    John (Columbia)
    John (Elbert)
    John (Gwinnett)
    Lewis (Hall)
    Mormon (Gwinnett)
    Nathaniel, Jr. (Gwinnett)
    Nathaniel, Sr. (Gwinnett)
    Silas (Gwinnett)
    Suzanny (Elbert)
    Thomas A. (Gwinnett)
    William (2) (Gwinnett)
Dobson, Henry (Habersham)
    John (Jasper)
    Joseph (2) (Habersham)
    Neely (Habersham)
    Street (Habersham)
Dodd, Catherine (Madison)
    Dennis (Hall)
    Isaac (Baldwin)
    James (Elbert)
    James (Oglethorpe)
    Jesse (Hall)
    Patterson (Hall)
    Robert (Jefferson)

Sarah (Elbert)
William (Habersham)
William (Hall)
Zachariah (Hall)
Dodge, Nehemiah (Wilkes)
Dodson, Cloe (Wilkes)
    Daniel (Morgan)
    Elisha (Clarke)
    John (Wilkes)
    William (Columbia)
Doget, George (Oglethorpe)
Doggett, Thomas (Clarke)
    William (Clarke)
Dogin, Olemon (Jackson)
    William (Jackson)
Doles, Benjamin (Baldwin)
    Jesse (Baldwin)
    John (Wilkinson)
Dollar, James (Elbert)
Dolly, B.(ind.) (Chatham)
    James (Chatham)
    Lunean (Bryan)
    Priscilla (Chatham)
Dolton, B. (Richmond)
Dolvin, James (Greene)
Dominer, Frederick (Wilkinson)
    John (Wilkinson)
Domino, (ind.) (Chatham)
Donald, Abraham (Early)
    William R. (Chatham)
Donaldson, Hugh (Emanuel)
    John (Pulaski)
    Robert (Bulloch)
    Robert (Jefferson)
    William (Jefferson)
    William (Pulaski)
Donagdon, John (Jones)
Donalson, William (Screven)
Donely, Elizabeth (Wilkinson)
Donisldcy(?), Andrew
                (Hancock)
Donnell, Isaac (Jasper)
    Levi (Jasper)
Donner, John (Baldwin)
Donoho, Charles (Chatham)
Donton, Johns (Habersham)
Dony, Lowden (Hancock)
Dooley, Bennet (Elbert)
    William (2) Elbert
Doolittle, Silvanus C. (Clarke)
Dooly, James (Habersham)
    John M. (Lincoln)
    Thomas (Columbia)
Dorch, Davis (Washington)
Dorlick, S. (Richmond)
Dorman, Eph. (Jones)
Dormon, John (Clarke)
Dorough, Thomas (Morgan)
Dorsett, Elijah (Hall)
    John (Hall)
    Joseph (Hall)

Dorsett, Thomas (Hall)
William (Richmond)
Dorsey, John (Jones)
Jonathan (Jones)
Mathew (Jones)
Thomas B. (Oglethorpe)
Walter B. (Oglethorpe)
Dorsset, A. (Chatham)
Dorsy, Lowden (Hancock)
Dortes, Henry H. (2) (Jones)
Dortrey, Demsey (Appling)
Doss, Claborn (Jasper)
Edward (Jackson)
George (Jackson)
James (Putnam)
Joel (Elbert)
John (Jasper)
Mark (Jackson)
Dossey, John (Greene)
Doster, Benjamin (Warren)
James (2) (Putnam)
Jonathon (Warren)
Thomas (2) (Putnam)
William (2) (Hancock)
William (Jackson)
William (Warren)
Dostor, Stephen (Jones)
Dotson, Asaph (Walton)
David (Chatham)
Mathew (Chatham)
Neely, Jr. (Habersham)
William (Chatham)
Doty, Mr. (Chatham)
Douberly, Joseph (Tattnall)
Douding, William (Wayne)
Dougherty, Charles (Jackson)
Neil (Columbia)
Michail (Columbia)
Patrick (Columbia)
Doughrty, Nancy (Tattnall)
Doughtee, William (Greene)
Douglas, Amos (Chatham)
Benjamin (Chatham)
Benjamin (McIntosh)
David (Chatham)
David (Jones)
Frederick (Tattnall)
George (Jones)
James George (Wilkes)
James (Jones)
Appling James (Wayne)
John (Chatham)
John (Jones)
King (Wayne)
Mary Ann (Jones)
Samuel C. (Richmond)
Spencer (Wilkinson)
W. B. (Burke)
William (Jones)
William (Montgomery)
Willis (Jones)

Wright (Tattnall)
Douglass, Alexander (Screven)
Edward (Emanuel)
Francis (Morgan)
Frederick (Emanuel)
John (Columbia)
John (Emanuel)
Jonah (Bryan)
Martha (Wilkes)
Seaborn (Emanuel)
Thomas (Wilkes)
Douville, Capt. P. (Chatham)
Dove, Richard (Burke)
Dover, Francis (Habersham)
Thomas (Glynn)
William (Jones)
Dover(?), Johnson (Habersham)
Dow, Mrs. (Chatham)
Azarah (Jasper)
Dowdell, L. (Jasper)
Dowdle, James (Putnam)
Dowdy, Aaron (Hall)
Amos (Hall)
Balam (Hall)
Benjamin (Jackson)
Henry (Oglethorpe)
Martin (Oglethorpe)
Richard (Oglethorpe)
Robert (Hall)
Wiley (Screven)
Richard (Screven)
William (Hall)
Dowell, Thomas (Chatham)
Dowley, M. (Chatham)
Dowlin, Thomas P. (Burke)
Dowling, Sabray (McIntosh)
William (Liberty)
Downer, Joseph, Jr. (Elbert)
Joseph, Sr. (Elbert)
Downey, Joseph (Gwinnett)
Downie, Mathew (Putnam)
Downing, Edmond (Wilkinson)
George (Wilkes)
William (Lincoln)
Dowman, William P. (Laurens)
Downs, Isaac (Columbia)
Isaac (Warren)
Jacob (Columbia)
James (Jasper)
John (Emanuel)
John (Jasper)
Josiah (Jasper)
Polly (Morgan)
S. Kelly (Jasper)
Silas (Warren)
Sylas (Jones)
William (Camden)
William (Warren)
Willis (Emanuel)
Dowse, Samuel (Burke)
Dowzier, B. M. (Chatham)

Doyl, Jesse (Lincoln)
Doyle, Alex (Jasper)
Dennis (Baldwin)
Rosetta (Chatham)
Thomas (Jasper)
William (Burke)
Dozier, Green S. (Columbia)
James P. (Baldwin)
John (Columbia)
Nancy (Warren)
Richard (Warren)
Thomas (Columbia)
Woody (Jasper)
Drake, Alfred (Putnam)
Archable (Oglethorpe)
Elias (Burke)
Epp (Hancock)
James (Oglethorpe)
James (Telfair)
Lemuel (Jefferson)
Robert (Jefferson)
Turner (Madison)
William (Hancock)
Drane, Stephen (Columbia)
William (Columbia)
Draper, James (Warren)
Joshua (Warren)
Thomas (Putnam)
Drawdy, Daniel (Irwin)
Thomas (Irwin)
William (McIntosh)
Drawhorn, James (Jones)
Richard (Jones)
Dregers, Matthew (Liberty)
Dreggors, Henry (Liberty)
J. M. (Liberty)
Drew, Asa (Burke)
John S. (Emanuel)
John S. (Jasper)
Josiah (Burke)
Mary (Emanuel)
William (Burke)
Willis (Laurens)
Wilson (Burke)
Drewry, Cathe (Chatham)
Driggers, Alex (Bulloch)
William (Emanuel)
Driggors, Ann (McIntosh)
Drigors, James (Liberty)
Drinkwater, Bathine (McIntosh)
Daniel (Emanuel)
W. W. (Richmond)
Driskel, Elgale (Jackson)
Nancy (Jackson)
Driskell, William (Hancock)
Wooten (Hancock)
Driskey, Jacob (Jasper)
Driver, Bud (Jones)
David (Washington)
Giles (Jones)
Goodridge (Jones)

⟨ 42 ⟩

Driver, Jacob (Putnam)
  John (Jones)
  Susan (Montgomery)
  William (Lincoln)
Drummond, Henry (McIntosh)
  W. (Chatham)
Drury, Brady (Morgan)
  Edwin (Hancock)
  Samuel (Putnam)
Dryson, John (Wilkes)
Dubberley, Allen (Putnam)
Duberry, John (Jasper)
  Thomas (Putnam)
Dubige, Pulliam (Wilkinson)
DuBignon, C. P. (Glynn)
Dublain, George N.
    (Washington)
Dubolgin, Mr. (Chatham)
Dubose, Joseph (Baldwin)
  Margarett E. (Lincol.n)
  Rubin (Washington)
Dubourg, Andrew (Baldwin)
Duck, David (Jasper)
  John (Morgan)
  Jonathon (Hancock)
Duckworth, Elizabeth (Hancock)
  Jeremiah (Hancock)
  Joseph (Jones)
  Rebekah (Warren)
Ducy, Yearly (Jasper)
Dudley, Arthur (Washington)
  Eden (Washington)
  Edward (Putnam)
  Elam (2) (Washington)
  George (Screven)
  Ignatius (Elbert)
  James (Elbert)
  John T. (Elbert)
  Warren (Chatham)
  William (Hancock)
  William B. (Madison)
  William G. (Pulaski)
  William J. (Effingham)
Dudly, Kinchen C. (Burke)
  Thomas (Hancock)
Dufaurd, A. (Chatham)
Duffee, Robert S. (Jefferson)
Duffel, James (Oglethorpe)
Duffer, Thomas (Jones)
Duffet, William (Jones)
Duffy, Daniel (Putnam)
  Frederick (Putnam)
  P. (Chatham)
Dugar, Susan (Chatham)
Dugas, G. (Richmond)
  S. P. (Burke)
Dugass, Gustave (Richmond)
Duggan, John (Washington)
  John H. (Washington)
  William (Washington)
Duggar, Sampson (Hancock)

Dugger, Chesley (Bulloch)
  David (Effingham)
  John (Effingham)
  William (Bulloch)
Duggins, John (McIntosh)
Duglas, James (Appling)
  John (Telfair)
Duglass, James (Putnam)
Duke, Mrs. (Chatham)
  Azariah (Burke)
  Charles (Morgan)
  Charles (Walton)
  Charles (Wilkes)
  Daniel (Burke)
  David (Morgan)
  Drewry (Burke)
  Edmond (Walton)
  Edmond (Clarke)
  Eldridge (Morgan)
  Epps (Morgan)
  Green (Jackson)
  Green (Jefferson)
  Hardeman (Jasper)
  Henry (Clark)
  Henry (3) (Morgan)
  James (Burke)
  James (Morgan)
  James (2) (Walton)
  John (3) (Morgan)
  John (Putnam)
  John (Tattnall)
  John M. (Putnam)
  John T. (Morgan)
  Joseph (Morgan)
  Kesiah (Wilkes)
  Mary (Burke)
  Robert (Walton)
  Robert G. (Putnam)
  S. H. (Jasper)
  Stephen (Jasper)
  Stolla (Wilkes)
  Taylor (Morgan)
  Thomas (Morgan)
  Thomas (Oglethorpe)
  Turner (Burke)
  William (Morgan)
  William (2) (Walton)
  William (Washington)
Dukes, (torn) (Laurens)
  Frederick (Jasper)
  Green (Jones)
  Nancy (Bulloch)
Dukson, William (Jackson)
Dumas, David (Putnam)
  Jeremiah (Jones)
  Moses (Putnam)
  Williams (Putnam)
Dun, John (Columbia)
  Joseph (Hall)
Dunagan, Ezekial (Hall)
Dunagon, Abner (Habersham)

  Hiram (Habersham)
Dunan, James M. (Putnam)
Dunaway, Edward (Jackson)
  James (Lincoln)
  Mary (Warren)
  William (Wilkes)
Dunbar, George (Richmond)
  Harriet (Chatham)
Duncan, (ind.) (Laurens)
  Benjamin (Putnam)
  Daniel (Morgan)
  Edmond, Sr. (Jones)
  George (Jones)
  Hyram M. (Baldwin)
  Isaac (Jones)
  James (Jasper)
  John (Hall)
  John (Wilkes)
  Joseph (Putnam)
  Mathew (Putnam)
  Miles (Wilkes)
  Moses (Elbert)
  Moses (Lincoln)
  Person (Elbert)
  Robert (Wilkinson)
  Tapley (Wilkes)
  Thomas (Laurens)
  William (Jones)
Dunevan, Daniel (Baldwin)
Dunevant, (ind.) (Warren)
  Nancy (Washington)
Dunford, Daniel (Burke)
  Susannah (Burke)
Dunham, Jacob H. (Liberty)
  Samuel (Richmond)
  William (McIntosh)
  William A. (McIntosh)
Dunison, Burwell (Wilkes)
Dunkin, Jane (Greene)
Dunlap, Patrick L. (Gwinnett)
  William (Elbert)
Dunn, Asaham (Jones)
  C. C. (Richmond)
  David (Oglethorpe)
  Dudley (Oglethorpe)
  Elizabeth (Columbia)
  Gatewood (Columbia)
  Gatewood (Oglethorpe)
  Henry (Hancock)
  James (Greene)
  Jane (Burke)
  Jeremiah (Jones)
  John (Burke)
  John, (Columbia)
  John (Elbert)
  John (2) (Hall)
  John (Hancock)
  John, Jr. (Jasper)
  John, Sr. (Jasper)
  John (Jones)
  John (Oglethorpe)

Dunn, John (Walton)
  Joseph (Jones)
  Larken (Walton)
  Mary (Burke)
  Mary (Columbia)
  Michael (Hall)
  Nancy (Pulaski)
  Nehemiah (Jones)
  Sharlot (Jones)
  Thomas (Hall)
  Thomas (Oglethorpe)
  William S. (Columbia)
Dunnahoo, James (Oglethorpe)
Dunning, John (Chatham)
Dunson, W. (Jackson)
Dunston, Charles (Jackson)
  Eliz. (Jackson)
Dunwoody, James (McIntosh)
  John, slaves of (Liberty)
Dupreast, Elizabeth (Wilkinson)
Dupree, Burgess (Putnam)
  Daniel (Oglethorpe)
  G. (Glynn)
  Harod (Jefferson)
  James (Jefferson)
  Jesse (Putnam)
  Jessee (Washington)
  John (Putnam)
  John (Washington)
  Lewis J. (Oglethorpe)
  Louis I. (Jackson)
  Mathew (Wilkinson)
  Timothy (Washington)
Dupon(?), Peter (Chatham)
Dupont, William (Chatham)
Duran, Seth (Bulloch)
Durant, Francis (McIntosh)
Durbin, Sarah (Jackson)
Durdan, Washington (Baldwin)
Durden, Elisha (Wilkinson)
  Francis (Washington)
  Henry (Emanuel) *Henry (Appling)*
  Jacob (Emanuel)
  Jesse (Columbia)
  John (Columbia)
  Miles (Columbia)
  William (Emanuel)
  William (Jones)
  William (Wilkinson)
Dure(?), Michael (Jasper)
Durham, Abner (Jasper)
  Anderson (Jackson)
  Jeptha (Telfair)
  John (Telfair)
  Mathew (Jones)
  Samuel (Greene)
  Thomas (Wilkinson)
  William (Greene)
Durkee, Augs. F. (Chatham)
Durouzeaux, James (Jefferson)
  Stephen (Jefferson)

  Peter (Jefferson)
Durrah, James (Putnam)
Durrence, Elizabeth (Tattnall)
  Jesse (Tattnall)
  Joseph (Tattnall)
  Peggy (Tattnall)
  William (Tattnall)
Durret, Rice (Jones)
Dutton, Henry (Bulloch)
  James (Elbert)
  Thomas (Elbert)
Duveryou, Peter (Camden)
D'Villers, Betty (Chatham)
Dyall, George (McIntosh)
  John (McIntosh)
  Thomas (McIntosh)
  Zelphy (McIntosh)
Dyas, John, Jr. (Tattnall)
  John, Sr. (Tattnall)
Dyberry, Giles (Jasper)
Dye, Abel (Warren)
  Avery (Burke)
  Benjamin (Burke)
  Brown (Elbert)
  Burrell (Elbert)
  David (Elbert)
  Hopkin (Burke)
  John (Emanuel)
  Martin M. (Burke)
  Randol (Putnam)
  Stephen (Hall)
Dyer, Anthony (Jasper)
  Elizabeth (Wilkes)
  James (Hancock)
  John (Greene)
  Obid (Greene)
  Rachel (Washington)
Dyess, Henry (R. S.) (Liberty)
  John, Jr. (Liberty)
Dykes, Alen (Wilkinson)
  Elias (Pulaski)
  Elizabeth (Pulaski)
  George (Wilkinson) *see below*
  Henry (Pulaski)
  Jacob (2) (Pulaski)
  Jesse (Effingham)
  Jordan (Pulaski)
  Josiah (Pulaski)
  Mary (Pulaski)
  Nathaniel (Pulaski)
  Samuel (Pulaski)
  Warren (Wilkinson)
Dyre, Thomas (Baldwin)
Dyson, Isaac (Warren)

E

Eades, Elizabeth (Oglethorpe)
  Randolph (Jackson)
Eadon, Thomas (Irwin)
Eads, Reuben (Oglethorpe)
Eady, Henry (Jasper)

  Henry (Wilkinson)
  John (Wilkinson)
  John B. (Jasper)
  Samuel (Jasper)
Ealey, Samuel (Greene)
Earde, William W. (Jasper)
Early, Ann A. (Greene)
  Anselon (Jasper)
  E. (Chatham)
  Jesse (Washington)
  Joel (Greene)
  Joseph (Jasper)
Earnest, Elisha (Clarke)
  John (Clarke)
Easley, Ann L. (Greene)
Easly, William P. (Walton)
Eason, (ind.) (Oglethorpe)
  Abram (Morgan)
  Abraham (Appling)
  Eliz. (Jasper)
  Isaac (Wilkes)
  John (Hall)
  John (Oglethorpe)
  John (2) (Wilkes)
  Joseph (Morgan)
  Parker (Wilkes)
  Penelope (Wilkinson)
  Rice (Walton)
  Seth (Jefferson)
  Thomas (Morgan)
  Whitmell (Jasper)
  William (Tattnall)
East, Benjamin (Jefferson)
  Stephen (Jackson)
Easter, Baxter (Jasper)
  George (Appling)
  John C. (Baldwin)
Easterland, Shaderick (Wilkinson)
Easterling, Henry (Jackson)
Easters, Davd. (Putnam)
  George (Wilkes)
  Joshua (Gwinnett)
  Miles (Gwinnett)
  William (Gwinnett)
Eastrige, Elisha (Jackson)
Easts, Jeams (Putnam)
Eastus, Zachary (Jasper)
Eastwood, Elijah (Washington)
  John (Walton)
  Lawrence (Walton)
Easwood, Andrew (Habersham)
Eatheridge, John (Wilkinson)
  Lewis (Wilkinson)
  Samuel (Wilkinson)
Eathridge, Thomas (Wilkinson)
Eaton, John (Habersham)
  Reubon (Hall)
  William (Habersham)
Eavans, Burwell (Wilkinson)
  Josiah G. (Wilkinson)

George (Appling)
Giles (Appling)

Eavans, Stephen (Wilkinson)
Ebberhart, Addam (Oglethorpe)
Eberhart, George (Madison)
  Jacob (Oglethorpe)
  James (Madison)
  Susannah (Madison)
Echols, (ind.) (Wilkes)
  Abraham (Habersham)
  Absalom (Jasper)
  Darius (Habersham)
  Edward (Wilkes)
  Edward, Jr. (Wilkes)
  Elijah (Lincoln)
  Elijah (Wilkes)
  Elizabeth (Gwinnett)
  James (Wilkes)
  John (Jasper)
  Levi H. (Wilkes)
  Mary (Wilkes)
  Milner (Clarke)
  Nathan (Wilkes)
  O. (Jasper)
  Reuben (Wilkes)
  Robert M. (Walton)
  Samuel B. (Columbia)
  Samuel D. (Walton)
  Thomas (Wilkes)
  William (Gwinnett)
Eckles, Joshua (Morgan)
Ecles, R. W. (Chatham)
Ector, Hugh (Putnam)
  Wiley B. (Putnam)
Eddenfield, David (Telfair)
Eddridge, William (Baldwin)
Eddy, Russel (Columbia)
  William (Chatham)
Eden, Melinda (McIntosh)
  Thomas (McIntosh)
Edenfield, Jesse (Emanuel)
Edinfield, John (Emanuel)
  Thomas (Emanuel)
Edens, Job (Elbert)
Edgar, Elizabeth (Walton)
Edge, James (Wilkes)
  John (Jasper)
  Lyon (Jones)
  M. (Jasper)
  Obadiah (Jasper)
Edington, D. (Richmond)
Edins, Blakley (Pulaski)
  Ephraim (Pulaski)
Edleman, David (Walton)
Edmond, William (Wilkes)
Edmonds, Anthony (Oglethorpe)
  James (Oglethorpe)
  Jesse (Jones)
  John (Morgan)
  John (Oglethorpe)
  John L. (Lincoln)
  Penelope (Wilkes)
Edmondson, Edmond (Putnam)

Fanning (Oglethorpe)
  Griffen (Columbia)
  James (Gwinnett)
  John (Oglethorpe)
  John (Putnam)
  Joseph (Gwinnett)
  Nancy (Bulloch)
  Philemon (Oglethorpe)
  Thomas (Putnam)
  Thomas (Warren)
  William (Putnam)
Edmonson, C. (Jasper)
  James (Columbia)
  Thomas (Jasper)
  Samuel (Greene)
  Sam (Jasper)
  William (Greene)
Edmunds, Ambrose (Warren)
  William (Burke)
Edmundson, William (Warren)
Edmunson, James (Morgan)
  Philip (Morgan)
  Thomas (Clarke)
Edson, James (Oglethorpe)
Edward, James (Emanuel)
  John (Jasper)
Edwards, (ind.) (Wilkes)
  Ambrose (Greene)
  Ambros (Jones)
  Andrew (Hancock)
  Anny (Jackson)
  Asa (Putnam)
  Auguston (Elbert)
  Benjamin (Oglethorpe)
  Britton (Washington)
  Christopher (Telfair)
  Cullen (Telfair)
  David (Putnam)
  Elizabeth (Oglethorpe)
  Ethelred (Hancock)
  Henry (Telfair)
  Henry L. (Oglethorpe)
  Isaac O. (Elbert)
  J. W. (Bulloch)
  Jacob (Greene)
  James (Elbert)
  James (Telfair)
  James H. (Jasper)
  John (Effingham)
  John (Elbert)
  John (2) (Jones)
  John (Lincoln)
  John (Oglethorpe)
  John (2) (Putnam)
  John (Telfair)
  John (Washington)
  John M. (Oglethorpe)
  Littlebury B. (Oglethorpe)
  Maria (Chatham)
  Mary (Columbia)
  Nathan T. (Irwin)

Obediah (Effingham)
  Peter (Hall)
  Phebe (Columbia)
  R. (2) (Jasper)
  Rachel (Jackson)
  Rebekah (Emanuel)
  Reuben (Oglethorpe)
  Samuel (Jasper)
  Solomon (Clarke)
  Stephen (Hall)
  Stirling (Columbia)
  Synthia (Oglethorpe)
  Thomas (Habersham)
  Thomas (Telfair)
  Timothy (Richmond)
  William (Effingham)
  William (Greene)
  William (2) (Jones)
  William (Putnam)
  William (Tattnall)
  William L. (Baldwin)
  William W. (Oglethorpe)
Edy, Eliza (Lincoln)
  James (Lincoln)
Ehily, Michael L. (Jones)
Eicktson, Swenah (Montgomery)
Eidson, Bain (Oglethorpe)
  Shilton (Oglethorpe)
  Thomas (Wilkes)
  Thomas, Sr. (Wilkes)
Eilands, David (McIntosh)
  James E. (McIntosh)
  Nancy (Jones)
  Ruthe (Jones)
  Stephen (Jones)
  William (McIntosh)
Eilon, Susannah (Chatham)
Eirick, Mary (Chatham)
Elbert, Sarah (Richmond)
  William (Wilkes)
Elder, Edward (Elbert)
  Edward (Jasper)
  Howel (Clarke)
  Robert B. (Putnam)
  Sterling (Clarke)
  William (Putnam)
Elders, James (Liberty)
Elenburger, Charles
          (Habersham)
Elendan, Thomas M., Sr.
          (Walton)
Elender, William M. (Walton)
Eley, John (Richmond)
Elgin, Kesekiah R. (Wilkes)
Elington, Garland (Elbert)
Elinon, James (Jones)
Eliot, George (Oglethorpe)
  Robert (Early)
  Thomas (Early)
Eliott, Thomas (Walton)
Elison, William (Walton)

(45)

Elkin, Mary (Jones)
Elking, Young (Wilkinson)
Elkings, John (Tattnall)
Elkins, John (Chatham)
    Thomas (Effingham)
    William (Oglethorpe)
Ellenton, Elizabeth (Baldwin)
Ellette, Mrs. E. (Hancock)
Elliby, Dick (Burke)
    Elizabeth (2) (Burke)
Ellington, (ind.) (Laurens)
    David E. (Wilkes)
    Enock (Greene)
    Hezekiah (Wilkes)
    Jane (Wilkes)
    Joseph (Jackson)
    Josiah (Putnam)
    Leonard (Hall)
    Robert (Morgan)
    Sarah (Wilkes)
    Stephens (Wilkes)
    William (Jackson)
Elliott, (ind.) (Hall)
    Alexander (Morgan)
    Alexander (Richmond)
    Alexander D. (Greene)
    Andrew (Baldwin)
    Benjamin (Washington)
    David (Morgan)
    Drewry (Burke)
    Mrs. E. (Hancock)
    George (Morgan)
    George W. (Greene)
    James (Hall)
    James (Morgan)
    James (Warren)
    John (2) (Burke)
    John (Liberty)
    John (Walton)
    John (Wilkes)
    Nelson (Putnam)
    heir of R. E. (Chatham)
    Rebecca (Chatham)
    Robert H. (Morgan)
    Silas (Burke)
    Stephen Est. of
        (Chatham)
    Thomas (Elbert)
    Thomas (Lincoln)
    Thomas (Morgan)
    Wm. & R. (Chatham)
    William (Lincoln)
Ellis, Austin (Baldwin)
    Fielding (Baldwin)
    Elisha (Putnam)
    Iddo (Putnam)
    Isaac (Hall)
    Isaac (Jones)
    James (Hancock)
    James (Jasper)
    Jane (Hancock)

    Jiles (Camden)
    John (Jasper)
    John (Telfair)
    Levi (Jones)
    Levin (Hancock)
    Major (Washington)
    Mathew (Greene)
    Moses (Camden)
    Nathan (Oglethorpe)
    Nathan (Putnam)
    Prucilla (Jones)
    Richard (Jones)
    Robert (Warren)
    Richard W. (Baldwin)
    Sarah (Warren)
    Shadereck (Putnam)
    Shadereck, Sr. (Putnam)
    Stephen (Jackson)
    Stephen (Putnam)
    Thomas (Camden)
    Thomas (Glynn)
    Thomas (Greene)
    Walter (Hall)
    William (Appling)
    William (2) (Baldwin)
    Wiliam (Greene)
    William (Oglethorpe)
    William, Sr. (Oglethorpe)
    William (Telfair)
Ellison, Charity (Gwinnett)
    Francis (Gwinnett)
    James (Chatham)
    Moses (Gwinnett)
    Polly (Gwinnett)
    Robert (Gwinnett)
    Samuel (Gwinnett)
    Watson (Gwinnett)
    William (Gwinnett)
Ellisson, Samuel (Jackson)
Elliston, George (Burke)
    Joseph (Burke)
    Robert (Burke)
Ellit, William (Wilkes)
Ellot, Carnelas (Oglethorpe)
Ellotson, Jacob (Burke)
Ellyson, Francis (Jackson)
    Samuel (Jackson)
Elrod, Adam (Hall)
    Christopher (Hall)
Elsberry, Benjamen (Clarke)
    Benjamin (Oglethorpe)
    Lindsey (Gwinnett)
Elsey, Charles (Madison)
Elsworth, John (Richmond)
Elton, Abram (Washington)
    Andrew (Jackson)
    Charles (Washington)
    John (Washington)
    Robert (Washington)
Ely, John (Washington)
    Michael (2) (Hancock)

Emanuel, Alexander (Screven)
    Berry (Screven)
    David (Screven)
Embree, John (Columbia)
Embry, Isaiah (Oglethorpe)
    Joseph (Oglethorpe)
    Mirel (Clarke)
    Tall (Oglethorpe)
    William (Oglethorpe)
Emerson, William (Jones)
Emery, Lemuel (Jasper)
Emmery, John (Jackson)
Emory, Elijah (Clarke)
England, Charles (Habersham)
    David (Habersham)
    Elijah (Habersham)
    Joseph (Habersham)
English, Cornelos (Tattnall)
    Eli (Laurens)
    Henry (Greene)
    Henry (Oglethorpe)
    James (Warren)
    James (Wilkinson)
    John (Habersham)
    John (Jones)
    Joseph (Tattnall)
    Lovy (Appling)
    Matthew (Warren)
    Parnemus (Oglethorpe)
    R. (Jasper)
    Sampson (Hancock)
    Simpson (Washington)
    William (Wilkinson)
Ennis, Mr. (Chatham)
    Charles (Hancock)
    James (Washington)
    John (Camden)
    Mary (Wilkinson)
    Nathaniel (Hancock)
    Peggy (Burke)
Eno, Richard (Richmond)
Ensley, Samuel (Greene)
    William (Greene)
Epperson, James (Oglethorpe)
    John (Jackson)
Eppinger, James (Chatham)
    John (Chatham)
Epps, Thomas (Clarke)
Ericon, Nancy (Jones)
Erley, Henry (Oglethorpe)
    Sarah (Oglethorpe)
Erly, Jacob (Oglethorpe)
Ernest, Thomas T. (Jefferson)
Ernst, Godlip (Effingham)
Ervin, Joseph M. (Jackson)
    Josiah (Jones)
    William (Jones)
Erwin, Leander A. (Clarke)
    Richard (Burke)
    Robert (Burke)
Esball, Nancy (Appling)

Espey, James (Clarke)
James (Putnam)
John Clarke)
Espy, Joseph (Oglethorpe)
Robert (Jackson)
Thomas (Jackson)
Thomas (Morgan)
Estes, Allen (Baldwin)
Jiles (Appling)
Etchison, Nathaniel (Madison)
Eters, Peter (Habersham)
Etheridge, Allen (Baldwin)
Rebecca (Liberty)
Robert (Wilkinson)
Wiley (Wilkinson)
William (Wilkinson)
Ethrage, William (Putnam)
Ethridge, Caleb (Baldwin)
Elijah (Jones)
Edmond (Jones)
Edward (Wilkinson)
Enoch (Washington)
Marmaduke (Baldwin)
Merett (Wilkinson)
Nathan (Jones)
William (Baldwin)
Eubank, Caleb (Columbia)
Esther (Columbia)
Garner (Jefferson)
George (Jefferson)
John (Columbia)
Richard (Columbia)
William, Jr. (Columbia)
William, Sr. (Columbia)
Eubanks, Edward (Hancock)
John (Hall)
John (Hancock)
Nancy (?) (Hancock)
William (Lincoln)
Eugin(?), T.(?) (Camden)
Evan, Peter (Tattnall)
Evans, (ind.) (Chatham)
Andelen (Jasper)
Ansalum L. (Jones)
Arden (Morgan)
Banister (Warren)
Benjamin (Laurens)
Boswell Y. (Putnam)
Britian (2) (Hancock)
Charles (Jones)
Charles (Lincoln)
Daniel (Burke)
Daniel J. (Burke)
Darky (Richmond)
David (Jasper)
David (Laurens)
E. Y. (Putnam)
Edward H. (Putnam)
Elam (Elbert)
Elijah (Putnam)
Elisha (Pulaski)

Elisha (Wilkes)
Elizabeth (Baldwin)
Elizabeth (Wilkes)
Evan (Jasper)
Frederick (Jefferson)
G. W. (Richmond)
George (Pulaski)
George W. (Burke)
Henry(?) (Lincoln)
Henry (Pulaski)
Humphrey (Columbia)
James (Wilkes)
Jesse (Warren)
John (Gwinnett)
John (2) (Jackson)
John (Jones)
John (Morgan)
John (Walton)
John (Wilkes)
John A. (2) (Hancock)
John C. (Morgan)
Joshua (Jasper)
Luellen (Wilkes)
Martha (Putnam)
Richard (Burke)
Richard H. (Burke)
Robert (Putnam)
Robert (Wilkes)
Ruel, Sr. (Screven)
Sterling (Hancock)
Thomas (Baldwin)
Thomas (Bulloch)
Thomas (Jones)
Thomas (Putnam)
Thomas (Wilkes)
William (Gwinnett)
William (Morgan)
William (2) (Putnam)
William (Wilkes)
William D. (Putnam)
Willmouth (Putnam)
Eve, (ind.) (Richmond)
J. (Richmond)
Evens, Jeremiah (Oglethorpe)
Joseph (Greene)
William, Jr. (Greene)
William, Sr. (Greene)
Everatt, Matthew (Oglethorpe)
Everett, Joshua (Bulloch)
Josiah (Pulaski)
Thomas (Columbia)
Turner (Pulaski)
Samuel (Hall)
Everitt, Aaron (Bulloch)
Hardy (Screven)
Jehu (Bulloch)
John (Bulloch)
John, Sr. (Bulloch)
Joseph (Jackson)
Solomon (2) (Jasper)
William (Screven)

Evers, Gibson (Wilkinson)
Peter (Effingham)
William (Effingham)
Eves, Rhody (Elbert)
Evins, David (Madison)
John (Oglethorpe)
Robert (Madison)
Thomas (Madison)
William (Madison)
Evinson, Abraham (Elbert)
Eli (Elbert)
George (Elbert)
Evrit, Jehu (Telfair)
Ewing, John (Hancock)
Johnathan (Hancock)
Samuel (Hancock)
Exley, John (Effingham)
Solomon (Effingham)
Exum, Benjamin (Wilkinson)
James (Wilkinson)
Eyden(?), Elisha (Oglethorpe)
Ezard. Margaret (Gwinnett)
William (Gwinnett)
Ezell, H. G. (Jasper)
Timothy (Laurens)
W. (Jasper)

F

Fabian, Est. of (Liberty)
Fagg, T. W. (Jasper)
Fagin, Uriah (Early)
Fahm. Jacob (Chatham)
Fail, William (Jones)
Fails, Mary (Jones)
Fain, Ebenezer (Habersham)
Jessie (Morgan)
John (Elbert)
John (Habersham)
John (Morgan)
Matthew (Telfair)
Mercer (Habersham)
Robert (Chatham)
Thomas (Telfair)
William (Morgan)
William (Screven)
Fair, Peter (Baldwin)
Fairchild, William (Jasper)
Fairchilds, Rachel (Wilkinson)
Fairchiles, John T. (Wilkinson)
Faircloth, (Screven)
Allen (Laurens)
Benjamin (Emanuel)
Benjamin (Laurens)
Etheldred (Emanuel)
Francis (Pulaski)
Peter (Laurens)
Reddin (Burke)
William (Pulaski)
Fairfess, James (Jones)
Fairley, John (Jones)

Falanel(?), Covington (Screven)
Falkner, Job (Walton)
Fallen, John H. (Wilkes)
Fallens, Charles (Wilkes)
Faller, Wargreen V. (Jasper)
Fallford, Valentine (Laurens)
Falligant, Louis (Chatham)
Fambraugh, Thomas
    (Oglethorpe)
Famby, Thomas (Wilkes)
Fann, Jesse (Pulaski)
Fannin, Charles (Elbert)
    Jacob (Putnam)
    Jacob, Sr. (Putnam)
    Jeptha (Morgan)
    John H. (Putnam)
    Traverse (Laurens)
Fanning, Benjamin (Elbert)
    John (Elbert)
    Laughlin (Elbert)
Fannon, William (Walton)
Fanton William (Washington)
Farechildes, Cader (Screven)
Farel, I. (Chatham)
Faris(?), George D. (Chatham)
Faries Faris, William (Habersham)
Farkner, John (2) (Jasper)
Farley, Alexander (Putnam)
    Charles (Jasper)
    Frances (Morgan)
    James (Jasper)
    John (2) (Jasper)
    Mathew (Putnam)
    N. (Jasper)
Farlin, Fleet (Wilkes)
Farmer, Amelia (Laurens)
    Benjamin (Elbert)
    Daniel (Wilkes)
    Elizabeth (Jones)
    Enoch (Warren)
    Henry (Oglethorpe)
    Isaac (Burke)
    James (Burke)
    James (Hancock)
    James (2) (Gwinnett)
    James (Wilkes)
    John (Elbert)
    John (Gwinnett)
    John (Morgan)
    John (Washington)
    Nancy (Burke)
    Nathan (Morgan)
    Samuel (Morgan)
    Sarah (Chatham)
    Uriel (Wilkes)
    Verity (Burke)
    William (Screven)
Farmsworth, James (Wilkes)
Farnell, Elisha (Pulaski)
Farr, (ind.) (Warren)
    Dorian (Warren)

John (Chatham)
Mary (Wayne)
Farrar, Henry (Pulaski)
    James (Lincoln)
    Mary (Putnam)
    Thomas (Lincoln)
Farrel, Bender (Burke)
Farrior, William (Chatham)
Farron, Darcus (2) (Morgan)
Farrow, Jesse (Burke)
    John (Morgan)
    Stephen D. (Morgan)
    Thomas Jefferson (Morgan)
Farsf(?), Manet (Chatham)
Fase, Willis (Wilkinson)
Fason, William (Hancock)
    William (Washington)
Fauche, Jonas (Greene)
Faucett, Elmore (Greene)
Faulk, Henry (Elbert)
Faulkner, William (Elbert)
Faver, Isiah (Putnam)
    Mary (Wilkes)
    Mathew (Wilkes)
    Reuben (Wilkes)
    William (Putnam)
Favier, Capt. P. (Chatham)
Favors, William, Sr. (Putnam)
Feagan, Henry R. (Jones)
    Samuel (Jones)
Feagin, Moses (Habersham)
    William (Habersham)
Fears, Ezekiel (Jasper)
    James (Warren)
    Richard (Hancock)
    William (Greene)
Feaster, William (Bryan)
Featherton, Edward
    (Montgomery)
Federick, Louis (Putnam)
    Stephen (Putnam)
Fefst, Washing (Jasper)
Fell, Fred S. (Chatham)
    Samuel E. (Elbert)
Feller, Mary (Warren)
Felp, Sinhler (Elbert)
Felps, Francis (Hall)
    John (2) (Putnam)
    Joseph D. (Putnam)
    Polly (Oglethorpe)
    William (Jones)
    William (Pulaski)
Felt, Joseph (Chatham)
Felton, Edward (Walton)
    Hezekiah (2) (Hall)
    Howard(?) (Hall)
    John (Greene)
Felts, Carey (Jones)
    Hartwell (Warren)
    James (Putnam)
    Simeon (Putnam)

William (Putnam)
Femby, Nathan (Oglethorpe)
Fench, Robert (Putnam)
Fendale, T. H. M. (Richmon
Fendly, John (Tattnall)
Fenel, John (Jasper)
Fenell, John (Wilkes)
Fenn, Isaac (2) (Hancock)
    William (Clarke)
Fennall, Hardy L. (Madison
Fennel, Michel (Emanuel)
    William (Morgan)
Fenno, William (Chatham)
Fergerson, James (Oglethor
    Johnson (Morgan)
    Joseph (Jones)
Ferguson, Isaac (Emanuel)
    Isaac (Wilkes)
    Lucy (Wilkes)
    Mary (Liberty)
    Neill (Jasper)
    Norman(?) (Elbert)
    William (Chatham)
    William E. (Bryan)
Ferin, Eli (Washington)
Fernander, L. C. (Jasper)
Ferrel, John (Hall)
Ferrell, Bennett (Wilkinson
    Hubbard (Hancock)
    John (Jones)
    Michaelberry (Jones)
    Micajah (Elbert)
    Williamson (Wilkinson)
Ferrile, Solomon (Putnam)
Ferrill, Bird (Hancock)
    John (Jasper)
Fetzer, John G. (Effingham
Fetzir, Madalen (Effingham
Few, Benjamin (Walton)
    Clement (Morgan)
    Hannah (Columbia)
    Ignatius (Columbia)
    Ignatius (Morgan)
    James (Walton)
    John (Richmond)
    Mary (Columbia)
    Thomas (Richmond)
Fezzle, Jane (Washington)
Fickling, Barnell W. (Warr
Fielder, Elizabeth (Hall)
    Elizabeth (Putnam)
    George (Walton)
    Samuel (Morgan)
    Sarah (Morgan)
    Thomas (Morgan)
Fields, (ind.) (Laurens)
    Gediah by B. A. Busb
    Overseer (Libert
    Horatio (Hancock)
    Mary (Burke)
    Miles (Burke)

Fields, Morgan (Gwinnett)
  Sion (Morgan)
  Thompson (Warren)
  William (Gwinnett)
Figg, Mary (Jefferson)
Files, Adam I. (Walton)
Finch, B. (ind.) (Oglethorpe)
  Ichabod (Warren)
  John (Hall)
  John (Jasper)
  John C. (Oglethorpe)
  Liddy (Madison)
  William (Jackson)
  William (2) (Oglethorpe)
Fincher, Benjamin (Jasper)
  Isaac (Jasper)
  James (Walton)
  Joshua (Walton)
  Josiah (Gwinnett)
  William (Jasper)
Findlay, Sarah (Glynn)
Findlewood, Christopher
      (Telfair)
Findley, Isabella (Wilkes)
  John (Burke)
  John (Richmond)
Finlay, William (Walton)
Finley, George (Walton)
  James (Greene)
  Jane (Greene)
  John (2) (Morgan)
  Margaret (Greene)
  Robert (Greene)
  Samuel (Greene)
  Samuel P. (Oglethorpe)
Finn, Vincent D. (Gwinnett)
Finney, Arthur (Jones)
  Benjamin (2) (Jones)
  Drury (Jones)
  Henry (Jones)
  James (Jones)
  Sarah (Jones)
  Sterling (Morgan)
  Uphamy (Jones)
  William (Morgan)
Finny, Sarah (Burke)
Fior, Edmund (Burke)
Firewill, Benjamin (Putnam)
Firns, Henry H. (Screven)
Fish, James (Chatham)
  Joseph John (Chatham)
  Nathan (Jasper)
Fisher, Benjamin P. (Wilkes)
  Charles (Washington)
  Metcalf (Washington)
Fishler, Charles (Chatham)
Fisk, Sarah (Walton)
Fitch, Catherine (Camden)
  John (Camden)
Fitchet, John (Camden)
Fitts, John (Elbert)

Fitzgerald, David (Burke)
  John (Burke)
FitzJarrell, Willis (Greene)
Fitzpatrick, Mrs. (Chatham)
  Benjamin (Morgan)
  David (Morgan)
  Elizabeth (McIntosh)
  Hamner (Morgan)
  Joseph (Greene)
  Joseph (Jackson)
  Joseph (Morgan)
  Perkins (Morgan)
  R. (Jasper)
  Rene (Jasper)
  Reney (Greene)
  William (Greene)
Fiveash(?), Elisha (Appling)
Fiveash, John (Tattnall)
  Sion (Montgomery)
Flaherty, Thomas (Jasper)
Flake, J. M. (Richmond)
  Mary (Putnam)
  William (Screven)
  William (Richmond)
  William (Warren)
Flanagan, John (Jackson)
  Thomas (Chatham)
  William, Jr. (Hall)
  William, Sr. (Hall)
Flanders, John R. (Emanuel)
  Jordan (Emanuel)
  William (Emanuel)
Flaneghan, Phillip (Putnam)
Flanigan, Sussannah (Jackson)
  Thomas (Habersham)
Flannigan, John (Jones)
  Malinda (Jones)
Fleeting, John (Jefferson)
  Margaret (Jefferson)
Fleetwood, John (Richmond)
Fleming, George (Camden)
  Henry (Elbert)
  James (Baldwin)
  James (Jefferson)
  James (2) (Warren)
  John (Jefferson)
  John (Lincoln)
  John (Washington)
  John A. (Columbia)
  Moses (Elbert)
  Robert (Jefferson)
  Robert (Lincoln)
  Robert A. (Warren)
  Samuel (3) (Jefferson)
  Samuel (Lincoln)
  Samuel (Warren)
  William, est. of (Liberty)
  William (Hall)
  William (Lincoln)
  William (Madison)
Flemister, John (Jasper)

Fletcher, Mrs. (Chatham)
  Ezekiel (Lincoln)
  George (Liberty)
  George (Tattnall)
  John (Clarke)
  John (Telfair)
  John, Jr. (Telfair)
  Joseph (Hancock)
  Joseph (Telfair)
Fletcher, Mary (Telfair)
  Richard (Columbia)
  Thomas (Jasper)
  Thomas (Oglethorpe)
  Wilie (Walton)
  William (Bulloch)
  William, Sr. (Bulloch)
  Zebra (Jones)
Flewellen, Alexander (Putnam)
  Archilus (Warren)
  James (Warren)
  Shadarach (Warren)
  William (Jones)
Flewelling, Taylor (Richmond)
Flinn, Elizabeth (Columbia)
  James (Warren)
Flint, Aquilla (Columbia)
  Augustin W. (Wilkes)
  George W. (Wilkes)
  Jane (Columbia)
  John (Wilkes)
  Thomas H. (Columbia)
  William (Morgan)
Floid, Alexander (Oglethorpe)
  William R. (Oglethorpe)
Florence, (ind.) (Lincoln)
  David (Lincoln)
  John (Lincoln)
  Obariat (Lincoln)
  Thomas (Lincoln)
Flournoy, Frances (Morgan)
  Joseph (Putnam)
  Obediah (Wilkes)
  Peter F. (Putnam)
  Capt. R. (Chatham)
  Robert (Chatham)
  Samuel (Wilkes)
  Thomas (Richmond)
  William (Putnam)
Flowers, (ind.) (Laurens)
  Abner (Jones)
  Charles (Liberty)
  Edward (Jasper)
Flowers(?), Elijah (Pulaski)
Flowers, Hardy (Habersham)
  Harwell (Jones)
  John (Jones)
  John (Liberty)
  Joseph (Emanuel)
  Joseph (Liberty)
  William (Wayne)
Floyd, Benjamin (Oglethorpe)

Floyd, Clement (Oglethorpe)
Dolphen (Jones)
Elizabeth (Chatham)
Elizabeth (Oglethorpe)
Enoch (Jackson)
Frederick (Pulaski)
Gallant (Pulaski)
Gilford (Greene)
Grambury (Liberty)
Jabus (Madison)
James (Burke)
Jessie (Liberty)
John (Burke)
John (Camden)
John (Clarke)
John (Oglethorpe)
John (Putnam)
Joseph (Pulaski)
Lewis (Madison)
Marguett (Wilkes)
Matthew (Burke)
Richard (Oglethorpe)
Robert (Madison)
Shadrack (Lincoln)
Stephen P. (Screven)
Thomas (Burke)
Thomas (Jones)
Thomas (Wilkes)
Thomas E. (Chatham)
William (Madison)
Floynoy, Williiam (Jasper)
Fluellen, John (Baldwin)
Fluellin, Nancy (Baldwin)
Fluker, Baldwin (Washington)
Isaac (Wilkes)
John (Jasper)
Flurme, G. B. (Jasper)
Flurnoy, Marcus (Jefferson)
Flynn, John (Columbia)
Michael (Columbia)
Foard, Abraham (Baldwin)
Brandon (Baldwin)
Stephen (Laurens)
Thomas (Baldwin)
William (Laurens)
Foitt(?), James (Wayne)
Fokes, John (Jefferson)
Fokez, Amos (Jefferson)
William (Jefferson)
William L. (Jefferson)
Folds, George (Columbia)
John (Jasper)
Richard (Burke)
Foley, Edward (Jefferson)
Joshua (Camden)
Folk, James (Wilkinson)
Jesse (Jones)
John (Laurens)
Folker, James (Chatham)
Folsom, (ind.) (Pulaski)
Benjamin (Bulloch)

Edith (Pulaski)
Lawrence (Pulaski)
Nathaniel (Laurens)
William (Pulaski)
Folsome, Ebenezer (Laurens)
Fendren, James (Walton)
Fontain, Enos (Jefferson)
Fontaine, Benjamin (Warren)
John (Warren)
Foose(?), Jessee (Washington)
Footman, Edward (Bryan)
Richard H. (Bryan)
Forbes, Benjamin (Washington)
John (McIntosh)
John (Washington)
Ford, Daniel (Habersham)
Daniel (Oglethorpe)
Elisha (Elbert)
Isaac (Elbert)
James (Wilkes)
John (Jefferson)
John (Elbert)
John (Irwin)
John (Pulaski)
Robert (Lincoln)
Sally (Habersham)
Samuel (Jefferson)
Thomas (Jones)
Valentine (Hancock)
William (Jones)
William (Wilkinson)
William (Warren)
Fordham, Benjamin (Wilkinson)
Forehand, David (Washington)
Drewry (Burke)
Jerry (Washington)
Jordon (Washington)
Foreman, David (Pulaski)
Elizabeth (Jefferson)
John (Putnam)
Moore (Jefferson)
William B. (Jefferson)
Forester, John (Habersham)
Forgarty, Cornelius (Jones)
Formby, Aaron (Morgan)
Obediah (Morgan)
Forrester, Moss (Madison)
Thomas (Madison)
Forrister, Joel (Greene)
Willis (Greene)
Forster, Jeptha (Jasper)
John (Lincoln)
Forstson, Jesse (Elbert)
Forsyth, James (Laurens)
John (Hancock)
Phillip (Hancock)
Forsythe, James (Hancock)
John (Hancock)
Phillip (Hancock)
Fort, Edwin (Hancock)
Elias (Chatham)

John (Laurens)
John (Washington)
John (Wayne)
Owen (Jefferson)
Tomlinson (Baldwin)
Forth, Joel L. (Burke)
John T. ((Burke)
Thomas (Burke)
Fortner, Sarah (Emanuel)
Fortson, Benjamin (Elbert)
James (Elbert)
Richard (Elbert)
Thomas (Elbert)
Foshee, Elijah (Hall)
Fossett, Anderson (Columbia)
George (2) (Columbia)
Foster, (ind.) (Pulaski)
Achilles (Hall)
Ardin (Wilkes)
Arthur (Columbia)
Arthur (Greene)
Arthur (Morgan)
Elizabeth (2) (Hancock)
Federick, Jr. (Putnam)
Federick, Sr. (Putnam)
Francis (Hancock)
Francis (Wilkes)
George W. (Greene)
James F. (Greene)
Jesse (Morgan)
John (Clarke)
John (Columbia)
John (Jasper)
John (2) (Putnam)
John (Oglethorpe)
John (Washington)
John S. (Elbert)
Joseph S. (Wilkes)
Joshua (Columbia)
Levi (Clarke)
Lewis (Wilkes)
Lucy (Chatham)
Martha (Wilkes)
Richard (Burke)
Sarah (Hancock)
Susan (Greene)
Thomas (Hancock)
William (Jasper)
William (Jefferson)
William (Liberty)
William (Putnam)
William I. (Hancock)
William S. (Wilkes)
Fouche, George (Wilkes)
Jonathon (Wilkes)
Fountain, Dempsy (Burke)
Elthered (Jefferson)
Henry (Emanuel)
James (Chatham)
James (Wilkinson)
Isariah (Wilkinson)

Fountain, Margaret (Chatham)
Owen (Emanuel)
Sarah (Jefferson)
Susanna (Wilkinson)
William (Emanuel)
William (Jefferson)
Fouracres, Jesse (Camden)
Moon (Camden)
Fowler, Benjamin (Oglethorpe)
Cody (Clarke)
Eddy (Jackson)
George (Jefferson)
James (McIntosh)
Jeremiah (Washington)
John (Jefferson)
John (McIntosh)
John (Washington)
John M. (Jasper)
Joshua (Richmond)
Minta (Clarke)
Polly (Gwinnett)
Rachel (Elbert)
Richard (Habersham)
Samuel (Hall)
Samuel (Jackson)
Thornton (Wilkinson)
Zaphamah (Warren)
Fox, Ann (Richmond)
Benjamin (Morgan)
Jacob (Chatham)
John (Richmond)
Mary (Richmond)
Richard W. (Morgan)
Richard W. (Putnam)
William B. (Chatham)
Foxey(?), William (Putnam)
Foy, Rhoda (Columbia)
Foye, (torn) (Laurens)
Foyil, Elizabeth (Jefferson)
Frail, Elizabeth (Columbia)
Fanny (col.) (Columbia)
Richard (Telfair)
France(?), William (Richmond)
Frances, Rachel (Effingham)
Francis, Cordel (Washington)
James (Richmond)
Frank, (col.) (Columbia)
William, (Wilkes)
Franklin, Bird (Hall)
David (Morgan)
Edward (Screven)
Edwin P. (Baldwin)
Felix D. (Warren)
Frances (Morgan)
Francis (Elbert)
Goodman (Jones)
James (Washington)
Job (Elbert)
John (Glynn)
John (Putnam)
Joseph (Jones)

Josiah (Washington)
Louis (Jackson)
Mary G. (Morgan)
Singleton (Hancock)
Vashti (Washington)
Franklin(?), William (Bulloch)
Franklin, William (Oglethorpe)
Zepohemiah (Warren)
Fransette, Abram (Laurens)
Frapp, John L. (Jackson)
Fraser, Alex (Chatham)
Donald (Liberty)
Est. of E. (dec'd) (Liberty)
Ely (Jasper)
Robert (Richmond)
Simon, Sr. (Liberty)
Simon A. (Liberty)
William (Liberty)
Frasier, Andrew F. (Liberty)
Archibald (Screven)
Barnet (Wilkes)
James (Richmond)
John (Wilkes)
William (2) (Wilkes)
Frazer, John (Lincoln)
Frazier, Arthur (Lincoln)
David (Lincoln)
Elizabeth (Pulaski)
Nancy (Hancock)
Joshua (Putnam)
Samuel (Lincoln)
Freason, James (Jones)
Thomas (Jones)
Frederick, J. (Richmond)
James (Wilkinson)
Thomas (Bulloch)
Frederick, Mary (Pulaski)
Freeland, Lewis (2) (Jasper)
Mary (Habersham)
Freeman, Allen (Clarke)
Ann (Greene)
Benjamin (Jackson)
Baily (Jasper)
Bailey (Morgan)
Boswell (Jones)
Daniel (Jasper)
Daniel (Columbia)
Fanny (Washington)
Francis (Habersham)
Francis (Wilkes)
Gabriel (Morgan)
Garrod (Screven)
George (Jones)
George W. (Wilkes)
Henry (Chatham)
Henry (Wilkes)
Hugh (Putnam)
James (Jones)
James (Jasper)
James (Putnam)
James (Wilkinson)

John (Jasper)
John (Jones)
John (Washington)
John (Wayne)
John (Jefferson)
John (Oglethorpe)
John (Wilkinson)
John (2) (Greene)
Johnson (Clarke)
Joseph S. (Wilkes)
Jisse(?) (Jasper)
Laban F. (Wilkes)
Martha (Baldwin)
Noah (Oglethorpe)
Robart (Oglethorpe)
Robert (Hall)
Robert (Jones)
Samuel (Oglethorpe)
Thomas (Jackson)
Thomas (Wilkes)
William (Oglethorpe)
William (Wilkes)
William H. (Wilkes)
French, Dempsey (Laurens)
James (Warren)
James (Wilkinson)
John (Jones)
Liddey (Wilkinson)
R. (ind.) (Emanuel)
Robert (Emanuel)
Thomas (Emanuel)
Frenel, Thomas (Warren)
Frestham(?), Abraham (Hall)
Fretwell, Charles (Jefferson)
James (Jasper)
John (Putnam)
Leonard (Putnam)
Leonard (Walton)
Richard (Walton)
William (Walton)
Freyermouth, John (Effingham)
Peter (Effingham)
Frier, Henderson (Bulloch)
Frizzle, Thomas (Washington)
Fromainto, Z. (Chatham)
Frost, James (Burke)
John (Wilkinson)
Johnson (Clarke)
Ruth (Hall)
Sarah (Wilkinson)
Fruin, James (Glynn)
Fruman, William (Baldwin)
Fruny, Elizah (Baldwin)
William (Baldwin)
Fry, Benjamin (Jasper)
Catherine (Chatham)
Jesse (Chatham)
Mary (Gwinnett)
Fryer, Aaron (Bryan)
Elizabeth (Chatham)
Fielding (Burke)

Fryer, John (Burke)
  Robert (Burke)
  Winnifred (Burke)
  Zachariah L. (Burke)
Fryier, Jemina (Washington)
  William (Washington)
Fudg, John (Richmond)
Fudge, Benjamin (Jasper)
  David (Columbia)
  Jacob (Columbia)
  Solomon (Columbia)
  Stephen (Jackson)
Fuerth, Dr. H. (Chatham)
Fugerson, Benjamin
            (Washington)
  Daniel (Washington)
Fuhett, Alex (Oglethorpe)
Fulcher, Armstard (Richmond)
  Austin (Jackson)
  Dillon (Jackson)
  James (Jackson)
  James (Richmond)
  John (Burke)
  Rebukah (Montgomery)
Fulford, Araan (Laurens)
  John (Laurens)
Fulgham, Jackson (Pulaski)
  Stephen (Morgan)
Fuller, Abner (Columbia)
  Abraham (Columbia)
  Alford (Greene)
  Benjamin (Columbia)
  Benjamin (Gwinnett)
  Benjamin (Liberty)
  Chloe (Washington)
  David (Greene)
  Elijah (Greene)
  Elizabeth (Columbia)
  Ezekiel (Habersham)
  George W. (Morgan)
  Green (Greene)
  Isaac (Baldwin)
  Isham (Columbia)
  Isiah (Hancock)
  James (Morgan)
  John (Baldwin)
  John (2) (Morgan)
  Jones (Baldwin)
  Joshua, Sr. (Columbia)
  Samuel (Columbia)
  Samuel (Putnam)
  Semmeon (Putnam)
  Spivy (Warren)
  Thomas (McIntosh)
  Truman (Clarke)
  Uriah (Morgan)
  William (Columbia)
  William A. (Warren)
  Wilson (Chatham)
Fullerwood, E. (Jasper)
Fullilove, John (Oglethorpe)

Ludwell (Wilkes)
Fullwood, (ind.) (Laurens)
  Andrew (Telfair)
  James (Appling)
  Thomas (Wayne)
  Wilkins (Telfair)
Fulsome, John (Hancock)
  Benjamin (Jasper)
Fulton, Elijah (Gwinnett)
  James (Clarke)
  James B. (Hall)
  John (Liberty)
  John (Oglethorpe)
  William (McIntosh)
Fulwood, Andrew (Screven)
  John (Wilkinson)
  Robert (Clarke)
Funderburg, Henry (Gwinnett)
Funderburke, Abel (Warren)
  Jacob (Wilkinson)
  John (Jones)
Fuqua, Henry (Laurens)
  John (Laurens)
  William (Gwinnett)
Fuquay, Moses (Liberty)
Furlow, Charles (Morgan)
  David (Greene)
  John (Greene)
Furman, Joel (Madison)
Furnel, B. (Chatham)
Furr, Paul (Hall)
Futch, Jacob (Bulloch)
  Isaac (Bulloch)
  Oniumus (Bryan)
  Solomon (Bulloch)
  Thomas (Bulloch)
  William (Tattnall)
  William, Jr. (Tattnall)
Futral, Benjamin (Greene)
Futrell, Micajah (Effingham)

G

Gaar, George (Elbert)
Gabard, Thomas (Burke)
Gabbard, George (Putnam)
Gaddis, John, Jr. (Gwinnett)
  John, Sr. (Gwinnett)
  Thomas C. (Jones)
Gadis, Hezekiah (Jackson)
Gady, William (Hall)
Gafford, Susannah (Jones)
  Zachariah (Jones)
Gailey, Andrew (Madison)
Gailor, John (Gwinnett)
  Margaret (Gwinnett)
Gainer, James (Washington)
  Martha (Washington)
  Michael (Washington)
  William (Washington)
Gaines, Ann T. (Elbert)

Duncan (Burke)
  Francis (Elbert)
  Livingston P. (Elbert)
  Richard S. (Elbert)
  Robert T. (Elbert)
  Theophilus (Burke)
  William (Elbert)
Gainey, Micajar (Walton)
  Richard (Pulaski)
Gains, George G. (Pulaski)
  John (Richmond)
Gaither, Brice (Putnam)
  Greenburg (Putnam)
Galagin, William (Camden)
Galbraith, Joseph (Oglethorpe)
Gallaway, Britton (Oglethorpe)
  William (Oglethorpe)
Gallen, Radford (Greene)
Gallman, I. (Jasper)
  James (Jasper)
  Jesse (Jasper)
  Silas (Jasper)
Galloway, (Burke)
Galoway, Thomas (Oglethorpe)
Galpin, Green (Columbia)
Galtany, Gehue (Jones)
  John (Jones)
Gamage, Solomon (Baldwin)
Gambell, James (Baldwin)
Gamble, Hugh T. (Jefferson)
  Isaac (Jones)
  John (Jones)
  Rachel (Jefferson)
  Roger L. (Jefferson)
  Thomas (Putnam)
Gamell, James (Lincoln)
  John (Lincoln)
  William (Lincoln)
Gammage, Ast (Jones)
  Charity (Wilkes)
  Nancy (Wilkes)
  Nathaniel (Jones)
Gammon, Elizabeth (Jones)
  Joel (Jones)
  Jonathan (Oglethorpe)
  Joseph (Chatham)
  Samuel (Jones)
  Willis (Jones)
Ganahl, Joseph (Richmond)
Gandy, (ind.) (Montgomery)
Ganey, Edmond (Emanuel)
Gann, John (Clarke)
  Mary (Clarke)
  Micajah (Clarke)
  Nathan, Jr. (Clarke)
  Nathan, Sr. (Clarke)
  Sally (Walton)
  William (Clarke)
  William, Jr. (Clarke)
  William, Sr. (Clarke)
Gant, Est. (Lincoln)

Gant, Charles (Lincoln)
Gantt, Britton (Putnam)
Gany, McLendon (Tattnall)
   Reddick (Tattnall)
Garatt, Jonathon (Walton)
Garaway, Thomas (Habersham)
Garbett, Elisha (Pulaski)
   William (Pulaski)
Garce, Breton (Jasper)
Gardener, Mary (Richmond)
   Thomas (Richmond)
Gardiner, James (Richmond)
   John (Chatham)
   Thomas (Chatham)
Gardner, Aaron (Emanuel)
   Elizabeth (Morgan)
   Ethelred (Walton)
   Ezekiel (Washington)
   Gray B. (Pulaski)
   Isham (Washington)
   Jason (Columbia)
   John (Jones)
   John E. (Washington)
   Lecia (Washington)
   Samuel (Wayne)
   Samuel (Wilkes)
   Sterling (Hancock)
   Sterling (Warren)
   Thomas (Habersham)
   William (Madison)
   William (Morgan)
   William (Richmond)
Garet, Mary (Burke)
Garette, Samuel (Washington)
Garisson, David (Wilkinson)
Garland, Henry (Putnam)
   Patrick (Putnam)
   William D. (Hancock)
   William T. (Hancock)
Garlick, Samuel (Burke)
Garlington, Joseph (Oglethorpe)
Garmany, Joseph (Columbia)
Garnel, A. (Jasper)
Garner, Daniel (Morgan)
   Francis (Walton)
   Henry (Washington)
   James (Jefferson)
   John (Greene)
   John (Richmond)
   John G. (Putnam)
   Luke (Clarke)
   Mark (Putnam)
   Martin (Jackson)
   Presley (Morgan)
   Stephen (Putnam)
   Stephen (Washington)
   William (Hall)
   William (Greene)
Garnett, Eli (Lincoln)
   Elizabeth (Columbia)
   John (Columbia)

John (Screven)
Joseph (Chatham)
Nancy (Columbia)
Rebecca (Columbia)
Samuel (Chatham)
Thomas (Chatham)
Garol, Mr. (Chatham)
Garr, Adam (Elbert)
   Joel (Morgan)
   Lewis (Morgan)
Garrard, Jacob (Jackson)
Garrason, Darius (Effingham)
   Isaac (Effingham)
   Michael (Effingham)
Garret, Samuel (Telfair)
Garrett, Asa (Washington)
   Catherine (Richmond)
   Charles (Morgan)
   Charly (Morgan)
   Daniel (Hall)
   George (Jasper)
   Jacob (Putnam)
   Jacob (Warren)
   James (Gwinnett)
   James (Hall)
   James (Madison)
   Jeremiah (Wilkinson)
   John (Greene)
   John (Jasper)
   John (Wilkinson)
   Joseph (Hancock)
   Nancy (Jackson)
   Nathanl C. (Jackson)
   Richard (Jackson)
   Robert (Wilkinson)
   Thomas (2) (Jasper)
   Thomas (Walton)
   Thomas B. (Greene)
   Thomas B. (Hall)
   William (Putnam)
Garrison, Allen (Hall)
   Caleb (Habersham)
   Nehemiah (Hall)
   Zebulon (Hall)
Garritt, William (Putnam)
Garrot, Caswell (Early)
   John (Wilkes)
Garrott, Benjamin (Jasper)
Garry, Polly (Hall)
Gartman, (ind.) (Pulaski)
Garven, S. (Richmond)
Garvin, David (Habersham)
   Henry (Oglethorpe)
   Richard (Oglethorpe)
Gary, Hartwell (Hancock)
   M. E. (Jasper)
   Nancy (McIntosh)
   Richard (Hancock)
   William (Jasper)
Casaway, James (Wilkes)
   John (Gwinnett)

Gaskett(?), Charley (Jones)
Gaskin, David (Telfair)
   Fisher (Telfair)
Gaskins, George (Lincoln)
Gasten, Alexander (Greene)
Gastin, Mathew (Putnam)
Gaston, Thomas (Jasper)
   William (Chatham)
Gate, M. (Chatham)
Gates, Benjamin (Jones)
   Benjamin (Wilkinson)
   Edward (Lincoln)
   Elisha (Jackson)
   Horatio (Baldwin)
   James (Jones)
   James (Pulaski)
   William (Chatham)
Gatewood, Frances M. (Putnam)
Gather, Vachel (Lincoln)
Gathright, William (Jackson)
Gatland, Sarah (Appling)
Gatlen, Stephen (Greene)
Gatlin, Edward (Morgan)
   Furney D. (Pulaski)
   Levi (Morgan)
   Mary (Greene)
   Stephen (Pulaski)
Gatling, Moses (Warren)
Gatrelle, Francis (Wilkes)
   John (2) (Wilkes)
   Joseph (Wilkes)
   William (Wilkes)
Gatten, Shade (Greene)
Gauding, John (2) (Hancock)
Gauldin, Jonathon (Liberty)
   Richard (Hancock)
   William (Hancock)
Gauldoin, Alexander (Elbert)
Gaup(?), William (Appling)
Gause, Martha (Tattnall)
Gautry(?), J. B. (Chatham)
Gay, (torn) (Laurens)
   Allen (Jasper)
   Amelia (Jones)
   G. (Jasper)
   Joel (Burke)
   Joshua (Emanuel)
   Joshua (Gwinnett)
   Mary (Burke)
   Mathew (Emanuel)
   Rachel (Pulaski)
   Reason (Jones)
   S. H. (Jasper)
   Simon (Emanuel)
   T. B. (Jasper)
   Thomas (Burke)
   Thomas (Jasper)
   William (Jasper)
   William (Jefferson)
   William (Telfair)
Gayley, James (Hall)

Gayley, Joseph (Hall)
Gaylor(?), Theophilas (Habersham)
Gazaway, Enoch (Hall)
  Jesse (Habersham)
  Thomas (Habersham)
Gear, William (Greene)
Geddens, Benjamin (Bulloch)
Gee, Peter R. (Putnam)
  Samuel (Elbert)
Gegar(?), Jeremiah (Effingham)
Geiger, Cornelius (Wayne)
  Felia (Wayne)
  John (Lincoln)
  Nicholas (Lincoln)
Geisling, Charles (Warren)
  Samuel (Warren)
  Richard (Warren)
Genkins, John (Jones)
Genning, Coleman (Jackson)
Genobley, (ind.) (Effingham)
Gent, Peter (Baldwin)
Gentry, Allen (Hall)
  Elisha (Walton)
  John (Hall)
  Martin (Walton)
  Wyatt (Elbert)
George, Benjamin (Jackson)
  Bucks, (Jasper)
  David (Burke)
  David (Walton)
  Elisha (Putnam)
  Eliza (Jasper)
  Henry (Jasper)
  James (Jones)
  James F. (Jones)
  Jean (Jackson)
  Jesse (Jackson)
  Jesse (Jasper)
  Jesse (Walton)
  Jonathon (Chatham)
  Jourdain (Columbia)
  Price (Appling)
  Rufus K. (Jones)
  Suky (Jackson)
  Tabitha (Putnam)
  Traver (Jackson)
Geralds, Susan (McIntosh)
Gerard(?), Jonah (Chatham)
Germade, James (Warren)
  Timothy (Warren)
Germany, Robert (Jasper)
  William (Morgan)
Gerrald, James (Columbia)
  Randle (Columbia)
  Tilmon (Columbia)
Gesseran, R. (Jasper)
Gestmond, Daniel (Telfair)
Getmain, William (McIntosh)
Ghee, Drewry (Madison)

Ghiles, John (Warren)
Gholston, B. (ind.) (Chatham)
  Benjamin (Madison)
  Dabney (Madison)
  John (Putnam)
  Leonard H. (Madison)
  Zachariah (Madison)
Gibbons, Ann (Laurens)
  Henry (Camden)
  John (Chatham)
  Sarah (2) (Chatham)
  Thomas (Chatham)
  Thomas (Screven)
  William (Chatham)
Gibbs, Herod (2) (Morgan)
  Jeremiah (Hall)
  John (Montgomery)
  Doct. I. C. (Liberty)
  Martha (Morgan)
  Thomas (Irwin)
  Thomas S. (?) (Hancock)
  Shadrack (Montgomery)
  William (Elbert)
  William (Montgomery)
Gibs, John (Telfair)
Gibson, (torn) (Laurens)
  A. H. (Wilkes)
  Chastine (Wilkes)
  Churchill (Warren)
  Daniel (Wayne)
  Elizabeth (Columbia)
  F. G. (Richmond)
  Frances (Jones)
  George (Wilkes)
  George W. (Jones)
  Henry (Columbia)
  Henry B. (Wilkes)
  Isaiah (Jackson)
  James (Gwinnett)
  James (Wilkinson)
  James F. (Putnam)
  James P. (Jasper)
  John (2) (Warren)
  John (Wilkes)
  John C. (Jasper)
  John L. (Jasper)
  John W. (Liberty)
  Margaret (Warren)
  Michael (Glynn)
  Michael (Morgan)
  Patrick (McIntosh)
  Richard (Wilkes)
  Sarah (Columbia)
  Shadrack W. (Columbia)
  Solomon (Greene)
  Springer S. (Wilkes)
  Sylvanus (Wilkes)
  Thomas (Jefferson)
  Thomas (Warren)
  Thornton (Warren)
  Walter (Wilkinson)

  William (Camden)
  William (Wilkes)
  William C. (Jasper)
Giddens, Francis (Wilkes)
Giddons, John (Wayne)
Gideon, William (Jackson)
Gideons, Edward (Pulaski)
Gigniliaitt, Charles (McIntosh)
  Gilbert Est. of (McIntosh)
  Henry (McIntosh)
  James (McIntosh)
  John M. (Glynn)
Gigsby, Duncan (Jones)
Gilbart, Thomas (Wilkinson)
  William (Wilkinson)
Gilbert, Mrs. (Chatham)
  Byrd (Wilkinson)
  Edmond (Jones)
  Edward (Jackson)
  Ezekiel (Morgan)
  Hill H. (Walton)
  Instant (Morgan)
  Isaac (Madison)
  James (Gwinnett)
  Jesse (Jefferson)
  Jesse (2) (Walton)
  John (Madison)
  John (Wilkinson)
  John B. (Chatham)
  John G. (Hancock)
  Mary (Wilkes)
  Richard (Wilkes)
  Richard W. (Morgan)
  Sarah (Hancock)
  William (Chatham)
  William (Madison)
  William (2) (Morgan)
  William (Richmond)
  William (Washington)
  William (Wilkes)
Gilbreath, Daniel T. (Greene)
Gilchrist, Hannah (Effingham)
Gilder, John S. (Irwin)
Giles, Elijah (Jones)
  John (2) (Hancock)
  Joseph G. (Jones)
  Richard (Walton)
  Robert (Wilkinson)
  William (Putnam)
Gilgore, John (Lincoln)
  Jerimiah (McIntosh)
  John (Morgan)
  Joseph (Morgan)
  Peter (Jones)
  Ralph (Lincoln)
  Robert (McIntosh)
  Sarah (Screven)
  Thomas Y. (Gwinnett)
  William (Jasper)
  Young (Walton)
Gill, Eleanor (McIntosh)

Gill, James (Telfair)
Gillam, Ezekel (Oglethorpe)
Gillespie, Robert (Oglethorpe)
Gillets, Francis (Chatham)
Gilley, Henry (Montgomery)
Gilliam, Thomas (Jasper)
Gillian, John (Wilkinson)
Gilliland, Hugh (Hancock)
Gillipund(?), John (Chatham)
Gillis, Bender (Emanuel)
   John B. (Glynn)
   Norman (Montgomery)
Gillispie, John (Chatham)
Gillmen, Elizabeth (Oglethorpe)
Gillmore, James (Putnam)
   John H. (Jasper)
   Mary (Putnam)
   Robert (Jasper)
   William (Morgan)
Gills, William (Wilkes)
Gillum, Miles (Washington)
   Robert (Greene)
   Thomas (Oglethorpe)
Gilly, Charles (Habersham)
   John (Early)
   Lendy (Montgomery)
   Roderick (Telfair)
   Willis (Habersham)
Gilman, Samuel (Lincoln)
Gilmer, John (Oglethorpe)
   John (Tattnall)
   John (Wilkinson)
   Pachy (Oglethorpe)
   Thomas L. (Wilkes)
   William (Oglethorpe)
Gilmor, Henry (Wilkinson)
   George (Wilkinson)
   Martha (Wilkinson)
   Stephen (Wilkinson)
   William (Wilkinson)
Gilmore, Alice (Hall)
   David (Hall)
   Hugh (Jefferson)
   Hugh (Washington)
   James, Sr. (Hall)
   James (Hall)
   James (2) (Washington)
   Jane (Hall)
   John (Hall)
   John (2) (Jasper)
   John (Jefferson)
   John (Washington)
   John H. (Jasper)
   Samuel (Jasper)
   Stephen H. (Morgan)
   Thomas (Washington)
   Umphrey (Morgan)
Gilpin, Benjamin (Putnam)
   John (Morgan)
Gilson, Samuel (Morgan)
Gilston, David (Morgan)

Gilstrap, Henry (Burke)
   John (Pulaski)
   William (Burke)
Gilt, Thomas (Chatham)
Ginble, Jacob (Putnam)
Gindrat, John (Richmond)
Ginn, Isaac (Elbert)
   Jesse (Elbert)
   Ruffin (Elbert)
   Silvana (Elbert)
Gipson, Hugh (Oglethorpe)
   Luke (Oglethorpe)
Girard, H. (Chatham)
Girardeau, Ann (Liberty)
   William (Liberty)
Giredou, Lewis (Chatham)
Girtman, Andrew (Jefferson)
   David (Emanuel)
   Joice (Emanuel)
Gisson(?), N. B. (Chatham)
Givings, George (Appling)
Gladdin, James (Washington)
Glascock, E., Overseer for
        (Burke)
   Edward (Richmond)
   George (Habersham)
   Thomas (Richmond)
   William (Richmond)
Glase, Abner (Oglethorpe)
   Thomas (Oglethorpe)
Glasier, Charles R. (Putnam)
Glass, James (Morgan)
   Levi, Sr. (Laurens)
   Manson (Walton)
   Mary (Jones)
   Thomas (Morgan)
   William (Jones)
Glasson, Henry (Clarke)
   James (Clarke)
   John (Morgan)
Glatigny, J. (Chatham)
Glaze, Daniel (Habersham)
   David (Lincoln)
   John (Putnam)
   John (Lincoln)
   Jonathan (Putnam)
   Milly (Lincoln)
   Nancy (Hall)
   Ruben (Oglethorpe)
   Thomas (Habersham)
   William (Habersham)
   William (Lincoln)
Glazier, H. (Jasper)
Gleen, Thomas (Hancock)
Glen, Jemicy (Habersham)
Glenn, Betsy (Jackson)
   Betsy (Oglethorpe)
   James (Elbert)
   James (Jackson)
   John (Jackson)
   John (Oglethorpe)

   John, Jr. (Oglethorpe)
   John (Washington)
   John W. (Jackson)
   Joseph (Elbert)
   Joseph (Oglethorpe)
   Otway (Washington)
   Thomas (Oglethorpe)
   Thomas (Washington)
   William (Morgan)
   William (Putnam)
   William (2) (Oglethorpe)
   Wm. Sr. (2) (Oglethorpe)
   Wyley (Jackson)
Glente, F. est. of (Chatham)
Glisson, Dennis (Burke)
   Lydia (Burke)
   Pheron(?) (Burke)
   Tilly (Burke)
Glisten, Joseph (Tattnall)
Glisters, Allen (Montgomery)
Gloover, Henry (Putnam)
   John (Putnam)
   John P. (Putnam)
   Thomas W. (Putnam)
   William (Putnam)
Glover, Eli (Jasper)
   Frederick (Warren)
   Jesse (Jefferson)
   John (Jasper)
   Joseph B. (Wilkes)
   Larken (Warren)
   Preston (Hall)
   Robert (Madison)
   Washington (Warren)
   William (Wilkes)
Gnann, (ind.) (Effingham)
   Andrew (2) (Effingham)
   Benjamin, Sr. (Effingham)
   Jacob (Effingham)
   Jacob, Jr. (Effingham)
   John Christian (Effingham)
   Jonathon (Effingham)
   Jonathon, Sr. (Effingham)
   Solomon (2) (Effingham)
   Timothy (Effingham)
Goad, Priscella (Putnam)
Goalding, Benjamin (Wilkinson)
Goar, Maning H. (Madison)
Gobert, Benjamin (Jefferson)
Godard, Frederick (Jones)
   Joseph (Jones)
   Samuel (Jones)
Goddard, Joel (Jones)
Godbee, Alfred A. (Burke)
   Elbert (Burke)
   Henry (Burke)
   James (Burke)
   Mary (Burke)
   Stephen (Burke)
   William (Burke)
Goddart, Elias (2) (Morgan)

Goddart, Thomas (Morgan)
Godfrey, Enoch (Burke)
 Francis H. (Jefferson)
 George (Walton)
 Thomas (Walton)
 William (Laurens)
Godin, Mary (Screven)
Godley, James (Jasper)
Godwin, Alan (Washington)
 Arnold (Wilkinson)
 Barnaby (Hancock)
 Elias (Washington)
 Jacob (Wayne)
 James (Baldwin)
 Jeremiah (Putnam)
 John (Hancock)
 Joseph (Putnam)
 Leon (Wilkinson)
 Mary (Montgomery)
 Sally (Putnam)
 William (Montgomery)
 William N. (Putnam)
Goff, Isaac (Appling)
 John (Tattnall)
 John (Telfair)
 Samuel (Emanuel)
 Samuel (Richmond)
 William (Emanuel)
Going, Alexander (Walton)
 William (col.) (Columbia)
Gold, Nancy (Richmond)
Golden, Abbot (Lincoln)
 Caleb (Lincoln)
 Elizabeth (Warren)
 Henry (Warren)
 Isaac (Baldwin)
 James (Lincoln)
 Jesse (Oglethorpe)
 John (Lincoln)
 Leaton (Lincoln)
 Mark, Jr. (Lincoln)
 Mark, Sr. (Lincoln)
 Thomas W. (Oglethorpe)
 William (Lincoln)
Golding, James (Chatham)
 John R. (Clarke)
Goldman, Francis (Lincoln)
Goldsby, A. C. (Madison)
 Charles M. (Effingham)
 Joshua (Jackson)
Goldsmith, Benjamin (Chatham)
 Elizabeth (Chatham)
 John (Putnam)
 William (2) (Chatham)
 William H.(Putnam)
Goldwire, John (Effingham)
Golesby, Barnet (Lincoln)
 Isiah (Oglethorpe)
 James (Oglethorpe)
 Kerby (Oglethorpe)
 Miles (Oglethorpe)

 Richard (Oglethorpe)
 Waide (Oglethorpe)
 William (2) (Oglethorpe)
Golightly, James (Pulaski)
Golphin, Frances (Burke)
Golsby, Thornton B.
 (Oglethorpe)
Goner, Rhodds (Effinghah)
Good, John (Putnam)
Goodall, Samuel (Baldwin)
 Samuel (Jones)
 Seborn (Screven)
Goodbread, John (Camden)
 Philip (Camden)
 Thomas (Camden)
Goode, Mackaness (Baldwin)
 Nicholas (Elbert)
 Samuel W. (Wilkes)
Gooden, John (Hall)
Goodeson, James (Wilkes)
Goodett, Thomas (Jasper)
Goodgame, Alexander
 (Washington)
Goodlow, Thomas (Jones)
Goodman, Jessee (Early)
 John (Madison)
 Moses (Bulloch)
Goodon, Jacob (Jefferson)
Goodrich, James (Pulaski)
 West (Putnam)
Goodrum, Lydia (Washington)
Goodser(?), Margaret
 (Richmond)
Goodson, Abraham
 (Washington)
 Jordan (Warren)
 Josiah (Bryan)
 Nancy (Putnam)
 Noel (Putnam)
 William (Warren)
Goodwin, Charles (Burke)
 David (Warren)
 George (Wilkes)
 Henrietta (Greene)
 Isaac (Gwinnett)
 James (Jones)
 John (Gwinnett)
 Jonathan (Jones)
 Joseph (Greene)
 Lewis (Jones)
 Martha (Chatham)
 Matthews (Burke)
 Neeley (Gwinnett)
 Shadrach (Jones)
 Tellitha (Chatham)
 William (Burke)
Goodwyn, Timothy (Wilkinson)
Goodwynn, Isaac (Wilkinson)
Googer, James (Greene)
 Stephen (Hancock)
Gooldsby, Drury (Columbia)

Goolsby, James B. (Jasper)
 John (2) (Jasper)
 Reuben (Elbert)
 Thomas (Jasper)
 William (Jasper)
Goram, Henry (Jones)
Gorcem, Nathaniel (Jones)
Gordain, James F. (Oglethorpe)
Gordin, Charles P. (Putnam)
 James C. (Oglethorpe)
Gordon, Mrs. (Chatham)
 Alexander (Jefferson)
 Alexander (Richmond)
 Alexander (Tattnall)
 Benjamin (Putnam)
 Benjamin (Washington)
 Charles (Hall)
 George (Chatham)
 George A. (Madison)
 James (Putnam)
 James (Jefferson)
 James T. (Hancock)
 Jane (Chatham)
 John (Clarke)
 John(?), (Elbert)
 John (Jefferson)
 John (Morgan)
 John (2) (Warren)
 Joseph (Habersham)
 Lucretia (Chatham)
 Philamon (Oglethorpe)
 Posey (Morgan)
 Richard (Washington)
 Robert (Burke)
 Silas (Morgan)
 William (2) (Burke)
 William (McIntosh)
 Zachariah (Jones)
Gordred, Samuel (Jasper)
Gordy, Eli (Burke)
 Elizabeth (Burke)
 Elizabeth (Emanuel)
 James (Burke)
 Leonard (Hancock)
 Moses (Burke)
 Peter (Baldwin)
 Thomas (Hancock)
 William (Hancock)
Gore, Jacob (Hancock)
 Pharis (Hancock)
Gorham, Richard (Chatham)
 Willis (Jefferson)
Gorman, Claburn (Hall)
 John (Hall)
 William (Camden)
Gornto, Nathan (Screven)
Gortman, Daniel (Elbert)
Gosden, Ezekiel (Oglethorpe)
Goslin, James P. (Baldwin)
Gosling, Barnet (Baldwin)
 Samuel (Warren)

(56)

Goss, Benjamin (Habersham)
H. F. (Morgan)
Horatio L. (Elbert)
Isham (Oglethorpe)
Jesse (Morgan)
John (Habersham)
Goss(?), John (Jones)
Goss, Matthew (Hall)
Susan (Morgan)
Thomas (Habersham)
Wiley (Gwinnett)
Gossett, John (Madison)
Gotier, Mary A. (Chatham)
P. W. (Jasper)
Goucher, Susan (Lincoln)
Gougue, Nathan (Greene)
Gould, Charlotte (McIntosh)
Jacob F. (Chatham)
James (Glynn)
William G. (McIntosh)
Goulding, Palmer (Liberty)
Peter I. (Burke)
Gower, Abel (Clarke)
Gowing, John (Greene)
Goyne, Drewry O. (Wilkes)
Grabill, Henry (2) (Hancock)
Michael (Hancock)
Grace, Elizabeth (Burke)
John, Jr. (Tattnall)
John, Sr. (Tattnall)
Joshua (Hancock)
Sarah (Hancock)
Silas (Hancock)
Thomas (Tattnall)
William (Richmond)
William (Tattnall)
William (Warren)
Graddy, Arthur (Pulaski)
Grady, Charlotte (Hall)
Frederick (Washington)
Mary (Jackson)
Needham (Elbert)
Graham, Mrs. (Liberty)
Alexander (Telfair)
Andrew (Burke)
Diegle (Telfair)
Duncan (Laurens)
Duncan (Liberty)
Duncan (Telfair)
Elisander (Appling)
Green (Irwin)
Hugh (Effingham)
Isabel (Telfair)
James (Bryan)
James (Hancock)
John (Effingham)
John (Oglethorpe)
Nancy (Irwin)
Nancy (Pulaski)
Neil (Telfair)
Sarah (Burke)
Alexander (Appling)

Tabithy (Irwin)
William (Wilkes)
Grammer, Peter (Hancock)
Granade, John (Jefferson)
Granberry, Loamme (Warren)
Grand, Frances (Chatham)
Grandeur, Langle (2) (Jones)
Grandmaison, William
(Chatham)
Granger, Absalem (Oglethorpe)
Grant, Charles A. (Hancock)
Grant(?), Christia (Richmond)
Grant, Daniel (Camden)
Daniel (Greene)
Isaac (Burke)
Isaac (Screven)
J. (Richmond)
James (Glynn)
James (Hancock)
Jane (col.) (Wilkes)
Jinny (W. C.) (Wilkes)
John (Habersham)
John O. (Pulaski)
Jordan (Jasper)
Joseph (Hancock)
Joseph (Putnam)
Mary (Burke)
Numan (Wilkes)
Peter (Early)
Philip (col.) (Columbia)
Priscilla (Chatham)
Robert (Glynn)
Robert (McIntosh)
Sampson (Wilkes)
Thomas (Jasper)
Thomas (Putnam)
Thomas M. (Jones)
William (Habersham)
William (2) (Wilkes)
Grantham, Benjamin (Telfair)
Cornelius (Montgomery)
Daniel (Irwin)
Mary Ann (Wayne)
Grantland, Eliza A. (Baldwin)
Seaton (Baldwin)
Grasch(?), P. (Chatham)
Grasy, James (Jones)
Grave, Thomas (Walton)
Graves, C. est. of (Columbia)
David (Jasper)
John G. (Wilkes)
John L. (Jasper)
John W. (Clarke)
Lewis (Jasper)
Lewis (Morgan)
Mary (Richmond)
Robert C. (Wilkes)
Suasannah (Morgan)
Gravett, Charles (Jackson)
Obadiah (Jackson)
Randolph (Hall)

William (Jackson)
Gravor(?), Valentine (Chatham)
Gray, Absalom (Jackson)
Archibald (Greene)
Bazil (Burke)
Daniel (Lincoln)
Daniel (Tattnall)
Edmund (Burke)
Enoch (Washington)
Gibson (Burke)
Green (Putnam)
Hezekiah (Elbert)
Isaac (Gwinnett)
James (Jones)
James (Lincoln)
James (2) (Putnam)
James, Jr. (Warren)
James, Sr. (Warren)
John (Burke)
John (2) (Columbia)
John (Elbert)
John (Jones)
John W. (Glynn)
John W. (Liberty)
Jonathon (Gwinnett)
Joseph (Elbert)
Joseph (Washington)
Joseph (Wilkes)
Mary (Wilkinson)
Mincha (Burke)
Morton (Hancock)
Peter (Jones)
Priscilla (Baldwin)
Rebecca (Columbia)
Richard (Morgan)
Samuel (Jones)
Samuel (Lincoln)
Seaborn B. (Putnam)
T. V. (Chatham)
Thomas (Bryan)
Thomas (Putnam)
Thomas, Jr. (Putnam)
Thomas (Walton)
Thomas (Wilkinson)
Thomas, Jr. (Wilkinson)
William (Bryan)
William (Burke)
William (2) (Putnam)
Graybill, John (Hancock)
Philip (Glynn)
Grayham, David (Madison)
Jesse (Jackson)
Joseph (Madison)
Josiah (Madison)
Moses (Jackson)
Thomas (Madison)
William (Madison)
Windsor (Jackson)
Grayson, John R. (Chatham)
Greason, Abraham (Warren)
James (Warren)

Creathouse, Abrm. (Clarke)
Greaves, Ellis (Lincoln)
Green, Widow (Morgan)
Abram (Burke)
Alexis (Screven)
Allen (Jones)
Alston H. (Morgan)
Benjamin (Gwinnett)
Benjamin (Jefferson)
Burrell (Jasper)
Carter (Hall)
Green(?) Carter(?) (Richmond)
Green, Charley (Warren)
D. (Jasper)
Daniel (Camden)
Daniel (McIntosh)
David (Jackson)
David, Jr. (Warren)
David E. (Burke)
Eanoch (Jones)
Elias (Jackson)
Elisha (Green)
Elisha (Putnam)
Elizabeth (Oglethorpe)
Ezekiel (Jackson)
Forrest (Jackson)
George (Lincoln)
Hartwell B. (Morgan)
Isaac (Jones)
J. D. (Richmond)
James (Hall)
James (Jones)
James (Putnam)
Jesse (Laurens)
John (Bulloch)
John (Camden)
John (Hancock)
John (Jones)
John (Oglethorpe)
John (2) (Putnam)
John (Walton)
John W. (Hall)
Joseph (Jones)
Joseph A. (Hancock)
Joseph P. (Walton)
Larkin (Gwinnett)
Lemuel (Greene)
Lewis (Bulloch)
Marey (Richmond)
McKeen (Washington)
Mial (Oglethorpe)
Moses (Burke)
Nancy (Putnam)
Peter (Walton)
Rebecca (Jefferson)
Richard (Jones)
Richard D. (McIntosh)
Robin (Screven)
Shadrack (Hall)
Shepherd (Jefferson)
Thomas, Sr. (Greene)

Thomas (2) (Jasper)
Thomas (Putnam)
Thomas (Wilkes)
Thomas B. (Morgan)
Thornberry (Hancock)
Capt. W. (Chatham)
W. B. (Burke)
Warren (Burke)
William (Bulloch)
William (Jasper)
William (Oglethorpe)
William (Screven)
William (2) (Walton)
William (Washington)
William H. (Chatham)
Greene, Mrs. (Chatham)
Augustin (Greene)
Eliza (Washington)
F. H. (Greene)
Harmon (Chatham)
John (Chatham)
John (Oglethorpe)
John H. (Baldwin)
Myles (Baldwin)
Nancy (Warren)
Peter B. (Pulaski)
Robert (Gwinnett)
Ruthe (Greene)
Stephen E. (Chatham)
William (Baldwin)
William (Greene)
William (Gwinnett)
Greenter(?), James W.
(Chatham)
Greenway, Elijah (Elbert)
Lucretia (Burke)
William (Burke)
Greenwood, Baker (Clarke)
Hugh (Habersham)
John (Oglethorpe)
Thomas (Greene)
Thomas B. (Oglethorpe)
Greer, Abraham (Greene)
Aquilla (Clarke)
Aquilla (Greene)
Aron, Sr. (Warren)
Asal (Greene)
Carlton (Wilkinson)
David (Washington)
Francis M. (Greene)
George (Washington)
Gilbert (Greene)
Henry (Greene)
James (Clarke)
James (Greene)
James (Jasper)
John (Jasper)
Leonard (Greene)
Moses (Greene)
Robert (Chatham)
Thomas (Bulloch)

Thomas (Greene)
Dr. Thomas (Greene)
Thomas (Jasper)
William (3) (Greene)
William (Morgan)
Greeson, William (Gwinnett)
Gregory, Arabella (Columbia)
Charles (Chatham)
E. (Richmond)
Hardy (Burke)
Hardy (Putnam)
Jesse (Screven)
John (Emanuel)
Lewis (Richmond)
Martha (Burke)
Mary (Chatham)
Nancy (Lincoln)
Richard (Emanuel)
Richard (Greene)
Richard (Hancock)
Richard (Putnam)
Samuel (Emanuel)
Gregory(?), William (Chatham)
Gregory, William (Columbia)
William (Washington)
Dr. William B. (Morgan)
Greison, Abraham, Jr.
(Warren)
Grenade, Jonson (Warren)
Stephen (Columbia)
Gresham, Archibald (Greene)
Archibald (Wilkes)
Charles (Wilkes)
Davis E. (Morgan)
Edmond (Jackson)
Edward (Lincoln)
Ferdinand (Jones)
George M. (Gwinnett)
James D. (Wilkes)
Job (Burke)
John (Hall)
John (Lincoln)
John (2) (Oglethorpe)
John H. (Wilkes)
Josiah (Morgan)
Kaufman (Wilkes)
Littleberry (Morgan)
Marmoduke (Jones)
Micajah (Morgan)
Thomas (Wilkes)
Greson, John (Gwinnett)
Grey, John (Camden)
Greyham, Archibald (Camden)
Gribbin, Mrs. (Chatham)
Jean (Chatham)
John (Chatham)
Grice, Easter (Pulaski)
Gabriel (Madison)
Silas (Hancock)
Grider, Jacob (Tattnall)
Grier, James (Clarke)

Grier, James (Morgan)
Jason (Putnam)
Robert (Wilkes)
Griffeth, Caleb (Habersham)
David (Oglethorpe)
George (Oglethorpe)
John L. (Madison)
Robert (Madison)
Griffey, Jonathan (Jasper)
Griffin, (ind.) (Burke)
(ind.) (Laurens)
Abner (Laurens)
Allen (Washington)
Anderson (Greene)
Ann (Wilkes)
Asa (Hall)
Asa (Warren)
Beverly A. (Jones)
Buckner (Lincoln)
Charles (Putnam)
Civil (Montgomery)
Claborn (Putnam)
Comford (Richmond)
D. (Chatham)
David (Emanuel)
David (Washington)
Dempsey (Hancock)
Drury (Wilkes)
Elizabeth (Columbia)
Enoch (Washington)
Hardy (Hall)
Isom G. (Hall)
James (Montgomery)
James (Tattnall)
James (Washington)
Jerimiah (Columbia)
John (Burke)
John (Columbia)
John (Early)
John, Jr. (Hancock)
John (Putnam)
John (Telfair)
John (Oglethorpe)
John M. (?) (Columbia)
Joseph (Lincoln)
Josuah (Jasper)
Lewis (Warren)
Lewis (Washington)
Nancy (Pulaski)
Mary (Washington)
Moses (Glynn)
Nathan (Morgan)
Nathaniel (Columbia)
Noah (Burke)
Noah (Telfair)
Reuben (Emanuel)
Richard (Hancock)
Robert F. (Baldwin)
Sally (Washington)
Samuel (Camden)
Samuel (Tattnall)

Sarah (Burke)
Shade (Irwin)
Silas (Oglethorpe)
Sol (Jackson)
T. (Richmond)
Tempie (Telfair)
Walden (Effingham)
William (Gwinnett)
William (Jones)
William (Putnam)
William (Washington)
Griffis, Charles (Appling)
John (2) (Emanuel)
Samuel (Appling)
Griffith, Ann (Camden)
Ann (Oglethorpe)
David H. (Oglethorpe)
James (Jones)
James (Madison)
Margaret (Chatham)
Morgan (Morgan)
Griger, John (Bulloch)
Grigg, William (Baldwin)
Grigger, Abraham (Bryan)
Griggs, Asa (Putnam)
Hillory (Jones)
James (Jasper)
James (Jones)
Jesse W. (Hancock)
John (Badlwin)
John (2) (Putnam)
Lee (Hancock)
Linnah (Hancock)
Nancy (Hall)
Nathaniel (2) (Hancock)
Rhodom S. (Baldwin)
Robert (Hancock)
Robert, Jr. (Hancock)
Thomas (Hancock)
William (2) (Hancock)
William, Sr. (Hancock)
William (Jasper)
William N. (Wilkinson)
William W. (Hancock)
Wolsey (Jasper)
Grigsby, Betsy Anne (Greene)
Grimes, Mrs. (Chatham)
Jessie (Greene)
John (Putnam)
Morris (Jefferson)
Robert (Wilkes)
Sterling (Greene)
Thomas est. of (Greene)
Thomas (Jones)
Thomas M. (Madison)
Thomas W. (Greene)
William (Jackson)
William G. (Greene)
Grimsley, Joseph (Baldwin)
Richard (Early)
Zachariah (Lincoln)

Grinage, Joshua (Lincoln)
Grinard, Sarah (Oglethorpe)
Grindle, James (Hall)
Griner, Andrew (Effingham)
James (Bulloch)
James (Screven)
John (Bulloch)
John (Screven)
Jonathan (Bulloch)
Samuel (Screven)
Timothy (Screven)
William (Screven)
Grinnell, Peter (Jasper)
Grinstead, William (Pulaski)
Grisham, Benjamin, Jr. (Wilkes)
James D. (Oglethorpe)
Martha W. (Oglethorpe)
Robert (Oglethorpe)
William (Oglethorpe)
Grisop, James (Wilkes)
Grissom, David (Jasper)
Isom (Jasper)
James (Jasper)
John, Jr. (Jasper)
John (Jasper)
Griswell, Jesse (Gwinnett)
Griswold, Jiles (Richmond)
Samuel (Jones)
Grizard, Joseph (Warren)
Grizzle, Clement (Warren)
Stephen (Columbia)
Thomas W. (Warren)
Willis (Warren)
Groce, Shepherd (Lincoln)
Gromet, Mary (Effingham)
Gronmis, Charles (Jones)
Groom, Emmiry (Washington)
Jessee (Washington)
Major (Washington)
Wyllie (Washington)
Grooms, Benjamin (McIntosh)
Colson (Bulloch)
Groover, Charles (Bulloch)
David (Bulloch)
John, Jr. (Bulloch)
John, Sr. (Bulloch)
Solomon (Bulloch)
William (Bulloch)
Grose, G. (Jasper)
Grosmanger, Mrs. Stephens
(McIntosh)
Gross, Edmon (Screven)
Hannah (Lincoln)
Mund (Jefferson)
Rody (Screven)
Solomon (Jones)
William (Screven)
Grovenstein, Lewis (Effingham)
Grover, Hannah E. (Effingham)
Groverstein, Mary (Effingham)
Groves, Joseph (Jackson)

Groves, Robert (Madison)
Samuel (Madison)
Stephen (Madison)
Grubbs, Thomas (Burke)
Gruber, John (Bryan)
Grubs, Benjamin (Camden)
Grumbly, G. (Richmond)
Grunbee, Samuel (Baldwin)
Grunnod(?), E. (Chatham)
Gruver, William C. (Jasper)
Guerard, P. (Chatham)
Guerinean, Mrs.(Chatham)
Guerre, (ind.) (Chatham)
Guerrey, Margarett (Wilkinson)
Guerry, James (Wilkinson)
Guess, David (Hall)
Presley (Elbert)
Thomas (Wilkes)
Guest, Benjamin (Burke)
E. B. (Burke)
(?), Henry (Wilkinson)
Gugel, Daniel (Chatham)
Mary (Chatham)
Guger, Samuel (Lincoln)
Guiger, Samuel (Bryan)
Guilder, Jacob (Walton)
Senot (Walton)
Guilford, Colson (Tattnall)
Isaac (Tattnall)
John (Tattnall)
Guill, Augustus (Oglethorpe)
Guilmarken, John (Chatham)
Guiminan, John (Richmond)
Guine, Hiram (Warren)
Gukie, James G. (McIntosh)
Gullall, Peter (Lincoln)
Gulley, John (Elbert)
Valentine (Elbert)
William (Elbert)
Gumm, Jacob (Baldwin)
Gunby, George (Columbia)
Leven (Camden)
William (Columbia)
Gunn, Bradford (Oglethorpe)
David (Jones)
Esther (Chatham)
Gabriel (Morgan)
James (Jefferson)
Jesse (Jefferson)
Jesse (Morgan)
Jesse T. (Morgan)
John (Jones)
Moses (Jones)
Nancy (Morgan)
Nicholas (Greene)
Richard, Jr. (Warren)
Richard, Sr. (Warren)
Telathy (Warren)
Thomas (Jones)
William (Burke)
William (Warren)

Gunnels, Willis (Jones)
Gunter, Charles (Hall)
Gidion (Hall)
Isom (Jasper)
James (2) (Elbert)
John (Elbert)
Needham (Liberty)
Polly (Hall)
Richard (Liberty)
Gurley, William (Walton)
Gusling, Benjamin (Warren)
Guthery, John (Hall)
Lee (Hall)
Sarah (Oglethorpe)
Thomas (Hall)
William (Greene)
Guthrie, Frances (Morgan)
Jane (Warren)
Nancy (Morgan)
William (Washington)
Guttiare(?), Mrs. (Chatham)
Guy, Hillary (Columbia)
Guy, James, Sr. (Columbia)
John (Columbia)
John Y. (Columbia)
Lemuel (Columbia)
Guye, Joel (Lincoln)
Guyer, Ernest William)
(Effingham)
Guyse, Peter (Lincoln)
William (Lincoln)
Guyton, John (Laurens)
Gwin, Humphrey (Walton)
Gwinnett, William (Jasper)
Gwynn, William (Burke)

H

Habersham, (ind.) (Chatham)
Joseph (Chatham)
Dr. Joseph (Chatham)
R. (Chatham)
R. W. (Chatham)
Robert (Chatham)
Sally (Chatham)
Habin, Elijah (Telfair)
Hack, Thomas (Oglethorpe)
Hackett, Edward (Jones)
Hackney, John (Greene)
Joseph (Wilkes)
Joseph P. (Wilkes)
Nathan (Morgan)
Stephen (Morgan)
William (Greene)
Hadaway, Alix (Wilkes)
Amos (Wilkes)
David (Jones)
John (Jones)
Levi (Putnam)
Haddix, John (Jasper)
Haddock, Admiral

Amos (Jones)
Charles (Pulaski)
Luke (Pulaski)
William (Pulaski)
Zachriah (Camden)
Haddon, Mary (Jefferson)
Haden, Turnel(?) (Wilkinson)
Hadley, Simon (Montgomery)
Simon D. (Montgomery)
John (Burke)
Hadly, Elizabeth (Burke)
Hadnett, James (Jasper)
Hagan, (ind.) (Elbert)
Adam (Telfair)
Hagan(?), Benjamin (Wilkes)
Hagan, Daniel (Walton)
Henry (Appling)
Michael (Putnam)
Hagans, Francis (Appling)
John (Appling).
Hagen, Peter (McIntosh)
Haggis, Andrew (Jasper)
Hagin, Absolem (Bulloch)
Edward (Clarke)
Enoch (Bulloch)
Ethelrid (Bulloch)
Jesse (Bulloch)
Malachi (Bulloch)
Solomon (Bulloch)
Hagins, John (Camden)
Nancy (Jasper)
Hagle, Zazariah (Wilkes)
Hagler, Jacob (Walton)
Hague, Sidney (Putnam)
Hagwood, James (Warren)
Haig, William (Chatham)
Hail, Nathaniel (Putnam)
Tharp (Burke)
Haile, Hosea (Clarke)
Joel (Clarke)
John (Clarke)
Wiley (Clarke)
Hailey, Ambrose (Morgan)
J. A. (Wilkes)
William (Elbert)
Haille, John (Clarke)
Hails, John (Madison)
John (Oglethorpe)
Haims, Joshua (Jasper)
Hainey, George (Jackson)
Hainy, Peter (Jackson)
Hair, William (Wayne)
Haires, Jeptha V. (Elbert)
Hairgroves, (ind.) (Laurens)
Isaac (Wayne)
Merich (Laurens)
Hairston, Peter (Gwinnett)
Thomas (Jasper)
William (Gwinnett)
Hakin, Elijah (Emanuel)
Halbrook, Fleming (Elbert)

Halcomb, R. L. (Camden)
Hale, (ind.) (Hancock)
　Miss (Chatham)
　Amos (Chatham)
　Benjamin (Richmond)
　Dixon (Hancock)
　Elephalet (Warren)
　Hugh (Putnam)
　J. (Richmond)
　James (Clarke)
　James (Morgan)
　John (Chatham)
　Lernard (Hancock)
　Martin L. (Hancock)
　M. (ind.) (Putnam)
　Mary (Putnam)
　Moab (Clarke)
　Obediah (Clarke)
　Patience (Hancock)
　Samuel (Richmond)
　Thomas (Jones)
　William (2) (Pulaski)
　William G. (Jasper)
Haley, James (Elbert)
　John (Elbert)
　Reuben (Elbert)
Hall, (ind.) (Montgomery)
　Mrs. (Richmond)
　Abraham (Appling)
　Alexander (Greene)
　Armajor (Wilkinson)
　Benjamin (Hancock)
　Benjamin (Wilkinson)
　D. (ind.) (Chatham)
　Daniel, Jr. (Wilkinson)
　Daniel, Sr. (Wilkinson)
　Daniel M. (Wilkinson)
　David (Burke)
　David (Camden)
　Dempsey (Jefferson)
　Elisha (Wilkinson)
　Enoch (Appling)
　Frances (Greene)
　George (Greene)
　George (Jackson)
　Hardy (Emanuel)
　Henry (Elbert)
　Hiram (Hall)
　Huriah (Jackson)
　I. D. (Jasper)
　Ignatius (Montgomery)
　Isaac (Wilkinson)
　James (Burke)
　James (Emanuel)
　James (2) (Hancock)
　James (Richmond)
　James (Wilkinson)
　Jeremiah (Madison)
　James (Jefferson)
　Jessey (Wilkinson)
　John (Chatham)

　John (Columbia)
　John (Greene)
　John (Hancock)
　John (Jasper)
　John (Madison)
　John (Telfair)
　John (Walton)
　John (Wilkinson)
　John B. (Gwinnett)
　John C. (Greene)
　Jonathen (Camden)
　Jordon (Montgomery)
　Joseph (Jefferson)
　Juniper (Emanuel)
　Juniper, Sr. (Emanuel)
　Levi (Putnam)
　Lewis (Tattnall)
　Lewis (Telfair)
　Lydia (2) (Washington)
　Mary (Chatham)
　Mary (Greene)

Nathaniel (Appling)

　Polly (McIntosh)
　Reading (Jefferson)
　Robert (Elbert)
　Robert (Morgan)
　Samuel (Greene)
　Sarah (2) (Burke)
　Sion (Irwin)
　Solomon (Laurens)
　Stanley (Walton)
　Susan (Chatham)
　Thomas (Camden)
　Thomas (Jefferson)
　Thomas (Laurens)
　Thomas (Oglethorpe)
　Thomas (Putnam)
　Thomas B. (Richmond)
　Toliver (Elbert)
　William (Clarke)
　William (Emanuel)
　William (Gwinnett)
　William (Irwin)
　William (Jefferson)
　William (Laurens)
　William, Sr. (Wilkinson)
　William (2) (Washington)
　William K. (Pulaski)
　Willis (Putnam)
　Wingate (Baldwin)
　Zacheriah (Putnam)
　Zilphay (Burke)
Hallas, Thomas (Jasper)
Hallin, L. L. (Telfair)
Hallman, John (Tattnall)
Halloway, Daniel (Oglethorpe)
Halomon, Eaton (Hancock)
Halsey, Benjamin L. (Jefferson)
Halsted, David (Jones)
Halsworth, Joseph (Jones)
Ham, Jesse (Liberty)
　William (Bryan)

Hamack, Benjamin (Morgan)
Hamalton, Samuel (McIntosh)
Hamber, Robert (Jasper)
Hambleton, (ind.) (Montgomery)
　James W. (Gwinnett)
　John (Laurens)
　Newland (Montgomery)
Hambrick, James (Jasper)
　Joseph (Gwinnett)
　S. (Jasper)
　Susannah (Jones)
Hambrike, John (Jackson)
Hamby, Edmund (Morgan)
　John (Walton)
　Levi (Morgan)
　Mary (Gwinnett)
Hamel, Clarke (Wilkes)
　Dennis (Lincoln)
　George (Wilkes)
　James (Wilkes)
Hamell(?), E. (Richmond)
Hamelton, David (2) (McIntosh)
Hames, John (Hall)
　John, Jr. (Hall)
　William (Hancock)
Hamil, Clarke (Wilkes)
Hamil(?), Isaac (Pulaski)
Hamil, John (Jasper)
Hamilton, Agnes (Wilkes)
　Andrew (Gwinnett)
　Ann (Chatham)
　Archy (Gwinnett)
　Cader (Putnam)
　Duke (Hancock)
　Duncan (Washington)
　Edwin (Putnam)
　Francis (Walton)
　George (Hancock)
　George M. (Wilkes)
　John (Clarke)
　John (Hall)
　John (Jones)
　John (2) (Putnam)
　John (Warren)
　Joseph (Gwinnett)
　Lewis (Gwinnett)
　Moses (Morgan)
　Nathan (Walton)
　Peter (Clarke)
　Robert (Elbert)
　Robert (Hall)
　Sampson (Hall)
　Samuel (Washington)
　Shurrod (Jones)
　T. P. (Jasper)
　Thomas (Columbia)
　Thomas A. (Jones)
　Walter (Hancock)
　William (Chatham)
　William (Habersham)
　William (Morgan)

Hamilton, William (Pulaski)
William A. (Gwinnett)
Hamley, Henry (Jasper)
Hamlin, Catharine (Jones)
John (Jones)
Richard (Jones)
Hamm, Aaron (Burke)
Gidion (Elbert)
James (Elbert)
Hammack, Margarett (Wilkes)
Hammel, Hugh (Gwinnett)
Hammens, James (Oglethorpe)
Hammet, James (Oglethorpe)
John (Jefferson)
Hammett, James (Wilkes)
Hammock, Benedict (Jones)
Benjamin (Walton)
Caty (Walton)
Emanuel (Tattnall)
Harrison (Jones)
Jacob (Jones)
James (Jones)
John (Jones)
John (Lincoln)
John (Wilkes)
Jonathan (Jones)
Joshua (Walton)
Lewis (Jones)
Reuben (Wilkes)
Robert (Warren)
Robert (Wilkes)
Robert B. (Jones)
Simeon (Jones)
Thomas (Lincoln)
William (2) (Jones)
William (Wilkes)
Willoughley (Jasper)
Hammon, Alfred (Elbert)
Ambrose (Hall)
Hammond, A. (Baldwin)
Abner (Jackson)
Abraham (Wilkes)
Daniel (Jackson)
John (Wilkes)
Joseph (Jackson)
Mark (Jackson)
Raleigh (Greene)
Richard (Wilkes)
Robert (Greene)
William (Greene)
Hammonds, Isaac (Morgan)
Charles (Oglethorpe)
Elijah (Hall)
John (Hall)
Sussannah (Walton)
William (Hall)
Hamner, Willton (Putnam)
Hamnott, James (Jasper)
Hampton, Andrew (Laurens)
Benjamin (Walton)
David H. (Madison)

George (Madison)
James (Burke)
James (Jackson)
John (Hancock)
John Jr. (Jackson)
John Sr. (Jackson)
John (Walton)
John M. (Wilkes)
Joseph (Jackson)
Mary (Washington)
Simeon (Burke)
Thomas (Burke)
Waid (Richmond)
Hamreck, Moses (Lincoln)
Hamrick, Peter (Lincoln)
Hamson, Helta(?) (Hancock)
Hamuck, John (Jasper)
Hancock, Bennet (Wilkes)
Cader (Tattnall)
Clement (Putnam)
Clemmont (Wilkinson)
Durham (Tattnall)
Elizabeth (Hall)
Enoch (Jones)
Isac (Habersham)
Isom (2) (Jasper)
James (Emanuel)
James (Tattnall)
Jestine (Tattnall)
Joel (Oglethorpe)
John (Wilkinson)
Joseph (Oglethorpe)
Joseph (Wilkinson)
Nancy (Wilkes)
Nero (Burke)
Phillip (Jasper)
Robert (Gwinnett)
Sintha (Jones)
Tabithy (Wilkes)
William (2) (Jackson)
William (Oglethorpe)
William (Tattnall)
William (Wilkinson)
Hand, Abraham (Washington)
Christopher (Oglethorpe)
Henry (Columbia)
Henry (Screven)
Isaac (2) (Jasper)
James (Jasper)
John (Columbia)
John (Jasper)
John J. (Burke)
Robert (Camden)
Spencer (Oglethorpe)
Hand(?), William Appling)
Hand, William (Columbia)
William (Walton)
William W. (Madison)
Handburg, Israel (Burke)
Handley, James (Washington)
Jarret (Elbert)

Handsend, Thomas S. (Elbert)
Handsford, John (Elbert)
Handy, Nathaniel (Oglethorpe)
Hanes, Anthony (Richmond)
Haney, Charles (Oglethorpe)
Dicken (Morgan)
Milley (W. C.) (Wilkes)
William (Pulaski)
Hanigan, Joel (Walton)
Hankins, (ind.) (Pulaski)
Hanks, Christian (Chatham)
Dunston (Jasper)
Rhoda (Pulaski)
Hanley, James Jr. (Washington)
Hanna, William (Madison)
Hannah, James (Elbert)
John (Burke)
William (Jefferson)
Hannam, William (Jasper)
Hanner, Matthew (Morgan)
Susannah (Walton)
William (Walton)
Hanning, John (Screven)
Hannon, John (Columbia)
Samuel (Columbia)
T. S. (Richmond)
Hansard, William (Elbert)
Hansell, William (Chatham)
William Y. (Baldwin)
Hansen, E. P. (Richmond)
Hansford, Charles P. (Jones)
George (Jones)
John M. (Jasper)
Stephen (Morgan)
Susannah (Jones)
Hanson, Elizabeth (Wilkes)
James (Morgan)
Jesse (Walton)
John M. (Wilkes)
John W. (Morgan)
Richard T. (Oglethorpe)
Samuel (Morgan)
Samuel (Walton)
Trapley (Morgan)
Thomas (Jackson)
Thomas (Walton)
William (Morgan)
William (Walton)
Hanton, George (Jasper)
Hanuk, R. (Jackson)
Hany, P. (ind.) (Baldwin)
Haragan, George (Gwinnett)
Haraldson, Reuben
(Montgomery)
Haralson, Vincent (Walton)
Harbin, John (Elbert)
Nathaniel (Habersham)
Sarah (Elbert)
Thomas (Habersham)
William (Elbert)
Wyly (Habersham)

Harbison, William (Richmond)
Harbuck, James (Warren)
  Michael (Warren)
  Nicholas (Warren)
Harcraw, Samuel (Elbert)
Harcrow, Hugh, Jr. (2) (Elbert)
Hardain, Thomas (Wilkinson)
Hardarck, George W.
              (Columbia)
Hardaway, Francis (Warren)
  James H. (Greene)
  Keth (Warren)
  Washington (Warren)
Hardee, James (Washington)
  Theophilus (Washington)
  Whittty (Washington)
Hardeman, Felix (Jasper)
  John (Oglethorpe)
  Thomas (Putnam)
Harden, Adam (Putnam)
  Arabelak (Oglethorpe)
  David (Hall)
  Edward (Chatham)
  John (Hall)
  Johnson (Oglethorpe)
  Martin (Early)
  Robert (Clarke)
  Robertsen (Oglethorpe)
  Sanlen (Putnam)
  Sarah (Oglethorpe)
Hardeson, Elizabeth
              (Washington)
Hardie, Henry (Habersham)
  John (Camden)
  John (Montgomery)
  Thomas E. (Camden)
Hardiman, John (Morgan)
  Thomas (Washington)
Hardin, Benjamin (Columbia)
  Benjamin (Morgan)
  Edward (Wilkes)
  Isaac B. (Burke)
  Hoedson (Putnam)
  James (Warren)
  James (Washington)
  John (Washington)
  Josiah (Wilkes)
  Sarah (Putnam)
  Thomas (Columbia)
  Thomas K. (Bryan)
  Winny (Tattnall)
Harding, James (Habersham)
  Nancy (Habersham)
Hardison, Cullen (Jones)
  Frederick (Washington)
  John (Washington)
  William (Washington)
Hardman, Allin (Oglethorpe)
  Charles (2) (Oglethorpe)
  Elbert (Oglethorpe)
  Farnam (Oglethorpe)

Felix (Oglethorpe)
H. (ind.) (Oglethorpe)
Isaah (Oglethorpe)
Samuel (Oglethorpe)
William (2) (Oglethorpe)
William Jr. (Oglethorpe)
Hardridg, John (Hall)
Hardwell, Samuel (Jasper)
Hardwick, Andrew (Burke)
  David (Walton)
  Garland (Jackson)
  James (Walton)
  John (Jackson)
  John W. (Jasper)
  Judith (Jasper)
  Leonard (Habersham)
  Richard (Wilkes)
  William (Hancock)
  William P. (Jefferson)
Hardy, Allen (Wilkinson)
  C. (ind.) (Jasper)
  Charles (Jackson)
  Collins (Washington)
  David (Lincoln)
  Edward (Lincoln)
  Jesse (Lincoln)
  John (Jones)
  John Jr. (Lincoln)
  John Sr. (Lincoln)
  John (Washington)
  John (Wilkinson)
  Josiah (Jasper)
  Louis (Jackson)
  Preston (Jackson)
  Sally (Lincoln)
  Thomas Jr. (Washington)
  Thomas Sr. (Washington)
  William (Washington)
  William (Wilkinson)
  William B. (Jasper)
Hare, Edmond (Early)
Hareback, Henry (Gwinnett)
Hargraves, William
              (Washington)
Hargrove, Benjamin C.
              (Putnam)
  Howell (Jefferson)
  Jacob (Burke)
  Joseph (Liberty)
  Pleasant W. (Jefferson)
  Richard (Oglethorpe)
  S. E. Estate (Effingham)
Hargroves, Hardy (Wilkinson)
  Henry (Emanuel)
Haris, Benjamin (Walton)
Harison, Ann (McIntosh)
Harkins, Robert (Morgan)
  William (Jones)
Harkness, James (Morgan)
  Mary (Jones)
Harlin, Zachariah (Wilkes)

Harlow, Southworth (Burke)
Harmen, S. (2) (Richmond)
Harmon, Abraham (Chatham)
  Bartholomeu (Jones)
  James (Greene)
  Job (Elbert)
  John (Habersham)
  John (Jones)
  Mary (Chatham)
  William N. (Jefferson)
Harms, John (Chatham)
Harn, John (Bryan)
  Reuben (Oglethorpe)
  Thomas (Camden)
  William (Bryan)
Harnage, Jacob (McIntosh)
Harnesberger, Adam (Lincoln)
Harnsberger, Mary (Lincoln)
Harod, Ethelred (Jefferson)
Harp, Arthur (Putnam)
  Dinon (Baldwin)
  William (Jones)
Harper, Mrs. (Lincoln)
  Allen (Morgan)
  Ann (Morgan)
  Bedford (Elbert)
  Benjamin (Hancock)
  Benjamin (Jefferson)
  Benjamin I. (Hancock)
  Carlton B. (Elbert)
  Charles (Elbert)
  Edward (Putnam)
  Edward (Warren)
  Elizabeth (McIntosh)
  Everet (Walton)
  Frederick (R. S.) (Liberty)
  George (Hall)
  George (Jones)
  Halcom G. (Greene)
  Henry A. (Elbert)
  James (Wayne)
  James (Wilkes)
  John (McIntosh)
  John (Putnam)
  John (Wilkes)
  John J. (Wilkes)
  John W. (Clarke)
  Joseph (Clarke)
  Josiah (Elbert)
  Leonard (McIntosh)
  Milachiah (Appling)
  Nathaniel (Wilkinson)
  R. (Jasper)
  Richard (Elbert)
  Robert (Hall)
  Robert (Lincoln)
  Sabiry (McIntosh)
  Samuel Sr. (Greene)
  Samuel (Jasper)
  Samuel B. (Greene)
  Shadrack (Liberty)

Harper, Sherord (Clarke)
  Solomon (Wilkes)
  Tabitha H. (Hall)
  Wilkins (Jasper)
  William (Hall)
  William (Hancock)
  William Sr. (2) (Hancock)
  William (Lincoln)
  William (Putnam)
  William (Richmond)
  William P. (Hancock)
  William T. (Putnam)
Harralson, Elijah (Greene)
  Jonathon (Greene)
Harrel, Abner (Camden)
  Alexander (Jefferson)
  Hardy (Jefferson)
  John (Bulloch)
  Mary (Appling)
  Sarah (Jefferson)
Harrell, Asa (Pulaski)
  Charles (Warren)
  Elisha (Emanuel)
  Ethelred (Pulaski)
  Henry (Jones)
  Holody H. (Warren)
  Jacob (Pulaski)
  James (Wilkinson)
  Jesse (Pulaski)
  Jessee (Washington)
  John (Liberty)
  John (Warren)
  John (Wilkinson)
  Kader (Warren)
  Levi (Pulaski)
  Moses (Pulaski)
  Rheuben (Wilkinson)
  Samuel (Jasper)
  Simon (Warren)
  Solomon (Washington)
  Thomas (Warren)
  Venus (Jasper)
  William (Pulaski)
  William (Warren)
  Zachariah (Warren)
Harries, John (Camden)
Harrigan, Elizabeth (Screven)
Harril, William (Telfair)
Harrill, Abraham (Warren)
  George (Washington)
Harrilson, Bradley (Morgan)
Harrington, (ind.) (Gwinnett)
  James (Hall)
  Stephen (Screven)
Harrinton, Peter (Jones)
Harris, (ind.) (Wilkes)
  Absolom (Hancock)
  Adeline (Chatham)
  Agnes (Morgan)
  Alexander (Richmond)
  Alsey (Early)

Angin (Habersham)
Ann (Columbia)
Ann (Richmond)
Archibald (Jones)
Augustin (Baldwin)
Bailey (Jones)
Benjamin (Burke)
Benjamin (Gwinnett)
Buckner (Gwinnett)
Charles (2) (Chatham)
Charlotte (Chatham)
Churchwell (Washington)
Harris(?), Claborn (Baldwin)
Harris, Daniel (Gwinnett)
David (Putnam)
Doctor (Chatham)
Mrs. E. (Hancock)
Edmond S. (Putnam)
Edward (Greene)
Edward (Hall)
Edward (Jasper)
Edwin (Warren)
Ehud (Jones)
Eli (Putnam)
Elias (Baldwin)
Elisha (Wilkinson)
Elizabeth (Columbia)
Elizabeth (Glynn)
Elizabeth (Gwinnett)
Elizabeth (Hancock
Elizabeth (Oglethorpe)
Ely (Wayne)
Euphamia (Jones)
Ezekiel (Wilkes)
Francis (Wayne)
Gabriel (Putnam)
George (2) (Walton)
George Sr. (Walton)
George (Warren)
Gideon (Burke)
Giles (Madison)
Gillium (Greene)
Graves (Morgan)
H. (Richmond)
Hampton (Bryan)
Henry (Glynn)
Henry (Hancock)
Henry (Warren)
Hiram C. (Gwinnett)
Isom (Jasper)
J. B. (Camden)
James (Clarke)
James (Greene)
James (Jones)
James (Laurens)
James (McIntosh)
James (Morgan)
James (2) (Washington)
Jeremiah (Richmond)
Jesse (Gwinnett)
Jesse (Jackson)

Jesse (Pulaski)
Jesse (Walton)
Jessie (Wilkinson)
John (Columbia)
John (Elbert)
John (Glynn)
John (2) (Hall)
John (Jones)
John (Morgan)
John (Oglethorpe)
John S. (Oglethorpe)
John (Screven)
John G. (Putnam)
John N. (Greene)
Joseph (Bulloch)
Joseph (Jackson)
Joseph (Morgan)
Joseph B. (Jackson)
Joseph C. (Putnam)
Joshua (Jones)
Jourdan (Morgan)
Jureat(?) (Columbia)
Lard (Putnam)
Louis (Richmond)
Mary (Chatham
Maryan (Liberty)
Mathew (Greene)
Micajah (Morgan)
Morris (Greene)
Moses (Glynn)
Nathan (Warren)
Nathaniel (Oglethorpe)
Neidham (Jasper)
Nelly (Richmond)
Overton (Oglethorpe)
Pascal (Wilkinson)
Peter (Jasper)
Peterson (Hancock)
Polly (Chatham)
Dr. Raymond (Liberty)
Richard (Jones)
Robert (Greene)
Robert (Wilkes)
Robert G. (Greene)
Roderick (Putnam)
S. W. (Putnam)
Samuel (Clarke)
Samuel Sr. (2) (Hancock)
Samuel (Morgan)
Samuel (Washington)
Samuel (Wilkes)
Silvy (Putnam)
Stephen (Gwinnett)
Stephen (Oglethorpe)
Stephen (Wilkes)
Tery (Oglethorpe)
Thomas (Elbert)
Thomas (Jackson)
Thomas (Jones)
Thomas (Putnam)
Thomas W. (Pulaski)

Harris, Thompson (Gwinnett)
Virginia (Clarke)
Walter (Richmond)
Wiley I. (Putnam)
William (Effingham)
William (2) (Greene)
William (2) (Jones)
William (Madison)
William (Oglethorpe)
William (Pulaski)
William (Telfair)
Willie (Warren)
Wilmot E. (Greene)
Harrison, Benjamin (Pulaski)
Benjamin (Warren)
Mrs. Caty (Greene)
Charles (Jones)
Colman (Jackson)
David (Putnam)
Henry (Warren)
J. W. (Richmond)
James (Columbia)
James (Morgan)
Jeremiah (2) (Jasper)
Jesse (Putnam)
John (Chatham)
John (Oglethorpe)
John (Putnam)
John (Warren)
Jonathan (Jones)
Joseph (Jackson)
Joseph (Jones)
Joseph (2) (Putnam)
Joseph (2) (Washington)
Joseph (Wilkes)
Josephus (Gwinnett)
Kenchen (Warren)
Martin (Chatham)
Mary (Columbia)
Moses (Wilkinson)
Nancy (Warren)
Nathaniel (Putnam)
Reuben (Hall)
Reuben (Putnam)
Richard (Columbia)
S. G. (Laurens)
Samuel (Columbia)
Shepherd (Warren)
Sullivan (Columbia)
Thomas (Chatham)
Thomas (Glynn)
Thomas (Pulaski)
Tyrrel E. (Columbia)
William (Chatham)
William (Columbia)
William (2) (Jones)
William (Putnam)
William (Wilkinson)
Harrocks, Catherine (Chatham)
Harrol, William (Hancock)
Harrold, John (Gwinnett)

Harrup, James (Greene)
Joseph (Columbia)
Mannen (Greene)
Thomas (Columbia)
Harry, James O. (Jasper)
John (Warren)
Zephaniah (Jasper)
Harryson, Edward (Jackson)
John (Jackson)
Harston, H. B. (Elbert)
Hart, Mrs. (Chatham)
Archibald (Oglethorpe)
Barny (Washington)
Benjamon (Putnam)
David (Emanuel)
Hart(?), Eliza (Chatham)
Hart, Frederick (Gwinnett)
Henry (Camden)
Henry (Pulaski)
Isaac (Hancock)
Isaac (Warren)
John (Jones)
Jonathon (Washington)
Levy (Chatham)
Peggy (Gwinnettt)
Robert (Jones)
Samuel (Pulaski)
Susan (Hancock)
Thomas (Burke)
Thomas (Emanuel)
Thomas (Greene)
Thomson (Putnam)
William (Emanuel)
William (Gwinnett)
William (Morgan)
William (Warren)
Hartell(?), John (Pulaski)
Hartey, John (Jackson)
Hartley, Burwell (Washington)
Hilliry (Washington)
James Sr. (Washington)
Joseph (Putnam)
Robert (Hancock)
Hartlin, George (Jackson)
Harton, Lott (Hancock)
Nancey (Hancock)
Hartsfield, Allen (Jasper)
Alsy (Wilkes)
Andrew (2) (Oglethorpe)
Elizabeth (Clarke)
James (Oglethorpe)
Wiley (Jasper)
William (Oglethorpe)
Hartstein, Mrs. (Chatham)
Harvee, Judith (Clarke)
Harvel, Anderson (Putnam)
Jackson (Morgan)
Sarah (Baldwin)
Harves, Majus (Jones)
Harvey, Mrs. (Chatham)
Elizabeth (Richmond)

German (Columbia)
Isaac (Bryan)
Isaac (Jones)
Jeremiah (Putnam)
John (Bryan)
John (Clarke)
John (Jones)
Moses (Jones)
Moses (Putnam)
Richard (2) (Bryan)
Samuel (Bryan)
Sarah (Columbia)
Sebastain (Jones)
Thomas (Early)
Harvie, Daniel (Wilkes)
Harvil, James (Gwinnett)
James (Walton)
James R. (Putnam)
Harvill, Nancy (Warren)
Harville, Samuel (Liberty)
Zebulan (Liberty)
Harvy, Blassingame (Burke)
Caleb W. (Jefferson)
G. B. (Burke)
Isaac (Baldwin)
James Sr. (Lincoln)
John C. (Baldwin)
Rebecca (Baldwin)
Stephen (Baldwin)
Thomas D. (Jefferson)
Harwell, Absalom (Burke)
Harry (Jones)
John (Hancock)
Mark (Oglethorpe)
Robert (Jasper)
Samuel (Jasper)
William (Jasper)
Hascall, E. N. (Jasper)
Hasco, James (Chatham)
Hase, Martain (Wilkinson)
Haskins, John (Jones)
Silas (Jones)
Haslip, Winnefred (Jefferson)
Hass, George (Baldwin)
Henry (Baldwin)
Hassel, Edward (Columbia)
Hassell, Fanney (Jones)
Hasteen, William (Washington)
Hasten, Harison (Greene)
Hastens, John (Greene)
Hataway, Balam (Warren)
Hatcher, Edward (Burke)
H. (Richmond)
James (Wilkinson)
John Jr. (Wilkinson)
John Sr. (Wilkinson)
Josiah (Burke)
Martha (Habersham)
Mary (2) (Richmond)
Millany (Jefferson)
Moses (McIntosh)

Hatcher Robert (Wayne)
 William (Wilkinson)
 William Jr. (Wilkinson)
Hatchett, William (Oglethorpe)
Hatenay, David (Washington)
Hatfield, Richard (Wilkinson)
Hathcock, Hosiah (Elbert)
Hathorn, Elizabeth (Morgan)
 Hugh (Wilkinson)
 James (Morgan)
 John (Wilkinson)
 Thomas (Putnam)
 William (Putnam)
 William (Wilkinson)
Hatley, Byman (Jones)
 James (2) (Jasper)
 Jane (Hall)
Hatlin, William (Telfair)
Hatton, Oliver (Jasper)
Haupt, Henry (Chatham)
 John (Chatham)
Havens, (ind.) (Effingham)
Haw, John (Jasper)
Hawes, Burwell (Oglethorpe)
 Isaac (Lincoln)
 Mariah (Oglethorpe)
 Sabia (Burke)
 Spencer (Lincoln)
Hawk, Andrew (Jasper)
 Charles (Richmond)
 Frederick (Madison)
 Henry (Oglethorpe)
 Jacob (Jasper)
 Peter (Jasper)
Hawkins, Alexander
 (Oglethorpe)
 Benjamin (Putnam)
 Benjamin (Washington)
 Charles (Hall)
 Edward (Hall)
 Ezekiel (Jones)
 John (Morgan)
 John (Oglethorpe)
 John (Putnam)
 Jessey (Wilkinson)
 Lavina (2) (Jones)
 Martha (Pulaski)
 Nicholas (Putnam)
 Roger (Jones)
 Stephen (Jones)
 Susannah (Jones)
 Thomas (Appling)
 Thomas (2) (Putnam)
 William (Clarke)
 William (Washington)
 Willis (Morgan)
Hawpe, George (Jackson)
Haws, Nancy (Jones)
 Peyton (Lincoln)
 Richard (Jones)
Hawthorn, William (Pulaski)

Hay, Charley (Jasper)
 Felix G. (Wilkes)
 Gilbert (Wilkes)
 Hardy (Burke)
 Isaac (Jefferson)
 Job G. (Hall)
 Samuel (Jackson)
 William (Jasper)
 William (Wilkes)
Hayden, C. H. (Chatham)
Hayes, Alexander (Early)
 David (Wilkes)
 Elijah (Habersham)
 George (Clarke)
 James (Pulaski)
 John (Jasper)
 Richard (Burke)
 Sarah (Emanuel)
 Sussannah (Emanuel)
 William (Habersham)
 William Sr. (Habersham)
Haygood, James (Morgan)
 Parten (Habersham)
Hayles, Mary (Oglethorpe)
Hayley, Holiday (Washington)
Hayman, Stephen (Burke)
 William (Burke)
Haymans, Henry (Bryan)
 Jeremiah (Bryan)
 Stanton (Bryan)
Haynes, Abraham (Greene)
 Daniel (Greene)
 Elijah (Morgan)
 Ezekiel (Washington)
 Francis (col.) (Columbia)
 G. B. (Gwinnett)
 Henry (Morgan)
 James (Morgan)
 Jasper (Oglethorpe)
 John (Lincoln)
 John (Morgan)
 Joshua (Morgan)
 Leven (Washington)
 Moses Jr. (Elbert)
 Nathan (Washington)
 Parmenas (Clarke)
 Richard (col.) (Columbia)
 Richard (Oglethorpe)
 Thomas (Elbert)
 Thomas (Hancock)
 Thomas (Warren)
 Waller G. (Elbert)
 William (Elbert)
 William (Morgan)
Hayney, Bridger (Madison)
Haynie, James (Oglethorpe)
Hayns, Robart (Oglethorpe)
Hays, Boon (Jackson)
 Edward (Putnam)
 Elizabeth (Early)
 George (Jackson)

Howel (Wilkes)
 Isaac (Washington)
 James (Gwinnett)
 James (Putnam)
 James (Wilkes)
 James L. (Jackson)
 John (Early)
 Jonathan (Morgan)
 Leonard (Madison)
 Lewis (Gwinnett)
 Quinny (Washington)
 Samuel (Washington)
 Thomas S. (Putnam)
 William (Madison)
 William (Morgan)
Hayslett, Andrew (Gwinnett)
Hayslip, John (Burke)
 Kendal G. (Burke)
 Susannah (Burke)
Hayward, Augustus (Putnam)
 Josh (Jasper)
 Louis (Putnam)
Hazard, William J. (McIntosh)
Haze, Edmund (Warren)
 John (Warren)
Hazlehurst, Robert (Glynn)
Hazzard, French (Jackson)
 William Wigg (Glynn)
Head, Charles (Hall)
 Edmond (Jones)
 George W. (Elbert)
 James (Hall)
 James (Jasper)
 James (Morgan)
 James (Putnam)
 James P. (Elbert)
 John (Glynn)
 John (Hall)
 John (Putnam)
 John S. (Elbert)
 Lewis G. (Morgan)
 Margaret (Morgan)
 Richard (Hall)
 Richard (Jones)
 Samuel (Wilkes)
 Tavner (Elbert)
 Thomas (Putnam)
 Thomas (Wilkes)
 William (Elbert)
 William (Jasper)
 William R. (Jasper)
 William (Jones)
 William R. (Morgan)
Headon, George (Jackson)
Heard, Abraham (Greene)
 Barnabas (Elbert)
 Bernard (Wilkes)
 Daniel C. (Wilkes)
 Elizabeth (Elbert)
 Ephraim (Morgan)
 Faukner (Morgan)

Heard, Franklin C. (Greene)
George (Greene)
George (Morgan)
George W. (Elbert)
James (Clarke)
James (Greene)
Jesse (Wilkes)
Jesse F. (Wilkes)
John (Greene)
John (Jasper)
John (Oglethorpe)
John (Wilkes)
John G. (Morgan)
John P. (Walton)
Joseph (Morgan)
Joseph (Wilkes)
L. G. (Jasper)
Samuel (Jasper)
Stephen (Morgan)
William (Clarke)
William (2) (Morgan)
William (Walton)
William (Wilkes)
Woodson (Greene)
Heardin, John (Putnam)
Hearn, Asa (Jasper)
Benjamon (Putnam)
Elijah (Putnam)
Elisha (Jasper)
Elisha (Putnam)
Frances S. (Morgan)
George (Morgan)
Isaac (Jasper)
Jacob (Putnam)
Jonathan (Putnam)
Joshua (Putnam)
Lott (Putnam)
Samuel (Putnam)
Seth (Putnam)
William (Jasper)
Hearnden, Reuben (Putnam)
Hearndon, Edward Sr. (Elbert)
Susannah (Elbert)
Hearstile, John (Gwinnett)
Heath, Benjamin (Jones)
Colson (Putnam)
Colson Jr. (Putnam)
Daniel (Washington)
Drucilla (Burke)
Gillford (Putnam)
Henry (Burke)
James (Burke)
James (Jones)
Jeremiah (Jasper)
John (Habersham)
John (Jones)
John B. (Jones)
Jordan (Burke)
Joseph (Jackson)
Pleasant (Jones)
Richard (Burke)

Richard (Jasper)
Rigdon (Wilkinson)
Samuel (Burke)
Tinsley (Wilkinson)
Thomas (Putnam)
W. (Jasper)
William B. (Jones)
William (Putnam)
Winnefred (Emanuel)
Heathe, Sarah (Washington)
Heatherford(?), John
(Wilkinson)
Heck, John (Effingham)
Hedrich, Casper (Hall)
Hedrick, John (Hall)
Hedspeth, Richard (Wilkes)
Heeth, Chappel (Warren)
Hartwell (Warren)
Henry (Warren)
Jetferson P. (Warren)
Heeth(?), Richard Hall)
Heeth, Membrame (Hall)
Richard (3) (Warren)
Royster (Warren)
Sarah (Warren)
Thomas (Warren)
Heethe, Benjamin (Jefferson)
Heflin, Joshua (Putnam)
Wilie (Walton)
William (Putnam)
Wyatt (Walton)
Hefner, John (Habersham)
Heggie, Archibald (Columbia)
Heidt, (ind.) (Effingham)
Abel (Effingham)
Chris Jr. (Effingham)
Chris Sr. (Effingham)
John (Effingham)
Heineman, Mrs. (Chatham)
Heirs, Thomas (Wilkes)
Heislar(?), Samuel (Burke)
Hellim, John (Emanuel)
Hellow, Sally (Jones)
Helman, Joshua (Warren)
Helmley, David (Effingham)
Joshua (Effingham)
Helon, George (Warren)
Helsaback, Frederick (Morgan)
Helsapeck, Henry (Morgan)
Helsom(?), Mrs. (Chatham)
Helton, Abraham (Washington)
Elisha (Jones)
James (Washington)
John (Walton)
Richard (Washington)
Sterling (Clarke)
Helverston, James (Wayne)
Helveston, John (Effingham)
Helviston, John C. (Chatham)
Helvy, Barbary (Jefferson)
Hemley, Miss (Chatham)

Hemp, Benjamin A. (Greene)
Hemphill, James (Jackson)
Jonathan (Jackson)
Marcus (Morgan)
Robert (Jackson)
Samuel (Madison)
Thomas (Lincoln)
Tillman (Morgan)
Henage, Benjamin (Wilkes)
Henary, Robert (Morgan)
Henden, Isham (Oglethorpe)
Henderson, Widow (Morgan)
Archibald (Columbia)
Archibald (Morgan)
Daniel (Hall)
Daniel (Irwin)
Daniel (Jones)
David (Appling)
David (Jackson)
E. (Jasper)
George (Burke)
Greenville (Morgan)
Henry (Wilkes)
James (Jasper)
John (Elbert)
John (Hancock)
John (Irwin)
John (Jackson)
John (Jasper)
John (Jones)
John (Pulaski)
Joseph (Elbert)
Joseph (Jones)
Joseph (Lincoln)
Joseph (Walton)
Joseph (Wilkes)
L., Jr. (Jasper)
Lodwick (Morgan)
M. (2) (Jasper)
Michael (Screven)
Nancy (Telfair)
Robert (2) (Hall)
Robert (2) (Jackson)
Robert (Lincoln)
Henderson (?), Richard(?) (2)
(Wilkes)
Samuel (Jackson)
Samuel (Jasper)
Simion (Elbert)
Simeon (Wilkes)
Thomas (Jackson)
William (2) (Elbert)
William (Habersham)
William (Putnam)
William (Wilkes)
Hendley, Horton (Pulaski)
James (Screven)
Thomas H. (Richmond)
William (Pulaski)
Hendly, John (Emanuel)
Hendon, David (Lincoln)

Hendrick, Berry (Madison)
Catherine (Wilkes)
Drewry (Putnam)
Elisha (Warren)
Elizabeth (Wilkes)
Gideon (Walton)
Gustavius (Baldwin)
Isaac (Morgan)
Jesse (Elbert)
Jesse Jr. (Elbert)
John (Madison)
John D. (Lincoln)
Leon (Elbert)
Micajah (Gwinnett)
Seraz (Walton)
Sylvanis (Lincoln)
William (Elbert)
William (Greene)
William (Madison)
Whitehead (Elbert)
Hendricks, Hillary (Hall)
James (Putnam)
Jesse Sr. (Elbert)
John (Tattnall)
Joseph (Montgomery
Joseph (Wilkes)
Hendrickson, Elizabeth (Glynn)
Hendrix, Camel (Madison)
Daniel (Bulloch)
Elias (Madison)
Falton (Madison)
Hanah (Jackson)
James (Jackson)
John (Screven)
Sarah (Bulloch)
Hendry, Alexander (Screven)
George (Morgan)
John (Liberty)
Hendry(?), Nelly (Screven)
Hendry, Pamelia (Morgan)
Robert Jr. (Liberty)
William (Liberty)
Henkerson, M. (Jasper)
Henley, James Jr. (Putnam)
James Sr. (Putnam)
James (Walton)
John (Morgan)
Henly, Abner (Wilkes)
Edmond (Hall)
Joshua (Putnam)
Micajah (Lincoln)
Philip (Lincoln)
William (Walton)
Henney, Mary (Camden)
R. K. (Camden)
Henningbow, Betsey
(Washington)
Henoir, John (Burke)
Mary (Burke)
Henrick, Benjamin (Jasper)
Henry, Alexander (Elbert)

Alexander (Screven)
Amariah (Hall)
Benjamin (Elbert)
Benson (Morgan)
Charles (Elbert)
Daniel (Hancock)
Henderson (Greene)
I. (Chatham)
Isaac (Chatham)
James (Jackson)
John (Chatham)
John (Elbert)
John (Gwinnett)
John (Warren)
Joseph Jr. (Hancock)
Joseph Sr. (Hancock)
William (Elbert)
William (Gwinnett)
William (Jackson)
Hensley, John P. (Jones)
Henson, Mrs. Chatham)
Jesse (Hall)
Joseph (Habersham)
Samuel (Jackson)
William (Clarke)
Herb, Catharine (Chatham)
Herben, Jesse (Jackson)
Herbert, J. (Richmond)
Moses (Chatham)
Herckaby, James (Jones)
Herd, Dorath (Wilkinson)
Elexander (Walton)
Herin, John (Oglethorpe)
Herington, Richard Jr.
(Screven)
Herman, Daniel (Chatham)
Jessah (Madison)
Hern, Joseph (Washington)
Stephen (Washington)
Wyatt (Washington)
Hernden, Robertson
(Oglethorpe)
Herndon, Edward Jr. (Elbert)
James (Elbert)
James (Wilkinson)
John (Hall)
Michael (Elbert)
Walker (Jones)
Heron, John (Habersham)
William (Habersham)
Herrick, John (Chatham)
Herrin, Alex (Jasper)
Jonathon (Madison)
Herring, Arthur (Jasper)
Edmond (Pulaski)
James (Elbert)
Jesse (Jefferson)
John (Jefferson)
Peter (Hancock)
Herringden, Silas (Hancock)
Herrington, Drury (Hall)

Ephraim (Emanuel)
Jabes (Screven)
John (Jefferson)
John (Jones)
John (Pulaski)
Luke (Hancock)
Martin (Burke)
Moses (Emanuel)
Richard Sr. (Screven)
Wiley A. (Hall)
William (Emanuel)
William (Pulaski)
Herriott(?), Catherine
(Chatham)
Herst, Miller (Hall)
Herston, William (Wilkinson)
Hervey, Benjamin (Effingham)
Hester, Abraham (Jasper)
Daniel (Lincoln)
David (Burke)
Eunice (Hancock)
Jasper (Laurens)
Joseph (Effingham)
Michael (Putnam)
Robert (Jasper)
Samuel (Clarke)
Steven (Clarke)
Stephen (Laurens)
Thomas (Jasper)
William B. (Jones)
Wyatt (Greene)
Zachariah (Jones)
Hesterly, Frances (Hall)
Isom (Hall)
Heston, Elisha (Jasper)
Hestor, Stephen (Effingham)
Hetley, John (Jasper)
Hewbanks, Isaac (Warren)
Hewell(?), Jesse (Clarke)
Hewett, John (Gwinnet)
William (Jackson)
Hews, Matthew (Jefferson)
Hewston, Thomas (Morgan)
Hexton, John (Elbert)
Hey, Warren (Emanuel)
Hick(?), Christopher
(Richmond)
Hickaby, Charles (Jasper)
Hichendon(?), William
(Wilkinson)
Hickey, Benjamin (Putnam)
John (Chatham)
Hicklen, Ruben (Washington)
Hickman, Edward (Wilkinson)
I. C. (Jasper)
Joshua (Camden)
Josiah (Jackson)
Martha (Elbert)
Mary (Bryan)
Stephen (Burke)
Walker (Elbert)

(68)

Hicks, Abner (Wilkinson)
Amos (Hancock)
Amos (Morgan)
Asa (Jones)
Daniel (Baldwin)
Daniel (Clarke)
Daniel (Wilkinson)
Edmond (Columbia)
Eli (Liberty)
Elizabeth (Richmond)
Hicks(?), Henry (Lincoln)
Hicks, Isaac (Oglethorpe)
James (Gwinnett)
Jeremiah (Liberty)
John (Camden)
John (2) (Hall)
John (Warren)
John (Wilkes)
John H. (Baldwin)
John J. (Morgan)
Joseph (Jasper)
Josiah (Hall)
June (Emanuel)
Matthew (Gwinnett)
Nathaniel (Columbia)
Robert (Jones)
Rubin (Laurens)
Thomas (Chatham) Ralph
Thomas (Greene) (Appling)
William (Liberty)
Wylly (Habersham)
Hicky, James (Burke)
Hicky(?), Ralph (Appling)
Hidon, (torn) (Laurens)
Hidgon, John S. (Warren)
Primel (Emanuel)
Robert (2) (Laurens)
Higganbotham, Elizabeth
(Madison)
Higgenbotham, Oliver (Morgan)
Higginbotham, Bartley (Elbert)
Jacob (Elbert)
John S. (Elbert)
Samuel (Glynn)
William (Elbert)
Higgins, Benjamin (Gwinnett)
Enock (Habersham)
Henry (Habersham)
James (Greene)
Joel (Gwinnett)
Joseph (Gwinnett)
Reuben (Gwinnett)
Higgons, John (Habersham)
Higgs, John (Tattnall)
William (Tattnall)
High, John (Greene)
Highnote, Benjamin (Jones)
Henry (Warren)
Highsaw, Joel (Walton)
Highsmith, Daniel (Tattnall)
James (Elbert)

John (Elbert)
Hight, Henry (Warren)
Howell, Jr. (Warren)
Howell Sr. (Warren)
Julius (Warren)
Willis (Warren)
Hightour, Pleasant A (Baldwin)
Hightower, Aaron (Clarke)
Daniel (Jones)
Henry (Telfair)
Henry (Walton)
Jonathon (Walton)
Philemon (Elbert)
Reuben (Elbert)
Stephen (Greene)
William (Baldwin)
William (Clarke)
William (Putnam)
Higins, Reuben (Habersham)
Higson, P. (Jasper)
Hildebrand, D. (Jasper)
William (Jasper)
Hildescran, D. (Jasper)
Hiley, Charles (Jasper)
John (Jasper)
Hill, Abraham (Oglethorpe)
Abraham (Warren)
Abraham (Wilkes)
Asa (Putnam)
B. B. (Jasper)
Benjamin (Warren)
David B. (Baldwin)
Daniel (Laurens)
Edward (Gwinnett)
Elias (Walton)
Elijah (Burke)
Enoch (Washington)
Fielding (Warren)
Francis (Warren)
Frederick (Columbia)
G. (Richmond)
Gilham (Burke)
Granberry (Burke)
Green (Screven)
Henry (Jones)
Henry (Oglethorpe)
Henry (Warren)
Hinchy (Columbia)
Isaac Sr. (Clarke)
Isaac (Jones)
Isaac (Putnam)
Isaac (Walton)
James (Gwinnett)
James (Jasper)
James (2) (Morgan)
James (Warren)
James A. (Baldwin)
James A. (Jasper)
Jeptha (Jones)
John (Hall)
John (Gwinnett)

John, Jr. (Gwinnett)
John, Sr. (Gwinnett)
John (Jasper)
John (2) (Morgan)
John (3) (Richmond)
John (Putnam)
John (Wilkes)
Joseph(Gwinnett)
Joseph (Warren)
Joseph (Wilkinson)
Joseph L. (Baldwin)
Joshua (Gwinnett)
Manning D. (Putnam)
Mary (Lincoln)
Mary (Putnam)
Miles (Oglethorpe)
Mountain (Warren)
Phillis (Chatham)
Polly (Putnam)
Priscilla (Elbert)
R. (Richmond)
Rachel (Hall)
Robert (2) (Putnam)
Robert (Warren)
Robert, Sr. (Warren)
Robert H. (Baldwin)
Samuel B. (Jackson)
Sarah (Oglethorpe)
Sion L. (Putnam)
Theopeles (Oglethorpe)
Theopolus (Richmond)
Thomas (Hall)
Thomas (Richmond)
Waid (Putnam)
Wiley (Wilkes)
William (Bryan)
William (Gwinnett)
William (Lincoln)
William, Sr. (Warren)
William B. (Laurens)
William C. (Warren)
Hillard, Kinchen (Laurens)
Martin (Washington)
Nancy (Washington)
Silas (Bulloch)
Hilley, Thomas (Elbert)
Hillhouse, David P. (Wilkes)
Hilliard, Henry (Burke)
Jane (Burke)
Richard (Wilkes)
Hilliard(?), Robert (Lincoln)
Hilliard, Silas (Tattnall)
William (Hancock)
William (Pulaski)
Hillier, John (Hancock)
Hillis, James (Burke)
John (Burke)
William (Burke)
Hills, James (Chatham)
Hillsman, Bennett (2)
(Hancock)

(69)

Hillyard, Elizabeth (2)
(Wilkes)
William M. (Wilkes)
Hillyer, Rebecca (Wilkes)
Hilman, Winder (Warren)
Hilsman, Micajah (Morgan)
Hilson, John (Warren)
Lewis (Warren)
William (Warren)
Hilton, Abraham (Habersham)
James (Habersham)
Sarah Ann (Jefferson)
William (Jones)
Hims, Thomas (Putnam)
Hinds, A. (Richmond)
J. E. Richmond)
Hindeman, Israel (Wilkes)
Michael (Wilkes)
Hineley, (ind. (2) (Effingham)
Hinely, Israel (Effingham)
Job (Effingham)
Hines (ind.) (Laurens)
Augustus (Screven)
Charlton (Liberty)
David (Liberty)
Howell (Effingham)
J. M. (Richmond)
James (Burke)
James (Jasper)
John, Jr. (Burke)
John, Sr. (Burke)
John B. (Baldwin)
Joseph (Burke)
Lewis (Bryan)
Mary (Elbert)
Nathaniel (Greene)
Richard (Washington)
Stephen (Burke)
William (Camden)
William (Effingham)
Hinesley, Thomas (Walton)
Hing, Benjamin (Jasper)
Hingson, John (Wilkes)
Hinly, Mary (Burke)
Hinnard, William (Clarke)
Hinning, John (Clarke)
Hinsley, Brittian (Jones)
Robert (Jones)
Hinson, (ind.) (Richmond)
James (Clarke)
James (Telfair)
Hinton, Christopher (Warren)
Henry (Warren)
Jacob (Clarke)
James (Clarke)
James (Wilkes)
John (Wilkes)
Lewis (Walton)
Noah (Wilkes)
Peter (Elbert)
Thomas (Elbert)

Thomas (Warren)
Wood (Jackson)
Hipkin, Henry (Appling)
Hirbin, John H. (Jackson)
Hitchcock, David (Hancock
Irwin (Hancock)
James (Morgan)
John (Oglethorpe)
Joseph (Effingham)
Meshack (Hancock)
William (Hancock)
William (Jasper)
Hite, Mary (Tattnall)
Shadrick (Emanuel)
Hitower, Elisha (Putnam)
Jacob (Putnam)
James (Putnam)
Milly (Putnam)
Pressley (Putnam)
William, Sr. (Putnam)
Hitson, James (Oglethorpe)
Hix, David (Elbert)
David (Walton)
William (Elbert)
Hixon, Elizabeth (Columbia)
George (Oglethorpe)
Timothy (Wilkes)
William (Columbia)
Hobbs, Mrs. (Chatham)
David (Columbia)
David, Sr. (Warren)
Drury (Bulloch)
Fanny (Warren)
James (Warren)
John (Jackson)
John (Warren)
Joseph (Walton)
Moses (Warren)
Robert (Greene)
William (Warren)
Hobby, Francis (Pulaski)
William I. (Richmond)
Hobson, Baker (Jackson)
C. (Jasper)
Caswell (Putnam)
Hardy (Warren)
John (Jasper)
Zachariah (Warren)
Hoddy, Nelly (Hancock)
Hodg, William (Morgan)
Hodge, Abel (Baldwin)
Archibald (Greene)
Caty (Jackson)
David (Columbia)
David (2) (Jasper)
Drury (Jones)
Henry (Washington)
James (Jackson)
James (Jasper)
John, Jr. (Greene)
John, Sr. (Greene)

John (Morgan)
John (Washington)
John E. (Walton)
Robert (Pulaski)
William (Madison)
Hodgen, Hannah (Warren)
Mary ((Warren)
Hodges, Benjamin (Bulloch)
Elias (Jefferson)
Elizabeth (Burke)
Foreman (Washington)
George C. (Washington)
Jesse (Putnam)
John (Screven)
John (Washington)
Joseph (Bulloch)
Joseph (Clarke)
Joshua (Bulloch)
Lemuel (Washington)
Nancy (Burke)
Nathan (Tattnall)
Nathan (Washington)
Nathaniel (Bulloch)
Richard (Jefferson)
Robert, Jr. (Liberty)
Samuel (Tattnall)
Sherwood (Clarke)
William (Clarke)
William (Liberty)
William (Tattnall)
William (Washington)
Hodnet, John (Walton)
Hodo, Salley (Warren)
Hog, Jacob (Warren)
Robert (Chatham)
Hogan, Elijah (Wilkinson)
Griffin (Laurens)
Isham (Baldwin)
James (Jefferson)
James (Lincoln)
John (Jackson)
Lyly (Columbia)
Mary (Columbia)
Ridgeway (Jones)
Shadrack (Jackson)
Thomas (Warren)
Thomas M. (Jasper)
Hogans, John (Camden)
John (Emanuel)
Samuel (Emanuel)
Hoge, Solomon (Columbia)
Stephen (Columbia)
William (Columbia)
Hogen, James (Wayne)
Hogg, Catherine (Chatham)
Hogg(?), Charles (Hancock)
Hogg, Hannah (Chatham)
Hugh T. (Greene)
Jeter A. (Greene)
Mary (Chatham)

(70)

Hogg, Samuel (Greene)
Hogue, James (Hall)
    Jonathon S. (Greene)
Hogwood, Benjamin (Clarke)
    Polly (Clarke)
    William (Clarke)
Holaway, Asa (Oglethorpe)
Holcom, John (Putnam)
Holcomb, H. B. (Baldwin)
    J. C. (Richmond)
    Joel (Putnam)
    John (Hall)
    John G. (Chatham)
    Thomas (Hall)
    William (Hall)
Holcombe, Absalam
    (Habersham)
    Hampton (Habersham)
    Henry (Habersham)
    Henry D. (Habersham)
    John (Habersham)
    Joseph (Habersham)
    Samuel (Habersham)
    Sherod (Habersham)
Holden, Daniel (Camden)
    Jesse (Columbia)
Holden(?), Joseph (Camden)
Holder, John (Clarke)
    John (Habersham)
    John S. (Jefferson)
    William (Warren)
Holderfield, John (Gwinnett)
Holdstock, James (Putnam)
Holebrook, Sally (Gwinnett)
Holiday, Allen (Wilkes)
    Ivel (Wilkes)
    John (Wilkes)
    Mickleberry (Tattnall)
    Orsan (Wilkes)
Holifield, A. (Jasper)
    William R. (Jasper)
Hollan, David (Tattnall)
Holland Arch'd. (Jasper)
    Betsey (Putnam)
    Clarissa (Chatham)
    Daniel (Burke)
    Elisha (Jackson)
    Elisha (Warren)
    George W. (Jasper)
    Henry (Tattnall)
    Henry I. (Jasper)
    Isaac (Putnam)
    Jacob (Wilkinson)
    James (Pulaski)
    James, Jr. (Pulaski)
    James H. (Jasper)
    Jeremiah (Burke)
    Jerutha (Pulaski)
    John (Jackson)
    John (Putnam)
    John (Tattnall)

Benjamin (Appling)

    John R. (Putnam)
    L. C. (Jasper)
    L. L. (Jasper)
    Lewis (Pulaski)
    Lucretia (Hall)
    Moses (Pulaski)
    Thomas (Greene)
    William (Warren)
    William R. (Chatham)
Holleman, Lewis (Warren)
Holley, Amos (Morgan)
    Richard H. J. (Morgan)
    Soloman (Richmond)
    William (Bulloch)
Holliday, Abner (Burke)
    Dickerson (Lincoln)
    Ferny (Burke)
    Joseph (Burke)
    Martha (Jackson)
    Milner (Burke)
    Thomas (Burke)
    William (Burke)
Holliman, Benjamin (Pulaski)
    James (Columbia)
    Lewis (Columbia)
    Samuel (Columbia)
    Thomas (Washington)
Hollinger, James (Hall)
Hollingstree, J. (Richmond)
Hollingsworth, Vallentine
    (Emanuel)
    William (Baldwin)
    William (Camden)
    Zebulon, Jr. (Tattnall)
    Zebulon, Sr. (Tattnall)
Hollingshead, Hugh (Lincoln)
Hollis, James (Morgan)
    John (Morgan)
    Richard (Putnam)
    Silas (Chatham)
    William (Jasper)
Holliway, James (Bulloch)
    Jeremiah (Bulloch)
    William (Bulloch)
Hollman, Col. (Chatham)
Holloday, Abraham (Putnam)
    John, Sr. (Jones)
Hollomon, David (Putnam)
    Edward (Lincoln)
    John (Jefferson)
    John (Putnam)
    William (Pulaski)
Hollon, Benjamin (Appling)
Holloway, Anthony (Putnam)
    David (Burke)
    Edward (Putnam)
    H. (Jasper)
    James (Jones)
    James (2) (Putnam)
    Jesse (Jasper)
    John, Jr. (Jones)

    Paul (Putnam)
    Peter (Putnam)
    Samuel (Putnam))
    William (Jasper)
    Zacheriah (Putnam)
Holly, Ephraim (Wilkinson)
    Eritha (Elbert)
    Gracy (Hancock)
    Hazel (Irwin)
    Henry (Washington)
    James (Burke)
    James (Putnam)
    John (Burke)
    John (Hancock)
    Nathaniel (Jones)
    William (Emanuel)
Holman, Rich (Jasper)
Holmes, (ind.) (Elbert)
    Est. of (Liberty)
    Gideon (Hall)
    Hannah (Lincoln)
    James (Habersham)
    James (Liberty)
    James P. (Jasper)
    John (Jasper)
    Joseph (Wilkes)
    Joshua (Wilkes)
    Josiah B. (Wilkes)
    Lewis (Washington)
    Mary (Wilkes)
    Nathaniel G. (Washington)
    Richard (Jasper)
    Samuel (Wilkes)
    Sarrah (Liberty)
    William (col.) (Wilkes)
Holms, Benjamin (Morgan)
    James (Pulaski)
    Robert (Oglethorpe)
Holoburtin, David (Wilkes)
Holomon, Harmon (Hancock)
    Hannah (Hancock)
Holsey, Gideon (Hancock)
    Susannah (Hancock)
Holt, Arrington (Washington)
    Asa (Jefferson)
    Bowbow (Madison)
    David (Putnam)
    Elizabeth (Oglethorpe)
    Hines (Baldwin)
    James (Greene)
    Larken (Habersham)
    Lyons S. (Chatham)
    Milton (Putnam)
    Peyton (Putnam)
    Pulaskit (Putnam)
    Richard (Gwinnett)
    Roley (Putnam)
    Sarah (Baldwin)
    Shadrac (Haberham)
    Simon (Putnam)
    Singleton (Putnam)

Holt, Tarpley (Putnam)
Thomas (Washington)
W. W. (Richmond)
William (Elbert)
William (Habersham)
William (Jasper)
William (Putnam)
William B. (Greene)
Holton, Isaac (Burke)
James (Burke)
Josiah (Burke)
Mark (Emanuel)
Milbing (Emanuel)
Peter (Wilkinson)
Robert (Laurens)
Stephen (Washington)
Thomas (Burke)
William (Washington)
Holtzclaw, Elijah (Oglethorpe)
Henry (Wilkes)
John (Wilkes)
Rhoda (Wilkes)
Silas (Wilkes)
Willaford (Oglethorpe)
Holwell, Theophelus (Screven)
Holyfield, Alice (Jasper)
Holzendorff, J. L. K. (Camden)
Holzendorff, John (2)
(McIntosh)
William B. (McIntosh)
Hombuckle, N. H. (Jasper)
Homes, David (Wilkinson)
Honey, Byrs (Gwinnett)
William (Gwinnett)
Honeycut, Myrick (Columbia)
Hood, (torn) (Laurens)
Burwell (Wilkes)
Edward (Hancock)
Elisha (Walton)
James (Early)
John (Columbia)
John (Wilkes)
Lucy (Washington)
Sien (Washington)
Thomas (Richmond)
William (Washington)
William M. (Jones)
Hoof, Robert (Oglethorpe)
Hook, Daniel (Jefferson)
Lucy (Washington)
Hooker, Nathan F. (Wilkes)
Stephen (Tattnall)
Hooks, Asa (Wilkinson)
Charles (Putnam)
Daniel (Wilkinson)
Dixon (Putnam)
Hellery (Putnam)
James (Putnam)
James (Wilkinson)
Jessey (Wilkinson)
John (Wilkinson)

Jonathon (Wilkinson)
Sally (Washington)
Thomas (Putnam)
William (Burke)
William (Emanuel)
William (Wilkinson)
Hooper, Andrew (Hall)
John (Putnam)
Mathew (Habersham)
Hoopugh, James (Jackson)
Hooten, Henry (Jones)
John (Jasper)
L. (Jasper)
Lucy (Jones)
Hoover, Jacob (Wilkinson)
John (Wilkinson)
Hope, John (McIntosh)
William (McIntosh)
Hopegood, Les (Jackson)
Milly (Jackson)
Hopkin, Silas (Wilkes)
Hopkins, Aaron (Walton)
B. B. (Richmond)
Dennis (Madison)
Francis (McIntosh)
Gibson (Wilkes)
Isaac (Wilkes)
James (Wilkes)
Jesse (Washington)
John (Emanuel)
John (Wilkes)
John A. (Morgan)
John A. (Wilkes)
Josiah (Madison)
Susanna (Clarke)
Susannah (Warren)
Timothy (Camden)
Hopper, Rolley (Oglethorpe)
Samuel (Oglethorpe)
Thomas (Oglethorpe)
Hops, Margaret (Wayne)
Hopson, Absolem (Pulaski)
Hardy (Jasper)
William (Washington)
Hordon, Edward (Jasper)
Horkins, William (Walton)
Horn, (torn) (Laurens)
(ind.) (Washington)
Abraham (Elbert)
Britain (Wilkinson)
Cullen (Jefferson)
Harris (Jones)
Henry E. (Putnam)
Howell (Jones)
Isaac (Greene)
Isaac (Morgan)
Isaac (Wilkinson)
Isabel (Chatham)
James (Baldwin)
Jesse (Gwinnett)
John (Washington)

John (Wilkinson)
Judy (Washington)
Larry (Emanuel)
Levi (Baldwin)
Margaret (Wilkinson)
Orin (Emanuel)
Richard (McIntosh)
Sarah (Morgan)
Simeon (Jones)
Thomas (Jones)
Thomas (Wilkinson)
Thomas H. (Washington)
Hornaday, Isaiah (Jones)
Hornberry, John (Glynn)
William (Glynn)
Hornby, Elender (Richmond)
James (McIntosh)
William (McIntosh)
Horne, Aquilla (Hall)
Eli (Pulaski)
Joab (Pulaski)
Michael (Pulaski)
Horner, Clement (Clarke)
Horning, (ind.) (Effingham)
Horry, Henly (Wilkes)
Horsinsky, L. (Chatham)
Horton, Daniel (Washington)
Edwin (Habersham)
Elisha (Jasper)
Frederick (Washington)
Howell (Washington)
Isaac (Hall)
James (2) (Hancock)
James (Jackson)
James (Jones)
Jeremiah (Elbert)
Jerry (Jackson)
Josiah (Jones)
Kittral (Washington)
Levi (Washington)
Lott (Hancock)
Nancy (Hancock)
Procer (Jackson)
Robert (Hancock)
Samuel (Hancock)
Sarah (Hancock)
Sherod (Jackson)
Stephen (Gwinnett)
Thomas (Elbert)
Thomas, Sr. (Elbert)
William (Elbert)
William (Putnam)
William (Washington)
Hoscall, David (Jasper)
Hosdy, Aquilla (Jasper)
Hotchkiss, Daniel (Effingham)
Hott, Cader (Greene)
Houghton, Joshua (Greene)
Reuben (Greene)
Tabitha (Greene)
Thomas (Greene)

Houghton, Thomas (McIntosh)
Willis (Greene)
House, Clayborn (Gwinnett)
James (Richmond)
John (Jackson)
Littleberry (Jackson)
N. (Richmond)
Samuel (Jackson)
Sarah (Clarke)
Thomas (Jackson)
William (Hall)
Wiliam H. (Jasper)
Willie (Madison)
Hously, William (Richmond)
Houston, Isaac (Glynn)
Mary Ann (McIntosh)
Robert (McIntosh)
William (Glynn)
Houstonn, Ann (Chatham)
Houze, James (Jackson)
How, Robert (Putnam)
Howard(?), Absalom (Jasper)
Howard, Benjamin (Greene)
Charles (Washington)
D. (Richmond)
David S. M. (Putnam)
David (Jones)
Edmon (Camden)
Elisha (Appling)
Elizabeth (Columbia)
Elizabeth (Oglethorpe)
Elizabeth (Screven)
Ellender (Baldwin)
Ezra S. (Putnam)
Frances (Columbia)
George (Liberty)
Groves (Oglethorpe)
Hardy (Jackson)
Harmon (Washington)
Hawkins (Putnam)
Henry (McIntosh)
Henry (Oglethorpe)
Henry (Washington)
H. (ind.) (Clarke)
J. (Richmond)
James (Jones)
James (Washington)
James, Sr. (Washington)
John (2) (Baldwin)
John (Liberty)
John (2) (Morgan)
John (Putnam)
John (Walton)
John (Washington)
John H. (Baldwin)
Joseph (Morgan)
Joshua (Washington)
Lemuel (Washington)
Michael (Jones)
Mordecai (Oglethorpe)
Moses (Screven)

Nancy (Laurens)
Nauflight (Washington)
Nicholas (Greene)
Patsy (Columbia)
Samuel (Jasper)
Samuel (Liberty)
Samuel (Putnam)
Samuel (Washington)
Samuel L. (Wilkinson)
Sarah (Wilkinson)
Simton (McIntosh)
Solomon (Washington)
Solomon, Jr. (Washington)
Starling (Greene)
Thomas (Lincoln)
Thomas (Oglethorpe)
Thomas (Warren)
Thomas (Wilkinson)
Vining (Wilkinson)
William (Burke)
William (Wilkinson)
Willis (2) (Jefferson)
Howe, David (Jones)
Eliza. (Chatham)
Lott (Lincoln)
Howel, Casandria (Screven)
Cathrine (Camden)
Charles (Camden)
David (2) (Wilkinson)
Elizabeth (Walton)
Lily (Clarke)
Mahaley(?) (Screven)
Michael (Habersham)
Pheba (Wilkinson)
Samuel (Putnam)
Soloman (McIntosh)
William (Walton)
Wyatt (Oglethorpe)
Howell, Burdig (Gwinnett)
Burwell (Pulaski)
Casper (Greene)
David (Jones)
Ethelred (Pulaski)
Hollida (Morgan)
J. G. (Liberty)
James (Greene)
Jesse (Clarke)
John (Pulaski)
Joseph (2) (Hancock)
Joseph (Warren)
Joshua (Warren)
Lewis (Lincoln)
Lewis (Warren)
Mary (Hancock)
Mathew (Hancock)
McKinney (Hancock)
Meshack (Hancock)
Nathaniel (Greene)
Penelope (Wayne)
Rachel (Hancock)
Samuel D. (Elbert)

Sarah (Jones)
Theopholis (Wilkinson)
Thomas (Pulaski)
Thomas T. (Jones)
Tomas (Camden)
W. (Jasper)
William T. (Hancock)
Wright (Pulaski)
Howill, Woodward (Greene)
Howingtor., Wilson (Madison)
Howley, M. (Jasper)
Howsley, Nedia (Jones)
Howton, I. (Richmond)
Hoxey, Asa (Wilkes)
Thomas (Putnam)
Hoy, Quinton (Baldwin)
William (Baldwin)
Hoyle, John (2) (Hancock)
William (Jefferson)
William S. (Hancock)
William T. (Hancock)
Hubbard, Benjamin (Wilkes)
Elisha (,Morgan)
Elizabeth (Greene)
Jacob (Walton)
James (Chatham)
J. (ind.) (Hall)
John (Chatham)
John (Elbert)
John (Hall)
John (Oglethorpe)
Joseph (Oglethorpe)
Manoah (Baldwin)
Richard (Hall)
Stephen (Telfair)
Thomas (Greene)
William (Putnam)
William (Wilkes)
Woodson (Putnam)
Hubbert, Bennet (Oglethorpe)
Harmon (Warren)
Hiram (Warren)
Irvin (Oglethorpe)
Robert (Oglethorpe)
Hubbord, Haley (Camden)
Winniford (Camden)
Huchen, Uriah (Laurens)
Huchinson, Joseph (Richmond)
Huckaby, Cosby (Jones)
James B. (Jasper)
John (Wilkes)
Josiah (Hancock)
Phelis (Jones)
Phillip (Wilkes)
Sarah (Hancock)
William (Gwinunett)
William (Jones)
Huckle, Christopher (Wilkes)
Huckoby, William (Oglethorpe)
Huddleson, George (Oglethorpe)
Huddlesten, Isaac (Hancock)

Huddleston, Allen (Morgan)
James (Jones)
John (Oglethorpe)
Huddleston, Willis (Oglethorpe)
Huddleton, Joseph (Morgan)
Hudgeon, Beverly (Hall)
Hudggins, Thornton
(Wilkinson)
Hudgins, Ansel(?) (Jones)
Bartholmew (Wilkes)
James (Habersham)
John (Wilkes)
Josiah (Jones)
William, Jr. (Wilkes)
William W. (Wilkes)
Hudgon, Wyley (Jackson)
Hudlasten, Robert (Oglethorpe)
Hudler(?), Timothy (Bulloch)
Hudman, Hezakiah (Gwinnett)
Jannett (Jones)
John (Gwinnett)
William (Gwinnett)
Hudson, (torn) (Laurens)
Alexander (Elbert)
Ashbury (Jefferson)
Benjamin (Elbert)
Benjamin (Jefferson)
Benjamin (Washington)
Booker (Elbert)
Byrd (Jefferson)
Charles (Putnam)
David, Jr. (Elbert)
David, Sr. (Elbert)
Denils(?) (Hancock)
Elbert (Jefferson)
Elijah (Jefferson)
Ephraim (Jefferson)
Evan (Washington)
Hudson(?.), Francis (Richmond)
Hudson, Frederick (Greene)
Gilum (Elbert)
Hall (Jefferson)
Hamilton (Chatham)
Irby (Putnam)
Isiah (Lincoln)
James (Habersham)
James T. (Jefferson)
Job (Putnam)
John (Burke)
L. (Putnam)
Mally (Elbert)
Richard (Jasper)
Richard (Jefferson)
Robert (Screven)
Thomas (2) (Hancock)
Thomas (Walton)
Sam (Screven)
Sarah (Putnam)
Sion (Morgan)
William (Elbert)
William, Sr. (Elbert)

William (Hancock)
William (Jones)
Hudspeth, A. (Jasper)
George (Oglethorpe)
James (Jasper)
Mark (Jasper)
Huduell, John (Pulaski)
Huey, John (Jones)
Huff, Abner (Warren)
Andrew (Hancock)
Clayton (Warren)
Daniel (Putnam)
Edward (Baldwin)
George (Greene)
Green (Hancock)
Harrison (Clarke)
James (Hancock)
James (Jones)
James (Putnam)
Jeremiah (Wilkes)
John (Greene)
John (Richmond)
Jonathon (Warren)
Martha (Warren)
Mathews (Wilkes)
Peter (Oglethorpe)
Roulph (Putnam)
Tabitha (Jasper)
Thomas (Putnam)
Travie (Putnam)
Whitfield (Jasper)
William (Jones)
William (Wilkes)
Hugany, John (Jones)
Hugdon(?), E. H. (Chatham)
Huggins, Daniel (Washington)
David (2) (Jackson)
Philip (Pulaski)
William (Jackson)
Hugh, Bernard (Wilkes)
John (Jasper)
Hughes, Edward (Chatham)
Jane (Burke)
John (Chatham)
John (Jones)
Robert (Habersham)
Sarah (Jones)
Hughey, James (Jackson)
James (Morgan)
John (Morgan)
Joseph (Morgan)
Robert (Jackson)
Samuel (Jones)
William (Morgan)
Hughs, Ann (Wilkes)
David Z. (Greene)
Elizabeth (Richmond)
George (Wilkes)
Isaac (Morgan)
John (2) (Hancock)
Macajah (Morgan)

Mary (Wilkes)
Peter (Morgan)
Simon (Morgan)
Thomas (Laurens)
Thomas (Montgomery)
William (Liberty)
William (Morgan)
Huguly, Charles (Lincoln)
John, Jr. (Wilkes)
Huicase(?), Emanuel
(Effingham)
Huks, John, Jr. (Warren)
John, Sr. (Warren)
Hulbert, John (Hancock)
Warner (Walton)
Hulet, Henry (Telfair)
Hulett, William (Screven)
Hulin, Martha (Richmond)
Huling, Elizabeth (Wilkes)
Hull, Ambros (Camden)
Asbury (Clarke)
Ezekial (Burke)
Joseph (Camden)
Mary (Wayne)
Thomas (Putnam)
Hullim, Duke (Elbert)
Hulman, John (Elbert)
William (Elbert)
Hulsey, (ind.) (Hall)
Adley (Hall)
Adonijah (Hall)
Adonijah, Sr. (Hall)
Asa (Clarke)
Charles (2) (Hall)
Dewey (Hall)
Elijah (Hall)
Hiram (Hall)
James (Hall)
Jennings (Gwinnett)
Jesse (Hall)
Joel (Hall)
Micajah (Hall)
William (Hall)
Human, Alexander (Madison)
Ana (Madison)
Humber(?), John (Jackson)
Humphres, George (Morgan)
Humphrey, Benjamin (Jasper)
H. L. (Baldwin)
James (Warren)
John (Gwinnett)
John (Jones)
John (Oglethorpe)
Thomas (Hancock)
Thomas (Jasper)
William (Hancock)
Humphries, George (Gwinnett)
Mathew (Hancock)
Nancy (Clarke)
Robert (Jefferson)
Shadrack (Gwinnett)

(74)

Humphries, Uriah (Jackson)
William (Burke)
William (Morgan)
Humphris, Isaac Walton)
James C. (Baldwin)
Hunden, Joseph (Clarke)
Hundley, John (Wilkes)
Huneycut, Henry (Putnam)
Hungerford, Dana (Greene)
Hunshan, Thomas (Washington)
Hunt, (ind.) (Laurens)
Aaron (Jasper)
Adderson (Putnam)
Daniel (Jones)
David (Wilkes)
George (2) (Greene)
George, Sr. (Greene)
Gerkins (Jasper)
Henry (Columbia)
Henry (Morgan)
Henry (Putnam)
James (Elbert)
James (Hancock)
Joel (Putnam)
John (Clarke)
John (Greene)
John (Jasper)
John R. (Jones)
Littleton (Jackson)
Michael C. (Baldwin)
Moses (Elbert)
Nancy M. (Elbert)
Nathaniel (Chatham)
Silas (Clarke)
Thomas (Washington)
Timothy (Greene)
Turna, Jr. (Jasper)
Turna, Sr. (Jasper)
William (Habersham)
William (Jones)
William (Laurens)
William (Morgan)
William H. (Clarke)
Ziba (Columbia)
Hunter, Abram (Screven)
Adam (Wilkinson)
Alex (Chatham)
Alex (Clarke)
Archibald R. L. (Hancock)
David (Irwin)
Edward (Jefferson)
Elijah (Irwin)
Elisha (Greene)
Elizabeth (Lincoln)
Ephriam (Screven)
James (Appling)
James (2) (Chatham)
James (Jasper)
Jane (Hancock)
Jesse (Clarke)
Job (Warren)

John (McIntosh)
John (2) (Morgan)
Joseph (Appling)
Mrs. M. (Chatham)
Margaret (Chatham)
Mary (Lincoln)
Redin (Irwin)
Seth (Columbia)
Silas (?) (Appling)
Starky (Lincoln)
Thomas (Jackson)
William (Camden)
William R. (Hancock)
Huntingdon, R. (Richmond)
Huntington, A. S. (Richmond)
Hubert, Hardy (3) (Jones)
Hurd, Eliza (Jackson)
William (Jackson)
William (Jefferson)
Hurley, David (Emanuel)
Hurry, John (Morgan)
Hurst, Bryant (Screven)
Felix (Effingham)
Hardy (Washington)
Henry (2) (Washington)
Humphrey (Washington)
Jacob (Screven)
James (Washington)
Jesse (Burke)
John (Burke)
Major (Burke)
Major (Screven)
Thomas (Effingham)
William (Burke)
William (Columbia)
William (Effingham)
William (Screven)
Hurt, Benjamin (Warren)
Charles (Putnam)
Elisha (Warren)
Joel (Oglethorpe)
William (Hancock)
Huse, Dempsey (Hancock)
John (Wilkinson)
Josiah (Pulaski)
Reddick (Wilkinson)
Thomas (Wilkinson)
William (Wilkinson)
Husler, Daniel (Jones)
Husley, Joseph (Walton)
Huson, Thomas (Baldwin)
Hust, Harmon (Burke)
Hustay, Rebekah (Warren)
Huston, Frances (Burke)
James (Morgan)
John, Sr. (Jasper)
Valentine (Jackson)
Hutchens, Elijah (Jefferson)
Elizabeth (Burke)
Simon (Jefferson)
Thomas (Wilkes)

William (Burke)
William (Tattnall)
Hutcherson, James (Elbert)
William (Baldwin)
Hutcheson, James (Columbia)
Seaborn T. (Columbia)
Hutchings, Edward (Hancock)
Hutchingson, William
(Columbia)
Hutchington, John (Emanuel)
Hutchins, Burrel (Jackson)
Robert (Jones)
Hutchinson, Adam (Richmond)
Daniel (Warren)
Elijah (Telfair)
John (Jackson)
Lewis (Emanuel)
N. (Warren)
Nathaniel (Washington)
Richard (Washington)
Samuel B. (Morgan)
William (Washington)
Hutchison, Ambrose (Greene)
Sarah (Chatham)
William (Jasper)
Hutchons, John (Hall)
Huton, Arnold (Jasper)
John (Jasper)
Hutson, Archibald (Clarke)
Charles (Clarke)
Charles (Jackson)
Hillary (Warren)
James (McIntosh)
John (Early)
John (Hall)
John (McIntosh)
Leavin (Jackson)
Mary (Richmond)
Robert (Jasper)
Ward (Oglethorpe)
William (Jackson)
Hutto, Benjamin (Telfair)
George (Laurens)
John (Laurens)
Hyatt, James (Baldwin)
Hyde, David (Hall)
Jonathan L. (Jones)
Hyers, Joseph (Tattnall)
Hylliard, Majer (Washington)
Hyms, William (Hancock)
Hynard, John (Walton)
Hynes, Micajah L. (Hancock)
Moses (Elbert)
William (Hancock)
Hynor, Louis (Jackson)

I

Iaism(?), William (Hall)
Ihly, John I. (Effingham)
Iler, William (Bulloch)
Indzor, John (Jackson)

(75)

Inge, William (Warren)
Ingland, Thomas (Oglethorpe)
    William (Oglethorpe)
Inglatt, John (Putnam)
Inglish, Jacob (Richmond)
    John (Jones)
    Sally (Richmond)
    William (Bryan)
Ingraham, David (Wilkinson)
    George (Putnam)
    Pressley (Putnam)
    Thomas (Putnam)
Ingram, Abram (Greene)
    Bartholmew (2) (Hanock)
    Celia (Jefferson)
    Miss E. (Richmond
    Felmon (Hall)
    Harmon (Hall)
    James (Jefferson)
    John (Hall)
    John (Jefferson)
    John (Hancock)
    John, Jr. (Hall)
    John, Sr. (Hancock)
    Little (Hall)
    Martin (Hall)
    Mary (Jefferson)
    Thomas (Hancock)
Inlow, Lewis (Hall)
    Sebastain (Warren)
Inman, Alfred (Burke)
    Daniel (Burke)
    Elizabeth (Habersham)
    Ezekiel (Burke)
    John (Tattnall)
Inseep, George (Elbert)
Irby, Abram (Grene)
    Herod (Greene)
    William (Jefferson)
Irehdon(?), Simon (Chatham)
Irons, Louis (Wilkes)
    McKenny (Elbert)
Irvin, Hannah (Wilkes)
    Isaiah (Wilkes)
    Joseph (Jackson)
    Leavin (Jackson)
    Thomas (Pulaski)
    William (Emanuel)
    William (Jones)
Irvine, Mrs. (Chatham)
    Alexander (Chatham)
    John R. (Effingham)
Irwin, Alexander (Washington)
    Benjamin (Jasper)
    Christopher (Morgan)
    Francis (Jasper)
    George (Morgan)
    James (Jackson)
    James (Morgan)
    Jared (Washington)
    John (Jefferson)

John (Washington)
John L. (Washington)
Joseph Baldwin)
Joshua (Putnam)
    William (Washington)
Isaac, Robert (Chatham)
Isdale, James I. (Warren)
Isham, Jane (Jackson)
    John (Morgan)
    Margaret (Morgan)
Ishley, Marah (Burke)
Islands, Nancy (Baldwin)
Isler, John (Madison)
    John (Wilkinson)
    Nathan (Wilkinson)
Isom, Edward (Hall)
Israil(?), Prucilla (Jones)
Ivey, Barney (Baldwin)
    Benjamin (Warren)
    Elias (Greene)
    James (Putnam)
    James S. (Pulaski)
    Robert (Baldwin)
    Sarah (Greene)
    Thomas (Habersham)
    Turner (Wilkinson)
Ivy, (ind.) (Warren)
    Adam (Columbia)
    Benjamin (Gwinnett)
    Charles (Wilkes)
    Ephraim (Warren)
    Isaac (Jackson)
    Jenkins (Warren)
    Jeremiah (Walton)
    Jesse (Warren)
    John (Warren)
    Jordan (Greene)
    Myrick (Warren)
    Peebles (Warren)
    Randol (Warren)
    Wilkerson (Columbia)

J

Jack, James (Elbert)
    James (Wilkes)
    Margaret (Clarke)
    Patrick (Elbert)
Jackson, Absalom (Jones)
    Alexander (Jones)
    Allen W. (Warren)
    Ailsey (Warren)
    Allsy (Washington)
    Aron (Warren)
    Benjamin (Gwinnett)
    Benjamon (Putnam)
    C. (Jasper)
    Catherine (Bulloch)
    Charity (Jasper)
    Charles (Clarke)
    Charles (Washington)

Daniel (Clarke)
Daniel (Morgan)
Daniel (Oglethorpe)
Daniel E. (Grecne)
David (Greene)
David (Gwinnett)
David (Jones)
Deborah (Wilkes)
Druty (Baldwin)
Eben (2) (Chatham)
Edmund (2) (Hancock)
Edward (Gwinnett)
Edward (Washington)
Elijah (Habersham)
Elinor (Columbia)
Enoch (Jasper)
Frederick (Camden)
Hartwell (Wilkes)
Henry (Clarke)
Henry, Jr. (Hancock)
Henry, Sr. (Hancock)
Henry (Wilkinson)
Isaac (Greene)
Isaac (Putnam)
Isaac (Wilkinson)
Isaac R. (Walton)
Jabez (Jefferson)
Jacob (Baldwin)
James (Burke)
James (Clarke)
James (Columbia)
James (Hall)
Jackson(?) James (Hancock)
Jackson, James (2) (Jefferson)
James (Warren)
James (Wilkes)
Jeremiah (Greene)
Jessey (Wilkinson)
Jethro (Putnam)
Job (Greene)
Jobo (Hancock)
Joel (Wilkinson)
John (Camden)
John (Chatham)
John (2) (Clarke)
John (Greene)
John (Gwinnett)
John (Jasper)
John (Jones)
John (Liberty)
John (Putnam)
John (Screven)
John (Tattnall)
John B. (Jackson)
John W. (Warren)
Joseph (Jefferson)
Joseph (Putnam)
Joseph (Wilkinson)
Joshua (Wilkes)
Kenchin (Washington)
L. (Camden)

Jackson, L. B. (Oglethorpe)
Lewis (Warren)
Littleton (Walton)
Mark (Greene)
Mark (Putnam)
Mary (Jasper)
Mary (Jones)
Mary (Putnam)
Moses (Greene)
N. (Jasper)
Nancy (Jasper)
Nathan (Wilkinson)
Nathaniel (Habersham)
Nathaniel (Morgan)
Obediah (Burke)
Peter (Morgan)
Peter L. (Putnam)
Phillip (Hancock)
R. (ind.) (Chatham)
Richard (Jefferson)
Robert (Early)
Robert (3) (Morgan)
Robert (2) (Putnam)
Samuel (Clarke)
Samuel (Warren)
Samuel W. (Jasper)
Sarah (Wilkes)
Seaborn R. (Warren)
Stephen (Greene)
Thomas (Hall)
Thomas (Hancock)
Thomas (Jasper)
Thomas (2) (Warren)
Thomas M. (Morgan)
Warren (Jasper)
Warren (Putnam)
Warren (Washington)
Wiche (Wilkes)
Wilkins (Jones)
William (2) (Clarke)
William (Gwinnett)
William (Hancock)
William (Lincoln)
William (Morgan)
William (Richmond)
William (Warren)
William (Wilkinson)
William F. (Columbia)
William H. (Jefferson)
Woody (Oglethorpe)
Wright (Habersham)
Jacobs, Elisha (Walton)
John (Wayne)
Jos'h. (Jasper)
Mordice (Jones)
Sharack (Washington)
Thomas (Walton)
Jaillett, Peter (Baldwin)
Peter F. (Baldwin)
Jamerson, John (Jackson)
James, Archibald (Jones)

Arden (Wilkinson)
Benjamin (Chatham)
Cary (Oglethorpe)
Charles (Irwin)
Charles (Walton)
David (Jones)
David R. (Elbert)
Gabriel (Oglethorpe)
George (Oglethorpe)
J. (Richmond)
James slaves of (Liberty)
James (Warren)
Jane (Chatham)
Joel H. (Jones)
John (Hall)
John (Jasper)
John (Warren)
Joseph (Walton)
Josiah (Walton)
Levi (Chatham)
Philip (Warren)
Robart (Oglethorpe)
Stephen (Walton)
Thomas (Elbert)
William (Walton)
Jameson, Rosana (Jackson)
Thomas (Jackson)
William (Jackson)
Jamison, John (Burke)
Jancurson(?), Eli (Madison)
Janell, John (Wilkes)
Janes, Absolem (Greene)
William (Wilkes)
Jarad, John (Lincoln)
Peter (Lincoln)
Jarman Berry (Jefferson)
John (Jefferson)
Reuben (Jefferson)
Tresse (Gwinnett)
Jarrat, Devereux (Habersham)
Jarrel, George (Madison)
James (Madison)
Jarrell, Irby (Warren)
Jacob (Greene)
Redden (Greene)
Thomas (Greene)
William (Greene)
Jarrett, Rebecca (Balwin)
Jarrett(?), William (Lincoln)
Jarrett, William (Putnam)
William D. (Baldwin)
Jarrill, James (Jasper)
Jarrit, Patsy (Jackson)
Jarrot, David (Habersham)
Nicholas (Wilkes)
Thomas (Wilkes)
Jarrott, Archelus (Elbert)
Jarvis, Edward (Chatham)
John W. (Jones)
Patrick (Burke)
Jaudnon, Thomas D. (Screven)

Jay, William (Columbia)
Jean, Green (Baldwin)
John (Pulaski)
Jeffers, George (Morgan)
James (Screven)
Jefferson, Thomas (Jones)
Jefferys, Lee (Jasper)
William (Jasper)
Jeffords, John (Screven)
Jeffors, John (Habersham)
Jeffreys, Thomas (Jasper)
Jelke, William (Pulaski)
Jemerson, William (Putnam)
Jemison, Samuel (Pulaski)
Jenell, Margaret (Wilkes)
Jenkins, Abishai (Burke)
Arthur (Warren)
Ashford (Emanuel)
Benjamin (Baldwin)
Catharine (Wilkes)
Charles (2) (Hancock)
Charles C. (Emanuel)
Charles J. (Madison)
Drury (Washington)
Edmond (Jasper)
Elijah (Morgan)
Evan (Washington)
Frances (Jones)
Francis (Wilkes)
Hezekiah (Washington)
J. (Richmond)
James (Effingham)
James (Putnam)
James J. (Oglethorpe)
John (Greene)
John (Jones)
John (Madison)
John (Montgomery)
John J. (Jefferson)
John R. (Lincoln)
Joseph (Appling)
Joseph (Gwinnett)
Joseph (McIntosh)
Lewis (Greene)
Lewis (Washington)
Moses (Washington)
Nicholas (Habersham)
Owen (Washington)
Peyton (Morgan)
Polly W. (Baldwin)
Royal (Morgan)
Sampson (Burke)
Samuel (Elbert)
Stephen (Burke)
Thomas (Habersham)
Tommie (Screven)
Uriah (Washington)
Walter S. (Baldwin)
Washington (Morgan)
William (Jackson)
Jenks, Allen L. (Walton)

Jenks, Burrell (Jasper)
  John (Jasper)
Jennings, (ind.) (Gwinnett)
  Caty D. (Columbia)
  Charles (Lincoln)
  Elijah (Oglethorpe)
  James (Lincoln)
  Miles (Morgan)
  Moody (Lincoln)
  Robert (Morgan)
  Thomas (Lincoln)
Jennins(?), Henry (Hall)
Jenson(?), Joseph (Pulaski)
Jerneghan, James (Putnam)
  William (Putnam)
Jernican, Ezechel (Irwin)
Jernigan, Aaron (Tattnall)
  Ezekiel (Irwin)
  Hardy (2) (Hancock)
  Harry (Telfair)
  Mary (Hancock)
  Moses (Irwin)
  Nathan (Appling) (2)
Jerry, Ambrose (col.) (Wilkes)
Jeter, Barnett (Elbert)
  Beademen (Laurens)
  Dudler (Elbert)
  James (Lincoln)
  John, Sr. (Greene)
  John (Morgan)
  Presley (Lincoln)
  Samuel (Lincoln)
  Thomas (Morgan)
  William (Lincoln)
Jett, Daniel (Greene)
  James (Gwinnett)
  Stephen (Gwinnett)
Jewell, Hinchen (Emanuel)
  Humphrey (Emanuel)
  Moses (Emanuel)
  Zachariah (Emanuel)
Jewet, Mrs. (Chatham)
Jewett, E. A. (Chatham)
Jiles, Alexander (Washington)
  Jacob (Washington)
  James (Putnam)
  Jeremiah (Putnam)
  Thomas (Putnam)
  William (Putnam)
  William (Washington)
Jinkens, Daniel (Oglethorpe)
  Sterling (Wilkes)
Jinkins, James (Greene)
  Nathaniel (Gwinnett)
  Robert (Putnam)
  Rutha (Greene)
  Sussannah (Jefferson)
Jinks, Western (Gwinnett)
  William (Gwinnett)
  William (Oglethorpe)
  Willis (Gwinnett)

Jinn, Jourdan (Gwinnett)
Jinnings, Henry (Oglethorpe)
  Robart (Oglethorpe)
  William (Oglethorpe)
Jinnins, L. (ind.) (Oglethorpe)
  Nelson (Oglethorpe)
Jipson, Benjamin (Greene)
Joana, (col.) (Columbia)
Jocoby, Samson (Habersham)
John, Daniel (Hancock)
  James H. (Wilkinson)
  William (Wilkinson)
  Zachariah (Wilkinson)
Johns, Bartley C. (Hall)
  George (Camden)
  Hannah (Camden)
  Isaac (Wayne)
  Jeremiah (Wayne)
  Jesse (Burke)
  John (Madison)
  Obadiah H. (Putnam)
  Robert (Columbia)
  William (Camden)
  Zachariah (Wilkinson)
Johnson, (ind.) (Oglethorpe)
  (ind.) (Columbia)
  (ind.) (Liberty)
  A. F. (Jackson)
Johnson(?), Aaron (Clarke)
Johnson, Aaron (Jefferson)
  Aaron (Pulaski)
  Abner (Greene)
  Abraham (Wilkes)
  Alexander (Putnam)
  Allen (Tattnall)
  Allen S. (Greene)
  Amos (Jones)
  Ann (Bryan)
  Archibald (Appling)
  Arthur (Jones)
  B. (ind.) (Wilkes)
  Bartholomew (Greene)
  Benjamin (Jones)
  Benjamin (Morgan)
  Benjamin, Jr. (Pulaski)
  Benjamin, Sr. (Pulaski)
  Cairey (Warren)
  Cary (Oglethorpe)
  Charlotte (Burke)
  Cintha (Richmond)
  Crawford (Columbia)
  Daniel (Appling)
  Daniel (Washington)
  Darling (Emanuel)
  David (Emanuel)
  David (Wilkinson)
  Edmund (Warren)
  Elaner (Richmond)
  Elijah (Burke)
  Elijah (Hall)
  Elijah (Washington)

  Elisha (Clarke)
  Elizabeth (Burke)
  Elizabeth (Jones)
  Elizabeth (Oglethorpe)
  Errick (Liberty)
  Francis (Chatham)
  George (Burke)
  George W. (Oglethorpe)
  George W. (Wilkes)
  Gilbert D. (Greene)
  Green (Jones)
  Green (Oglethorpe)
  Hardy (Emanel)
  Harvey (Putnam)
  Henry (Emanuel)
  Henry (2) (Jackson)
  Henry (Jones)
  Hickee (Warren)
  Howell (Columbia)
  Isaac W. (Oglethorpe)
  Isham (McIntosh)
  Israel (Washington)
  J.(?) W.(?), (Appling)
  Jabis (Jones)
  Jacob (Burke)
  Jacob (Hancock)
  Jacob (Wilkes)
  James (Elbert)
  James (2) (Emanuel)
  James (Habersham)
  James (2) (Hall)
  James (Hancock)
  James (McIntosh)
  James (Oglethorpe)
  James (Putnam)
  James (Walton)
  James (Washington)
  James (Wilkinson)
  James J. (Burke)
  Jane (Madison)
  Jared (Burke)
  Jared (Washington)
  Jeremiah (Oglethorpe)
  Jesse (2) (Jackson)
  Jesse (Putnam)
  Jesse (Screven)
  Jesse (Washington)
  Jessie (Greene)
  Joel (Walton)
  John (Emanuel)
  John, Sr. (Emanuel)
  John (2) (Jackson)
  John (Jones)
  John (2) (Liberty)
  John (2) (Oglethorpe)
  John (3) (Putnam)
  John (2) (Walton)
  John (Washington)
  John (Wilkes)
  John (Wilkinson)
  John C. (Jackson)

Jhohn, S? (Putnam)

John (Appling)

Johnson, John F. (Jackson)
John H. (Jackson)
Joseph (Putnam)
Joseph (4) (Wilkes)
Joshua (Screven)
Josiah (Gwinnett)
Josiah (Putnam)
Larkin (Oglethorpe)
Lee (Oglethorpe)
Lemuel(?) (Richmond)
Lewis (Jones)
Lewis (Laurens)
Little B. (Greene)
Lochlin (Putnam)
Luke (Oglethorpe)
Malcolm (Tattnall)
Marcus J. (Chatham)
Martha (Clarke)
Martha (Pulaski)
Martin (Emanuel)
Martin (Putnam)
Mary (Clarke)
Mary (Hall)
Mary (2) (Jones)
Matthew (Greene)
Mordecai (Warren)
Moses (Bryan)
Moses (Burke)
N. (Richmond)
Nancy (Jackson)
Nancy (Putnam)
Nathaniel (Chatham)
Nathaniel (Oglethorpe)
Noel (Oglethorpe)
Patrick H. (Putnam)
Peggy (Greene)
Peter (Hall)
Pleasant (Greene)
Polly (Greene)
Posey (Morgan)
Quinny (Washington)
Randolph (Tattnall)
Rebecca (Laurens)
Redmond (Jackson)
Reuben (Clarke)
Reuben (Oglethorpe)
Rhody (Jones)
Richard (Putnam)
Robert (2) (Greene)
Robert (Hall)
Robert (Jones)
Robert (Oglethorpe)
Sampson (Wilkinson)
Samuel (Greene)
Samuel (Lincoln)
Samuel (Oglethorpe)
Samuel (Putnam)
Samuel M. (Oglethorpe)
Sankey T. (Greene)
Sarah (Burke)

Seaborn (Emanuel)
Shadrac (Habersham)
Sherwood B. (Greene)
Silas (Laurens)
Stephen (Emanuel)
Stephen (Wilkes)
Thomas (Columbia)
Thomas (2) (Greene)
Thomas (Gwinnett)
Thomas (3) (Jackson)
Thomas (Jones)
Thomas (2) (Oglethorpe)
Thomas (Pulaski)
Thomas (Putnam)
Thomas (Washington)
Thomas W. (Putnam)
Timothy (Screven)
Uriah (Montgomery)
William (Bryan)
William (Clarke)
William (2) (Emanuel)
William (Hancock)
William (Jackson)
William (3) (Jones)
William (Oglethorpe)
William (Pulaski)
William, Jr. (Pulaski)
William (Tattnall)
William (Telfair)
William (2) (Washington)
William (2) (Wilkes)
William C. (Putnam)
William M. (Wilkes)
Willis (Columbia)
Willis (2) (Washington)
Johnston, Mrs. (Chatham)
Alexander (Elbert)
Andrew N. (Wayne)
Angus (Elbert)
Archabil (Elbert)
Benjamin (Jasper)
Benjamin H. (Morgan)
Burwell (Morgan)
D. est. of (Chatham)
D. (2) (Jasper)
D. (Richmond)
Daniel (Elbert)
Danuel (Jasper)
David (Chatham)
David (Clarke)
Edward (Hancock)
Elam (?) (Hancock)
Elizabeth (Hancock)
Elizabeth (Morgan)
Gideon (Baldwin)
H. G. (Jasper)
Isaac M. (Hancock)
Israel (Hancock)
Colonel J. (Chatham)
James (Chatham)
James (Hancock)

James (Jasper)
James (Jefferson)
James (2) (Richmond)
John (Chatham)
John (2) (Baldwin)
John (Hancock)
John (2) (Jasper)
John (Morgan)
John A. (Hancock)
Johnston (Elbert)
Jonas (Laurens)
Joseph (Jasper)
Lancelot (Morgan)
Larkin (Elbert)
Lewis (Chatham)
Luke (Hancock)
Malcolm (Hancock)
Malcolm (Elbert)
Margaret (Hancock)
Martha (Morgan)
Mary (Elbert)
Matthew (Jefferson)
Micajah (Hancock)
Moses (Burke)
Mournen (Hancock)
Nathan (Elbert)
Nicholas (Jasper)
Peter (Jasper)
Peter (Richmond)
Philip (Jefferson)
Prudence (Jasper)
Rachel (Chatham)
Reuben (Morgan)
Samuel (2) (Baldwin)
Sarah (Baldwin)
Silas M. (Morgan)
Susan (Elbert)
Sylvester (Jones)
Thomas (Elbert)
Thomas (Jefferson)
Timothy (Hancock)
W. (Jasper)
William (2) (Baldwin)
William (Clarke)
William (2) (Jasper)
William, Jr. (Jasper)
William, Sr. (Jasper)
William (3) (Morgan)
Johnstone, Susan (Chatham)
Johson, John, Jr. (Emanuel)
Joice, William (Washington)
Joiner, (torn) (Laurens)
Abraham (2) (Washington)
Absolom (Baldwin)
Benjamen (Putnam)
Edmund (Washington)
Elisha (Washington)
Gibson (Warren)
Hardy (Washington)
Jabez (Washington)
Jacob (Emanuel)

Jones, Mary (Columbia)
Mary (Hall)
Mary (Putnam)
Mary (Wilkes)
Mason (Oglethorpe)
Matthew (Chatham)
Mathew (Putnam)
Matthew (3) (Tattnall)
Micajah (Elbert)
Mitchell (Warren)
Moses (Lincoln)
Moses W. (Lincoln)
N. W. (Chatham)
Nathan (Jones)
Nathan (Morgan)
Nimrod (Columbia)
Peyton (Morgan)
Philip (Effingham)
Polly (Lincoln)
Rebecca (Habersham)
Rebecca (Jones)
Redisey (Putnam)
Reuben (Warren)
Richard (3) (Morgan)
Robert (Burke)
Robert (2) (Columbia)
Robert (Greene)
Robert (Pulaski)
Robert (Putnam)
Robert S. (Richmond)
Russel (Jackson)
Samuel (Gwinnett)
Samuel (Habersham)
Samuel (Laurens)
Samuel (Liberty)
Samuel, Est. of (Liberty)
Samuel (Lincoln)
Samuel (Pulaski)
Samuel (Warren)
Samuel (Wilkes)
Sarah (Bulloch)
Sarah (Warren)
Sarah R. (Jefferson)
Seabone (Baldwin)
Seaborn (Jefferson)
Seaborn (3) (Morgan)
Seaborn (Wilkinson)
Seaborn H. (Burke)
Simon (Burke)
Simon (Warren)
Smith, Est. of (Burke)
Solomon (Elbert)
Stanley (Elbert)
Stephen (2) (Morgan)
Stephen (Putnam)
Stephen (Warren)
Sterling (Warren)
Tabina (Jones)
Tandy C. (Jefferson)
Thomas (Bulloch)
Thomas (Burke)

Thomas (Chatham)
Thomas (Columbia)
Thomas (2) (Elbert)
Thomas (3) (Gwinnett)
Thomas (3) (Hancock)
Thomas (Jasper)
Thomas (2) (Jones)
Thomas, Jr. (Morgan)
Thomas, Sr. (Morgan)
Thomas (Putnam)
Thomas (Richmond)
Thomas (Warren)
Thomas, Sr. (Warren)
Thomas (Wilkinson)
Thomas B. (Warren)
Thomas H. (Burke)
Thomas T. (Wilkes)
Timothy (Morgan)
Uriah (Jones)
Walter (Columbia)
Warrington (Walton)
Washington (Hall)
Wiley (Columbia)
Wiley (2) (Elbert)
Wiley (Jasper)
Wiley (Wilkinson)
Wiley B. (Wilkes)
William (Burke)
William (2) (Columbia)
William (Emanuel)
William (Elbert)
William (Hall)
William (Hancock)
William (Jackson)
William, Jr. (Jasper)
William (2) (Jones)
William (3) (Morgan)
William (2) (Richmond)
William (Warren)
William (Washington)
William (Wilkes)
William (2) (Wilkinson)
William D. (Lincoln)
William H. (2) (Morgan)
Willis (Lincoln)
Winey (Richmond)
Wylly (Telfair)
Zachariah (Greene)
Jonons, Martha (Warren)
Jonson, Abner (Warren)
Henry (Warren)
Jacob (Warren)
James (Warren)
Joseph C. (Warren)
Martin (Warren)
Robert (2) (Warren)
Jonston, Aaron (Warren)
Benjamin (Warren)
Calvin (Warren)
Elisha (Warren)

James (Warren)
Lewis (Warren)
Jonston(?), Mary (Emanuel)
Jonston, Randle (Warren)
Reese (Warren)
Robert, Jr. (Warren)
Robert, Sr. (Warren)
Valient (Warren)
William (Warren)
William, Jr. (Warren)
Joor(?), Doct. (Chatham)
Jordains, Shadrick (Wilkinson)
Jordan, (ind.) (Laurens)
Benjamin (Jasper)
Daniel (Burke)
Dempsey (Greene)
Elijah (Greene)
Fleming (Jasper)
Henry (2) (Jasper)
James, Jr., (Jones)
James, Sr. (Jones)
John W. (Jones)
Larkin (Jones)
Overoff (Baldwin)
William, Jr. (Jones)
William (Jones)
William (Wilkinson)
Jorden, Thomas (Oglethorpe)
Jordin, Redin (Madison)
Jordon, Archibald (Habersham)
Asa (Habersham)
Asa (Washington)
Avan (Jefferson)
Benjamin (Washington)
Burrel (Washington)
Chaney (Lincoln)
David (Emanuel)
Edmond (Oglethorpe)
Fountain (Elbert)
Frederick (Jefferson)
Henry (Washington)
Isam (Irwin)
Israel (Warren)
Jacob (Lincoln)
Jacob (Washington)
James (2) (Elbert)
James (Hall)
James (Hancock)
Jane (Washington)
John (Emanuel)
John (Jefferson)
John (2) (Washington)
John C. (Walton)
Joseph (Emanuel)
William (Emanuel)
Matthew (Jefferson)
Reuben (Oglethorpe)
Robin (Washington)
Thomas (Washington)
Thomas G. (Jones)

(81)

Jordon, William (Elbert)
  William (2) (Washington)
  William H. (Wilkes)
  Zachariah (Baldwin)
Joseph, Samuel (Wilkes)
  Sid (Jones)
Josey, Henry (Wilkes)
Jott, Francis (Jones)
Jourdan, Abner (Morgan)
  Benjamin (Morgan)
  Charles (Gwinnett)
  Henry (Wilkinson)
  James (Gwinnett)
  James (Oglethorpe)
  James D. (Morgan)
  Jarret (Oglethorpe)
  Samuel (Gwinnett)
  Warren (Morgan)
  William (Wilkinson)
  Zachariah (Hancock)
Jourden, Absolem (Wilkinson)
  Edmond (Hancock)
  Em (ind.) (Hancock)
  Josiah (Oglethorpe)
  Nathan (Hancock)
  Richard (Wilkinson)
Jourdin, Green (Putnam)
Jourdon, Ann (McIntosh)
  Josiah (Oglethorpe)
  Sarah (Chatham)
  Thomas B. (Montgomery)
Joyce, Henry (Montgomery)
  Henry (Tattnall)
  John (Tattnall)
  Michael (Tattnall)
  Sabra (Tattnall)
Joyner, Charles (Wayne)
  William H. (Chatham)
Judah, David (Chatham)
Judkens, Zachariah (Hancock)
Judkins, George (Hancock)
Juel, James (Oglethorpe)
  Jane (Oglethorpe)
Jump, Elizabeth (Pulaski)
Junigian, Joseph (Telfair)
Junior, John (Jones)
  Matthew (Jones)
Justian, John (Hancock)
Justice, Aaron (Wilkinson)
  David (Jackson)
  Elsey (Laurens)
  Henry (Jackson)
  Isaac (Jones)
  John (Jackson)
  James (Jasper)
  James (Wilkinson)
  Moses (Wilkinson)
  Stephen (Jackson)
  Thomas (Wilkinson)
Justiss, Benjamin (Greene)

K

Kaggor, Charles (Elbert)
Kanady, Andrew (Greene)
  Jonathon (Greene)
Kaone(?), Charles (Chatham)
Karr, Isaac (Jackson)
  Robert (Jackson)
Kay, Joseph (Jasper)
Keaggy, George (Jones)
Keall, John (Wilkinson)
  Noab (Wilkinson)
Keating, Richard T. (Bryan)
Keaton, Ann (Richmond)
  Benjamin (Wilkinson)
  John H. (Walton)
  Lane (Richmond)
Keats, Georgia (Chatham)
Kee. Chiles T. (Elbert)
Keeling, Leonard (Elbert)
Keen, Mrs. (Chatham)
  David (Tattnall)
  Theophilus (Tattnall)
  William (Wayne)
Keenan, Lewis (2) (Jackson)
Keeton, Elizabeth (Hall)
Keiffer, Joel (Effingham)
Keith, David (Jasper)
  James (Jasper)
  Whiten (Jasper)
Kell, John (McIntosh)
Kellam, Gideon (Pulaski)
Keller, Godfrey (Jefferson)
  J. A. (Chatham)
  Paul (Chatham)
Kellett, John (Jasper)
Kelley, Aimey (Richmond)
  Daniel (Morgan)
  Daniel (Hall)
  Daniel (Putnam)
  James (Madison)
  Joel (Wilkinson)
  John (Appling)
  John (Putnam)
  Joseph (Elbert)
  Nelly (Richmond)
  Samuel (Wilkes)
  Sarah (Screven)
  William (2) (Elbert)
Kellgore, Allen (Oglethorpe)
Kellum, Archibald (Warren)
  George (Warren)
  Sarah (Oglethorpe)
  Russel (Washington)
Kelly, Col. (Chatham)
  (ind.) (Richmond)
  Capt. (Chatham)
  Miss (Chatham)
  Abner (Hancock)
  Abraham (Screven)
  Allen I. (Jasper)

John (Appling)

  Barnabas (Elbert)
  Charles (Walton)
  David (Elbert)
  E. (Richmond)
  Easton (Jones)
  Francis (Elbert)
  Francis O. (Jasper)
  George (Washington)
  Gibbs(?) (Hancock)
  Jacob (Wilkinson)
  James (Early)
  James (2) (Jasper)
  James (Jones)
  James (Pulaski)
  James (Warren)
  Jeremiah (Chatham)
  Jesse (Burke)
  Jesse (Early)
  Jesse (Walton)
  John (Burke)
  John (Clarke)
  John (Hancock)
  John (Jasper)
  John (Jones)
  John (Greene)
  John (Pulaski)
  John (Wayne)
  John (Warren)
  Joseph (Jones)
  Lewis (Jones)
  Lloyd (Hancock)
  Lyod (Jones)
  Malacki (Pulaski)
  Marvel (Walton)
  Moses (Richmond)
  Nancy (Gwinnett)
  Peggy (Hancock)
  Rachel (Gwinnett)
  (ind.) (Gwinnett)
  Randol (Early)
  Rebeccah (Screven)
  Redick (Walton)
  Robert (Bulloch)
  Sally (Jones)
  Shadrick (Oglethorpe)
  Stephen (Jefferson)
  Sussannah (Burke)
  William(?) (Chatham)
  William (Early)
  William (Elbert)
  William (Hall)
  William (Jackson)
  William (Oglethorpe)
  William (Pulaski)
  William (Wayne)
  William F. (Camden)
Kelsy, Joel (Hancock)
  Noah (Wilkes)
Kemble, Henry (Morgan)
  Peter (Morgan)
Kembro, William (Putnam)

Kemp, Benjamin (Wilkinson)
Berriman (Jackson)
David (Screven)
David E. (Wayne)
David N. (Wayne)
Elitha (Washington)
James (Tattnall)
John (Jones)
John (Screven)
John (Wayne)
John A. (Emanuel)
John R. (Glynn)
Joseph (Jones)
Joshua (Appling)
Mary (Washington)
Simeon (Baldwin)
Solimin (Screven)
William (Wilkinson)
Kemph, Talton (Screven)
Kempton, Edward S. (Liberty)
Ken, Joseph (Jones)
Kenady, Edward (Tatttnall)
James (Gwinnett)
John (2) (Jefferson)
John (Tattnall)
Seth (Hancock)
Stephen (Tattnall)
Thomas (Jefferson)
Thomas (Hall)
William (Jefferson)
Kenam, Alexander (Hancock)
David Leo (Jones)
Kenan, Lewis (Jefferson)
Thomas H. (Baldwin)
Kenard, John N. (Jasper)
Kenchley, M. (Chatham)
Kendal, David (Hancock)
Kendall, Henry (Hancock)
Thomas H. (Hancock)
Kendell, Isaac (Jasper)
Kendoll, Henry (Warren)
Kendren, Jordon (Wilkes)
Kendrick, Abel (Hall)
Alexander (Putnam)
Anderson (Putnam)
Ann (Greene)
Hezekiah (Putnam)
I. (Jasper)
Isham (Putnam)
James (Washington)
John (Hall)
John (2) (Putnam)
Johnathan (Putnam)
Jones (Putnam)
Mered (Putnam)
R. E. (Wilkes)
Kendricks, Har--y (Putnam)
Keneday, Alexander (Richmond)
Kenedy, Benjamin (Effingham)
Kennady, Robert (Elbert)
William (Elbert)
Kennan, Celia (Putnam)
Charles L. (Putnam)
John (Putnam)
Kennard, Charles (Chatham)
Kennebrew, Littleberry (Oglethorpe)
Robert (Putnam)
Kennedy, David (Bulloch)
David (Clarke)
David (Jones)
David (Washington)
Ely (Bulloch)
Franklin (Jackson)
James (Chatham)
James (Washington)
Jane (Washington)
Jesse (Clarke)
John (Chatham)
John (Jasper)
Judah (Chatham)
Samuel (Washington)
Kenneday, Thomas (Jasper)
William (2) (Jasper)
Kenney, Thomas, Jr. (Morgan)
Thomas, Sr. (Morgan)
Kennon, Charles (Morgan)
Richard (Morgan)
Thomas (2) (Morgan)
Warner L. (Columbia)
Kenny, Isaac (Wilkinson)
James (Clarke)
Tate (Lincoln)
William (Warren)
Kennymore, M. (Jasper)
Kent, Asa (Jackson)
Cain (Warren)
Charles (Oglethorpe)
Daniel (Oglethorpe)
Daniel, Sr. (Oglethorpe)
Easter (Pulaski)
Elijah (Oglethorpe)
Gilbert (Wilkes)
Jane (Oglethorpe)
Jenny (Wilkinson)
Jese (Telfair)
John (Morgan)
John (Wilkes)
John (Warren)
Lewis (Oglethorpe)
Peter (Wilkes)
Reuben (Putnam)
Robert Z. (Columbia)
Sampson (Oglethorpe)
Theophilas (Warren)
Thomas (Warren)
Thomas W. (Warren)
Kenum, James (Morgan)
Ker, Alexander M. (Chatham)
Kerbin, John (Oglethorpe)
Kermekle, John, Jr. (Jackson)
John, Sr. (Jackson)
Kernals, William (Wayne)
Kerr, Charles (Jasper)
David (Oglethorpe)
John D. (Greene)
Robert (Wilkes)
Thomas (Elbert)
William (Oglethorpe)
Kersey, James (Emanuel)
John (Emanuel)
Thomas (Emanuel)
Kerss, Stephen (McIntosh)
Kersy, Bud (Burke)
Kesant(?), Ann (Camden)
Kester, (ind.) (Effingham)
Ketching, B. (ind.) (Warren)
Fanny (Warren)
William (Warren)
Ketchings, John (Warren)
Ketchum, R. (Richmond)
Kettett, Solm (Jackson)
Kettles, (ind.) (Laurens)
Amy (Effingham)
John (Wilkinson)
Key (Ivy?) Eldridge (Columbia)
Key, F. W. (Jasper)
Geo. W. (Jackson)
Henry (Washington)
James (Elbert)
James (Washington)
Joseph (Jasper)
Robert (Chatham)
Samuel (Gwinnett)
Sarah (Gwinnett)
Tandy (Jackson)
Thomas (Jasper)
William (Burke)
William B. (Elbert)
Keyland, Jane (Burke)
Keys, James (Chatham)
Robert (Chatham)
Keyton, Charles (Wilkinson)
Jesse (Putnam)
Kezzick(?), David (Pulaski)
Kicklighter, Andrew (Bulloch)
Thomas (Bulloch)
Kidd, Abraham (Oglethorpe)
Absolem (Oglethorpe)
Henry (Burke)
James H. (Gwinnett)
John (Jackson)
John (Oglethorpe)
Richard (Oglethorpe)
William (2) (Oglethorpe)
Zachariah (Oglethorpe)
Kider, Benjamin (Morgan)
Kieffer, Ephraim (Effingham)
Kieth, Marshall (Columbia)
Kight, David (Gwinnett)
Henry (Gwinnett)
John (Gwinnett)
Noah (Gwinnett)
Samuel (Gwinnett)

Kihily, Christopher (Jackson)
Jacob (Jackson)
Kilbee, William T.
(Montgomery)
Kilcrease, Arthur (Jones)
Elijah (Jones)
Kile, James (Madison)
John (Madison)
Thomas (Gwinnett)
Kiley, Sally (Bryan)
Kilgo, James (Gwinnett)
Margaret (Walton)
Mathew (Walton)
William (Gwinnett)
Kilgore, Charles (Hancock)
John (Clarke)
John L. (Clarke)
Nancy (Hancock)
Ralph (Hancock)
Robert (Jasper)
Solomon (Clarke)
Williaim (Hancock)
Killbun, Woodard A. (Baldwin)
Killebrew, John (Warren)
William (Hancock)
Killerian, Daniel (Jasper)
Killgore, Benajah (Wilkes)
John (Putnam)
Robert (Wilkes)
William (Wilkes)
Killingsworth, Ambrose
(Hancock)
David (Columbia)
Freeman (Columbia)
John (Columbia)
William (Washington)
Kilpatric, David (Baldwin)
Samuel (Baldwin)
Kilpatrick, A. (Jasper)
Hugh (Jackson)
John (Burke)
Martha (Warren)
Richard (Baldwin)
Spencer (Burke)
Thomas (Morgan)
William (Jones)
Kimball, Buckner (Walton)
James (Burke)
James W. (Burke)
John (Hall)
Joseph (Burke)
Joshua (Burke)
Mary (Burke)
William (Burke)
Kimbell, Charles (Burke)
Kimbrel, Benjamin (Oglethorpe)
David (Oglethorpe)
John H. (Richmond)
Thomas (Oglethorpe)
Kimbro, John H. (Jones)
William (Clarke)

Kimbrough, Bradley (2)
(Greene)
Gracy (Greene)
John (Greene)
John (Jasper)
Jonah (Greene)
Shadrack (Jasper)
Thomas (2) (Greene)
Kimmy, John (Washington)
Kinard, Daniel (Montgomery)
Kindrick, John (Camden)
John (Columbia)
Jones (Wilkes)
Martha (Putnam)
Nancy (Columbia)
Robert (Hall)
Samuel (Putnam)
Kindricks, Leon (?) (Putnam)
King, A. E. (Richmond)
Alexander Greene)
Ann (Washington)
Benajer (Wilkinson)
Benjamin (Putnam)
Bennett (Wilkinson)
Curtis (Greene)
E. (Richmond)
Edward M. (Jones)
Eliflett (Pulaski)
Elijah (Baldwin)
Elisha (Baldwin)
Elisha (Washington)
Elizabeth (Morgan)
Elizabeth (Warren)
Ephraim (Burke)
George (Putnam)
George W. (Baldwin)
Harriet (Chatham)
Henry (Morgan)
Henry (Pulaski)
Henry (Putnam)
Jacob (Jones)
Jacob W. (Elbert)
James (Elbert)
James (Jasper)
James (2) (Putnam)
James M. (Jasper)
Joel (Wilkinson)
John (Baldwin)
John (Columbia)
John (Gwinnett)
John (Hall)
John (2) (Jackson)
John (Jefferson)
John (Jones)
John, Sr. (Jones)
John (2) (Washington)
John (Wilkinson)
John P. (Richmond)
John R. (Chatham)
Johnson (Wilkinson)
Joseph (Greene)

Joseph (Putnam)
Kintching(?), (Wilkes)
Martha (Putnam)
Martin (Jones)
Mary (Wilkes)
Micajah (Jefferson)
Nancy (Hancock)
Reuben (McIntosh)
Richard (Jasper)
Richard (Wilkes)
Robert (Elbert)
Roswell K. (McIntosh)
Samuel (Jackson)
Sarah (Clarke)
Tandy D. (Jasper)
Thomas (Laurens)
Thomas (McIntosh)
Thomas (Putnam)
Thomas (Washingtotn)
Thomas G. (Putnam)
Wiley (Emanuel)
William (Chatham)
William (Effingham)
William (2) (Elbert)
Dr. William (Greene)
William (2) (Greene)
William (Habersham)
William (Hall)
William (Montgomery)
William (Putnam)
William (Wilkes)
Wm. J. (Greene)
William J. (McIntosh)
Willis (Irwin)
Woody (Greene)
Zuriah (Elbert)
Kingham, Priscilla (Jackson)
Kingley, John G. (Chatham)
Kingtry, Daniel K. (Wilkinson)
Kingsley, James (Pulaski)
Kingson, Richard (Wilkes)
Kingston, John (Chatham)
Kinnebrew, H. (Columbia)
Henry (Elbert)
Kinner, Josiah (Jones)
Kinney, Agnes (Clarke)
David (Clarke)
George (Clarke)
James (Baldwin)
John (Clarke)
Kinnon, John (Jones)
Kinsey, Edward (Warren)
John (Warren)
Martin (Warren)
Peter (Habersham)
Kinsley, Alford (Wilkinson)
Kirbo, Saml. (Jackson)
Kirby, Arthur (Bulloch)
Moab (Liberty)

Kirk, Annie (Jones)
   Catharine (Gwinnett)
   George (Gwinnett)
   James (Jones)
   Jesse (Jasper)
   John (Jackson)
   John (Jones)
   John (Walton)
   Wiley (Jasper)
Kirke, Thomas (Washington)
Kirkland, Daniel (Tattnall)
   John (Camden)
   John (Emanuel)
   John S. (Emanuel)
   Joseph (Wilkes)
   Ralph (Pulaski)
   Richard (Bulloch)
   Sion (Emanuel)
   Snoden (Wilkes)
   William (Wilkes)
Kirklin, Benj. (Jackson)
   John (Jackson)
Kirkpatrick, James (Morgan)
   John (Jackson)
   John (Putnam)
   Robt. (Jackson)
Kirksey, Isaac (Pulaski)
Kirshaw, George (Liberty)
Kirsy, John (Burke)
Kirtler, Lemma (Jackson)
Kisa, George (Jones)
Kitchen, Stephen (Habersham)
Kitchens, B. (Jasper)
   C. (2) (Jasper)
   Chas. (Jasper)
   Eli (Jasper)
   Gary (Jones)
   Jacob H. (Putnam)
   James (Jasper)
   James, Sr. (Jasper)
   Joseph (Chatham)
   Joseph (Greene)
   Joseph L. (Bulloch)
   Sarah (Washington)
   T. (Jasper)
Kitching, Bartholemew
   (Warren)
   Willie (Warren)
Kitchings, Laurence (Warren)
Kite, Wm. (Jasper)
Kittle, Jeremiah (Hall)
Knappe, Francis (Chatham)
Knash, James (Jackson)
Kneeland, Elizabeth M.
   (Columbia)
Knight, Alexander (Bulloch)
   B. (Richmond)
   Carmenton (Jones)
   Charles (Washington)
   Coffield (Jefferson)
   E. (Richmond)

   Elias (Liberty)
   Enoch (Richmond)
   Ephraim (Morgan)
   F. (Jasper)
   Henry (Walton)
   Isaac (Gwinnett)
   James (Laurens)
   John (Jasper)
   John (Putnam)
   John (Richmond)
   Joseph (Bulloch)
   Joseph (Greene)
   Joshua (Morgan)
   Kenard (Jones)
   Presley (Gwinnett)
   Robert (Washington)
   Samuel (Wayne)
   Speir (Laurens)
   Sylvanus (Washington)
   Thomas (Bulloch)
   Thomas (Wayne)
   W. A. (Wayne)
   Walton (Richmond)
   William (Effingham)
   William (Jasper)
Knock, James (Chatham)
Knoles, Edmond, Jr. (Greene)
   Edmond, Sr. (Greene)
   Isaac (Greene)
   Joseph (Greene)
   Thomas, Jr. (Greene)
   Thomas, Sr. (Greene)
Knowland, Matthew
   (Oglethorpe)
Knowles, Amanuel (Irwin)
   James P. (Putnam)
   Thos., Jr. (Greene)
Knox, Andrew (Chatham)
   John (Lincoln)
   Robert (Wilkes)
   Samuel, Jr. (Jackson)
   Samuel, Sr. (Jackson)
   William (Jackson)
Knuckels, Alexander (Jackson)
Kofeman, Joseph (Chatham)
Kolb, (ind.) (Jones)
   Harryson (Jackson)
   Martin (Hall)
   Philip (Chatham)
   Sarah (Washington)
Kollock, Dr. Lem. (Chatham)
Kong(?), M. (Chatham)
Kornegay, George (Pulaski)
Kratty, John (Baldwin)
Krews, Benjamin (Jefferson)
Kruger, Frederick (Chatham)

L

Labroisan, D. (Chatham)
Labuzan, Charles (Richmond)

Lacee, Benjamin (Putnam)
Lacey, John B. (2) (Baldwin)
Lackey, Thomas (Greene)
   William (Wilkes)
Lacy, Archabald (Warren)
   Claburn (Early)
   George (Jones)
   Thomas (Morgan)
   Tilamon (Baldwin)
Laffler, Arnold (McIntosh)
Lafield, Josiah (Jones)
Lafiever, John (Jefferson)
Lafitte(?), Mrs. (Chatham)
   James B. (Richmond)
Lafong, Francis (McIntosh)
Lafont, A. (Chatham)
Laihan, Elijah (Jones)
Lain, Henry (Morgan)
   Noah (Oglethorpe)
   Samuel (Jasper)
Laine, Labern (Madison)
Lake, Abraham (Putnam)
   Elisha (Walton)
   James (Putnam)
   Joseph (Putnam)
Lamar, Basil (?) (Richmond)
   Catherine (Putnam)
   James (Jones)
   Jeremiah (Jones)
   John (Lincoln)
   John (2) (Putnam)
   E.Q.C. (Baldwin)
   Peter (Lincoln)
   Z. (Baldwin)
   Zachariah (Jones)
Lamb, Abram (Emanuel)
   Barnaba (Burke)
   Celia (Glynn)
   Daniel (Jefferson)
   Greene (Hancock)
   Hezekiah (Emanuel)
   Isaac (Jefferson)
   Jacob (Burke)
   Jacob (Jones)
   John (Glynn)
   John (Warren)
   Matthew (Jefferson)
   Reuben (Jefferson)
Lambert, (ind.) (Gwinnett)
   Mrs. (Chatham)
   Blakeley (Laurens)
   Caleb (Chatham)
   Easter (Wilkinson)
   Edwin (Walton)
   Elijah (Jackson)
   Elisha (Habersham)
   Isaac (Wilkes)
   James (Burke)
   James (Putnam)
   James (Screven)
   James (Walton)

Lambert, John (Columbia)
John (Jackson)
Lambert(?), L. (Richmond)
Lambert, Louis (Putnam)
Noah (Laurens)
P. (Richmond)
Quash (Chatham)
R. (Richmond)
S. (Richmond)
Sally (Jackson)
William (Morgan)
William (Screven)
Lambeth, James (Screven)
Lambot, Linsey (Richmond)
Lambright, James (Liberty)
Lamburt, George (Putnam)
Lamkin, Ann (Columbia)
James (Columbia)
John (Lincoln)
John (Richmond)
John L. (Telfair)
L. L. (Telfair)
Lab. L. (Telfair)
Lamon, Benjamin (Jones)
Lampe, (ind.) (Chatham)
Lampkins, S. (Richmond)
Lamplin, John (Jones)
Lampp, Lewis (Jefferson)
Michael (Jefferson)
Philip (Jefferson)
Lancaster, Benjamin
(Wilkinson)
Mahala (Burke)
Samuel (Greene)
Thomas (Hancock)
Washington (Pulaski)
William (Hancock)
Wright (Pulaski)
Lanceford, Josiah (Morgan)
Land, Frederick (Wilkinson)
Henry (Irwin)
Henry (Pulaski)
John (Warren)
Nathan (Irwin)
Landers, Clabon (Baldwin)
Humphrey D. (Elbert)
Lewis (Oglethorpe)
Luke (Putnam)
Merry A. (Lincoln)
Rensly (Columbia)
Samuel (Madison)
Sarah (Madison)
Tyree (Elbert)
Landforde, Caty (Morgan)
Landin, Elizabeth (Jefferson)
Landing, John (Burke)
Landram, Elizabeth (Warren)
Jacob (Warren)
Nancy (Warren)
William (Warren)
Landrew, Timothy (Jasper)

Landrum, Abner (Hall)
George (Early)
James (Hall)
James B. (Oglethorpe)
John (Oglethorpe)
John (Wilkes)
Joseph (Oglethorpe)
Lamkin (Jackson)
Micajah (Hall)
Thomas (Oglethorpe)
William (Oglethorpe)
Lane, Abram (Emanuel)
Allen (Morgan)
Betsey (Putnam)
Bryan (Tattnall)
Charles William (Baldwin)
Clenton (Putnam)
Edward (Emanuel)
Edward W. (Putnam)
Eleazer (Chatham)
Elexandre (Emanuel)
Garland (Habersham)
Henry (2) (Morgan)
Lane(?), Jacob (Hancock)
Lane, James (Burke)
Jeffry (Hancock)
Jesse (Walton)
Joel (Morgan)
John (Burke)
John (Hall)
John (Jefferson)
John (Lincoln)
Jonathan (Clarke)
Joseph (Morgan)
Micajah A. (Wilkes)
Rushing (Putnam)
Sarah (Pulaski)
Sarah (Putnam)
Thomas (2) (Burke)
Thomas (Elbert)
Thomas (Putnam)
William (Morgan)
Laneford, Enoch (Baldwin)
Lanere, Samuel (Bryan)
Laney, William (Gwinnett)
Lanford, Jesse (Baldwin)
Lang, Bezaleel (Clarke)
Charles (Pulaski)
Cornelius (Screven)
David (Camden)
David (Screven)
John (Jones)
Nathaniel (Bulloch)
Robert (Richmond)
Robert (Walton)
Solomon (Jasper)
William (Pulaski)
Langdon, Amos W. (Putnam)
Isaac (Wilkes)
John (Wilkes)
Thomas (Wilkes)

Langford, (ind.) (Warren)
Charley (Clarke)
Edmond (Hancock)
Edmund (Baldwin)
Elizabeth (Hancock)
George (Morgan)
George N. (Hancock)
Henry (Hancock)
Henry (Oglethorpe)
James (Clarke)
John (Hancock)
John (Jones)
Nicholas (Hancock)
Richard (Hancock)
William (Jackson)
Langham, Asy (Wilkes)
Richard (Washington)
William (Warren)
Langley, Catherine (Chatham)
James (Putnam)
Nowel (Wilkinson)
Langly, Miles (Jackson)
Thomas (Jackson)
Langston, (ind.) (Columbia)
David (Washington)
Dorcas (Washington)
Eloy (Columbia)
Jacob (Jackson)
James (Columbia)
James (Jackson)
Jesse (Elbert)
John, Jr. (Columbia)
John, Sr. (Columbia)
Moses (Morgan)
Samuel (Jackson)
Samuel M. (Jones)
Seth S. (Jefferson)
Langster, Peter (Wayne)
Languin, Robert (Morgan)
Laniar, Thomas B. (Gwinnett)
Lanier, Allen (Bulloch)
Benjamin (Bulloch)
David (2) (Morgan)
Frederic (Bulloch)
George M. (Clarke)
Hannah (Bulloch)
Henry (Greene)
James (Bulloch)
James (Jasper)
James (Morgan)
John (Bulloch)
John (Jasper)
John (Jefferson)
Lewis (Bulloch)
Lewis (Screven)
Nicholas (Hancock)
Robert (Jones)
Sampson (Morgan)
Sarah (Washington)
Zacus (Jones)
Laningdem, Thomas (Elbert)

Lankford, Jesse (Tattnall)
John (Tattnall)
Moses (Tattnall)
William (Tattnall)
Lankston, David (Oglethorpe)
Lanman, Travis (Greene)
Lanos, Charles Baldwin)
Lanson, Thompson
(Washington)
Lany, John (Jasper)
Laprad, John (Putnam)
Laramore, Peter (Tattnall)
Lard, A. (Jasper)
Lardon, Rosine (Chatham)
Large, John (Tattnall)
William (Tattnall)
Larisy, Moses (Screven)
Larissy, William (Screven)
Lark, S. (Richmond)
Larramore, John (Lincoln)
Polly (Lincoln)
Larrard, Bennett (Jasper)
Larrence, Abraham, Sr.
(Greene)
Abram, Jr. (Greene)
Britten (Greene)
John (Greene)
Larry, J. B. (Richmond)
John (Jones)
Larsen, Mrs. (Chatham)
Lary, Hinchy (Jones)
Larry (Jones)
Peggy (Hancock)
Thomas (Jones)
Las, M. (Jasper)
Lascier(?), Lewis (Camden)
Lasenby, Joshua (Warren)
Laseter. James (Clarke)
Joel (Clarke)
Lashley, (ind.) (Clarke)
Lashly, Elijah (Columbia)
Lasiter, Amos (Bulloch)
Robt. & Brittain (Clarke)
Lasitter, Jesse (Walton)
Laskay(?), Richard (Chatham)
Lasley, John (Hall)
Lucretia (Hall)
Silas (Wilkinson)
Thomas (Wilkes)
Laslie, Mae (Telfair)
Lasnett, James (Jasper)
Lason, John F. (Putnam)
Lassater. Mathew (Jasper)
Lasser, J. (Chatham)
Lassiter, Abraham (Wilkinson)
Ann (Jasper)
Benjamin (Gwinnett)
Edward (Burke)
George (Columbia)
Henry (Jasper)
Jacob (Wilkinson)

Lemuel (Burke)
Mary (Burke)
Russell (Laurens)
William (Burke)
Lasteno, Mary (Emanuel)
Lastinger, David (Bulloch)
Latemere, Benjamin F.
(Hancock)
Latemore Henry W. (Hancock)
John, Sr. (Hancock)
Thomas L. (Hancock)
Lathrop, B. (Chatham)
Lathrope, Eliza (Washington)
Lathrum, George (Gwinnett)
Latimer, George (Oglethorpe)
William (Warren)
Latimore, John S. (Hancock)
Robert (Hancock)
Latrent(?), Marey (Richmond)
Latson, Mary Ann (Liberty)
William F. (Liberty)
Lattey, David (Hall)
Latty, John (Jackson)
Lauchlin, Laslie (Telfair)
Laugham, James (Jasper)
Laughlin, William M. (Wilkes)
Laughridge, Elizabeth
(Gwinnett)
James (Gwinnett)
William (Gwinnett)
Laughter, Benjamin (Wilkes)
Henry (Wilkes)
Robert (Wilkes)
Laughton, David (Oglethorpe)
Lauingly(?), John (Jasper)
Laurens, Wiley (Baldwin)
Lavender, John (Wilkinson)
John S. (Pulaski)
Mary (Chatham)
Law, Alex (Jasper)
Benjamin (Liberty)
Est. of Charles (Liberty)
John F. T. (Jasper)
John (Jones)
Joseph, Jr. (Liberty)
Joseph, Sr. (Liberty)
Nathaniel (Liberty)
Robert (Jones)
Samuel S. (Liberty)
William (slaves) (Liberty)
Lawhorn, Simeon (Putnam)
Lawlace, Thomas (Putnam)
Lawler, John (Oglethorpe)
Lawless, John (Hall)
Nicholas (Chatham)
Lawlice, Jones (Morgan)
Lawrence, Allen (Putnam)
C. L. (Richmond)
D. (Jasper)
G. (Richmond)

Isham (Jefferson)
James (Gwinnett)
James (2) (Putnam)
John (Emanuel)
John (Gwinnett)
John (Washington)
Josiah (Chatham)
M. (Jasper)
Mary (Chatham)
Mary (Morgan)
Peter (Chatham)
R. (Jasper)
Richard (Jasper)
Samuel (Walton)
Sarah (Glynn)
Susan (Washington)
Thomas (Chatham)
Thomas (Jones)
William (Columbia)
William (Jasper)
William (Oglethorpe)
Laws, Isham (Morgan)
Joseph (Morgan)
Lawse, Jane (Wilkes)
Lawson, Mrs. (Chatham)
A. J. (Burke)
Adam (Putnam)
Arthur (Greene)
Booker (2) (Morgan)
D. (Jasper)
David (Jones)
David (Putnam)
David (Wilkes)
David (Wilkinson)
Dudley (Hancock)
Irvine (Jasper)
Ivy (Gwinnett)
John H. (Baldwin)
John (Telfair)
John (2) (Wilkes)
L. B. (Burke)
Margaret (Jefferson)
Pleasant (Wilkes)
Rachel (Putnam)
Sarah (Gwinnett)
Shelton (Wilkes)
Thomas B. (Hancock)
William (Jones)
Winright (Putnam)
Lay, Elijah (Jackson)
Elisha (Jackson)
Sampson (Madison)
William (Oglethorpe)
Zachariah (Jackson)
Laybon, John (Washington)
Layfield, John (Hancock)
Pricilla (Hancock)
Layman, W. C. (Wilkes)
Lazenby, Elias (Columbia)
Samuel (Columbia)

*Lard. Robert (Clarke)

Lea, John (Camden)
Jonathan (Clarke)
Vincen (Camden)
Leach, Robert (Wayne)
William (Lincoln)
Leak, John (Hancock)
Robert (Jasper)
Leake, Henry (Oglethorpe)
Lealey, William (Telfair)
Leapard, Holland (Jackson)
Leaptrot, Andrew (Bulloch)
Lears, Josiah (Jasper)
Wyatt, (Jasper)
Leary, Christopher (Gwinnett)
Leatheredge, I. (Jasper)
Leathers, John (Wilkinson)
Samuel (Hall)
Leaton, Adam (Jones)
Learesby, Trinity (Hancock)
(?), Thomas (Hancock)
Leckett, Benjamin (Jasper)
Lecontte, Louis (Liberty)
Lecroy, John (Habersham)
William (Habersham)
Ledbeater, Henry (Jasper)
Ledbetter, Benjamin (Jones)
Elizabeth (Putnam)
Isaac (Early)
James (Baldwin)
James W. (Hancock)
James (Putnam)
John (Putnam)
Joseph (Jones)
Mary (Burke)
Samuel (Jones)
Silas (Jones)
Timothy (Putnam)
Washington (Greene)
William (Baldwin)
Williamson (Clarke)
Ledlow, James (Jones)
John (Jones)
Lewis (Jones)
Ledwell, James (Habersham)
Lee, (ind.) (Laurens)
Abner (Morgan)
Abot (Bulloch)
Abraham (Morgan)
Andrew (Lincoln)
Ann (McIntosh)
Asalen (Wilkes)
Benjamin (col.) (Wilkes)
Bryan (Walton)
Bryant (Jones)
Bud (Washington)
Burvel (Clarke)
Charity (Emanuel)
Charles B. (Oglethorpe)
Daniel (Baldwin)
David (Bulloch)
Edward (Gwinnett)

Eli (Putnam)
Elias (Jefferson)
Elias (Washington)
Elijah (Putnam)
George (Appling)
Green (Morgan)
Green (Putnam)
Henry (Gwinnett)
Ira (Washington)
Jacob Jr. (Putnam)
Jacob Sr. (Putnam)
James (Appling)
James (Gwinnett)
James (Wilkes)
Jeneral (Bulloch)
Jesse (Morgan)
John (Appling) (2)
John, Jr. (Pulaski)
John, Sr. (Pulaski)
John, Sr. (2) (Putnam)
John (Screven)
John (Walton)
John (Wilkes)
John, Jr. (Wilkes)
John C. (Burke)
Joshua (Appling)
Joshua (Putnam)
Lewis (Appling)
Lewis (Wilkinson)
Lovard (Jefferson)
Lucinda (Morgan)
Martain B. (Wilkinson)
Nancy S. (Wilkes)
Needham (Jefferson)
Needham (Walton)
Noah (Wilkes)
Peter (Wilkinson)
Reuben (Jackson)
Robert (Pulaski)
Sampson (Washington)
Samuel (Gwinnett)
Seon (Putnam)
Sigmon (Oglethorpe)
Solomon (Walton)
Solomon P. (Wilkes)
Thomas (Baldwin)
Timothy (Walton)
William (Bryan)
William (Bulloch)
William (Chatham)
William (Greene)
William (Habersham)
William, Sr. (Wilkinson)
William, Jr. (Wilkinson)
William H. (Oglethorpe)
Wyatt (Clarke)
Leek, Thomas (Jefferson)
Leeper, Hugh B. (Madison)
John (Washington)
Lefler, Frances (Liberty)
Lefley, Wright (Effingham)

Leftwich, James H. (Oglethorpe)
Joel W. (Greene)
Legan, Willis (Morgan)
Legg, Agustus (Jackson)
Nathaniel (Jackson)
Thomas (Clarke)
Leggett, Alcey (Putnam)
Jeremiah (Walton)
Mathew (Putnam)
Leggit, Benjamin (Burke)
David (Burke)
Legon, David (Walton)
John (Columbia)
Legrand, Jesse (Elbert)
John N. (Elbert)
Leguinn, Samuel (Greene)
Leigh, Benjamin (Columbia)
James I .(Liberty)
Walter (Richmond)
Lekrour, (ind.) (Effingham)
Lemar, Harmony (Columbia)
John (Columbia)
Lemmons, Charity (Jones)
Lemon, Abraham (Jasper)
Lemons, Joseph (Morgan)
William (Walton)
Lenoir, Robt. C. (Burke)
Lenville, John (Gwinnett)
Leon(?), David (Chatham)
Leon, Lewis (Richmond)
Leonard, Benjamin (Baldwin)
Davis (Putnam)
Irbane (Greene)
James (Greene)
John (Greene)
John B. (Wilkes)
Joseph (Warren)
Patrick (Morgan)
Roderick (Morgan)
William (Oglethorpe)
Leopard, Jordan (Jackson)
Lepham, Francis H. (Wilkes)
Leprestree, Nicholas (2)
(Wilkes)
Leptrot, Aquilla (Washington)
Lequoux, Peter (Burke)
Leser, Samuel, Jr. (Elbert)
Samuel, Sr. (Elbert)
Lesley, William (Oglethorpe)
Leslie, Daniel (Telfair)
Lesset(?), Mrs. (Chatham)
Lessham, Mason (Jones)
Lester, Alexander (Oglethorpe)
Daniel (Bulloch)
Dennis (Baldwin)
Eli (Wilkinson)
Ezekiel, Jr. (Burke)
Ezekiel, Sr. (Burke)
George (Oglethorpe)
George D. (Jackson)
Hiram (Baldwin)

(88)

Lester, Isaac (Baldwin)
James D. (Putnam)
Jeremiah (McIntosh)
Jetho (Wilkes)
John (Burke)
John, Sr. (Jones)
John (Madison)
John (Pulaski)
John E. (Jones)
Josiah (Putnam)
Lucius (Oglethorpe)
Lucius, Jr. (Oglethorpe)
Noel (Burke)
Pleasant (Madison)
William (Pulaski)
William C.(Baldwin)
Lesueur, James (Lincoln)
Lesure, Drury M. (Baldwin)
Letterbetter, James W.
(Hancock)
Level, Edward (Hall)
Levens, Jacob (Camden)
Old (Camden)
Leverett, (ind.) (Lincoln)
B. (Jasper)
Elizabeth (Burke)
Gideon (Morgan)
Jesse (Jasper)
John (Gwinnett)
John (Morgan)
Matthew (Lincoln)
Mary (Lincoln)
Nancy (Wilkes)
Richard H. (Gwinnett)
Robert S. (Oglethorpe)
Thomas (Morgan)
Leverette, Joel P. (Wilkes)
Martha (Lincoln)
Leveritt, Abraham (Putnam)
Celia (Putnam)
Jeremiah (Jasper)
Jeremiah (Putnam)
Thomas (Putnam)
Levett, Thomas (Burke)
Levin, John (Appling)
Levins, Jacob (Morgan)
Jesse (Morgan)
Levistion, William (Hancock)
Levy(?), Green H. (Wilkes)
Morgan (Liberty)
Lewis, A. P. (Burke)
Abel (Burke)
Abram (Burke)
Asa (Washington)
Benjamin (Walton)
Christian (Morgan)
David (Habersham)
David (Hancock)
Eleazar (Burke)
Elizabeth (Baldwin)
Fauntleroy (Baldwin)

Fields (Jones)
George (2) (Hancock)
George (Jasper)
Haman (Hancock)
Hannah (Chatham)
Henry (Greene)
Hezekiah (Burke)
Ira (Washington)
Isaac (Washington)
Isaac (Wilkinson)
Isiah (Bulloch)
Jacob (Jones)
Jacob (Screven)
James C. (Bulloch)
James N. (Bulloch)
James, Sr. (Bulloch)
James, Jr. (Bulloch)
James (Burke)
James (Hancock)
Jeremiah (Elbert)
John (Baldwin)
John (Chatham)
John (Elbert)
John (Greene)
John (Jones)
John (Morgan)
John (Warren)
John C. (Burke)
John H. (Hancock)
Johnathan (Burke)
Jonathan (Jones)
Joseph (Emanuel)
Joseph (Hancock)
Josiah (Burke)
Lewis (Screven)
Littleberry (Burke)
Lorio R. (Baldwin)
Mary (Emanuel)
Mathew (Emanuel)
Nancy (Greene)
Nathaniel (Chatham)
Nicholas (Greene)
P. (Jasper)
Peter (Morgan)
Pierce (Jones)
R. C. (Richmond)
R. H. (Camden)
Rachel (Greene)
Rawlens (Wilkes)
Richard (2) (Greene)
Rich'd (Hancock)
Richard (Wilkinson)
Richardson (Hancock)
Robert (Chatham)
Samuel (Liberty)
Samuel (Washington)
Stephen (Tattnall)
Thomas (Jasper)
Thomas (Morgan)
Thomas (Richmond)
Thomas (Wilkinson)

Marius (?) (Putnam)
Wiley (Bulloch)
William (Baldwin)
William (Bulloch)
William, Jr. (Bulloch)
William (Burke)
William (Greene)
William (Hancock)
William (Morgan)
Zadoc (Columbia)
Zebulon (Walton)
Lials, Henry (Wayne)
Liddel, James (Jackson)
Liddle, William (Gwinnett)
Ligan, Thomas (Greene)
Ligget, Jordan (Burke)
Liggin, Marshall (Burke)
Light, Obadiah (Hall)
Lightfoot, James S. (Greene)
John A. (Hancock)
Philip (Burke)
Richard (Washington)
Thomas (Jones)
Lightner, Archibald (Emanuel)
Ligon, W. (Richmond)
William (Jefferson)
Liles, Benjamin (Glynn)
Charles (Columbia)
Jessey (Wilkinson)
John (Gwinnett)
Lillibridge, John (Chatham)
Oliver (Chatham)
Robert (Chatham)
Limburger, David (Effingham)
Mary C. (Effingham)
Lin, Charles M. (Columbia)
John (Columbia)
Linch, Benjamon (Putnam)
Charles (Putnam)
Cuthbut (Jasper)
Garill (Putnam)
Harvey (Putnam)
James (Greene)
John (Putnam)
Louis H. (Putnam)
Mary (Putnam)
Lindley, James (Walton)
Jonathon (Walton)
Lindly, Elizabeth (Walton)
Lindon, Matthew (McIntosh)
Lindsay, Abraham (Jasper)
Caleb (Warren)
David (Washington)
Dennis (Warren)
Lindsey, Abraham (Wilkes)
Ann (Jefferson)
Benjamin (Wilkes)
Hester (Montgomery)
Jacob (Wilkes)
James (Wilkes)
John (Montgomery)

(89)

Lindsey, John (Screven)
John (Wilkes)
John W. C. (Wilkes)
Mary (Emanuel)
Mary (Wilkes)
Polly (Warren)
Lindsy, Esther (Jackson)
Lindy, Dolphin (Jackson)
Lineard, John (Hall)
Lines, John (Wilkes)
Samuel (Liberty)
Lingo, Moses (Washington)
Pinkston (Washington)
Lingould, William (Baldwin)
Linman, John (Richmond)
Linn, John (Columbia)
William (2) (Jasper)
Linns, John G., Sr. (Hancock)
Linsay, Parham (Jasper)
Linsey, Adam P. (2) (Hancock)
Clabourn (Greene)
David (Greene)
Jacob (Jones)
James (Wilkinson)
Jeremiah (Greene)
John (Wilkinson)
P. (Jasper)
William, Jr. (Wilkinson)
William, Sr. (Wilkinson)
Linten, Alexander B. (Greene)
Linton, Dennis (Jones)
Lion, Elizabeth (Elbert)
Elizabeth (Wilkes)
Lions, Joseph (Wilkes)
Lipferd, H. T. M. M. (Elbert)
Lipham, Daniel (Putnam)
Lipharn, Abraham (Putnam)
Lippitt, Warren (Chatham)
Lipsey, James (Jones)
Rasco (Jones)
William (Emanuel)
Liptrot, James (Burke)
John (Burke)
Nelly (Burke)
Sarah (Burke)
Lisam, Richard M. (Jasper)
Lishness, A. (Bryan)
Lissenby, William (Burke)
Lister, James C. (Pulaski)
Literal, Richard (Hall)
Litner, A. (Jasper)
Litsey(?), Elijah (Screven)
Little, Archabald (Screven)
Archibald (Wilkes)
Edmond (Washington)
Elizabeth (Burke)
Forester (Jefferson)
George (Pulaski)
Jacob (Richmond)
Jesse (Putnam)
John (Lincoln)

John (Pulaski)
John C. (Wilkes)
Joseph (Jackson)
Josiah (Jackson)
Kinchen (Putnam)
Littleberry (Wilkes)
Louis (Putnam)
Robert (Putnam)
Sherrod (Wilkes)
Tabitha (Hancock)
Thomas (Hancock)
Thomas (2) (Wilkes)
William (Jefferson)
William (Pulaski)
William (Putnam)
William (Screven)
William (Wilkes)
Littlejohn, Abraham (Greene)
Thomas (Jasper)
Littleton, Enoch (Wilkes)
James (Wilkes)
John (Warren)
John (Wilkes)
Mary (Wilkes)
Moses (Lincoln)
Southery (Jones)
Lively, Charles (Morgan)
Elizabeth (Burke)
Mathew (Burke)
James D. (Burke)
Liverman, Mathis (Wilkinson)
Livermore, Brown (Wilkinson)
Livey, Lewis (?) (Camden)
Livingston, (torn) (Laurens)
Ann (Pulaski)
Barney (Telfair)
Isaac (Greene)
Jane (Putnam)
John (Greene)
John (Laurens)
John (Wilkes)
Mary (Laurens)
Mikell (Telfair)
Paul (McIntosh)
Peter L. (Burke)
Samuel (Greene)
Thomas (Jones)
William (Jefferson)
Livingstone, Joseph (Jefferson)
Lloyd, Nancy (Chatham)
John (Chatham)
Josiah (Chatham)
Mrs. T. (Chatham)
Lobdell, Jeremiah (Wilkes)
Loca, Benjamin (Jones)
Loche, Leonard (Laurens)
Lochren, James (Richmond)
Lock, Davico (Greene)
Francis (Gwinnett)
John (Gwinnett)
Richard (Emanuel)

Willis (Jones)
Locke, Abner (Baldwin)
David (Jones)
James (Jones)
John (Warren)
Locket, Royal (Baldwin)
Lockett, Abner (Jones)
David (Wilkes)
James (Jones)
Lucy (Jones)
Solomon (Warren)
Warren (Warren)
William R. (Warren)
Lockette, Thomas (Warren)
Lockhard, Samuel L. (Bulloch)
William (Bulloch)
Lockhart, Barton (Lincoln)
David (Jones)
Joel (Lincoln)
John (Lincoln)
William (Jones)
Locklin, Samuel (Columbia)
Lockwell, James (Jones)
Lockwood, William (Jasper)
Lodge, John (Burke)
Levi (Burke)
Lewis (Burke)
Ruth (Burke)
Loflin, Daniel (Putnam)
James (Lincoln)
James (Putnam)
John (Putnam)
Rosemond (Putnam)
Loften, James (Camden)
Loftin, (ind.) (Laurens)
William M. (Putnam)
Lofton, Eli (Jefferson)
James (Wilkinson)
William (Telfair)
Logan, Benjamin (Washington)
James G. (Jasper)
Logett(?), Sias (Wilkinson)
Logue, Charles (Warren)
James (Hancock)
William (Jefferson)
Loing, James, Jr. (Liberty)
Lokey, William (Madison)
Londay, McLean (Screven)
Londen, Elizabeth (Effingham)
Londy, Matthew (Jefferson)
Long, Alford (2) (Hancock)
Charity (Washington)
Coleman (Hancock)
Crawford (Hancock)
Evans (Baldwin)
George (Camden)
George T. (Morgan)
Harris (Wilkinson)
Henry, Sr. (Hancock)
Henry, Jr. (Jones)
Henry, Sr. (Jones)

Long, James (Madison)
James (Screven)
James (Washington)
James (Wilkinson)
Jesse L. (Jones)
John (2) (Hancock)
John (Jackson)
John (Jones)
John (Morgan)
John (Walton)
Jonathan (Putnam)
Lewis (Jones)
Littleton (Hancock)
Littleton (Jones)
Michael (Chatham)
Richard (Jones)
Richard H. (Wilkes)
Samuel, Sr. (Madison)
Samuel, Jr. (Madison)
Stafford (Wilkinson)
Thomas (Madison)
Thomas (Morgan)
William (Washington)
Longstreet, A. B. (Greene)
G. (Richmond)
Looper, Lewis M. (Pulaski)
Loper, (ind.) (Effingham)
Abel G. (Telfair)
Ara (Chatham)
Joshua (Bryan)
Lord, Abraham (Tattnall)
Claudias (Bulloch)
Henry (Hancock)
John (Washington)
Mathias (Clarke)
Nancy (Walton)
Robert (Clarke)
Samuel (Wilkinson)
William (Jackson)
William (Walton)
William (Wilkinson)
Lorry, Henry (Appling)
Lot, Daniel (Appling)
Lott, Arthur (Jefferson)
Delilah (Montgomery)
Ellis (Lincoln)
Jesse (Columbia)
Mark (Lincoln)
Robert (Hancock)
Louch, George (Hancock)
Louden, Robert (Jefferson)
Loughlin, William (Jackson)
Louis, Marey (Richmond)
Pierce B. (Jackson)
Louker, William (Madison)
Louther, Mary (Bulloch)
Loral, Dingley (Warren)
Love, Amos (Laurens)
Andrew (Jones)
Daniel (Telfair)
David (Morgan)

James (Effingham)
James (Walton)
John (Emanuel)
John (Greene)
John (Putnam)
John (Walton)
John C. (Telfair)
Josephus (Greene)
Mary (Jones)
William (Greene)
Lovejoy, E. (Jasper)
Minsy (Jackson)
Samuel (Jasper)
Simion (Jackson)
William (Jasper)
John (Jackson)
Lovel, Nancy (Columbia)
William (Columbia)
Lovelace, Allen (Columbia)
James (Columbia)
Jannet (Columbia)
Lovelady, John (Habersham)
Lovell, David (Effingham)
Loverick, Jordan (Lincoln)
Lovett, Duncan (Lincoln)
Fereby (Washington)
James (Hancock)
Lemuel (Hancock)
Richard (Warren)
Robert W. (Screven)
Thomas F., Jr. (Screven)
Thomas Z. (Screven)
Lovin, Arthur (Greene)
Gabriel (Oglethorpe)
Lydia (Pulaski)
Loving, James (Morgan)
John (Jackson)
Richard (Clarke)
Thomas (Clarke)
Lovingood, Harman (Elbert)
Lovings, Richmond (Tattnall)
Low, Ann (McIntosh)
Christopher (Chatham)
Edmund (Baldwin)
James (Baldwin)
James (Morgan)
James (Warren)
John (Jones)
Obedience (Baldwin)
Ralph (Putnam)
Samuel (McIntosh)
Sarah (Wilkes)
Stephen (Laurens)
Thomas (Elbert)
Thomas (Warren)
Vincent B. (Wilkes)
William (Hancock)
Lowder, Hamilton (Camden)
Lowe, Aaron (Jefferson)
Basil (Jefferson)
Benjamin (Jones)

Curtis (Columbia)
David (Columbia)
David (Greene)
Henry (Jones)
Isaac (Columbia)
John (Jones)
John (Washington)
Jno. E. (Jones)
William (2) (Jones)
William B. (Jones)
Lowery, John (Jefferson)
Shadrach (Jackson)
Simeon (Burke)
Thomas (Jefferson)
Thomas W. (McIntosh)
Lowremore, Sarah (Elbert)
Lowrens, Mary (Jones)
Lowrey, Andrew (Jefferson)
Christopher (Jefferson)
Henry (Gwinnett)
Joseph (Jefferson)
Patience (Jefferson)
Robert (Jefferson)
William (Jefferson)
Lowreymore, Samuel (Elbert)
Lowrimore, James (Elbert)
Lowry, Edmond (Elbert)
James (Jackson)
Levi (Jackson)
Meshack (Jasper)
Nathan (Jackson
William (Glynn) — Solomon (Appling)
Lowsalting, William (Walton)
Loyall, Charles (Wilkes)
Jesse (Jasper)
Loyd, Alston (2) (Hancock)
Charles (Morgan)
Daniel (Washington)
Elijah (Morgan)
George (Morgan)
Isham (Jones)
James (Camden)
James, Jr. (Jasper)
James, Sr. (Jasper)
James (Morgan)
Joseph (Morgan)
Joseph (Richmond)
Richard I. (Jasper)
Thomas, Sr. (Hancock)
Thomas (2) (Jasper)
Loyless, Henry (Warren)
James (Warren)
Lucas, Abraham B. (Wilkinson)
Barbary (Morgan)
Berry (Jones)
Edmond (Greene)
Frederick (Jones)
John (Baldwin)
John (Hancock)
John M. (Effingham)
Polly (Walton)

(91)

Lucas, Robert (Hancock)
  Samuel (Washington)
  William (2) (Hancock)
  William D. (Hancock)
  Willie (col.) (Greene)
Luce, Lewis (Jones)
Lucena, Thomas (Chatham)
Lucinda, Michael (Chatham)
Luck, Eldridge (Jackson)
Luckett, Thomas H. (Wilkes)
Luckey, James (Greene)
  John (Putnam)
Luckie, James (Oglethorpe)
Lucky, James (Jackson)
  James (Richmond)
  John (Richmond)
  Kezzihiah (Oglethorpe)
(?) Nathan (Richmond)
Lucky, Samuel (Wilkes)
  William (Columbia)
  William (2) (Putnam)
Luellin, Jonathan (Habersham)
  Joseph (Habersham)
Luffburrow, M. (Chatham)
Luggin(?), Chaten D.
         (Oglethorpe)
Luke, Daniel (Jasper)
  James (Columbia)
  John (Jackson)
  John Harper (Emanuel)
  Martin (Walton)
  Reubin (Columbia)
  Susanna (Clarke)
  Thomas (Columbia)
Lumkin, Polly and John
         (Jasper)
Lumpkin, Betsey (Madison)
  Dickerson (Jones)
  Edmund W. (Burke)
  George (Hall)
  George (Oglethorpe)
  Henry H. (Oglethorpe)
  James (Greene)
  John (Oglethorpe)
  Joseph (Oglethorpe)
  Philip (Burke)
  Robert (Hall)
  Robert (Morgan)
  Sack (Oglethorpe)
  Samuel (Oglethorpe)
  William (Greene)
  William (2) (Oglethorpe)
  William (Richmond)
  Wilson (Morgan)
Lumsby, Thomas (Hancock)
Lumsdel, John (Jasper)
Lumsol, Jeremiah (Jasper)
Lunceford, George (Elbert)
  William (Elbert)
Lunderson, Joseph (Jackson)

Lundy, Henry (overseer for)
         (Hancock)
  James (Hancock)
  Peyton L. (Hancock)
  Thomas (Hancock)
  William (Screven)
Lungino, James (Walton)
Lungins, Hugh (Putnam)
Lunsford, Bailey (Wilkes)
  Jacob (Wilkes)
  James (Elbert)
  John (Oglethorpe)
  Peter (Wilkes)
  William (Oglethorpe)
  William (Wilkes)
Luntsford, James (Putnam)
  Moses (Putnam)
Lupo, Moreland (Hancock)
Luther, G. (Richmond)
Lyle, Charly (Jackson)
  Delmus (Jackson)
  John (Jackson)
  Mathew (Walton)
  William (Jackson)
Lyles, Jesse (Hall)
  Philip (Hall)
  Randolph (Hall)
Lynch, David (Greene)
  George (Jasper)
  Henry (Burke)
  Isaac (Jackson)
Lyne, Elizabeth (Greene)
Lyner, Christopher (Habersham)
Lynn, Asa (Warren)
  David (Warren)
  John (Tattnall)
Lynum, William (Washington)
Lyon, Dixon (Columbia)
  Edmond (Columbia)
  Edmond (Lincoln)
  James (Clarke)
  John (Columbia)
  John (Jefferson)
  John (Richmond)
  Johnathon (Washington)
  Martha (Elbert)
  Nathan (Putnam)
  Norris (Oglethorpe)
  Peter (Burke)
  Thomas (Columbia)
  Thomas (Lincoln)
  William (Jefferson)
  William T. (Putnam)
Lyons, James (Richmond)
  Jesse (Putnam)
  Mikel (Camden)
Lysle, William (Jackson)

M

Maberry, Thomas W. (Elbert)
Mabry, Ephraim (Gwinnett)
  Gray (Greene)
  Jamison (Lincoln)
  Kinch P. (Greene)
  Reason (Jasper)
Mabury, Allen (Wilkes)
McAlister, John (Jones)
McAllester, James (Jasper)
McAllister, Charles (Warren)
  George W. (Bryan)
  Judge (Chatham)
McAllum, Hugh (Hancock)
McAlpen, Alexander (Greene)
McAlpin, Arch. (Chatham)
  Henry (Chatham)
Macan, Catherine (Burke)
  Margaret (Burke)
McAnless, William
         (Washington)
McAntone, James (Hall)
McArthur, John (2) (Hancock)
  John (Tattnall)
  Peter (Wilkinson)
McArty, John (Oglethorpe)
Macbeth, James (Pulaski)
McBride, David (Hall)
  David S. (Greene)
  James (Burke)
  James (Gwinnett)
  John (2) (Jefferson)
  John (Putnam)
  John (Wilkinson)
  Joseph (Greene)
  Levan (Wilkinson)
  Samuel (Jefferson)
  Thomas (Burke)
  Thomas (Jefferson)
  William (Jefferson)
McBryde, John (Jones)
  Robert (Jones)
McCain, William (Jasper)
McCall, (ind.) (Bulloch)
  (ind.) (Screven)
  Francis (Bulloch)
  George (Bulloch)
  George (Screven)
  Hugh (Chatham)
  John (Effingham)
  John (Telfair)
  John E. (Bulloch)
  Nathaniel (Pulaski)
  Robert (Bulloch)
  Thomas (Laurens)
  William (Screven)
McCallen, John (Greene)
McCalley, Allen(?) (Appling)
McCallum, William (Clarke)
McCalpen, William (Walton)

McCane, William D. (Elbert)
McCard, William (Jasper)
McCardal, John (Bulloch)
McCardell, Charlie (Jones)
   James (Effingham)
McCardin, Thomas (Morgan)
McCarthin, Charles (Telfair)
McCarthy, Roger (Jones)
McCarty, Mr. (Chatham)
   Ann (Chatham)
   Anthony (Morgan)
   Charles W. (Warren)
   James (Walton)
   John (Jackson)
   John (Walton)
   John (Wilkinson)
   Mary (Warren)
   Michael (McIntosh)
   Peter (Telfair)
   Reese (Warren)
   Sally (Oglethorpe)
   William, Jr. (Wilkinson)
   William, Sr. (Wilkinson)
McCasey, Andrew (Chatham)
McCathrines, Malcolm (Liberty)
McCay, Daniel (Putnam)
McCerley, William (Elbert)
McCissac, Archibald (Putnam)
McClain, Rubens (Oglethorpe)
   Samuel F. (Greene)
   Thomas (Oglethorpe)
McClane, Daniel (Emanuel)
McClarny, John (Lincoln)
McClean, Andra (Columbia)
McCleland, Andrew (Tattnall)
   William (Tattnall)
McClelland, John, Jr. (Liberty)
   John, Sr. (Liberty)
McClendon, Benjamin
   (Wilkinson)
   Bennaniah (Morgan)
   Daniel (Telfair)
   Haley (Wilkinson)
   Harry (col.) (Columbia)
   Jacob (Wilkinson)
   Jesse (Burke)
   Job (Wilkinson)
   Pherba (Wilkinson)
   Robert (Morgan)
   Samuel (2) (Morgan)
   Thomas, Sr. (Walton)
McCleskey, Benjamin (Hall)
   David G. (Hall)
   David H. (Hall)
   Jabel (Hall)
   James (Hall)
   James (Jackson)
McClester, John (Jackson)
   Joseph (Jackson)
McCliny, Ruben (Jackson)
McCluan, Arch. (Chatham)

McClung, John (Hall)
McClure, E. (Jasper)
   H. (Richmond)
McCollet, Ela___ (Emanuel)
McColloh, John (Hancock)
McCollum, Archd.
   (Montgomery)
   Rachal (Wilkinson)
McColor, Benjamin (Wilkinson)
   John (Wilkinson)
   Thomas (Wilkinson)
   William (Wilkinson)
McColum, Patrick (Wilkinson)
McCommen, James (Greene)
McConel, Joseph (Jackson)
McConnel, John (Hall)
   William (Wilkinson)
McConnell, (ind.) (Liberty)
   John (2) (Hall)
McCook, Alexander (Wilkinson)
   Daniel (Wilkinson)
   Mary (Wilkinson)
McCorcle, Archibald (Lincoln)
   John (Lincoln)
McCord, Elisha (Lincoln)
   James (Lincoln)
   John (Clarke)
   John (Lincoln)
   John (Wilkes)
   Mary (Clarke)
McCorkle, Robert (Columbia)
McCormac, John (Jasper)
McCormack, John (Elbert)
   Thomas (Wilkes)
McCormic, Alex(?) (Putnam)
McCormick, Mrs. (Chatham)
   Abner (Warren)
   David (Bryan)
   Jas. (Camden)
   James (Madison)
   James (Pulaski)
   John (2) (Pulaski)
   John (Warren)
   John (Wilkes)
   Mathies (Pulaski)
   Nancy (Columbia)
   W. (Chatham)
   William (Pulaski)
McCormies(?), Lemuel (Wilkes)
McCormis, Drewsiller
   (Montgomery)
McCorquedale, Daniel
   (Washington)
   Malcolm (Washington)
McCorrey, Edward (Emanuel)
McCosta, John B. (Putnam)
McCoullar, J. (Richmond)
McCoward, Joshua (Telfair)
McCowen, Alex (Oglethorpe)
   Duncan (Morgan)
   Finlaw (Morgan)

   John W. (Morgan)
   William (Morgan)
   William Davis (Morgan)
McCowin, Polly (Walton)
McCowley, James (Morgan)
McCoy, Abner (Putnam)
   Archibald (Putnam)
   E. (Morgan)
   Henry (Greene)
   Henry (Morgan)
   Hugh (Hall)
   Mrs. J. (Richmond)
   Jacob (Morgan)
   James (Oglethorpe)
   James (Putnam)
   John (Gwinnett)
   John (2) (Morgan)
   John (Pulaski)
   John (Warren)
   Leroy (Morgan)
   N. (Jasper)
   Nathaniel (Wilkes)
   Nathaniel (overseer)
   (Wilkes)
   Neil (Telfair)
   Rebecca S. (McIntosh)
   Robt. (Chatham)
   Robert (Putnam)
   Sarah (Jefferson)
   Thomas (Hall)
   Thomas (Morgan)
McCrackan, William (Jasper)
McCraig, Neil (Wilkinson)
McCraney, Daniel (Montgomery)
   Neil (Montgomery)
McCrannie, (ind.) (Liberty)
McCrarrey, Mary (Wilkinson)
McCrary, Bartley (Baldwin)
   Bartley, Jr. (Baldwin)
   Eze (Jackson)
   Lettis (Warren)
   Robert (Baldwin)
McCravy, D. S. (Jackson)
   Hanah (Baldwin)
   John (Baldwin)
   John (Telfair)
   Wiley (Baldwin)
McCray, M. (Warren)
McCrea, August (Richmond)
   Daniel (Appling)
McCreary, Fanny (Warren)
   John (Warren)
   Robert (Habersham)
   Samuel (Warren)
McCree, Sam'l. N. R. (Baldwin)
McCrimmon, Sarah A. (Bryan)
McCrone, Peter (Wilkinson)
McCuen, Thomas (Madison)
McCullar, H. (Richmond)
   J. (Richmond)
   Joseph (Emanuel)

McCullar, Samuel (Oglethorpe)
  Samuel (Richmond)
McCuller, (torn) (Laurens)
  Hardy (Emanuel)
McCullers, Burwell (Warren)
  Colston (Emanuel)
  John (Burke)
  Matthew C. (Burke)
  William (Walton)
McCulley, Thomas (Greene)
McCulloch, William (Gwinnett)
McCullock, Mary (Jones)
McCullor, John (Richmond)
McCullough, Jacob (Jefferson)
  William (Clarke)
McCurdy, James (Madison)
  John (Madison)
  John, Jr. (Madison)
McCurry, Angus, Jr. (Elbert)
  Angus, Sr. (Elbert)
  John (Elbert)
  Laughlin (Elbert)
McCutchen, Joseph (Hall)
  John (Hall)
  Robert (Hall)
  William (Hall)
McDade, J. (Richmond)
McDaniel, Alex (Hall)
  Bartley (Jones)
  Charles (Oglethorpe)
  Daniel (2) (Hancock)
  Daniel (Telfair)
  Daniel (Washington)
  David (Jackson)
  David (Laurens)
  Emily (Hancock)
  Ennis (Washington)
  Isaac (Jackson)
  Jacob (Jones)
  Jas. (Jackson)
  James (Wilkinson)
  John (Burke)
  John (2) (Clarke)
  John (Walton)
  John (Wilkinson)
  Margaret (Hancock)
  Mary (Washington)
  Moses (Hall)
  Nancy (Jones)
  Randa____ (Burke)
  Sarah (Pulaski)
  Susanna (Washington)
  Telman (Clarke)
  Thomas (2) (Washington)
  William (Jones)
  William (Wilkinson)
McDole, John (Greene)
McDonald, Absalom (Warren)
  Alexander (Elbert)
  Allen (Tattnall)
  Andrew (Warren)

Angus (Wayne)
Barbary (Putnam)
Brittain (Warren)
Charles (2) (Hancock)
Charles J. (Jones)
Daniel (Columbia)
Daniel, (McIntosh)
Daniel (Warren)
George (McIntosh)
Hugh (Habersham)
Ishmael (Warren)
James (Columbia)
James (Jackson)
Jeremiah (Tattnall)
John (Appling)
John (Baldwin)
John (Chatham)
John (Columbia)
John (2) (Elbert)
John (Jefferson)
John (Putnam)
John (2) (Tattnall)
John (Warren)
Mary (Warren)
Polly (Warren)
R. (Tattnall)
Robert (Glynn)
William (Early)
William (McIntosh)
McDonell, Joshua (Laurens)
McDonnell, John (Chatham)
McDonough, B. (Chatham)
  Henry (Chatham)
McDougal, Thomas (Jasper)
McDougall, Alexander
              (Washington)
  Daniel (Washington)
McDow, John (Hall)
McDowall, Patrick (Richmond)
  William (Jasper)
McDowel, Robert (Jackson)
  William (Jackson)
McDowell, D. and Cranford
              (Jasper)
  Isaac (Warren)
  John (Lincoln)
  John (Montgomery)
  M. (Jasper)
  Sussannah (Warren)
  Thomas (Jones)
  Thomas (Washington)
McDuff, Rich'd. Jasper
  Richard R. (Gwinnett)
  William (Hall)
McDuffe, Dugle (Telfair)
  Malcolm (Washington)
McDuffee, John (Washington)
  Murdoc (Telfair)
McDuffie, Duencan (Jones)
McDuffy, Archibald (Emanuel)
McDurmon, Ballard (Morgan)

McDurmott, Edward (Lincoln)
McEachin, John (Montgomery)
McEllers, Joseph (Walton)
McElray, William (Oglethorpe)
McElroy, James (Morgan)
  Samuel (Oglethorpe)
McElvin, Alias (Montgomery)
  William (Bryan)
McElvy, William (Tattnall)
McErven, Robert (Gwinnett)
McEver, Andrew (Madison)
  Brice (Hall)
  John (Jackson)
  John (Jackson)
  Jos. (Jackson)
  William (Jackson)
McEvoy, Edward (Greene)
McEwen, James H. (Gwinnett)
McEwin, James (Oglethorpe)
  John (Oglethorpe)
McEwing, Thomas (Jackson)
McFaddin, Davis (Putnam)
McFail, Eli (Liberty)
  Judah (Liberty)
McFaling, James H. (Warren)
McFarlan, Peter (Chatham)
McFarland, Daniel (Columbia)
  Douglas (Jones)
  Duncan (Chatham)
  J. B. (Tattnall)
  John (Chatham)
  John (Telfair)
  Rachel (Columbia)
  Washington (Habersham)
McFarlen, Aaron H. (Jones)
  Charles (Wilkinson)
  Peter (Jones)
  Usa (Jones)
  William (Jones)
McFarlin, Sarah (Camden)
  William (Hall)
McFerson, Martin P. (Jones)
McGahagin, William
              (Effingham)
McGahee, Daniel (Washington)
  David (Columbia)
  John (Columbia)
  William (Columbia)
  William B. (Pulaski)
  Willis (Columbia)
McGainer, (ind.) (Laurens)
McGanghey, James (Putnam)
McGar, Owen (Richmond)
McGarvey, Dorcas (Chatham)
McGathy, Jane (Jasper)
McGea, Mary (Richmond)
Mcgee, Anselem (Elbert)
McGee, Ephraim (Warren)
M'gee, Henry (Screven)
McGee, James (2) (Morgan)
  John (Columbia)

(94)

McGee, Levin (Putnam)
Milbry (Warren)
Reuben (Warren)
William (2) (Hancock)
McGehee, Davis (Jones)
Mcgehee, Hugh (Elbert)
McGehee, James (Baldwin)
James (Irwin)
Jane (Jasper)
Jonah (Jones)
Joseph (Jones)
Thomas (Jones)
William (Baldwin)
McGhee, Abner (Oglethorpe)
John (Oglethorpe)
McGibone, William (Greene)
McGilany, James (Hancock)
McGill, James (Chatham)
Milly (Lincoln)
Morris (Lincoln)
Peter (Montgomery)
McGillis, Randolph (Camden)
McGilvery, D. (Chatham)
McGinis, James (Jackson)
McGinley, Meshac (Baldwin)
McGinnis, James (Gwinnett)
William (Jackson)
McGintry, Washington
(Wilkinson)
McGinty, Alexander (Greene)
Isaac (Putnam)
John (Wilkes)
John A. (Wilkes)
Robert (Baldwin)
Robert (2) (Hancock)
Shadrack (Putnam)
Thomas (Wilkinson)
William (Baldwin)
McGish, James (Jones)
McGlaning, George (Warren)
McGlawn, Edmond (Putnam)
Hardy (Putnam)
Jeremiah (Putnam)
McGlochlan, John (Warren)
McGlohan, Adam (Jefferson)
McGlothlin, D. C. (Richmond)
McGomick, Seth (Walton)
McGommery, Margarett
(Wilkinson)
McGough, John (Greene)
Robert (2) (Jones)
William (Greene)
McGouirk, Benjamin (Walton)
David (Walton)
John (Walton)
Mossy (Walton)
McGourik, William (Walton)
McGowan, Joseph (Liberty)
McGowen, John (Jefferson)
John (Liberty)
McGowin, Alexander (Screven)

McGowing, William
(Wilkinson)
MacGran, B. (Chatham)
McGran, R. (Chatham)
McGranberry, Samuel (Jones)
McGrath, Thomas (Richmond)
McGraw, John (Jones)
Jno. P. (Jones)
McGready, Archibald (Hall)
McGregor, Charles (McIntosh)
McGregory, Dempsey (Pulaski)
McGriff, Patrick (Pulaski)
Richard (Pulaski)
Thomas (Pulaski)
McGrigor, Duncan (Tattnall)
McGruder, G. (Richmond)
McGuan (?), Thomas
(Richmond)
McGuin, Frederick (Gwinnett)
McGuire, Charlie I. (Screven)
D. (?) (Chatham)
Thompson (Hall)
William D. (Elbert)
Zemma (Hall)
McGuirter, John (Hancock)
McCurd, William (Jones)
McHargue, Alex (Jackson)
John (Greene)
John (Jackson)
McHenry, James (Chatham)
McHume, Malcom (Richmond)
McIin (?), Michael (Jackson)
McIllroy, Henry (Jasper)
Isaac (Jasper)
James (Jasper)
James, Sr. (Jasper)
John I. (Jasper)
McIlray, Billy (Oglethorpe)
Sarah (Oglethorpe)
McInsey, John (Telfair)
McIntial, Hu (Telfair)
McIntire, Duncan (Telfair)
M'Intire, James (Habersham)
Joseph (Habersham)
McIntosh, Agness (McIntosh)
Alexander (McIntosh)
Allex (Montgomery)
Ann (McIntosh)
Barbara (McIntosh)
D. (Jasper)
Daniel (Greene)
David (Morgan)
Elisa (Chatham)
Hamden (McIntosh)
Hety (McIntosh)
J. H. (Camden)
James (Wilkes)
Jesse (Morgan)
Dr. John (McIntosh)
Genl. John (McIntosh)
Lachlain (McIntosh)

Peter (2) (Chatham)
Robert (Liberty)
William H. (McIntosh)
William I. (McIntosh)
McIntyre, Daniel (Montgomery)
McInvale, James (Jones)
McIsac, Duncan (Putnam)
John (Putnam)
McKay, George (Burke)
Hugh (Jones)
John (Telfair)
MacKay, Littleton (Wilkes)
McKean, Mrs. (Chatham)
Rev. John (Liberty)
Robert (Greene)
Robert (Richmond)
McKebon, Edward (Oglethorpe)
McKee, Alexander (Wilkinson)
Betsey (Madison)
John (Putnam)
Thomas (Jones)
McKeehew, Zaccheus (Jasper)
McKeen, H. (Jasper)
McKeller, Archibald (Emanuel)
McKenel, George (Wilkes)
McKennan, John (Hancock)
McKenney, Moses (Warren)
McKennis, Lydia M. (Jones)
McKenny, George (Baldwin)
John, Jr. (Lincoln)
John, Sr. (Lincoln)
Kinchin (Warren)
Travis (Lincoln)
McKensey, John (Jones)
McKensie, John (Jones)
William (Morgan)
McKenstry, Alexander
(Richmond)
McKenzey, George (Jefferson)
McKenzie, D. W. (Chatham)
Keneth (Putnam)
Peter (Putnam)
Samuel (Lincoln)
McKessac, James (Putnam)
McKessicks, William (Jones)
McKever, Alexander (Liberty)
McKewin, Isaac (Madison)
McKey, Littleton (Wilkes)
Rebecca (Wilkinson)
William (Wilkinson)
Mackey, Patrick (Jackson)
Mrs. R. (Chatham)
Mackie, Thomas (Jones)
Macking, John (Habersham)
McKinley, Archd C. (Greene)
Joseph (Washington)
McKinne, Benjamin (Baldwin)
Daniel (Screven)
William (Baldwin)
McKinney, Michael (Columbia)
Roger (Screven)

McKinnie, Barna (Richmond)
   D. (Richmond)
   Eli (Jones)
   James (Jasper)
   John (Richmond)
McKinnis, Archibald (Irwin)
McKinnon, Archd.
        (Montgomery)
   Charles (Telfair)
   Duncan (Montgomery)
   John (Chatham)
   John (Montgomery)
McKinny, Charles, Sr.
        (Jackson)
   Charles (Jackson)
   Eli (Lincoln)
   Michael (Columbia)
   Mordecai (Lincoln)
   Samuel (Jackson)
   William (Columbia)
   Zachariah (Columbia)
McKinon, Jeston (Fem) (Jones)
McKinsey, Aaron (Jones)
   Dice (Hall)
   Daniel (Montgomery)
   Robert D. (Screven)
McKlahannon, John (Hall)
McKlehanon, John (Jackson)
McKleroy, James (Clarke)
   John (Madison)
   Mary (Madison)
   Needham (Clarke)
   Peltin (Madison)
Macklin, Edmund (Baldwin)
Mackling, Jane (Wilkes)
McKnight, James (Gwinnett)
   James (Jackson)
   John (Walton)
   Matthew (Gwinnett)
   William (Walton)
McKorkle. John (Lincoln)
McKoy, David (Jasper)
McKrary, Mary (Jasper)
Macks, James (Jones)
Mckuroy, Lewis (Madison)
Macky, John (Jones)
McLain, Ephrain (Gwinnett)
   John (Morgan)
Maelamar, C. (Jasper)
McLamore, George (Hancock)
Maclamore,
  (McLamore), Wilson (Jones)
Mclane, Harry (Camden)
McLane, James (Jones)
   James (Oglethorpe)
   Jesse (fem.) (Jones)
   John (Putnam)
McLarin, Harrison (Morgan)
McLary, James (Putnam)
McLaughlin, Benjamin (Wilkes)
   David (Oglethorpe)

   John (Oglethorpe)
McLaws, James (Richmond)
McLealand, Silas (Tattnall)
McLean, Captn. (Chatham)
   Allen (Jasper)
   James (Richmond)
   John (Chatham)
   John (Richmond)
   John (Warren)
   Laughlin (Washington)
McLeis (?), John (Putnam)
McLellan, William (Hancock)
McLelon, Thomas (Gwinnett)
McLemon, Jones (Hancock)
McLenden, Dennis (Putnam)
   Frances (Putnam)
   Jacob (Jasper)
McLendon, (ind.) (Laurens)
   Allen (Jasper)
   Burwell (Jones)
   E. (Jasper)
   Eldad (Wilkes)
   Elizabeth (Jones)
   I. (Jasper)
   Isaac (Wilkes)
   John (Jones)
   Lewis (Wilkes)
   Mason (Washington)
   Medado (Wilkes)
   Milly (Jones)
   P. (Jasper)
   Simon (Wilkes)
   Simpson (Wilkes)
   Wiley (Jasper)
   William (Wilkes)
McLennan, John (Pulaski)
McLenon, Andrew (Camden)
   Charles (Camden)
McLeod, Angus (Montgomery)
   Angus (Washington)
   Daniel (,Lincoln)
   Daniel (Washington)
   Mrs. E. (Chatham)
   James (Montgomery)
   John (Glynn)
   John (Tattnall)
   John (Telfair)
   Malcom (Clarke)
   Murdoc (Montgomery)
   Murdock (Pulaski)
   Neil (Washington)
   Norman, Jr. (Telfair)
   Norman (Telfair)
   Wiley (Appling)
   William M. (Montgomery)
McLeode(?), Isabella
        (Chatham)
Mcleroy, John (Madison)
McLesky, James (Wilkes)
   Thomas (Wilkes)
McLin, John (Bryan)

McLochlan, John (Montgomery)
McLoud (Jones)
McLouden, Joseph (Jasper)
McLoudon, Amos (Jasper)
   Joel (Jasper)
   Stephen (Jasper)
McLowdan, Holden (Appling)
McLucky, Hyram (Jones)
McLure, Samuel B. (Gwinnett)
McLurin(?), Robert (Jackson)
McLusky, L. (Oglethorpe)
McMahan, Barnett (Walton)
   John (Walton)
McMahon, Moses (Burke)
McMaley, Neal (McIntosh)
McManning, Robert
        (Richmond)
McMath. ____jah (Warren)
   Hackabah (Warren)
   Joseph (Warren)
   Philip (Wilkinson)
   William (Jones)
McMelon, Alexander
        (Wilkinson)
McMichael, Eliz'th (Jasper)
   G. (Jasper)
   I. (2) (Jasper)
   John (2) (Jasper)
   M. (Jasper)
   P. (Jasper)
   Shad (Jasper)
McMichel, William (Walton)
McMicken, Nathaniel (Wilkes)
McMilen, Danel (Camden)
McMillan, Angus (Montgomery)
   Archbald (2)
        (Montgomery)
   Archibald (Putnam)
   Neil (Montgomery)
McMillen, A. (Washington)
   Amon (Jones)
McMillin, James (Telfair)
   William (Telfair)
McMillon, Hector
        (Montgomery)
McMullan, Elizabeth (Elbert)
   Jeremiah (Elbert)
   Lewis (Elbert)
   Neal (Elbert)
   Patrick (Elbert)
   Thomas (Elbert)
   William (Elbert)
McMullen, John (Baldwin)
   John (Gwinnett)
   Micajah (Greene)
McMullin, James (Jackson)
   Marget (Jackson)
   Peter (Jackson)
McMurphy, Daniel (Richmond)
McMurran, John (Montgomery)
McMurray, David (Jasper)

McMurray, John (Morgan)
McMurrey, William (Wilkinson)
McMurrin, (torn) (Laurens)
McMurry, David (Wilkinson)
James (Greene)
John (Jasper)
William (Morgan)
McNabb, Daniel (Tattnall)
McNail, Samuel (Jefferson)
McNair, Daniel (Warren)
Gilbert (Wilkinson)
John (Warren)
John (Wilkinson)
Robert (Warren)
Samuel (Columbia)
McNall, Robert (Burke)
William (Burke)
McNaly(?), William (Bulloch)
McNar, Duncan (Telfair)
McNares, James,
Slaves of) (Columbia)
McNatt(?), Benj. L. (Burke)
McNeal, Archibald (Putnam)
Daniel (Jefferson)
Daniel (Laurens)
James (Jones)
John (Wilkinson)
Neil (2) (Putnam)
McNealy, Esther (Burke)
McNeece, James (Jackson)
McNeece(?), William
(Warren)
McNeel, Henry (Hall)
McNeely, Eleanor (Jefferson)
Samuel (Jefferson)
William (Jefferson)
McNees, William (Clarke)
McNeff, Charles (Chatham)
McNeil, Archibald (Columbia)
Daniel (Columbia)
Duncan (Columbia)
James (Putnam)
Neil (Telfair)
William (Columbia)
McNeir, John (Columbia)
McNiel, Archibald
(Washington)
Mary (Washington)
Nancy (Warren)
McNight, (ind.) (Wilkes)
Charles (Wilkes)
McNish, John (Chatham)
Roderick (Tattnall)
McNorrell, Fielding (Burke)
Henry (Burke)
Macombs, N. (Richmond)
R. (Richmond)
Macon, William G. (Hancock)
McQueen, John (Chatham)
John (Montgomery)
John (Washington)

Lydia (Chatham)
William (2) (Chatham)
McQueur, Lewis (Morgan)
McQuire, Anderson (Elbert)
David (Greene)
Joseph (McIntosh)
William (Elbert)
McRab, John (Pulaski)
McRae, Alexander (Telfair)
Catherine (Telfair)
Christopher (Telfair)
Daniel (Montgomery)
Farquhard (Montgomery)
John (Telfair)
Philip (Telfair)
McRay, Archibald (Telfair)
McRay(?), Eppa (Hancock)
McRight, John (Hall)
McRory, John (Effingham)
McRoy, Curtis (Morgan)
McSwain, Dennis (Morgan)
Edmond (Walton)
Elizabeth (Morgan)
John (Columbia)
McTear, Kindall (Warren)
McTerrell, John (Liberty)
McTyre, Frizel (Burke)
Mculer, Samuel (Oglethorpe)
McVay, David (Washington)
John (Jackson)
John (Washington)
Phany (Jackson)
McWaid, John (Screven)
McWater, Thomas (Chatham)
McWatty, Thomas (Jefferson)
McWhir, Rev. William (Liberty)
McWhirter, James (Hall)
William (Jackson)
McWhorter, Daniel (Habersham)
George (Habersham)
Hugh (Oglethorpe)
John (Oglethorpe)
William (Oglethorpe)
McWilliams, Daniel (Putnam)
McWire, Abner (Jackson)
Absalom (Jackson)
Fred'k (Jackson)
Madcalf, Henry (Jackson)
John (Jackson)
Madden, Calep (Richmond)
David (Morgan)
Dennis (Morgan)
Maddison, Thomas (Warren)
Maddix, John (Jasper)
Maddon, John (Baldwin)
William (Baldwin)
Maddox, (ind.) (Laurens)
Anthony (Greene)
B. W. (Jasper)
Benjamin (Elbert)
Chandler (Elbert)

Clabourn (Greene)
Claborn (Jackson)
Daniel (Hall)
George (Jones)
Hamlin D. (Gwinnett)
Hardy (Morgan)
James (Putnam)
Jesse (Putnam)
John (Gwinnett)
John (Putnam)
Joseph (Columbia)
Joseph (Putnam)
Josiah E. (Greene)
Leonard (Columbia)
Loston (Elbert)
Mary (Putnam)
Nathan (Pulaski)
Samuel (Jones)
Samuel (2) (Putnam)
Sarah (Emanuel)
Seaborn (Jackson)
Spencer (Putnam)
U. W. (Columbia)
Walter (Columbia)
William (Hancock)
William (Putnam)
William B. (Columbia)
Madray, Joseph (Burke)
Madry(?), Benjamin (Burke)
Mady, Joel (Jasper)
William (Jasper)
Maffin, James (Columbia)
Magee, Daniel (Pulaski)
William (Warren)
Magnam, Charley (Jones)
Magnan, John Baptiste
(Chatham)
Magruder, Archibald
(Columbia)
George, Jr., (Columbia)
Hezikiah (Columbia)
John (Burke)
John (Columbia)
Martha (Coolumbia)
William (Columbia)
Zadock (Columbia)
Maguire, John (Richmond)
Maher, Owen (Chatham)
Maho, Alfred (Telfair)
Mahon, Robert (Habersham)
Mahone, John R. (Hancock)
Peter F. (Putnam)
Roland (Putnam)
Thomas (Putnam)
William (Hancock)
Mahoney, George (Lincoln)
James (Lincoln)
Mary (Lincoln)
Mainer, George H. (Screven)
John (Morgan)

(97)

Mainer, William (Morgan)
Mainor, Hardy (Burke)
   William (Morgan)
Mairs, Winney (Wilkinson)
Majors, Richard (Jackson)
Malbritt, Nathaniel (Emanuel)
Malcom, James (Morgan)
   John (Baldwin)
   John (Morgan)
Malcolm, David (Walton)
   Ganalody (Morgan)
Malcomb, George (Morgan)
   James (Morgan)
Mald, Christopher (Wilkes)
Malden, Elias (Burke)
Maldon, Wesley (Hall)
Malgreene, Jacob (Pulaski)
Mallard, Daniel (Emanuel)
   Elijah (Columbia)
   John (Burke)
   Liddia (Liberty)
   Thomas (Liberty)
Mallet, James (Baldwin)
Mallett, Abraham (Effingham)
   Gideon (Effingham)
Mallie, Peter (Chatham)
Mallone, Robert (Putnam)
Mallory, Thomas (Burke)
   Thomas (Greene)
   William (Wilkes)
Mally, (ind.) (Baldwin)
Malone, B.(ind.) (Emanuel)
   Cheny (Washington)
   Daniel (Jones
   Edward D. (Morgan
   Elizabeth (Walton)
   Francis (Jasper)
   James (Columbia)
   John (Jasper)
   John (Putnam)
   Jones (Jasper)
   Madison (Washington)
   Martin (Columbia)
   Morgan (Columbia)
   Polly (Greene)
   R. (Richmond)
   Robert (Early)
   Sherrod (Jasper)
   Thomas (Columbia)
   William (Gwinnett)
   William (Richmond)
Malory, John (Greene)
   John (Hancock)
   William (Greene)
Malphrus, (ind.) (Liberty)
Malphus, Hardy (Washington)
   Maurice (Washington)
Malposs, John (Jasper)
Malpus, Hall (Appling)
Maltbie, William (Gwinnett)
Mammam, James (Oglethorpe)

Man, Caty (Morgan)
   David (Wilkinson)
   James (Jasper)
   John M. (Wilkinson)
   Malissa & Nancy (col.)
      (Wilkes)
   Rebecca (Morgan)
   William (Appling)
Manders, Samuel (Gwinnett)
Manderson, John (Wilkinson)
   John H. (Wilkinson)
Maner, John L. (Screven)
Manes, Benjamin (Wilkinson)
   Samuel (Wilkinson)
Mangan, James (Jones)
Mangham, James C. (Glynn)
   William (Putnam)
   Willis (Putnam)
Manghan, James M. (Putnam)
Mangum, William (Jackson)
Manifee, George (Jackson)
Manley, John A. (Oglethorpe)
   Joseph (Oglethorpe)
   William (Bryan)
Manly, David (Putnam)
   John (Putnam)
   William (Clarke)
Mann, Baker (Morgan)
   David (Greene)
   James (Elbert)
   Jessie (Greene)
   Joel (Elbert)
   Joel (Morgan)
   John (Elbert)
   John (Putnam)
   Jonathan I. (Putnam)
   Lewis (Columbia)
   Luke (Bryan)
   Reuben (Morgan)
   Mrs. S. (Richmond)
   S. H. (Richmond)
   Susan (Oglethorpe)
   Thomas (Bryan)
   <u>Thomas (Gwinnett)</u>
   William H. (Elbert)
Mannel, Charles (Chatham)
Mannga, Warren (Baldwin)
Mannin, James (Hancock)
Manning, Adam (Putnam)
   Benjamin (Pulaski)
   Benjamin, Sr. (Washington)
   Benjamin, Jr. (Washington)
   Casu (Washington)
   Isaac (Washington)
   Isaih (Putnam)
   Joseph (Glynn)
   Littleton (Putnam)
   Martha (Glynn)
   Reuben (Washington)
   Sophia(?) (Washington)
   Wright (Pulaski)

[handwritten annotation in left margin of second column: William (Appling)]

Manohanan, James (Jones)
Mansfield James (McIntosh)
Mansil, George (Pulaski)
Manson, Hugh (Jefferson)
   James (Wilkinson)
   John (Jefferson)
   William (Jefferson)
Mantz, Philip H. (Richmond)
Mapp, James (Hancock)
   John (Greene)
   Littleton (Hancock)
   Mary (Hancock)
   Robert H. (Hancock)
Marable, Richard (Clarke)
Marbury, Daniel (Wilkes)
Marbury(?), Patience
      (Richmond)
Marcellin, Capt. (Chatham)
   M. (Chatham)
March, George (Glynn)
   Nathan (Warren)
Marchant, Isaac (Jefferson)
Marchman, Ebe (Putnam)
   James (2) (Hancock)
   John (McIntosh)
   Stephen (Putnam)
Marcus, Hannah (Putnam)
   Mary (Baldwin)
   William (Putnam)
Marible, Champin (Oglethorpe)
   William (Oglethorpe)
Marie, Peter (Chatham)
Mariner, Benjamin (Jones)
Mark, John (Jones)
Markes, Joseph (Jones)
Marks, Henry (Columbia)
   John H. (Jasper)
   L. H. (Richmond)
   Stephen (Warren)
Marlan(?), Anthony
      (Oglethorpe)
Marler, Irma (Emanuel)
Marlow, George (Wilkes)
   James (Wilkes)
   James H. (Wilkes)
   Jeremiah (Wilkes)
   John (Jackson)
   Laborn (Wilkes)
   Mary (Screven)
   Paul (Effingham)
Marrable, Hartwell (Morgan)
   John (Morgan)
Marraut, (ind.) (Chatham)
Marron, Constantine (Morgan)
Mars, Alexander (Wilkinson)
Marsh, Bascom (Richmond)
   James (Emanuel)
   James (Warren)
   John (Burke)
   John (Jefferson)
   Rubin (Telfair)

Marsh, Sb(sic) (Burke)
  Taran (Jones)
Marshal, Ann Y. (Columbia)
  G. B. (Richmond)
  John (Putnam)
  Stephen B. (Putnam)
  William B. (Putnam)
Marshall, Doctor (Chatham)
  Abel (Wilkinson)
  Allen (Jones)
  Andrew (Chatham)
  Asa (Jones)
  Benjamin (Jasper)
  Francis (Clarke)
  Henry (Telfair)
  Jabus P. (Columbia)
  James(2) (Chatham)
  James (Telfair)
  John (Richmond)
  John (Telfair)
  John (Wilkinson)
  Joseph. Jr. (Jefferson)
  Joseph, Sr. (Jefferson)
  Jubal O. (Columbia)
  Luchens (Columbia)
  Matthew (Burke)
  Matthew (Jefferson)
  Mathew (Jones)
  Nakor (Putnam)
  Samuel (Columbia)
  Sarah (Columbia)
  Stephen (Putnam)
  William (Jefferson)
  William P. (Chatham)
  William S. (Burke)
Marston, Fred (Chatham)
Martain, (ind.) (Oglethorpe)
  Cluff (Oglethorpe)
  George (Wilkinson)
  Vinson (Wilkinson)
  Willey (Wilkinson)
Martand, Ward (Jasper)
Marten, Gabriel (Hancock)
Martin, A. (Jackson)
  Abram (Gwinnett)
  Absolon (Hall)
  Alexander (Clarke)
  Alexander (Jackson)
  Alexander (Liberty)
  Alexander (Oglethorpe)
  Alexander (Richmond)
  Allen (Jasper)
  Aly (Baldwin)
  Angis (Liberty)
  Ann (Hall)
  Asa (Putnam)
  Austin (Wilkes)
  Barton (Oglethorpe)
  Benjamin (Emanuel)
  Benjamin (Hall)
  Beverly (Elbert)

Charles (Washington)
David (Burke)
David (Screven)
David (Warren)
Druscilla (Warren)
E. (Jasper)
E. (2) (Richmond)
Elijah (Bulloch)
Elijah (Greene)
Elizabeth (Habersham)
Frances (Washington)
Francis (Jasper)
George (Greene)
George (Gwinnett)
George (Jefferson)
Gilly (Warren)
Henry (Appling)
Isaac (Clarke)
Isaac (Morgan)
J. (Richmond)
J. N. D. (Jasper)
Jacob (Hall)
Jacob (Jackson)
James (Bryan)
James (Columbia)
James (Greene)
James (Jackson)
James (Jefferson)
James (Warren)
James B. (Oglethorpe)
James G. (Oglethorpe)
Jesse (Hall)
Jesse (Oglethorpe)
John (Effingham)
John (2) (Elbert)
John (Hall)
John (Jackson)
John (Jasper)
John (Jefferson)
John (2) (Jones)
John (Liberty)
John (3) (Putnam)
John (Telfair)
John F. (Hancock)
John R. (Baldwin)
Jonathan (Jackson)
Joseph (Greene)
Joseph (Jefferson)
Joshua (Jackson)
Julius (Washington)
Leonard (Columbia)
Levi (Morgan)
Levi (Washington)
Lewis (Effingham)
Louisa (Chatham)
Margaret (Jefferson)
Marshall (Wilkes)
Martha (Emanuel)
Mary (Jefferson)
Mary (Morgan)
Maurice (Baldwin)

Micajor (Jones)
Murdoch (Gwinnett)
Nathaniel (Liberty)
Noah (Washington)
Peter (Habersham)
Peter (Jackson)
Reubim (Emanuel)
Richard (Washington)
Richard T. (Screven)
Robert (Columbia)
Robert, Sr. (Greene)
Robert (Jackson)
Robert D. (Jones)
Rovisa (Burke)
Sally (Clarke)
Sally (Oglethorpe)
Samuel (Gwinnett)
Samuel (Jackson)
Samuel L. (Bryan)
Stephen (Screven)
Susannah (Oglethorpe)
Sylas (Screven)
Thomas (Columbia)
Thomas (Emanuel)
Thomas (Hall)
Thomas (Jasper)
Thomas (Washington)
Wilford (Oglethorpe)
William (Emanuel)
William (2) (Greene)
William (Gwinnett)
William (Jackson)
Dr. William (Jackson)
William (Jasper)
William (Liberty)
William (Madison)
William (Putnam)
William (2) (Wilkes)
William W. (Warren)
Willis (Warren)
Wright (Hancock)
Yearly (Jasper)
Marton, William T. (Putnam)
Marwick, Joseph (Chatham)
Mase, James L. (Wilkes)
  Thomas (Morgan)
Mashbourn, Daniel
          (Washington)
Mashburn, Nancy (Jones)
Mason, (ind.) (Laurens)
Mason(?), Allen (Madison)
Mason(?), Jenny (Madison)
Mason(?), John (Madison)
Mason, Ann M. (Effingham)
  Caldemoore (Jones)
  Charles (Emanuel)
  David (Wilkes)
  Elizabeth (Putnam)
  George (Washington)
  Gideon (Jones)
  Henry (Jones)

Mason, Henry (Telfair)
James (Emanuel)
James (Jones)
John C. (Putnam)
L. (Chatham)
Levi (Telfair)
Peter (Emanuel)
Richard (Jasper)
Genl. Thomas (Hancock)
Thomas, Jr. (Hancock)
Walker (Hall)
Wellborn B. (Pulaski)
Wiliam (Elbert)
William (Hall)
William (Putnam)
Massa, James M. (Greene)
Massee, Needham (Jones)
Massengale, James (Greene)
Masser, Henry (Lincoln)
Massey, Abel (Washington)
Abraham (Washington)
Bonokias (Washington)
Reuben (Morgan)
Massie, A. (Chatham)
Massingale, Daniel (Columbia)
Masters, Bartholmus (McIntosh)
Mathers, William H. (Pulaski)
Mathew, Goss (Habersham)
Mathews, Asa (Wilkinson)
Benjamin (Wilkinson)
Burrell (Walton)
Cary (Clarke)
Edmond (Appling)
Edward (Chatham)
Gabriel (Clarke)
Henry (Burke)
Isaac (Clarke)
James (Bulloch)
James (Clarke)
James (3) (Wilkes)
James (Wilkinson)
Jarrott (Jasper)
Jeremiah (Clarke)
Jesse (Jackson)
John (Bulloch)
John (Jackson)
John (Wilkinson)
John D. (Screven)
Jonathon (Wilkinson)
Josiah (Baldwin)
Mary (Wilkes)
Richard (Jackson)
Ridley (Habersham)
Robert (Pulaski)
Sugar P. (Wilkinson)
Thomas (Early)
William (Jackson)
William (Pulaski)
William (Wilkinson)
Mathias, William (Oglethorpe)
Mathis, Britton (Putnam)

Charles L. (Oglethorpe)
Dicy (Hancock)
Elisha (Putnam)
Elisha H. (Putnam)
Green (Putnam)
Jacob Geo. (Oglethorpe)
John (4) (Washington)
Lewis (Washington)
Littleberry (Oglethorpe)
Lodowick (Washington)
Moses (Walton)
Robert (Hancock)
Sally (Washington)
Tempe (Washington)
Thomas (Putnam)
William (2) (Putnam)
Matin, Lemuel (Wilkes)
Matlock, Stephen (Tattnall)
Matox, John (Jasper)
Matthew, Rev. E. (Glynn)
Elisha (Jones)
J. D. (Jones)
Seaborn I. (Warren)
Matthews, (ind.) (Laurens)
Mrs. (Lincoln)
Allen (Jackson)
Andrews (Columbia)
Aquilla (Jefferson)
Arthur (Warren)
Benjamin (Jones)
Charles (Jefferson)
Charles (Morgan)
Edward (Warren)
Enoch (Morgan)
Ezekiel (Gwinnett)
George (Jones)
George G. (Greene)
Gideon (Jones)
Colby (Warren)
Henry (Gwinnett)
Isaac (Warren)
James (Jefferson)
Jane (Warren)
Jesse (Jones)
Jesse (Morgan)
Joel (Warren)
John (Jones)
John (Liberty)
John (Lincoln)
Joseph (Warren)
Josiah (Burke)
Kerom (Lincoln)
Mary (Wilkes)
Micager (Jones)
Moses (Jones)
Nowell(?) (Wilkes)
Peter (Burke)
Philip (Elbert)
Polly (Oglethorpe)
Richard (Morgan)
Robert (Wilkes)

Thomas (Gwinnett)
Thomas (Jefferson)
William (2) (Gwinnett)
William (Habersham)
William (Lincoln)
William (Wilkes)
Matton, David (Elbert)
Mattox, Aaron (Tattnall)
Charles (Wilkes)
Elijah (Tattnall)
H. (Richmond)
John (Gwinnett)
John (Tattnall)
Lanty (Wilkes)
Richard (Wilkes)
William (Wilkes)
Zachariah (Gwinnett)
Mauldin, Ryal (Jones)
Maulden, James (Liberty)
Maun, Daniel (Putnam)
Maund, Elizabeth (Burke)
Mallicae (Burke)
Maupas, Lewis K. (Chatham)
Maurel(?), Charlotte (Chatham)
Maurs, Abraham (col.)
(Columbia)
Simon (col.) (Columbia)
Maury, Mary (Madison)
Nathan (Madison)
Maxey, Barnes (Oglethorpe)
Garland (Jasper)
H. (ind.) (Oglethorpe)
Poney (Jasper)
Yelverton (Oglethorpe)
Maxfield, Felix (Washington)
Maxwell, Ann (Bryan)
Audley (Liberty)
Elijah (Elbert)
Elizabeth (Bryan)
Elizabeth (Wilkes)
James (Habersham)
James (Madison)
John (Elbert)
John B. (Bryan)
John H. B. (Liberty)
John J. (Bryan)
Jowel (Elbert)
Margaret (Bryan)
Margaret (Wilkes)
Mary (Chatham)
Simeon (Elbert)
Thomas (Elbert)
William (Elbert)
William (Liberty)
William (Wilkes)
May, (ind.) (Pulaski)
Benjamin (Jones)
Bukam (Warren)
Edmund (Washington)

May, James (Glynn)
Jeremiah (Warren)
Jethro (Washington)
John (Chatham)
John (Hancock)
John (Washington)
Jonas W. (Jefferson)
Nathan (Warren)
Peter (Warren)
Reuben (Warren)
Robert (Chatham)
Samuel (Wilkes)
Samuel C. (Warren)
Solomon (Wilkes)
Tempe (Washington)
Major W. (Greene)
William (Greene)
Mayaw, Mary (Wilkinson)
Maybank, Andrew (Liberty)
Mayfield, Abigal (Gwinnett)
Battle (Gwinnett)
Jacob (Jackson)
Obidiah (Clarke)
Maykim, Ninon (Warren)
Mayner, John (Jefferson)
Maynor, Jesse (Baldwin)
Mayo, Benjamin (Jackson)
Harmon (Jefferson)
James (Jackson)
Jonas (Jefferson)
Susannah (Pulaski)
William (Washington)
Mayow, Cypan (Wilkinson)
Eli (Wilkinson)
Elisha (Wilkinson)
Jessey (Wilkinson)
John (Wilkinson)
Nathan (Wilkinson)
Sheppard (Wilkinson)
Mays, John (Habersham)
John (Jasper)
John (Warren)
John W. (Lincoln)
Priscilla (Warren)
R. (Jasper)
Stephen (Jackson)
Valentine (Hancock)
William (Greene)
William (Gwinnett)
William (Lincoln)
William (Pulaski)
William (Warren)
Maze, Mattox (Putnam)
Mazo, Catherine (Glynn)
Christian (Glynn)
Meacham, Henry (Baldwin)
Mead, John (Madison)
Minor (Jackson)
Meaders, Absalem (Oglethorpe)
Isaac (Oglethorpe)

Meadorobrooks, William (Jones)
Meadow, Daniel (Burke)
Meadows, Abram (Morgan)
Benjamin (Jones)
Daniel (Greene)
Edmund (Jones)
Jacin (Jones)
William (Morgan)
William (Warren)
Meagher, Timothy (Chatham)
Meaks, Brittain (Baldwin)
Mealing, H. (Richmond)
Mealy, Mildred (Richmond)
Means, Alexander (Elbert)
Hugh (Morgan)
James (Jasper)
John (Morgan)
Mears, Abraham (Wilkinson)
John (Gwinnett)
John (Richmond)
Measels, Griffin (Telfair)
Meazles, Luke (Screven)
Luke (Wilkinson)
Mark (Wilkinson)
Meckeberry, James (Oglethorpe)
Medcalf, John (Jasper)
Meddars, Breen W. (Wilkinson)
Joel (Wilkinson)
Meddors, Jacob (Oglethorpe)
Meddows, Edward (Greene)
William (Greene)
Medford, George (Morgan)
William (Gwinnett)
William (Hancock)
Medlock, Charles (Hancock)
Isham (Gwinnett)
Meek, Allen (Emanuel)
Francois (Emanuel)
Jonas (Emanuel)
Meeks, (ind.) (Warren)
Archibald (Jones)
Littleton (Habersham)
Redding (Emanuel)
Meers, William (Hall)
Megar, Edward (Emanuel)
Megarity, Abner (Elbert)
Gardner (Elbert)
Kindred (Elbert)
Megee, Crafford (Walton)
Megehee, Samuel (Elbert)
Meggs, L. (Jasper)
Megill, Charles (Camden)
Mehathy, James (Gwinnett)
Thomas (Gwinnett)
Meigs(?), John (Hall)
Meiggs, Daniel (Richmond)
Mein, W. (Chatham)
Meizler, John (Camden)
Mekray, Andrew (Jasper)
Melams, James (Wilkes)

Melander, Charles (Liberty)
Melckham, Eliijah (Jones)
Mell, Benjamin, Jr. (Liberty)
Benjamin, Sr. (Liberty)
Thomas P. (Liberty)
Zachariah (Bryan)
Mellaloy, Joseph (Oglethorpe)
Melnas, R. H. (Jasper)
Melon, B. (Jasper)
Dudley (Jasper)
Joseph (Morgan)
Meloney, Samuel (Gwinnett)
Melson, Elijah (Jones)
Melton(?), Benjamin (Bulloch)
Melton, Daniel (Jones)
Henry (Bulloch)
James (Bulloch)
John (Columbia)
Joseph (Columbia)
Moses (Walton)
Robinson (Bulloch)
Seaborn (Putnam)
Tempy (Hall)
Thomas S. (Putnam)
Menard, Stephen (Wilkes)
Mence, R. (Jasper)
Mendes, John (McIntosh)
Menish, William (Camden)
Menor, William (Hall)
Menter, Richard (Jasper)
Meradith, Pleasant (Wilkinson)
Mercer, Christopher (Tattnall)
Colen (Jefferson)
Daniel (Greene)
Dennis (Washington)
Harmon (Greene)
Isabella (Richmond)
James (Jasper)
Jesse (Pulaski)
John (Greene)
John W. (Jasper)
Levi (Jasper)
Meredy (Telfair)
Mount M. (Oglethorpe)
Nathaniel (Pulaski)
Noah (Jones)
Stephen (Burke)
William (Wilkes)
William B. (Jones)
Williby (Burke)

Merchant, Jacob (Warren)
Mercier, Francis (Baldwin)
Meredeth, James (Richmond)
Robert (Richmond)
Meredith, John (Wilkinson)
Samuel (Wilkinson)
William (Wilkinson)
William H. (Burke)
Mereweather, Francis (Jackson)
Meridith, Joseph (Walton)

Merit, Abscilla (Burke)
Cotton (Burke)
Jesse (Burke)
William (Putnam)
Meriwether, Alexander
(Jefferson)
Savannah (Jefferson)
Thomas (Oglethorpe)
Meroney, William (Madison)
Merphy, John (Putnam)
Merrah, F. G. (Hancock)
Merrell, Sherwood (Morgan)
Merrett, Henry C. (Morgan)
John (Greene)
Thomas (Greene)
Toun (Elbert)
William (Morgan)
Merril, Benjamin (Gwinnett)
Merritt, Benjamin (Jones)
Jacob (Montgomery)
William (Greene)
Merriwether, David (Clarke)
Richard (Columbia)
William (Columbia)
Merriwither, G. M. (Jasper)
Merrlist, Jane (Chatham)
Merse(?), Claudine (Chatham)
Merser, Charles (Wilkinson)
Henry (Wilkinson)
Jesse (Hancock)
Mershon, William (Hancock)
Messicks, George (Washington)
Nehemiah (Washington)
Messor, Peter (Early)
Metcalf, Anthony (Burke)
Isaac (Burke)
William (Burke)
Methon, Thomas (Wilkinson)
Mets, Mary (Emanuel)
Redding (Emanuel)
Metter, Brazil (Hancock)
Metts, Frederick (Washington)
Levin (Washington)
Nathan (Wilkinson)
Wright (Washington)
Metzer, David (Effingham)
John I., Sr. (Effingham)
Miccan, Pleasant (Putnam)
Micheljohn, George (Baldwin)
Michell, Thomas (Montgomery)
Michem, John (Elbert)
Michson, William B. (Screven)
Mickel, Edward (Camden)
Micou, William (Richmond)
Middlebrook, David (Putnam)
Middlebrooks, Isaac (Morgan)
Isaac S. (Putnam)
Izere (Putnam)
John (Putnam)
Micajah (Hancok)
Robert (Jones)

Seins (Jones)
Thomas (Jones)
Middleton, Betsy C. (Elbert)
Charles (Chatham)
Hugh (Wilkinson)
John (Elbert)
John (Washington)
John H. (Richmond)
Margaret (McIntosh)
Owen (Wilkinson)
Robert (McIntosh)
Samuel (Emanuel)
Thomas (Habersham)
William (Greene)
William (McIntosh)
Mikeles, Peter (Camden)
Mikell, Alexander (Bulloch)
Dicy (Bulloch)
James (Bulloch)
Thomas (Bulloch)
William (Bulloch)
Mikle, Jacob (Oglethorpe)
William (Oglethorpe)
Miledg, Ann (Richmond)
Miles, Abraham (Washington)
Augustus N. (Greene)
Elisha (Jasper)
Gilham (Jones)
John (Baldwin)
Levisa (Burke)
Lewis (Morgan)
Rebecca (Greene)
Thomas (2) (Baldwin)
Thomas K. (Columbia)
William (Clarke)
William (Jasper)
Milford, Robert (Gwinnett)
Milican, James (Madison)
Milkey, Moses (Habersham)
Millagan, William C. (Hall)
Millar, Charles (Jackson)
Henry (Habersham)
John (Jackson)
John (Montgomery)
Joseph (Montgomery)
Samuel (Montgomery)
Sarah (Montgomery)
William (2) (Jackson)
William (Montgomery)
Millegan, Mary (Morgan)
Millen, Elisa (Chatham)
George (Chatham)
George D. (Chatham)
Miller, (torn) (Laurens)
Miller & Maxwell (McIntosh)
Miller, Alex (Bryan)
Alexander (Morgan)
Andrew (Warren)
Archibald (Appling)
Arthur (Chatham)
Benjamin (Jones)

Benjamin (Washington)
Benjah (Wilkes)
Brazil (Hancock)
Charles (Emanuel)
Charles (Hancock)
Charles (Jefferson)
David (Chatham)
David (Laurens)
David (Walton)
Dicey (Wilkinson)
Dudley (Jasper)
Ebenezer (Jackson)
Ede (Hall)
Elias (Hall)
Elijah (Jones)
Elizabeth (Wilkes)
Emson (Columbia)
Ezekiel (Baldwin)
Francis (Washington)
Frank (Clarke)
George (Jones)
Green (Jasper)
Hannah (Chatham)
Henrietta (Chatham)
Henry (Greene)
Hiram (Bryan)
Hopson (Jasper)
Isaac (Camden)
Isaac (Washington)
Jacob (Baldwin)
Jacob (Camden)
Jacob (Chatham)
Jacob (Putnam)
James (Hancock)
James (Jones)
James (Laurens)
James (Warren)
James (Wilkes)
Jeremiah (Jones)
Jesse (Baldwin)
Jesse (Warren)
Joel (Hall)
John (Bulloch)
John (Burke)
John (4) (Hall)
John (Jasper)
John (Jones)
John (Pulaski)
John (Putnam)
John (Richmond)
John (2) (Washington)
Jonathan (2) (Appling)
Johnathon (Hancock)
Jonathon (Laurens)
Joseph (Baldwin)
Joseph (2) (Chatham)
Lam (Telfair)
Lewis (Washington)
Lewis (Wilkes)
Martha (Warren)
Mary (Hancock)

Miller, Nath. (Baldwin)
O. (Jasper)
Preston (Hall)
Pugh (Washington)
Rich (Hall)
Richard W. (Screven)
Robert (Camden)
Robert (Hall)
Samuel (Chatham)
Samuel (Wilkes)
Solomon (Hancock)
Stephen (Wilkes)
Thomas (Bryan)
Thomas (Jones)
Thomas (McIntosh)
Thomas H. (Camden)
Wiley (Wilkinson)
William (Baldwin)
William (Bulloch)
William (2) (Hancock)
William (Jasper)
William (Madison)
William (Pulaski)
William (Telfair)
William (Wilkinson)
William C. (Hancock)
Willis (Jones)
Millerous, John (Putnam)
Millerson, William (Jones)
Millican, Delila (Madison)
John (Madison)
Thomas (Madison)
Milliford, Henry (Walton)
Milligan, Hugh (Jones)
Robert (Jones)
Milligin, John (Wilkes)
Millin, George (Burke)
James H. (Burke)
Milliner, Simeon (Morgan)
Milling, David T. (Jones)
Millirons, William (Warren)
Millirous, Henry (2) (Putnam)
John (Putnam)
Solomon (Putnam)
William (Putnam)
Mills, (ind.) (Pulaski)
Widdow (Screven)
Anthony (Burke)
C. (Richmond)
Charles C. (Morgan)
David (Tattnall)
Elizabeth (Burke)
Elizabeth (Camden)
Frederick (Effingham)
Frederick (Pulaski)
Mills(?), H. W. (Chatham)
Mills, Hardy (Pulaski)
Isaac (Jones)
Jacob (Screven)
James (Elbert)

James (Screven)
James (Washington)
Jemima (Laurens)
Mills, (or Wills), Jeremiah
(Telfair)
Mills, Jesse (Washington)
John (Gwinnett)
John (Irwin)
John, Sr. (Screven)
John (Washington)
John B. (Chatham)
Mary (Jones)
Mary (Screven)
Moses (Elbert)
Robert (Columbia)
Sarah (Wilkinson)
Stephen (Screven)
Thomas (Baldwin)
Thomas (Screven)
Thomas (Telfair)
Thomas (2) (Washington)
William (Elbert)
William (Hancock)
William, Jr. (Washington)
William C. (Chatham)
Millsaps, William (Walton)
Milner, John (Wilkes)
John B. (Wilkes)
John M. (Jones)
Johnathon (Oglethorpe)
Pitt (Jones)
Milsaps, Fuller (Jackson)
Hyrom (Jackson)
J. (Jackson)
Jacob (Clarke)
R. (Jackson)
Thomas (Jackson)
Milton, Catherine (Putnam)
Ethan (Clarke)
Hannah E. (Burke)
Homer V. (Jefferson)
Joshua (Jackson)
Peter (Burke)
Thomas (Pulaski)
William (Putnam)
Mimms, Benjamin (Laurens)
Elizabeth (Tattnall)
Joseph (Tattnall)
Leroy (Warren)
William (Washington)
Mims, (ind.) (Wilkes)
Anson (Wilkinson)
Calvin (Wilkinson)
David (Montgomery)
David (Telfair)
David (Warren)
John (Wilkinson)
Josiah (Chatham)
Martin G. (Pulaski)
Nadam (Baldwin)

Thomas (Wilkes)
Williamson (Baldwin)
Wright (Wilkinson)
Mincy, Abraham (Emanuel)
Minen, Meradeth (Wilkinson)
Miner, Nicholas (Gwinnett)
Mingledorf, J. G. (Effingham)
Minis, Abbe (Chatham)
Isaac (Chatham)
Miss Judah (Chatham)
Minne, R. W. W. (Pulaski)
Minor, Henry (Jones)
Mary (Baldwin)
Samuel W. (Clarke)
William (Hancock)
Minsey, Jacob (Bulloch)
Phillip (Bulloch)
Minshew, Jacob (Wayne)
Minter, Abner H. (Jones)
Anthony M. (Jones)
Antony (Baldwin)
James (Wilkinson)
John M. (Putnam)
Minton, Jesse (Hancock)
John (Wilkes)
Mills (Hancock)
Minyard, Betsy (Jackson)
Nicholas (Jackson)
William (Gwinnett)
Mirault(?), John (Chatham)
Mires, Abram (Hall)
Absolom (Morgan)
John (Hall)
William (Morgan)
Mise. Joseph (Jasper)
Saul (Elbert)
Mister, R. C. (Jasper)
Mitcham, Marcus (Jones)
Mitchel, Frances (Clarke)
Henry (Jones)
James (Appling)
James L. (Putnam)
John (Putnam)
John T. (Putnam)
Peter (Chatham)
Ransom (Putnam)
Robert (Chatham)
S. M. (Chatham)
Sally (Clarke)
Samuel (Putnam)
Thomas (Clarke)
Thomas R. (Clarke)
William, Sr. (Clarke)
William (Clarke)
William (Putnam)
Mitchell, A. (Richmond)
B. B. (Richmond)
Benjamin (Wilkinson)
D. B. (Baldwin)
Drury (Jones)

Mitchell, Edward (Greene) *Jesse (Appling)*
  Elizth (Jasper)
  Frances (Morgan)
  G. B. (Greene)
  George (Jasper)
  George (Morgan)
  Green (Hancock)
  Hartwell (Tattnall)
  Hench (Walton)
  Henry (Gwinnett)
  Henry (Hancock)
  Henry (Morgan)
  Henry D. (Telfair)
  Isaac (Greene)
  Isaac (Hall)
  Isaac (Wilkinson)
  Jacob (Greene)
  James (Greene)
  James (Hancock)
  James (Jackson)
  James (Morgan)
  Jesse (Oglethorpe)
  Joel (Jasper)
  John (Jones)
  John (2) (Morgan)
  John, Sr. (Warren)
  John (Warren)
  John (Wilkes)
  Joseph (Jasper)
  Julius C. B. (Jones)
  Mary (Wilkinson)
  Matthew (Morgan)
  Mourning (Wilkes)
  N. (Telfair)
  Nathaniel (McIntosh)
  Pleasant R. (Baldwin)
  Polly (Jones)
  Richard (Jasper)
  Robert (Hancock)
  Robert (Jasper)
  Robert (Jones)
  Robert (Warren)
  Stephen (Pulaski)
  Stephen M. (Chatham)
  Thomas (Jones)
  Thomas G. (Telfair)
  Thomas H. (Morgan)
  William (Jones)
  William (Warren)
  William, Jr. (Wilkinson)
  William, Sr. (Wilkinson)
Mitchill, A. G. C. (Washington)
Mitchum, Mary (Jones)
Mittaford, Hartville (Jones)
Mixen, Robert (Wilkinson)
Mixon, Allen (Bulloch)
  George (Burke)
  Jaimy(?) (Appling)
  Jesse (Telfair)
  Michael (Burke)
  Miles (McIntosh)

  Nancy (Burke)
Mize, Anderson (Putnam)
  Henderson (Putnam)
  James (Putnam)
  Shepherd (Putnam)
  Wiley (Putnam)
Mizell, William (Jones)
Mizle, Charlton (Camden)
  David (Camden)
  Joshua (Camden)
Mizzell, Hardy (Jones)
  Joseph (Jones)
  William (Jones)
Moasley, Edwin (Wilkes)
Moat, Daniel (Hall)
  David (Laurens)
Moats, William (Warren)
Mobary, Robert W. (Wilkes)
Mobbs, Jesse (Clarke)
* Mobely, _ _rantly (Montgomery)
Mobley, Isaac (Elbert)
  Jethro (Jasper)
  Ledford (Gwinnett)
  Lemuel (Wayne)
  Lewis (Wilkinson)
  Lud (Irwin)
  Reuben Rabb (Jones)
  Solomon (Appling)
  William (Jasper)
  Willy (Washington)
Mobly, Abner (Washington)
  Benjamin (Burke)
  Isaac (Jackson)
  John (Tattnall)
  Patience (Screven)
  Sarah (Burke)
  William (Tattnall)
Moch(?), Parry(?)
    (Wilkinson)
Mock, Andrew (Screven)
  Arthur (Burke)
  George (Jefferson)
  George (Screven)
  John M. (Effingham)
  Mattias (Putnam)
  Samuel (Jones)
  Thomas (Effingham)
Modesett, Isabel (Jones)
Mody, James (Liberty)
  John (Warren)
Moffat, Mary Ann (Lincoln)
Moffate, James (Jasper)
Moffatt, N. (Jasper)
Moinneville(?), Mary
    (Richmond)
Molden, Richard (Emanuel)
Molenmeux, Andrew
    (Habersham)
Molevaux, Abraham
    (Habersham)
Molfred, Thomas B. (Baldwin)

Molier, Clement (Warren)
Molp(?er), Jeremiah (Baldwin)
Molsby, John (Columbia)
Moman, Amy (col.) (Columbia)
  Jacob (Putnam)
  Mary (Morgan)
Momford, Thomas (Laurens)
Moncreaf, David (Greene)
  Samuel (Greene)
Moncrief, David (Morgan)
  John (Lincoln)
  Nancy (Lincoln)
  William (Columbia)
  William (Greene)
Monegham, John (Clarke)
Monford, Henry (Laurens)
Monfort, John (Greene)
Monger, Mrs. Lucy (Greene)
Mongin, Daniel N. (Chatham)
Mongomery, Hiram
    (Habersham)
Monham, Charley (Jones)
Monk, John (Jones)
  Miles (Appling)
  Silas (Columbia)
  Silas (Jones)
  Simeon (Putnam)
  Thomas (Jasper)
  William (Jones)
  Willie (Jones)
  Willis (Richmond)
Monkor, Benjamin (Gwinnett)
  Elijah (Gwinnett)
Monro, Solomon (Emanuel)
Monroe, David (Burke)
  Jane (Montgomery)
  Jesse (Habersham)
  Joseph (Burke)
  Thomas (Habersham)
Monrow, John (Emanuel)
Montcrief, Josiah (Wilkes)
  Mary (Wilkes)
  Thomas (Wilkes)
Montford, Isla (Laurens)
  Jeffry (Pulaski)
  John (Laurens)
  William (Laurens)
Montfort, Robert (Putnam)
  Theodereck (Putnam)
Montgomery, Absalom (Wilkes)
  Ann (Jefferson)
  Bartlet (Jackson)
  D. (Jasper)
  Elsey (Hall)
  H. (Jackson)
  Hugh (Warren)
  J. (Jasper)
  James (Baldwin)
  James (2) (Wilkes)
  Jane (Chatham)

(104)

* Mosely, Brantley R.S. (Montgomery)
Ancestor of J. E. Mosely, Jr.

Montgomery, Jane (Wilkes)
  John (2) (Madison)
  John (Richmond)
  Lewis (Washington)
  Mary (Wilkes)
  Rebecca (Wilkes)
  Robert (Jackson)
  Samuel (Laurens)
  T. M. C. (Jackson)
  William (Jackson)
Montyingo, Lewis (Washington)
Moody, Aierl(?) (Oglethorpe)
  Benjamin (Wayne)
  Daniel (Oglethorpe)
  Daniel (Washington)
  Granville (Warren)
  Isaac (Appling)
  Jablz (Jones)
  Jese (Appling)
  Jesse (Wayne)
  Joel (Greene)
  Joel (Liberty)
  John (Greene)
  John L. (Morgan)
  John M. (Oglethorpe)
  Shadrack (Liberty)
  Solomon (Glynn)
  Thomas (Appling)
  Thomas (Jones)
  Thomas (Oglethorpe)
  Thomas (Walton)
  W. (Richmond)
  William (Liberty)
Moon & How (Putnam)
Moon, Achilus (Madison)
  Bird (Madison)
  Boler (Jackson)
  David (Madison)
  Edom (Columbia)
  Jacob (Madison)
  James (Hancock)
  Jesse (2) (Columbia)
  John (Columbia)
  John (Madison)
  John, Jr. (Madison)
  Joseph (Columbia)
  Lewis S. (Columbia)
  Robert (Jackson)
  Thomas (Columbia)
  William (Chatham)
  William (Greene)
  William (Oglethorpe)
Moone, Alexander (Elbert)
Mooney, Isaac (Morgan)
  Sarah (Telfair)
Moons, Lewis (Emanuel)
Moony, Louis (Jackson)
Moor, Asa (Wilkinson)
  Cason (Washington)
  Mrs. Francis (Richmond)
  Israel (Morgan)

  John (Screven)
  Joseph (Morgan)
  Joseph (Richmond)
  Samuel (Wilkinson)
  Thomas (Elbert)
  Warren (Putnam)
  William (Morgan)
  William T. (Screven)
Moore, Alexander (Jackson)
  Annie (Emanuel)
  Asa (Columbia)
  Asa (Gwinnett)
  Augustus (Richmond)
  Barnard (Wilkes)
  Benjamin(?) (Hall)
  Benjamin L. (Jasper)
  Betsy (Columbia)
  Burnett (Greene)
  Carswell (Jefferson)
  Charity (Putnam)
  Charles (Oglethorpe)
  Charles (Wilkes)
  Clement (Baldwin)
  David (Greene)
  Dempsey (Jefferson)
  Donaldson (Washington)
  Drucilla (Jones)
  Ebenezer H. (Jones)
  Edward (Laurens)
  Elbert (2) (Jasper)
  Elijah (Baldwin)
  Elijah (Greene)
  Elisha (Wilkes)
  Elizabeth (Burke)
  Ethelred (Jefferson)
  Exander (Walton)
  George (Gwinnett)
  George (Putnam)
  George W. (Clarke)
  Gideon (Jones)
  Gilley (Greene)
  Henry (Jones)
  Hill (Wilkes)
  Hiram (Jasper)
  Hugh (Greene)
  Isaac (Greene)
  Isaac (2) (Jasper)
  Isaac (Madison)
  Jacaniah (Greene)
  Jacob (Glynn)
  Jacob (Hall)
  James (Burke)
  James (Emanuel)
  James (Glynn)
  James (Greene)
  James (3) (Jasper)
  James (Jones)
  James (Putnam)
  James (Wayne)
  James (Wilkes)
  James J. (Clarke)

  James R. (Jones)
  Jane (Greene)
  Jesse (Bulloch)
  Jesse (Jackson)
  Jesse (Wilkes)
  Joel (Greene)
  John (Baldwin)
  John (2) (Columbia)
  John (Emanuel)
  John (Greene)
  John (2) (Hall)
  John (Hancock)
  John (2) (Jasper)
  Gen'l. John (Jasper)
  John (Jones)
  John (Liberty)
  John (Oglethorpe)
  John (Pulaski)
  John (Walton)
  John (2) (Washington)
  John (Wilkes)
  John B. (Jones)
  John R. (Burke)
  Joseph (Greene)
  Joshua (Clarke)
  Joshua (Greene)
  Josiah (Washington)
  Lemuel (Greene)
  Lovid (Madison)
  Lui (Wilkes)
  Mark E. (Greene)
  Mary (Laurens)
  Mary (Wilkes)
  Mathew (Washington)
  Mathew (Wilkes)
  Murry (Effingham)
  Patience (Jackson)
  Patsy (Columbia)
  Phillip (Chatham)
  Pleasant (Burke)
  Prosley (Jones)
  Raburn (Wilkes)
  Ransom (Bullocn)
  Ransom (Greene)
  Richard (Habersham)
  Richard (Madison)
  Richard (Putnam)
  Robert (Greene)
  S. (Richmond)
  Sarah (Burke)
  Sarah (Elbert)
  Sarah (Greene)
  Sarah (Oglethorpe)
  Samuel (Jones)
  Seth (Wilkes)
  Shadrack (Washington)
  Spencer (Baldwin)
  Thomas (Burke)
  Thomas (Jefferson)
  Thomas (Laurens)
  Thomas (Wilkes)

Sarah (Appling)

Moore, Thomas (Wilkinson)
Turner B. (Burke)
Umey (wid.) (Wayne)
W. A. (Jasper)
Whittington (Baldwin)
Wilks (Gwinnett)
William (Burke)
William (Chatham)
William (Clarke)
William (Glynn)
William (Jackson)
William (Jones)
William (2) (Oglethorpe)
William (Putnam)
William (2) (Richmond)
William (Wilkes)
William A. (Chatham)
William A. (Jasper)
William C. (Putnam)
William H. (Oglethorpe)
William S. (Columbia)
Winfred (Burke)
Young (Greene)
Zachariah C. (Elbert)
Moorland, Jacob (Wilkinson)
Jessey (Wilkinson)
John, Jr. (Wilkinson)
John, Sr. (Wilkinson)
Moorman, (torn) (Laurens)
John (2) (Wilkes)
William (Wilkes)
William B. (Laurens)
Moran, Ellender (Baldwin)
Frances (Baldwin)
James (Jones)
Jesse (Baldwin)
Jesse (Jones)
John B. (Jasper)
William (Baldwin)
William (McIntosh)
Mordecai, Sampson (Chatham)
Samuel (Chatham)
More, Barnard (Wilkes)
David (Hancock)
Ebeneza (Hancock)
Elijah (Hancock)
James (Camden)
James W. (Walton)
John (Hancock)
John (Wilkes)
Luther (or Arthur)
            (Camden)
Mary (Wilkes)
Robert (2) (Wilkes)
Robert K. (Wilkes)
S. W. (Camden)
Sarah (Appling)
Morehore, Thomas (Jones)
Morel, Andrew (Chatham)
Ann (Chatham)
Diagon(?) (Chatham)

John (2) (Chatham)
John H. (Chatham)
Thomas N. (Chatham)
Musa (Chatham)
Moreland, Colson (Putnam)
Edmond (Jones)
Frank (Jasper)
Isaac (Putnam)
John (Putnam)
John, Sr. (Putnam)
Joseph (Putnam)
Rebecca (Jones)
Robert, Jr. (Pulaski)
Robert, Sr. (Pulaski)
Turner (Putnam)
Wood (Putnam)
Morevett, M. (Jasper)
Morgan, Rev. Asbury (Liberty)
Bethal (Madison)
Blake (Jackson)
Charlotte (Hancock)
Daniel (Oglethorpe)
David (Jones)
Eleanor (Chatham)
Elihue (Wayne)
Felix (Chatham)
G. (Richmond)
George (Warren)
H. C. (Jasper)
Hardy (Jefferson)
Hardy (Morgan)
Isham, Jr. (Elbert)
I. C. (Richmond)
James (Greene)
James (Wilkes)
James B. (Morgan)
Jeremiah (Gwinnett)
Jesse (Morgan)
Jessee (Early)
John (Jefferson)
John (Morgan)
John (2) (Putnam)
John (2) (Richmond)
John D. (Chatham)
Joseph (Gwinnett)
Joshua (Clarke)
Joshua (Wilkes)
Kisiah (Wilkes)
L. (Jasper)
Luke S. (Putnam)
Needham (Jefferson)
Nicholas (Morgan)
Richard (Baldwin)
Robert (Jackson)
Rock—heney(?) (Appling)
Sarah (Screven)
Simon (2) (Hancock)
Stephen (Jefferson)
Stokely (Jasper)
Tempy (Walton)
Thomas (Effingham)

William (Effingham)
William (Greene)
William (Hancock)
William (Jasper)
William (McIntosh)
William (Morgan)
William (Wilkes)
William C. (Elbert)
William S. (Putnam)
Morin, Peter (Chatham)
Morrall, John (Chatham)
Morrel, John (Jasper)
John (Jefferson)
Thomas (Jasper)
Morrell, Benjamin (Effingham)
Thomas W. (Columbia)
Morris, (ind.) (Pulaski)
(ind.) (Wilkes)
Austin (Gwinnett)
Benjamin (Hancock)
Bernard (Hall)
Burrell (Jasper)
Casawell (Jones)
Charles (Greene)
Charley (Jasper)
Daniel (Elbert)
E. (Richmond)
Frederick (Jefferson)
Garret (Clarke)
George (Jasper)
George (Warren)
Henry (Hall)
Henry (Morgan)
Henry (Pulaski)
Isaac (Oglethorpe)
Jacob (Washington)
James (Columbia)
James (2) (Jackson)
James (Jasper)
James (Walton)
James E. (Burke)
Jeremiah (Baldwin)
Jesse (Columbia)
Jesse, Sr. (Columbia)
Jesse (Screven)
John (Morgan)
John (Pulaski)
John (2) (Putnam)
John W. (Elbert)
Jonathon (Laurens)
Joseph (Elbert)
Joseph I. (Oglethorpe)
Joseph S. (Columbia)
Nathan (Hancock)
Nathaniel (Jones)
Obadiah (Columbia)
Obediah (Baldwin)
Sally (Lincoln)
Shadrack (Gwinnett)
Sherwood (Elbert)
Simon, Jr. (Greene)

Morris, Simon, Sr. (Greene)
Spencer (Walton)
Taylor (Jones)
Thomas (Columbia)
Thomas (Gwinnett)
Thomas (Jasper)
Thomas, Sr. (Jones)
Thomas (Richmond)
Thomas J. (Morgan)
Westly (Oglethorpe)
William (Hall)
William, Sr. (Jackson)
William (2) (Jackson)
William (Putnam)
William (Walton)
William (2) (Wilkes)
Morrison, Alexander (Jackson)
Archd. (Montgomery)
Daniel (Telfair)
David (Montgomery)
Ezra (Elbert)
George (Camden)
Hugh (Putnam)
James (Chatham)
James (Elbert)
James (Wilkinson)
John (Glynn)
John (Washington)
John B. (Burke)
Joseph (Walton)
Margaret (Jefferson)
Mary (Putnam)
Mary (Telfair)
Norman (Telfair)
Washington (Elbert)
William (Jasper)
Morrow, Arthur (Baldwin)
Eming (Morgan)
James (Walton)
John E. (Putnam)
Joseph (Morgan)
William H. (Walton)
Mors, Rebecca (Jasper)
Morse, Morgan (Liberty)
Mortan, Futrell H. (Chatham)
Morton, C. (Richmond)
Isaac P. (Jones)
Oliver (Jones)
Moseley, Benjamon (Putnam)
Elijah (Putnam)
Laborn (Morgan)
Stephen (Oglethorpe)
Mosely, Alanon(?) (Jasper)
Benjamin (Lincoln)
Benjamin (Morgan)
Elias (Jones)
Elisha (Jasper)
Henry (Jasper)
Jacob (Wayne)
Jesse (Morgan)
Jonathan (Morgan)

Joseph (Baldwin)
Mary (Clarke)
Mary (Jefferson)
Samuel G. (Wilkes)
Silas (Jasper)
Thomas (Jefferson)
Thomas (Jones)
Moses, Elisha (Warren)
John (Warren)
✳ Mosley, James (Morgan)
Lewis (Greene)
Nancy (Morgan)
Osborn (Morgan)
Thomas (Greene)
Thomas (Jasper)
Mosly, Eli (Walton)
Moss, Alexander (Lincoln)
Alfred (Clarke)
Daniel D. (Jefferson)
Ephraim (Elbert)
Eppes (Baldwin)
Gabriel (Hancock)
Hudson (Habersham)
John (Elbert)
John (Lincoln)
John (Wilkes)
John A. (Putnam)
Joseph (Clarke)
Lewis (Laurens)
Mary (Clarke)
Peter (Emanuel)
Peter (Wilkes)
William (Elbert)
William (Jefferson)
Mossa, A. W. (Jasper)
Mosseley, Thomas (Montgomery)
Mosser(?), John, (Screven)
Mote, Benjamin (Jackson)
Doley (Wilkinson)
Isaac (Chatham)
Levi (Habersham)
Silas (Columbia)
Motley, Benjamin (Washington)
Robert (Washington)
Moton, John (Wilkinson)
Thomas (Morgan)
Mott, Abraham (Camden)
Isaac (Camden)
James (Wilkinson)
John (Wilkinson)
Nathan (Washington)
Uriah (Wilkinson)
Zachariah (Wilkinson)
Motts, John (Camden)
Moughan, Thomas (Baldwin)
W. A. B. (Lincoln)
Mounger, Mrs. Frances (Clarke)
Mount, Edward (Chatham)
Mountain, Agnes (Jefferson)
Robert (Jefferson)
Thomas (Jefferson)

Thomas, Sr. (Jefferson)
Moxley, Benjamin (Burke)
Daniel (Burke)
Nathaniel (Burke)
Moye, Duran (Washington)
Furney (Screven)
George (2) (Washington)
Wilie (Jones)
Mozbay, Edmond (Hall)
Moze, Claxton (Habersham)
Heney (Habersham)
Zachariah (Habersham)
Muckaroy, Chereano (Jones)
Muckelon, William (Jones)
Mucklaroy, Jesse (Jones)
Muckle, Nathan (Jones)
Thomas (Jones)
Mulain, Nineon M. (Gwinnett)
Mulain(?), Thomas (Gwinnett)
Mulford, Wm. B. (Burke)
Mulholbrough, Alden
(Oglethorpe)
Mulkey, Betty (Habersham)
John (Hall)
Philip (Hall)
William (2) (Hall)
Mulky, Edny (Emanuel)
Isaac (Burke)
Littleberry (Wilkes)
Moses (Burke)
William (Burke)
Mullen, Isaac (Jefferson)
James (Columbia)
Mullians, John (Jones)
Thomas (Jones)
Mullican, Benjamin (Wilkes)
Mullin, John (Chatham)
Mullins, Bud (Hall)
Elias (Hall)
Elizabeth (Jackson)
Hardy (Jones)
James (Jones)
Jeremiah (Jones)
John (2) (Hall)
Levi (Jones)
Levics (Jones)
Malone (Hancock)
May (Hall)
Osburn (Hall)
Robert (Morgan)
Robert (Walton)
William (Hall)
William (Morgan)
Mulryne, Mrs. (Chatham)
Mulsha, Hyrum (Jones)
Mumford, Joseph (Laurens)
Robert (Lincoln)
Muncrab, Calip (Jones)
Muncrief, Arthur (Warren)
Laborn (Morgan)

(107)

✳ See footnote p. 104

Munden, Emanuel (Wayne)
William (Wayne)
Munk, George H. (Walton)
Murden, David (Morgan)
Malica (Greene)
Murf, Sarah (Lincoln)
Murfy, John (Jackson)
Murich, John (Wilkinson)
Mary (Wilkinson)
Murish, Amey (Wilkinson)
Murkison, John (Washington)
Murles, Antoine (Chatham)
Murphey, Ambrose (Wilkinson)
Murphrey, Solomon (Wilkinson)
William (Washington)
Murphy, Bartholmew (Jefferson)
Cornelius (Baldwin)
Daniel (Baldwin)
Daniel (Hancock)
Drury (2) (Hancock)
Drury (Putnam)
E. (Richmond)
Ellis (Baldwin)
H. (Richmond)
Hugh (Jefferson)
James (Burke)
James (Gwinnett)
James (Putnam)
James (Richmond)
John (Appling)
John (Burke)
John (Jefferson)
John (Jones)
John (Warren)
John (Wilkes)
John W. (Burke)
Josiah (Burke)
Lucy (Wilkes)
Miles (Columbia)
Morris (Jefferson)
Rev. Murdock (Liberty)
Nancy (Warren)
Pascall (Jasper)
Samuel (Warren)
Robert (Wilkes)
Murphy(?), Valentine
(Oglethorpe)
Murphy, William (2) (Burke)
William (Wilkes)
Wright (Burke)
Wright (Jones)
Murrah, Charles (Lincoln)
Moses (Lincoln)
Murraney, B. (Jasper)
Murray, (ind.) (Early)
(ind.) (Liberty)
Benj'h (Jasper)
David (Burke)
David (Lincoln)
G. (Richmond)
Jacob (Early)

James (Burke)
James (Lincoln)
John (Burke)
John (Putnam)
John (Richmond)
John (Washington)
John (Wilkinson)
Joseph (Warren)
Mary (2) (Burke)
Nancy (Warren)
Timothy (Burke)
Thomas (Lincoln)
Thomas W. (Lincoln)
William (Columbia)
Murrer, William (Wayne)
Murrey, John (Liberty)
John (Chatham)
Murrin, Mary (Richmond)
Murrow, John (Madison)
Murry, Alexander (Oglethorpe)
Anne (Hall)
Betty (Oglethorpe)
Thomas (Oglethorpe)
William (Oglethorpe)
Muse, Daniel (Putnam)
Pope (Wilkes)
Musgan, C. S. I. (Jasper)
Musgrove, H. (Richmond)
John (Jefferson)
John E. (Jefferson)
Larkin C. (Jefferson)
William (Pulaski)
Musick, Major (Jefferson)
Sellers (Appling)
Mussels(?), Jesse (Appling)
Musslewhite, William
(Washington)
Mustlewhite, Thomas (Pulaski)
Mutry, John (Screven)
Myars, Burwell (Jones)
John (Jones)
Myatt, William (Richmond)
Myers, Mrs. (Chatham)
Elizabeth (Chatham)
George (Habersham)
George B. (Elbert)
James (Glynn)
Thomas (Washington)
Myhan, Alvin (Morgan)
Jesse (Morgan)
Myhand, Thomas (Warren)
William (Warren)
Myrack, John (Warren)
Nathaniel (Warren)
Richard (Warren)
Myres, Elizabeth (Greene)
Henry (McIntosh)
Myrick, David (Jasper)
Evans (Jones)
Goodwin (Baldwin)
James (Baldwin)

Lewis (Appling)

John (Greene)
Josiah (Warren)
Robert (Oglethorpe)
William (Gwinnett)

N

Nabb, William B. (Emanuel)
Nace, Jonathan (Jones)
William (Jones)
Nail, Benjamin (Elbert)
John (Morgan)
Reuben (Tattnall)
Nally, Claon (Richmond)
Nance, Catharine (Columbia)
Nanman, Artemus B. (Tattnall)
Napier, Leroy (Putnam)
Thomas (Putnam)
Thomas T. (Putnam)
Napper, Drury (Effingham)
Naramore, Eli (Hall)
Nares(?), John (Burke)
Nase, Bird (Oglethorpe)
Nash, Acton (Wilkes)
Alice (Elbert)
George (Elbert)
George B. (Elbert)
James (Elbert)
James (Jones)
James (Montgomery)
John (Columbia)
Thomas I. (Madison)
Natt, Mary (Screven)
Natty(?), Henley (Lincoln)
Navy, Wilson (Burke)
Nazworthy, John (Burke)
Ogburn (Burke)
Neal, Basil (Columbia)
David (Warren)
Demarius (Morgan)
Harrell (Warren)
James (Warren)
James, Sr. (Warren)
Joel (Warren)
John (Warren)
Older (Greene)
Thomas (McIntosh)
Thomas (Warren)
Neblet, Susannah (Morgan)
Neblett, Edmond (Jones)
Nedam(?), Moses (Pulaski)
Neel, Elias (Emanuel)
James T. (Jefferson)
John (Emanuel)
Jonathon (Emanuel)
Mary (Emanuel)
Reubin (Emanuel)
Thomas (Emanuel)
Neele, Mrs. (Chatham)
Neelund, Polly (Washington)
Neely, David (Walton)

Neely, James (Jefferson)
  John (Jefferson)
  Thomas (Jones)
  Thomas, Jr. (Washington)
  Thomas, Sr. (Washington)
Neese, Godlip I. (Effingham)
Negus, Joseph (Putnam)
Neidlinger, Hannah (Effingham)
Neil, Andrew (Habersham)
Neilson, Jesse (Warren)
Neisler(?), Hugh (Clarke)
Neismith, James (Bulloch)
  John (Bulloch)
Neives, William (Putnam)
Nelams, Sarah (Wilkes)
Nellums, (torn) (Laurens)
Nelms, John (Elbert)
  Jonathon (Elbert)
  Jordon (Elbert)
  Mary (Burke)
  Nancy (Greene)
  Nathaniel (Elbert)
  Samuel (Greene)
  Thomas (2) (Greene)
  William (Elbert)
Nelson, Abraham (Greene)
  Abram (Hall)
  Alexander (Jones)
  Archibald (Walton)
  Cannaan (Jones)
  Daniel (Chatham)
  George (Hall)
  George (Hancock)
  George W. (Hancock)
  Henry (Screven)
  Isaac (Tattnall)
  Jeremiah (Hancock)
  John (Pulaski)
  John (Wilkes)
  Lydia (Columbia)
  M. (Richmond)
  Moses (Jackson)
  Nancy (Hall)
  Neel (Morgan)
  Richard (Chatham)
  Silvester (Jackson)
  Taylor (Greene)
  Thomas (Morgan)
  Thomas (Wilkinson)
  Ward (Wilkinson)
  William (2) (Morgan)
Nephew, James (McIntosh)
Nesbet, Jain (Wilkinson)
  John (Morgan)
Nesbit, Hugh (Richmond)
  Jeremiah (Gwinnett)
  John (Wilkes)
  William (Gwinnett)
Nesbitt, William (Chatham)
Nesmith, Charles (Burke)
  James (Screven)

Netherclift, Alex (Bryan)
Netherland, James (Richmond)
Nettles, Martin (Liberty)
  William (Liberty)
Neville, Peter (Chatham)
Nevills, Jacob (Bulloch)
Nevis(?), John (Baldwin)
New, Jacob (Madison)
  Jesse (Jackson)
  Joel (Madison)
  William (Telfair)
Newbern, John (Early)
  Nancy (Madison)
Newberry, James (Jones)
  James (Warren)
  Joshua H. (Hall)
  Levi (Columbia)
  Rebecca (Wilkinson)
  Thomas (Wilkinson)
Newburn, Archibald (Elbert)
Newby, Jesse (Jones)
  John (Jasper)
Newcomb, Capt. R. (Chatham)
Newell, Katy (Greene)
  Samuel (Morgan)
Newman, Argin (Warren)
  James (Liberty)
  James (Washington)
  Samuel (Warren)
  Thomoas (2) (Appling)
  Thomas. (Columbia)
  Thomas (Richmond)
  Walter (Washington)
  William (Columbia)
  William (Warren)
  Willis (Bulloch)
Newnan, Daniel (Putnam)
Newsen, Polly (Chatham)
Newsom, Amos (2) (Columbia)
  Asa (Warren)
  Bat (Telfair)
  Claburu (Columbia)
  Crawford (Warren)
  David A. (Greene)
  Green (Warren)
  Henry (Warren)
  James (Warren)
  Joel (Greene)
  Joel (Putnam)
  John (Putnam)
  John (Warren
  Jorday (Warren)
  Joseph (Putnam)
  Joshua (Warren)
  Kenchen (Washington)
  Randle (Columbia)
  Rhoda (Warren)
  Robert (Greene)
  Ron (Warren)
  Solomon (Warren)
  William (Warren)

Newsome, Olive (Chatham)
  William (Columbia)
Newson, Daniel W. (Warren)
  Hardy (Jones)
  Lewsy (Wilkinson)
Newton, Alice (Chatham)
  Aris (Jasper)
  Clary (Clarke)
  Daniel (Washington)
  Ebenezer (Clarke)
  George (Screven)
  James (Jasper)
  Josiah (Clarke)
  Moses (Jefferson)
  Moses (Screven)
  Phillip (Emanuel)
  Samuel (Screven)
Neyland, Charlotte (Burke)
  Henry (Burke)
Niblack, Thomas (Jackson)
Niblet, Tilbert (Jones)
Nicels(?), Mary (Glynn)
Nichelson, George P. (Greene)
  James (Wilkes)
Nicholas, Archibald (Gwinnett)
  Harris (Wilkinson)
  John (Hall)
  Samuel (Chatham)
  Thomas (Gwinnett)
Nicholes, John (Wilkinson)
  Nathaneil (Wilkinson)
Nichols, Abraham (Chatham)
  Abraham (Habersham)
  Allen L. (Baldwin)
  Ambrose (Gwinnett)
  Amos (Burke)
  Charles (Burke)
  David (Burke)
  David D. (Irwin)
  Emelia (Burke)
  George (Warren)
  Henry (Morgan)
  Isaac (Pulaski)
  James (Jones)
  Jonathan (Jasper)
  Ransom (Clarke)
  Thomas (Burke)
  Thomas (Oglethorpe)
  Troves (Jasper)
  William (Jones)
Nicholson, Britton (Walton)
  James (Putnam)
  Malcolm (Burke)
Nickels, John (Wilkes)
Nickelson, John (Greene)
  Margaret (Greene)
Nickerson, Ed (Chatham)
  James (Jones)
Nicks, Ve (Jackson)
Nickson, Thomas (Jackson)
Nicolau, Pascal (Glynn)

Nicols, Henry (Tattnall)
Nieghblack, William (Camden)
Niel, Harmon (Montgomery)
Nielly(?), Louis (Appling)
Nielson, George (Oglethorpe)
Night, Jesse (Burke)
   John (Emanuel)
   Matthew (Burke)
   Robt. (Burke)
   Westly (Burke)
   William (2) (Burke)
Nillsom, William (Oglethorpe)
Nipper, John (Pulaski)
Nisbet, James (Greene)
Nite, Elisha (Walton)
   John (Walton)
   John (Wilkinson)
   Robert (Wilkinson)
Niven, Daniel (Jones)
Nix, Anderson (Madison)
   Edward (Oglethorpe)
   George (Elbert)
   Jeremiah (Elbert)
   John (Habersham)
   Joseph (Elbert)
   William (Elbert)
   William (Pulaski)
Nixon, Benjn (Burke)
   John (Clarke)
   John (Wilkes)
   Joseph (Walton)
   Samuel (Wilkinson)
Noble, Rose (Chatham)
   Samuel (Pulaski)
Nobles, (ind.) (Laurens)
   Elizabeth (McIntosh)
   Joseph (Wilkinson)
   Robert (Laurens)
   Sally (Gwinnett)
   Tenison (Wilkinson)
   Thomas (Wayne)
   William (Morgan)
Noby, N. (Jasper)
Nolan, Rebecca (Morgan)
   Thos. F. (Jasper)
   William (Elbert)
Noland, George (Gwinnett)
   Isaac (Gwinnett)
   James (Gwinnett)
   James (Wilkes)
   Stephen (Gwinnett)
   William (Gwinnett)
Nolen, James (Gwinnett)
Noles, Abram (Lincoln)
   Ephraim (Burke)
   Parker (Jasper)
Nolley, Danil (Wilkinson)
Nolums(?), John (Putnam)
Nolwell, John (Screven)
Noris(?), James (Chatham)
Noris, Stephen (Putnam)

Norman, Elijah (Wilkes)
   H. (Lincoln)
   Jesse (Wilkes)
   John (Emanuel)
   John (Wilkes)
   John, Sr. (Wilkes)
   Joseph (Jackson)
   Joseph (Liberty)
   Polly (col.) (Wilkes)
   Samuel (Emanuel)
   Sarah (Lincoln)
   Thomas (Wilkes)
   William (Liberty)
   William (Lincoln)
   William (Putnam)
   William (2) (Wilkes)
Norris, (ind.) (Hall)
   A. (Wilkes)
   Abner (Warren)
   Archer (Clarke)
   Charles (Chatham)
   Elisha (Hall)
   Hardy (2) (Hancock)
   Isaac (Emanuel)
   James (Jones)
   James (Walton)
   James, Sr. (Warren)
   Jethro (Lincoln)
   Joel (Warren)
   John (Putnam)
   Martha (Putnam)
   Patrick (Chatham)
   Rebecca (Hall)
   Robert (Baldwin)
   Robert (Washington)
   Samuel (Greene)
   Sarah (Morgan)
   Thomas (Hall)
   William (Columbia)
   William (Hall)
   William (Jasper)
   William (Warren)
North, Anthony (Oglethorpe)
   Robert (Oglethorpe)
   William (Oglethorpe)
Northcot, A. (Jasper)
   Robert (Laurens)
Northcut, Nancy (Habersham)
Northen, Peter (Jones)
Northern, John (Elbert)
   Margaret (Jones)
   Samuel (Putnam)
   William (Jones)
Northington, James (Oglethorpe)
   John (Morgan)
Northon, B. (Jasper)
Norton, Eliza (Camden)
   Jacob P. (Hancock)
   Rev. James (Liberty)
   Nathan (Camden)
   Polly (Chatham)

   Sarah (Hall)
   William (Morgan)
   William (Oglethorpe)
Norwood, George (Morgan)
   George (Pulaski)
   John (Jasper)
   William (Pulaski)
   William (Wilkinson)
Nott(?), James H. (Clarke)
Nott, Nathaniel (Jones)
Nowel, James (Walton)
   Mary (Oglethorpe)
   Thomas (Oglethorpe)
Nowell, Ann (Chatham)
   James (Oglethorpe)
   John (2) (Oglethorpe)
Nowlan, David (Jackson)
   Hannah (Effingham)
   Sherod (Jackson)
Nowland, William (Jasper)
Nox, Allison (Columbia)
Noyoso(?), Peter (Chatham)
Numan, Daniel (Tattnall)
   Garret (Wilkes)
   John (Walton)
Nunely, William (Elbert)
Nungazer, George (Chatham)
   Nathaniel (Chatham)
Nunghridge, Thomas (Emanuel)
Nunis, Alexander (Burke)
   Anne (Camden)
Nunley, James F. (Elbert)
   John (Elbert)
   Walter (Elbert)
Nunn, Elijah (Gwinnett)
   Hiram (Burke)
   John (Wilkinson)
   Nimrod (Warren)
   William (Baldwin)
Nunnally, John (Clarke)
   Josiah (Clarke)
   Horatio (Greene)
Nunnely, Izriel (Greene)
Nuron, Eli (Walton)
Nusam(?), Joel D. (Hancock)
Nutt, Ann (Baldwin)
   Jonathan (Morgan)
   May (Clarke)
   Mathew (Pulaski)
   Samuel (Morgan)
Nutting, Samuel (Oglethorpe)

O

Oakes, John (Camden)
   Jonathan (Oglethorpe)
Oakman, William H.
      (Richmond)
Oar, William (Greene)
Oates, James (Clarke)
   Richard W. (Clarke)

Oats, Charles (Burke)
Obanion, Benjamin
          (Habersham)
  Bryant (Burke)
  Green (Habersham)
  John (Burke)
  John (Wilkinsono)
  William (Jones)
O'Barr, Thomas (Hall)
Obery, John (McIntosh)
  Reuben (McIntosh)
  Solomon (McIntosh)
O'Brian, Duncan (Habersham)
  John (Habersham)
  Wilson (Habersham)
Obriant, James (Baldwin)
O'Connor, Jeremiah (Chatham)
  M.(ind.) (Chatham)
Odam, Joshua (Burke)
Oden, Daniel (Wilkes)
Odingsell, Anth (Chatham)
Odle, Polly (Clarke)
Odnet, Charlotte (Chatham)
Odom, Alexander (Jones)
  Archibald (Emanuel)
  Benjamin (2) (Morgan)
  Dildatha (Early)
  Ellsanah (Columbia)
  Emory (Irwin)
  Gideon (Burke)
  James (Morgan)
  James (Pulaski)
  Laben (Burke)
  Marie (Pulaski)
  Moses (Pulaski)
  William (Morgan)
  Winburn (Putnam)
Odot, John (Chatham)
Odum, Dempsey (Washington)
  Jacob, Jr. (Washington)
  Jacob, Sr. (Washington)
  James (Bulloch)
  John (Telfair)
  John, Jr. (Washington)
  John, Sr. (Washington)
  Mary (Bulloch)
  William (Washington)
Oemler, A. (ind.) (Chatham)
Offutt, Archibald (Columbia)
  Obediance (Columbia)
  Sampson (Washington)
Ofton, William W. (Jasper)
Ogburn, Little B. (Wilkinson)
Ogden, Keziah (Richmond)
  Milly (Bryan)
  Soloman (Camden)
Ogellive, William (Oglethorpe)
Ogilbia, Peter F. (Oglethorpe)
Ogleby, Richard (Oglethorpe)
  William (Chatham)

Ogles, Jesse (Morgan)
  Nancy (Morgan)
Oglesby, Daniel (Tattnall)
  Drury (Elbert)
  Elihua (Liberty)
  George (Elbert)
  James (Emanuel)
  James (Screven)
  John (Wilkes)
  Leroy (Elbert)
  Richard (Tattnall)
  Robert (Elbert)
  Thomas (Elbert)
  Thomas (Madison)
  William (Elbert)
Ogletree, (torn) (Laurens)
  Absalom (Wilkes)
  Benjamin (Morgan)
  David (Wilkes)
  John (Putnam)
  John (2) (Wilkes)
  John B. (Jasper)
  Joseph (Jasper)
  Littleton (Greene)
  Philemon (Morgan)
  Richard (Hancock)
  Thomas, Jr. (Putnam)
  Thomas, Sr. (Putnam)
  William (Wilkes)
Oihers(?), Gresham
          (Oglethorpe)
O'Kelley James (Madison)
  Thomas D. (Madison)
O'Kelly, Elizabeth (Madison)
  James (2) (Oglethorpe)
  Mary (Oglethorpe)
Olary, John (Putnam)
Olcott, James I. (Effingham)
O'Leary, Corneluis (Putnam)
Oler, John (Baldwin)
Oliphant, Joseph (Burke)
Olivant, John (Telfair)
Olive, Berry (Columbia)
  Ichabod (Columbia)
  John (Columbia)
  John (Emanuel)
  Thomas W. (Columbia)
  Willey (Columbia)
Oliver, (ind.) (2) (Laurens)
  Asa (Washington)
  Benjamin (Jones)
  Caleb (Elbert)
  Caleb (Jones)
  Caty (Pulaski)
  Chas. (Jasper)
  Dyonisus (Elbert)
  Eadeth (Wilkinson)
  Elijah (Jackson)
  Elijah (Screven)
  James (Elbert)
  James (Hall)

  James (McIntosh)
  James (Pulaski)
  James (Screven)
  James (Warren)
  John (Clarke)
  John (2) (Jones)
  John (Oglethorpe)
  John (Screven)
  John G. (Emanuel)
  John M. (Washington)
  McCarty (Elbert)
  McDaniel (Laurens)
  Mary (col.) (Wilkes)
  Mathew (Washington)
  Moses (Screven)
  Peter (Elbert)
  Risdon (Laurens)
  Risden, Jr. (Screven)
  Rowan (Washington)
  S. H. (Richmond)
  Samuel (Jones)
  Samuel B. (Jackson)
  Simion (Elbert)
  Terry (Warren)
  Thomas (Elbert)
  Thomas (Screven)
  Whiting (Clarke)
  William (Emanuel)
  William (Screven)
  William F. (Chatham)
  William W. (Screven)
Olliff, Benjamin (Wilkinson)
Olliver, Andrew (Greene)
  John (Greene)
  William (Greene)
Olover, Shelton (Elbert)
  Thomas (Elbert)
O'Neal, (ind.) (Laurens)
  Bartlett (Clarke)
  Bertam (Habersham)
  Edmond (Putnam)
  Elijah (Washington)
  Harrison (Greene)
  Henry (Jones)
  Isham (Effingham)
  James (Morgan)
  John (Warren)
  Joseph (Gwinnett)
  Mary A. (McIntosh)
  Ross (Warren)
  Thomas (McIntosh)
  Thomas (Morgan)
  Wooten (Greene)
O'Neel, John (Jones)
O'Neil, James (Habersham)
  John (Glynn)
  Jurly(?) (Columbia)
  William, Jr. (Wayne)
  William, Sr. (Wayne)
O'Neill, Anestus (Bulloch)
  J. (Jasper)

O'Neill, Z. (Jasper)
   Zelphy (Bulloch)
O'Niel, William (Lincoln)
Oquin, John (Washington)
OQuinn, William (Burke)
Oran, John (Chatham)
Orear, Benjamin (Greene)
Orick, Celia (Putnam)
   James (Putnam)
Oriley, Michael (McIntosh)
Orme, John (McIntosh)
Orr, Allen (Jasper)
   Ally (Jackson)
   Burrell (Madison)
   Christopher (Wilkes)
   Daniel (Madison)
   Janet (Washington)
   Jessie (Morgan)
   John (Jackson)
   John (Washington)
   John (Wilkes)
   Jno. (Jackson)
   Phillip (Wilkes)
   Robert (Clarke)
   Robert (Hall)
   Williams (Washington)
Osborn, George (Jasper)
   George (Putnam)
   John (Wilkes)
   Thomas (Jasper)
   William (Jasper)
Osborne, Mrs. (2) (Chatham)
   Geo. (Jasper)
   James (Jasper)
   John (Clarke)
   William (Jasper)
Osbourne, John (Hancock)
Osburn, Britain (Gwinnett)
   James (Wilkinson)
Osby, James (Jones)
Osgood, William (Liberty)
Osley, Jesse (Elbert)
   Zachariah (Elbert)
Osling, Jessie (Greene)
   John (Greene)
Osteen, Caleb (Washington)
   Isaac (Camden)
   John (Camden)
   Michael (Gwinnett)
   Thomas (Washington)
   William (Liberty)
   William J. (Gwinnett)
O'Steene, John (Appling)
   Shadrack (Appling)
Ottrey, Archibald (Putnam)
Otwell, James (Hall)
   Sophia (Hall)
Ousley, Jesse C. (Putnam)
   John (Putnam)
   Micajah (Pulaski)
   William (Putnam)

Outlaw, Edward, Jr. (Emanuel)
   Edward, Sr. (Emanuel)
   James (Richmond)
Overbay, Freeman (Hall)
Overby, Susan (Columbia)
Overstreet, Daniel (Emanuel)
   John D. (Wilkes)
   Moses (Burke)
   Silas (Tattnall)
   William (Burke)
Overton, James (Walton)
   John (2) (Walton)
Ovington, John (Chatham)
Owen, Aaron ,(Baldwin)
   Barshaba (Elbert)
   Beecham (Putnam)
   Benjamin (Greene)
   Bricy M. (Clarke)
   Caleb (Burke)
   Davis (Oglethorpe)
   George (Elbert)
   George (Greene)
   Glenn (Oglethorpe)
   H. (Jasper)
   Jacob (Jasper)
   Jeremiah (Jackson)
   John (Burke)
   John (Habersham)
   John (Oglethorpe)
   Lemuel (Putnam)
   Nancy (Burke)
   Robert (Jasper)
   William (Burke)
   William (Greene)
Owens, Ann (Baldwin)
   Caleb (Washington)
   David (Jackson)
   E. (Richmond)
   Edmond (Putnam)
   Elizabeth (Walton)
   Geo. W. (Chatham)
   Henry (Jones)
   John (Lincoln)
   John J. (Baldwin)
   John N. (Putnam)
   Jonathan (Jones)
   Lorey (Jones)
   Obediah (Wilkes)
   Patience (Washington)
   Peter (Jones)
   Sarah (2) (Wilkes)
   Spencer (Jones)
   Stephen (Screven)
   Uriah (Washington)
   William (Jones)
   William (Walton)
   William (Wilkinson)
   Wm. H. (Baldwin)
   Williams (Pulaski)
Owings, Samuel (McIntosh)
Oxendine, Edney (Wilkinson)

Oxford, Edward (Jones)
   Tilman D. (Jones)
Oxley, Sarah Ann (Burke)
   William (Burke)
Ozburn, David (Jackson)
   Jesse (Jackson)
   John (Jackson)
   John, Jr. (Jackson)
   Ross (Jackson)
   Yerby (Jackson)

P

Pace, Barnabas (Elbert)
   Barnabas (2) (Morgan)
   Basil (Elbert)
   Bryan (Washington)
   Christopher (Telfair)
   Hardy (Putnam)
   Isaac (Gwinnett)
   James (Oglethorpe)
   James (Warren)
   John (Jackson)
   Nathaniel (Washington)
   Paris (Oglethorpe)
   Richard (Putnam)
   Samuel (Washington)
   Silas (Warren)
   Solomon (Putnam)
   Stephen (2) (Jasper)
   Stephen (Putnam)
   Thomas (Jasper)
   Thomas (Richmond)
   Thomas (Washington)
   Trion (Effingham)
   William (Columbia)
   William (Morgan)
   William, Jr. (Putnam)
   William (Warren)
Padget, (torn) (Laurens)
   Elijah (Tattnall)
   Elizabeth (Tattnall)
   Hopkin (Tattnall)
   John (Tattnall)
Padgett, Abram (Hall)
   Moses (Putnam)
   Rowley (Wilkinson)
   William (Putnam)
Page, Alan (Washington)
   Bery (Habersham)
   Jacob (Jefferson)
   James (Hancock)
   James (Washington)
   Jehue (Wilkes)
   John (Chatham)
   Level (Elbert)
   Martin (Elbert)
   Nathan (Washington)
   Solomon, Jr. (Washington)
   Solomon, Sr. (Washington)
   William (Baldwin)

Page, William (Elbert)
William (Glynn)
William (Habersham)
Paget, Elizah (Baldwin)
Pagett, William (Jasper)
Pain, (ind.) (Wilkinson)
Eliza (Wilkinson)
Flail (Oglethorpe)
H. D. (Jasper)
John (Wilkinson)
Jonathon (Wilkinson)
Joseph (Wilkinson)
William (Jasper)
Paine, Edward (Clarke)
James (Jackson)
John (Chatham)
Robert (Glynn)
Thomas (Habersham)
William (Columbia)
Paisley, Thomas (Glynn)
Palmer, Mrs. (Chatham)
Abel (Burke)
Amasa (Greene)
Benjamin (Burke)
Elisha (Greene)
Elisha (Lincoln)
George (Burke)
George (Chatham)
George (Lincoln)
Hesekiah (Hancock)
James (Greene)
James (Putnam)
John (Greene)
John (Liberty)
Martin, Sr. (Glynn)
Robert (Burke)
Russell (Greene)
Sally (Burke)
Wilson (Lincoln)
Palmeter, Paul (Elbert)
Palmon, Hezekiah (Hancock)
John (Hancock)
Palmore, Gru (Columbia)
Isaac (Columbia)
Joseph (Jones)
Nathaniel (Columbia)
William (Columbia)
Pamphrey, Isham (Wilkinson)
Pannel, Daniel (Jackson)
Pant, John (Telfair)
Papet, Catherine (Chatham)
Papot, Made. (Chatham)
Paradise, Elizabeth (Lincolin)
Parddis, William (Jefferson)
Pardeu, Huston (Camden)
Pardue, Benjamin (Jefferson)
James (Jefferson)
John (Jefferson)
William (Jefferson)
Parham, Dixon (Elbert)
Edmund (Warren)

Elijah (Warren)
Hadyn (Washington)
Isham (Elbert)
John (Putnam)
Jones (Putnam)
Lewis (Warren)
Matthew (Warren)
R. (Early)
Robert (2) (Warren)
Rolen (Baldwin)
Susan (Putnam)
Williamson (Baldwin)
Paris, Francis (Burke)
Jack (Burke)
Jane (Habersham)
Pelander O. (Warren)
Parish ____ard (Effingham)
Allen (Camden)
Charles (Washington)
Hampton W. (Baldwin)
Henry (Bulloch)
Hezekiah (Emanuel)
Isaac (Walton)
James (Washington)
John (Warren)
Joseph (Camden)
Moses (Hancock)
Peter (Putnam)
Prosser (Jefferson)
Samuel (Effingham)
Ting (Camden)
William (Morgan)
William (Warren)
Park, Andrew (Putnam)
Ezekiel E. (Greene)
Isham (McIntosh)
James (Greene)
James (Putnam)
John (Greene)
Joseph (Chatham)
Joseph (2) (Morgan)
Richard (Morgan)
Thomas (Putnam)
Parke, Hannah (Jackson)
Jean (Jackson)
John (Jackson)
Parker, Mrs. (Chatham)
Aaron (Clarke)
Aaron, Sr. (Clarke)
Aaron (Putnam)
Allen (Clarke)
Asa (Jefferson)
Beal (Putnam)
Benjamin (Emanuel)
Calib (Montgomery)
Daniel (Habersham)
Daniel (Jones)
David (Greene)
Dempsey (Greene)
Dicy (Greene)
E. B. (Camden)

Elisha (2) (Baldwin)
Elisha (Tattnall)
Emanuel (Greene)
G. (Richmond)
Gabril (Montgomery)
George (Baldwin)
George (Morgan)
George P. (Gwinnett)
George W. (Jackson)
Hardy (Emanuel)
Hardy (Jefferson)
Henry (Washington)
Isaac (Morgan)
Isiah (Gwinnett)
J. E.(?) (Washington)
Jacob (Burke)
James (Burke)
James (Walton)
James (Washington)
Jeptha P. (Putnam)
Jerre (Jackson)
Jesse (Emanuel)
John (Camden)
John (Clarke)
John (Hancock)
John (Putnam)
John (Warren)
Jonathon, Sr. (Laurens)
Joseph (Chatham)
Joseph (Elbert)
Joseph (Washington)
Joshua (Morgan)
Keder (Washington)
Leah (Walton)
Lewis (Burke)
Lewis, Jr. (Hancock)
Lewis, Sr. (Hancock)
Mary (Warren)
Moses (Jackson)
Mrs. O. (Chatham)
Phebe (Columbia)
Richard (Hancock)
Robert (Wilkes)
Robert (Wilkinson)
Samuel (Morgan)
Sarah (Jackson)
Simon (Burke)
Simon (Jefferson)
Starling (Bulloch)
Stephen (Gwinnett)
Stephen (Jefferson)
Stephen (Jones)
Tines (Columbia)
Dr. W. (Chatham)
West (Clarke)
William (Chatham)
William (Clarke)
William (Emanuel)
William (2) (Hancock)
William (Jackson)
William (Jefferson)

Parker, William, Jr. (Liberty)
William C. (Clarke)
William H. (Jasper)
William H. (Liberty)
Parkerson, Levan (Wilkes)
Parkey, Thomas (Wilkes)
Parkman, S. B. (Chatham)
Parks, Aaron (Columbia)
Abraham (Elbert)
Bird (Oglethorpe)
Fleman (Hall)
Estate of J. B. (Jasper)
James (Greene)
John, Sr. (2) (Columbia)
John, Jr. (Columbia)
Lewis (Lincoln)
Mary (Wilkes)
Robert (Wilkes)
Welcome (Jasper)
William (Jasper)
William (Lincoln)
Parland, John (Glynn)
Parmer, E. (Richmond)
Elizabeth (Jackson)
Fox (Emanuel)
Jacob (Jones)
Jonathan (Richmond)
Joseph (Early)
Thomas (Hancock)
Parnell(?), Joseph (Chatham)
Parner, Israel (Hancock)
Parr, John (Warren)
Parramore, James (Laurens)
James (Telfair)
John (Pulaski)
John (Telfair)
John E. (Early)
Noah (Telfair)
Reddin (Telfair)
William (Laurens)
William H. (Laurens)
Parris, Nathaniel H.
(Oglethorpe)
Treasea (Wayne)
Parrish, Ansil(?) (Bulloch)
Green (Telfair)
H. H. (Jasper)
Harris (Putnam)
John (Telfair)
Jonathan (Jones)
Neal (Telfair)
Philip S. (Pulaski)
Roda (Greene)
Parrot, Benjamin (Hancock)
Parrott, George (Walton)
Jessee (Greene)
John (Glynn)
John (Greene)
Parrymore, James (Washington)
Sarah (Washington)
Parson, Benjamin (Telfair)

Samuel (Jasper)
Parsons, Ann (Jefferson)
Frances (Camden)
James (Jasper)
Jones (Jasper)
Meriah (Camden)
Thomas (Jefferson)
Partin, Charles (Tattnall)
Parton, Britton (Jones)
Ezekiel (Jones)
Partrich, Daniel K. (Elbert)
Partrick, Luke (Walton)
Paul (Walton)
Solloman (Walton)
Partridge, Henry (Jefferson)
John (Jefferson)
Sarah (Wilkes)
William (Washington)
Partwater, D. (Jasper)
Party, Mary (Bryan)
Pascal, Isaiah (Wilkes)
John H. (Clarke)
Mary (Wilkes)
Samuel (Wilkes)
Paschal, Samuel (Morgan)
William (Lincoln)
Pase, Frederick (Wilkinson)
William (Wilkinson)
Pashall, Thomas (Lincoln)
Paskel, George (Oglethorpe)
Pasmoor, Alexander (Wilkinson)
Pasmore, Housman
(Washington)
Pasmor(?), John (Baldwin)
Pason, Evan (Habersham)
Pass, Andrew (Oglethorpe)
John (Clarke)
John B. (Putnam)
Mathew I. (Oglethorpe)
Patan, James M. (Irwin)
Patch, Rebecca (Liberty)
Pate, Barnet (Emanuel)
Cloah (Jefferson)
Edmund (Warren)
Edward (Morgan)
Elizabeth (Wilkes)
Harbul (Warren)
James (Jasper)
Jese (Jackson)
John (Washington)
Pater, Archabald (Jasper)
John (Jasper)
John (Walton)
Patern, Thomas (Wilkinson)
Paterson, Alexander (Wilkinson)
Jaoulín (Hancock)
Jesse (Habersham)
Joseph (Hancock)
Sarah (Hancock)
William (Hancock)
Patick, Rite (Wayne)

Patillo, John R. (Morgan)
Nancy (Morgan)
Patin, James (Chatham)
Patman, James B. (Oglethorpe)
Lenard (Oglethorpe)
Watson (Oglethorpe)
William (Oglethorpe)
William, Sr. (Oglethorpe)
Paton, Silas (Walton)
Patric, Clavendic (Baldwin)
Patrick, David (Oglethorpe)
I. & I. (Jasper)
John (Clarke)
John (Jackson)
John N. (Jasper)
Josiah (Oglethorpe)
Lemuel (Richmond)
Levy (Bulloch)
Robert (Morgan)
Robert (Putnam)
William (Emanuel)
William (Morgan)
William (Oglethorpe)
Patridge, Henry (Washington)
James (Jones)
Nicholas (Jones)
Thomas (Jones)
Patrige, John (Oglethorpe)
Patten, Catharine (Madison)
James H. (Madison)
Patterson, Charles (Morgan)
D. (Richmond)
Ezekiel (Jones)
Henry (2) (Oglethorpe)
James (Elbert)
James (Jackson)
James (Oglethorpe)
James (Screven)
Jesse (Elbert)
John, Sr. (Burke)
John (Elbert)
John (Jefferson)
John (Jones)
John S. (Jones)
Mark (Jones)
Mary (Jefferson)
Mary A. (McIntosh)
Nimrod (Elbert)
Robert (Jefferson)
Robert (Morgan)
Robert (Putnam)
Samuel (Burke)
Samuel (Elbert)
Samuel (Richmond)
Thomas (Jefferson)
Wilie (Jones)
William (Burke)
William (Chatham)
William (Effingham)
William (Elbert)
William (2) (Jackson)

(114)

Patterson, William (2)
    (Jefferson)
Patti, John (Habersham)
Pattillo, George H. (Greene)
  Henry (Morgan)
  Dr. Howard (Morgan)
  James (Greene)
  James (Morgan)
  John (Greene)
  John V. (Greene)
  Samuel (Morgan)
Pattishall, John (Wilkinson)
  Richard (Jones)
Pattman, John (Oglethorpe)
Patton, Benjamin (Oglethorpe)
  Lydia (Wilkes)
  Samuel (Oglethorpe)
  Sollomon (Oglethorpe)
  William (Jackson)
Patty, Elijah (Jasper)
Paul, Robert (Jones)
  William (Jones)
Paulet, B. G. (Burke)
Paulett, Richard (Clarke)
Paulk, John (Wilkinson)
  John, Jr. (Wilkinson)
  John, Sr. (Wilkinson)
  Micajor (Wilkinson)
  Samuel (Jefferson)
  Uriah (Wilkinson)
Paulson, Neals (Greene)
Paxton, Mrs. (Camden)
  John (Morgan)
Payne, B. (Richmond)
  John, Sr. (Greene)
  Joseph (Emanuel)
Payton, Howard (Madison)
  William (Madison)
  William (Oglethorpe)
Peace, Major (Hancock)
Peacock, (ind.) (Pulaski)
  (ind.) (Washington)
  Archibald (Washington)
  Bryant (Pulaski)
  Isham (Tattnall)
  Jessey (Wilkinson)
  John (Bulloch)
  John (McIntosh)
  John (Washington)
  John T. (Wilkinson)
  Jonathon (Washington)
  Levy (Wilkinson)
  Molton (Washington)
  Pierson (Washington)
  Samuel P. (McIntosh)
  Tinker John (Washington)
  Washington (Washington)
  William (Hancock)
  William (Jasper)
  William (Washington)
Peak, Henry (Hancock)

James (Habersham)
Leonard (Morgan)
Russel (Habersham)
Peale, William (Jasper)
Peaples, (Peeples) Henry
    (Jones)
Pearce, (ind.) (Gwinnett)
  Axom (Gwinnett)
  Benjamin (Richmond)
  Daniel S. (Wilkinson)
  Edmund (Gwinnett)
  Elizabeth (Wilkinson)
  Ezekiel (Gwinnett)
  Gedach (Gwinnett)
  Green D. (Screven)
  James (Gwinnett)
  Jesse (Wilkinson)
  John (Gwinnett)
  John (Jackson)
  John (Pulaski)
  John I. (Putnam)
  Joseph (Jackson)
  Loverick (Greene)
  Maria L. (Chatham)
  Samuel (Jasper)
  Sarah (Wilkinson)
  Seth (Jefferson)
  Sion (Gwinnett)
  Thomas (Putnam)
  Wiley (Gwinnett)
  William (Gwinnett)
Pearman, Robert (Morgan)
Pearre, Alexander (Columbia)
Pearre(?) James (Columbia)
Pearre, John (2) (Columbia)
  John (Elbert)
  Nathaniel (Columbia)
  William (Columbia)
Pears, William (Richmond)
Pearse(?), J. (Richmond)
Pearse, Lovet (Baldwin)
  Thomas (Wilkinson)
Pearson, Abel (Baldwin)
  Benjamin (Bulloch)
  Charles (Putnam)
  Edward (Warren)
  Elijah (Warren)
  Elizabeth (Wilkes)
  Enoch (Jasper)
  Francis (Walton)
  Francis (Wilkes)
  James (Warren)
  Jeremiah (Jasper)
  Jeremiah (2) (Jones)
  John (Screven)
  John M. (Jasper)
  Jonathon (Wilkinson)
  Littleton (Jones)
  Micheal (Wilkes)
  Nathan (Wilkinson)
  Peter (Wilkinson)

Ruth (Gwinnett)
Samuel (Putnam)
W. H. (Jasper)
William (Jones)
William (Putnam)
William H. (Jasper)
Peas, John (Jasper)
Peavines, Joseph (Habersham)
Peavy, Daniel (2) (Hancock)
  Dial (Walton)
  Elizabeth (Warren)
  Isom (Walton)
  Jacob (Telfair)
  James (Warren)
  Jane (Warren)
  John (Warren)
  Joseph (Clarke)
  Levy (Hancock)
  Thomas (Washington)
Peck, (ind.) (Hancock)
  John (Putnam)
  William (Chatham)
  William (Putnam)
Peddy, Betsey (Washington)
  Henry (Jasper)
  Julius C. (Washington)
  Madform (Jones)
Pedham, Nelson (Jones)
Pedigrin, James (Baldwin)
Peebles, Henery (Jefferson)
  Henry (Warren)
  Isaac (Warren)
  Thomas (Jefferson)
  Thomas (Warren)
Peek, Charles (Greene)
  Henry (Putnam)
  James (Greene)
  Locket (Greene)
  Robert (Greene)
  Solomon (Hall)
Peel, John (Jefferson)
  Richmond (Jefferson)
Peeler, Anthony (Greene)
  Jacob (Greene)
  Leonard (Columbia)
Peeples, Dudley (Morgan)
  Jehugh (Morgan)
  Joseph (Morgan)
Peery, David (Jasper)
Peevy, Allen (Jasper)
  Helton (Morgan)
  James (Putnam)
  Peter (Morgan)
Peff, Ann (Chatham)
Peirce, Briton L. (Burke)
Peler, Abner (Elbert)
Pelham, Richard (Chatham)
Pelotte, James (McIntosh)
Pelps, Albin (Jones)
Pembleton, Frances (Putnam)
Pen, George (Elbert)

Pen, Thomas H. (Richmond)
Pendarvis, Joseph (Wayne)
Pendavis, William (Glynn)
Pender, James (Richmond)
    Luraney (Jones)
    Wright (Jones)
Pendergrass, Hiram (Jasper)
    John (Jackson)
Pendleton, Coleman (Putnam)
    Jese (Appling)
    John B. (Clarke)
    William (Appling)
Pendley, Nimrod (Gwinnett)
Pendry, John (Jefferson)
Penfield, Josiah (Chatham)
Pengree, Thomas (Screven)
Penick, Robert (Morgan)
Penledge, Gideon (Effingham)
Penn, Benjamin (Elbert)
    Edmond (Oglethorpe)
    Francis (Madison)
    Francis (Oglethorpe)
    John, Jr. (Elbert)
    John T. (Oglethorpe)
    Moses (Oglethorpe)
    William (Elbert)
    William (Jasper)
Penney, Malichi (Greene)
Pennington, A. (Jasper)
    E. (Jasper)
    ✶ Elizabeth (Burke)
    Nancy (Jefferson)
    Neddy (Jones)
    Samuel (Morgan)
    ✶✶ Sion (Jefferson)
Penny, George (Chatham)
    Thomas M. (Morgan)
Pennyman, Joshua T. (Putnam)
Penroe, Ralph (Burke)
Penson, Baid (Oglethorpe)
Penthia(?), Mr. (Chatham)
Penticost, George (Jackson)
    Richard (Jackson)
    William (Jackson)
Penyea(?), John (Chatham)
Peoples, John (Jackson)
Pepper, Daniel (Jones)
    James G. (Glynn)
    John (Gwinnett)
    Parker, (Gwinnett)
    Samuel (Gwinnett)
Perch, Hartwell (Hancock)
Perdew, John (Putnam)
    John O. (Wilkinson)
Perdieu, William (Richmond)
Perdu, Joseph C. (Putnam)
Perdue, Daniel (Greene)
    George (Baldwin)
    James (Jones)
    James A. (Baldwin)
    Isaac (Jones)

    Thomas (Greene)
    William (Jones)
Perkens, John (Wilkinson)
Perkerson, Dempsey (Gwinnett)
    Jacob (Pulaski)
    Joel (Gwinnett)
    Sevesley(?) (Gwinnett)
Perkins, Aldman (Wilkes)
    Benjamin (Greene)
    Edward (Wilkes)
    Henry (Wilkes)
    John (2) (Jones)
    John (Wilkes)
    Joseph (Washington)
    Lunsford (Wilkes)
    Reason (Wilkinson)
    Robert (Clarke)
    Thomas (McIntosh)
    William (Morgan)
Permentor, Susan (Columbia)
    William (Jones)
    John (Jones)
Pernell, John (Washington)
    Scarbra (Washington)
Peron, Louis (Jackson)
Perrett, Nathaniel (Jones)
Perrey, Elias (Liberty)
    John (Liberty)
Perriman, Anthony A. (Elbert)
Perry, (ind.) (Laurens)
    Allen (Pulaski)
    Amos (Putnam)
    Ann (Jackson)
    Benjamin (Columbia)
    Burkley (Putnam)
    Byrd (Warren)
    George S. (Burke)
    Greene (Greene)
    Hardy (Burke)
    Hiram (Jackson)
    Humphry (Columbia)
    James (Tattnall)
    James (Washington)
    Jeremiah (Warren)
    Jesse (Jones)
    John (Columbia)
    John (Glynn)
    John (Laurens)
    John (Morgan)
    Jonathan (Columbia)
    Joseph (Burke)
    Levi (Baldwin)
    Levi (Columbia)
    Micajah (Warren)
    Michael W. (Baldwin)
    Nicholas (Baldwin)
    Peter (Clarke)
    Philip (Habersham)
    Sarah (Jackson)
    Shadrack (Washington)
    Thomas (Jackson)

    Thomas W. (Hancock)
    Walter (Wilkes)
    William (Columbia)
    William, Sr. (Columbia)
    William (Habersham)
    William (Jasper)
    William (Jones)
    William (Tattnall)
    Willis (Jackson)
    Zodack (Wilkes)
Perryman, Cornelius (Warren)
    David B. (Putnam)
    Elisha (Putnam)
    Elisha (Warren)
    James (Warren)
    John (Putnam)
    Robert L. (Pulaski)
    William G. (Putnam)
Persans, Thomas (Warren)
Persity, Mary (Camden)
Persol, John (Jackson)
Person, John C. (Clarke)
    Moses (Habersham)
    Ragland (Habersham)
Persons, Turner (Putnam)
    Turner, Jr. (Warren)
    Turner, Sr. (Warren)
Perteet, S. (Jasper)
Perthelot(?), Doct. (Chatham)
Pervatte, Peter (Liberty)
Pervice, Bennet (Wilkinson)
    Charles (Wilkinson)
Pervis, Jesse (Jefferson)
    Nancy (Jefferson)
    Needham (Jefferson)
    William (Emanuel)
    William (Jefferson)
Petarman, Benjamon
              (Oglethorpe)
Peteet, John (Wilkes)
    Richard (Wilkes)
    Robert(?) (Wilkes)
Petegrew, Robert (Hancock)
Peten, John (Wilkes)
    Louis (Wilkes)
Peters, Edmund (Morgan)
    Jesse, Sr. (Oglethorpe)
    John (Greene)
    John (Oglethorpe)
    Nathaniel (Jones)
    Nathaniel (Putnam)
    Simon (Wilkes)
    William N. (Oglethorpe)
Peterson, Benjamin W.
              (Morgan)
    Conrad (Richmond)
    James (Appling)
    John (Appling)
    John (Hall)
    Malcum (Montgomery)
    Polly (Burke)

✶ Jesse (Appling)
✶✶ William (Appling)

Peterson, Thomas (Hancock)
Petit(?), Mr. (Chatham)
   Mrs. (Chatham)
Peto, James (Chatham)
Pettice, Moses (Richmond)
Pettie, Constantine (Richmond)
Pettigrew, A. (Chatham)
Pettijohn, James (Jackson)
Pettit, John (Columbia)
   Purson (Columbia)
Pettus, Charles (Wilkes)
   John (Wilkes)
   Stephens (Wilkes)
Petty, Ambrose (Morgan)
   Eliza (Bulloch)
   Jeremiah (Jones)
   John ,(Morgan)
   John (Oglethorpe)
   Meredy (Screven)
   William (Jones)
Pettyjohn, A. (Jackson)
   Reuben (Jackson)
   William (Jackson)
Pevay, John (Warren)
Peveay, Joseph (Tattnall)
Pevey, Abraham (Chatham)
Pevy, Abraham (Warren)
Pew, Abel (Hancock)
   Catherine (Putnam)
Peyton, Cornelius (Madison)
   George (Madison)
   Moses (Madison)
Phair, Edward (Jackson)
   Samuel (Jackson)
Phelps, Aquila (2) (Jasper)
   Elizabeth (Liberty)
   Glen(?) (Clarke)
   Hillery (Jasper)
   James (Elbert)
   James E. (Liberty)
   Thomas (Elbert)
Phelson, Thomas (McIntosh)
Phepps, Richard (Elbert)
Pherris, Joab (Liberty)
Philipp, Burrel (Screven)
Philips, (torn) (Laurens)
   ----ham (Laurens)
   Adam (Jackson)
   Benjamin (Burke)
   Benjamin (Morgan)
   Charles (Jones)
   Charles (Morgan)
   Daniel (Jones)
   Dawson (Jones)
   George (Burke)
   Hardy (Morgan)
   Henry (Jackson)
   Isham (Jones)
   James (Morgan)
   Jessie (Morgan)
   John (Washington)

Joseph (Burke)
Joseph (Warren)
Joshua (Morgan)
Larkin (Morgan)
Lemuel (Morgan)
Levi (Jackson)
Obediah (Richmond)
Robert (Morgan)
Ruth (Warren)
Solomon (Jones)
Susan (Laurens)
Thomas (2) (Jackson)
William (2) (Morgan)
Zachariah (Morgan)
Phillip, John (Wilkes)
Phillips, (ind.) (Chatham)
   (ind.) (Effingham)
   (ind.) (Pulaski)
   Benjamin (Screven)
   Bluford (Putnam)
   Elijah (Jasper)
   Ephriam (Emanuel)
   George (Greene)
   George (Morgan)
   Hardy (Greene)
   Henry (Greene)
   Ichabod (Columbia)
   Irby (Wilkes)
   Isaac (Pulaski)
   Isham (Columbia)
   Isham (Pulaski)
   James (3) (Jasper)
   James (Morgan)
   James (Pulaski)
   Jesse B. (Greene)
   John (Jasper)
   John (Oglethorpe)
   John H. (Greene)
   John W. (Jasper)
   Jonathan (Jasper)
   Jonathan (Putnam)
   Leonard (Putnam)
   Leonard (Wilkes)
   Leroy (Jasper)
   Levi (Putnam)
   Lewis (Jasper)
   Mark (Emanuel)
   Martin (Putnam)
   Mary (Wilkes)
   Matthew (Morgan)
   Mathew (Oglethorpe)
   Nathan H. (Putnam
   Rial B. (Emanuel)
   Rial B. Sr. (Emanuel)
   Richard (Screven)
   Robert (Gwinnett)
   Sarah (Jasper)
   Solomon (Jefferson)
   Thomas (Jasper)
   Thomas (Richmond)
   Whitmel (Morgan)

Wilder (Columbia)
William (Morgan)
William (Pulaski)
William (Walton)
William (Wilkes)
Williaim C. (Montgomery)
Zacheriah (,Jasper)
Phinazy, John (Hall)
Phinizy, Jacob (Oglethorpe)
   John (Richmond)
Phipps, Joseph (Lincoln)
   Lewis (Elbert)
Phips, Lewis (Elbert)
Pickard, Micajah (Hancock)
   Silas (Jones)
Pickens, William (2) (Jasper)
Pickeren, Elijah E. (Screven)
Pickerion, John (Telfair)
Picket, James (Telfair)
Pickets, James, Jr. (Jones)
Pickett, Daniel (Chatham)
   James (Jones)
   Pruscilla (Jones)
   Thomas (Jones)
Picking, William (Richmond)
Picquet, Abner (Wilkes)
Pidge, Capt. (Chatham)
Pie, James (2) (Oglethorpe)
   Jesse (Oglethorpe)
   William (Oglethorpe)
Pierce, Adgworth (Wilkinson)
   Allen (Burke)
   Dorcas (Burke)
   Fellen (Putnam)
   George W. (Burke)
   Hugh (Habersham)
   John (Burke)
   Joshua (Screven)
   Mathew (Hancock)
   Reubern (Hall)
   Spotwood (Hancock)
   Stephen (Screven)
   Timathey (Wilkinson)
Piercson, Stephen (Hancock)
Piercy, Elizabeth (Morgan)
Pierman, Oren (Putnam)
   Whitmit (Putnam)
Pierson, Christopher
           (Washington)
   John (Chatham)
Pigg, John (Appling)
Pike, John (Walton)
   Mary (Baldwin)
   Mary (Putnam)
   William (Walton)
Pikins, William (Washington)
Pilbergh(?), John (Chatham)
Pilcher. Lewis (Washington)
   William (Chatham)
   William (Warren)
Piles. Gilbert (Glynn)

Piles, James (Glynn)
John (Glynn)
Mary (Glynn)
Samuel (Glynn)
William (Glynn)
Pilgrim, Michal (Habersham)
Pilkerton, John (Hall)
Pilman, John (Jones)
Pilton, Simon (Clarke)
Pincard, James (Jasper)
Pincher, Mary (McIntosh)
Pindugrass, Dolley (Greene)
Pine, Jacob (Oglethorpe)
Mary (Chatham)
Pines, William (Greene)
Pinkard, James (Jasper)
John (Jones)
P. (Jasper)
T. C. (Jasper)
Thomas (Greene)
Pinkardton, James (Putnam)
Pinkney, Thomas slaves of
(Liberty)
Pinks, David (Oglethorpe)
Pinkston, Basil (Washington)
Greenberry (Wilkes)
Gresham (Wilkes)
John (Hancock)
Pinnion, Jonathan (Hall)
Richard (Hall)
Pinsar, Joseph (Chatham)
Pinson, Mary (Oglethorpe)
Joseph (Jackson)
Thomas B. (Oglethorpe)
William (Oglethorpe)
Piper, John F. (Walton)
Zadock (Hancock)
Pipier, Antoine (Chatham)
Pipkin, Moses (Pulaski)
Prudence (Pulaski)
William (Pulaski)
Pirant, Charles (Jackson)
Piron, James (Jackson)
Pirtle, Isaac (Hall)
John (Hall)
Pitard, William (Oglethorpe)
Pitman, Albert (Laurens)
Edward (Hall)
Edward (Wilkes)
Henry (Wilkes)
Ichabod (Columbia)
James (Madison)
Sir James (Madison)
Jefferson (Columbia)
Jesse (Warren)
Jesse (Wilkes)
John (Columbia)
John G. (Jackson)
Maria (Columbia)
Marshal (Columbia)
Martin (Jackson)

Micajah (Wilkes)
Pleasant O. (Jackson)
Rebecca (Chatham)
Robert (Jefferson)
Timothy (Lincoln)
Timothy (Madison)
Pitt, John (Washington)
Pittard, Humphrey (Clarke)
Thompson (Clarke)
William (Oglethorpe)
Pittman, Arthur (Tattnall)
Daniel, (Columbia)
Daniel N. (Gwinnett)
James (Wilkinson)
Jeremiah (Putnam)
Jessey (Wilkinson)
John (Laurens)
Phillip (Wilkinson)
Pitts, Burton(?) (Pulaski)
Chany (Jones)
Elizabeth (Hancock)
Hardy (Warren)
Henry (Laurens)
James (Jones)
Jane (Washington)
John, Jr. (Telfair)
L. C. (Laurens)
Levi (Jones)
Mariah (Baldwin)
Nancy (Jones)
Nancy (Telfair)
Nicholas W. (Warren)
Obadiah (Jones)
Robert (McIntosh)
Samuel (Warren)
Wesley (Jones)
Plant, William (Wilkes)
Plask, James (Burke)
Plaster, Benjamin (Gwinnett)
Platt, David (Bulloch)
John (Bulloch)
Joshua (Bulloch)
Player, S. (Richmond)
Pledger, James (Elbert)
Johnson S. (Elbert)
Lemuel (Elbert)
Murrell (Elbert)
Thomas, Sr. (Elbert)
Thomas, Jr. (Elbert)
Plinton, David (Glynn)
Plummer, Thomas (Jones)
Plunkett, Silas (2) (Hancock)
Poder, Andrew (Wilkes)
Mary (Wilkes)
Poe, James (Habersham)
Samuel (Habersham)
William (Richmond)
Pointer, John (Wilkes)
Poiston, Clark D. (Jackson)
Poke, Hugh (Hall)
Polack, David (Chatham)

Poland, John (Telfair)
Polhill, James (Burke)
John G. (Burke)
Nathanl (Burke)
Thomas (Chatham)
Polk, Charles (Madison)
Evan (Jackson)
William (Jones)
Pollard, Frederick (Greene)
Hiram (Pulaski)
James (Greene)
Jane (Wilkes)
John (Morgan)
Joseph (Greene)
M. (Jasper)
Pugh (Greene)
Richard (Jasper)
Robert (Columbia)
Seaborn (Wilkes)
Thomas (Greene)
Thomas (Wilkes)
Pollock, Frederick (Chatham)
John (Screven)
John (Wilkinson)
Polock, George (Screven)
Pomberton(?), Alton (Burke)
Pond, John (Richmond)
Ponder, Amos (Jasper)
Dawson (Burke)
Elizabeth (Oglethorpe)
Ephraim (Burke)
James (Jasper)
James H. (Oglethorpe)
Jesse (Morgan)
John H. (Hall)
John L. (Jasper)
John M. (Oglethorpe)
Magatret (Jasper)
Richard (Burke)
Vitate (Oglethorpe)
William L. (Oglethorpe)
Ponsheir, William (Liberty)
Pool, Aaron (Jefferson)
David (Wilkes)
Eli (Habersham)
Hardy (Jefferson)
Henry, Jr. (Warren)
Henry, Sr. (Warren)
James (Jefferson)
James (Warren)
James (Wilkinson)
John S. (Wilkes)
Joseph (Jefferson)
Middleton (Washington)
Nathan (Hall)
Samuel (Columbia)
Samuel (Jackson)
Samuel (Jones)
Silas (Gwinnett)
Stovall (Wilkes)
Walter (Walton)

Pool, William (Wilkes)
Poolley, Benjamin (Baldwin)
Pope, (ind.) (Wilkes)
    Abner (Jefferson)
    Allen (Hancock)
    Archable (Oglethorpe)
    Burwell (Oglethorpe)
    Christian (Wilkes)
    Cullen (Jones)
    Elijah (Jefferson)
    Fereby (Washington)
    Fleet (Laurens)
    Henry (Jones)
    Henry (Wilkes)
    Henry N. (Clarke)
    Isaac R. (Jones)
    Jacob (Montgomery)
    Jacob (Putnam)
    James (Jones)
    Jesse M. (Jones)
    John (Jasper)
    John (Jones)
    John (Putnam)
    John (Warren)
    John (2) (Wilkes)
    Josiah (Oglethorpe)
    Josiah (Wilkes)
    Margaret (Wilkes)
    Mary (Clarke)
    Mary (Wilkes)
    Middleton (Oglethorpe)
    Robert (Clarke)
    Wiley (Oglethorpe)
    Doctor Willis (Jackson)
    Wilson (Greene)
    Wylee (Washington)
Poopham, John W. (Liberty)
Poppell, Pharoh (Tattnall)
Popwell, John (McIntosh)
Porch, Henry (Putnam)
    Sherwood (Clarke)
    Thomas (Jones)
    Thomas (Morgan)
    William (Clarke)
Port, Andrew (Richmond)
    Anthony (Jones)
Porter, Benjamin (Wilkes)
    Catherine (Jackson)
    Charles (Wilkinson)
    Elizabeth (Columbia)
    Elizabeth (Hancock)
    Fayette (Columbia)
    Frederick (Early)
    James (Effingham)
    Joel (Early)
    John (Jones)
    John (Oglethorpe)
    John F. (Wilkinson)
    John S. (Burke)
    Johnson (Greene)
    Mary (Wilkes)

Nobles (Wilkinson)
Olliver (Greene)
Robert (Wilkes)
Robert W. (?) (Chatham)
Samuel (Baldwin)
Silvester (Richmond)
Stanton (Columbia)
Susannah (Chatham)
Uriah (Jones)
Vinson (Putnam)
Watson (Morgan)
William (Oglethorpe)
William (Warren)
William (Washington)
William G. (Effingham)
Porterfield, Christopher
    (Madison)
    David (2) (Madison)
Portivine, John (Screven)
Portman, Fred (Chatham)
Portwood, Benjamin (Wilkes)
Posey, Benjamin (Pulaski)
    Druscilla (Pulaski)
    H. (Richmond)
    Hezekiah (Hall)
    Humphrey (Clarke)
    James (Jones)
    John (Telfair)
    John H. (Putnam)
    Richard (Clarke)
    Richard (Morgan)
    Squire (Jasper)
    Thomas (Elbert)
    Umphrey (Pulaski)
    Uriah (Hall)
Posner, Silry S. (Jefferson)
Poss, Christly (Wilkes)
    Christopher (Wilkes)
    George (Wilkes)
    Henry (Wilkes)
    John (Wilkes)
    John, Sr. (Wilkes)
    Samuel (Jasper)
Post, Joseph (Jasper)
    Samuel (Hall)
Postelle, Capt. (Chatham)
Posy, Greene (Jasper)
Potter, Augusta (Jasper)
    James (Chatham)
    John (Hancock)
    Matthew (Screven)
    Pleasant (Jasper)
    Samuel (Oglethorpe)
Pottle, (ind.) (Camden)
Potts, Henry (Jackson)
    Isaac (Habersham)
    James (Jasper)
    John (Warren)
    Moses (Jackson)
    Mosse (Jasper)
    Stephen (Jackson)

William (Jackson)
William (2) (Jasper)
William (Wilkinson)
Poulen, John (Chatham)
Pound, Joel (Hancock)
Pounds, Gerrad (Columbia)
    John (Gwinnett)
    John B. (Putnam)
    Mary (Gwinnett)
    Merriman (Putnam)
    William (Oglethorpe)
Pounsey(?), Sarah (Bulloch)
Pouyat, Doct. (Chatham)
Pow, James (Jasper)
    John (Lincoln)
Powe, Savannah (Wilkes)
Powel, Allen B. (McIntosh)
    George (Jasper)
    John (Jasper)
    Johnson (Jasper)
    Lewis R. (Hall)
    Millington (Putnam)
    N. B. (Jasper)
    Nelson (Wilkes)
    Seymor (Clarke)
    Sion (Jackson)
    William (Clarke)
    William (Habersham)
    William (Jasper)
Powell, (ind.) (Laurens)
    Mrs. (2) (Chatham)
    A. F. (Telfair)
    Alexander (Telfair)
    Allin (Jefferson)
    Ambrose (Washington)
    Ann Slave of (Liberty)
    Artemus (Burke)
    Benjamin (Burke)
    Benjamin (Emanuel)
    Benjamin (Wilkes)
    Charles (Laurens)
    Coleman (Jefferson)
    Elisha (Clarke)
    Elizabeth (Burke)
    Evan (Jasper)
    Francis, Jr. (Elbert)
    Francis, Sr. (Elbert)
    Francis (Lincoln)
    Francis (Wilkes)
    George (Washington)
    Hardy (Columbia)
    Henry (Laurens)
    Henry (Washington)
    James (Baldwin)
    James (Glynn)
    James (Habersham)
    James (Hancock)
    Jesse (Pulaski)
    John (Jefferson)
    John (Jones)
    John (Pulaski)

Powell, John (Richmond)
John (Telfair)
John (Warren)
Killis (Elbert)
Lewis (Burke)
Lewis (Columbia)
Moses (Jasper)
Nathan (Morgan)
Oliver C. (Madison)
Rachel (Columbia)
Rebecca (Laurens)
Reubin, (Jefferson)
Richard (Lincoln)
Richard (Warren)
Robert (Wilkes)
Sampson, Sr. (Emanuel)
Sampson, Jr. (Emanuel)
Silas (Emanuel)
Theophilus (Jefferson)
Thompson (Hancock)
William (Columbia)
William (Jefferson)
William (2) (Washington)
William R. (Elbert)
Power, David (Madison)
Francis (Jasper)
James (Madison)
Robert (Jasper)
Powers, Clem (Effingham)
Edmond (Putnam)
Hardy (Pulaski)
James (Chatham)
James (Columbia)
Jesse (Madison)
John (Columbia)
John (Effingham)
John (Greene)
John (2) (McIntosh)
Joseph (Camden)
Josiah (Gwinnett)
L. (Richmond)
Mikel (Oglethorpe)
Nichles (Oglethorpe)
Roger (Laurens)
William (Madison)
Powlain, Thomas M.
(Oglethorpe)
Poyner, Nathan (Wilkes)
Poythress, James (Screven)
Joseph (Warren)
Mundy (Screven)
William (Chatham)
William (Screven)
Prainir(?), Dabney (Elbert)
Prater, John (Jones)
Prather, Edward (Columbia)
Eliza (Wilkes)
Richard (Lincoln)
Thomas (Wilkes)
Pratt, Abram (Camden)
Bardel (Oglethorpe)

H. M. (Camden)
Hillary (Jones)
John (Camden)
John (Jones)
John (Oglethorpe)
Leonard (Warren)
Nathaniel (Camden)
Thomas (Jones)
Vincent (Warren)
William (Pulaski)
Prendergast, M. (Chatham)
Prescot, John M. (Richmond)
Milledg (Richmond)
Prescott, Anthony (Burke)
Morin (Putnam)
Samuel F. (Burke)
Sarah (Burke)
Thomas (Bulloch)
William (Burke)
Presley, Charles (Elbert)
John (Hancock)
Peter (Hall)
William (Habersham)
Presly, Elijah (Elbert)
James (Jackson)
Presnal, William (Walton)
Pressley, John (Putnam)
Moses (Putnam)
William (Putnam)
Preston, Nancy (Baldwin)
Thomas (Jasper)
Prestwood, Thomas S.
(Wilkinson)
Preswood, Robert (Baldwin)
Pretchett, Sarah (Hancock)
Pretor, John (Habersham)
William (Habersham)
Pretton, Giliam (Jasper)
Prevatt, James D. (Camden)
Prevette, William (Elbert)
Previtt, John (Elbert)
Price, Benjamin (Gwinnett)
Benjamon (Putnam)
Berry (Washington)
Britton (Screven)
Charles (Jackson)
Charles (Putnam)
Ephraim (Greene)
Evin (Greene)
Ezekiel (Jackson)
Frances (Putnam)
George (Oglethorpe)
James (Bulloch)
James (Washington)
Jesse (Eamnuel)
John, Jr. (Gwinnett)
John, Sr. (Gwinnett)
John (Hall)
John (Jasper)
John (Jefferson)
John (Washington)

Joseph (Jefferson)
Joshua (Washington)
Luke (Putnam)
Rice (Washington)
Richard (Washington)
Thomas (Hancock)
Whitamore (Jones)
William (Emanuel)
William H. (Greene)
William P. (Greene)
Prichard, John (Glynn)
Pressley (Morgan)
Prichet, Guilford (Burke)
Prichett, Joel (Gwinnett)
William (Jasper)
Pride, John (Baldwin)
Pridgen, Amile (Bulloch)
David (Bulloch)
Luke (Bulloch)
William (Montgomery)
Pridgeon, Luke (Telfair)
Thomas (Telfair)
Priest, Gabriel (Camden)
Martin D. (Morgan)
Priggen, James (Jasper)
Prilling, Henry (Emanuel)
Primrose, Elisabeth (Richmond)
James (Richmond)
Prince, George (Washington)
John (Greene)
L. H. (Wilkes)
Sarah (Jefferson)
Williaim (Chatham)
Pringle, James (Camden)
Prior, Asa (Morgan)
Elizabeth (Columbia)
John (Morgan)
Pritchard, James (Glynn)
Martha (Hancock)
William (Clarke)
William (Morgan)
Pritchet, Delsy (Wilkes)
Pritchett, Elizabeth (Madison)
John (Elbert)
Joshua (Gwinnett)
Phillip (Hancock)
Simond (Wilkinson)
Sion (Jackson)
Stephen (Wilkinson)
Privat, James D. (Wayne)
Procter, David (Wilkinson)
Joshua (Wilkinson)
Robert (Jones)
Stephen (Wilkinson)
William (Wilkinson)
Proctor, Abraham (Burke)
John (Early)
John (Wilkinson)
Jonas (Burke)
Samuel (Burke)
Sterling (Warren)

Proctor, William (Wilkes)
Prosser(?), J. H. (Chatham)
Prosser, Jesse (Baldwin)
    Olly (Washington)
Prothro, James (Elbert)
    Nathaniel (Elbert)
Prouty, C. (Richmond)
Prubach(?), Made (Chatham)
Prudell, David (Lincoln)
Prudet, Adam (Jasper)
Pruett, Hardin (Warren)
Pruit, John S. (Walton)
Pruitt, Benjamin (Gwinnett)
    David (Elbert)
    Henry (Hancock)
    Hebekiah (Jackson)
    Jacob (Jones)
    John (Jones)
    Joseph (Hancock)
    M. (Jackson)
    Martin (Jones)
    Mary (Hancock)
    Russell (Hancock)
    Samuel (Putnam)
    Solomon (Jones)
    Susanna (Elbert)
    William (Jones)
Pryor, Absalum (Jefferson)
    John H. (Madison)
    Marlow L. (Baldwin)
    Martin (Baldwin)
Psallet, (ind.) (Chatham)
Ptitt. Joseph (Walton)
Pucket, Edmond (Putnam)
    John (Greene)
    John (Gwinnett)
Puckett, Aaron B. (Pulaski)
    John (Hancock)
    Richard (Gwinnett)
Pudgesley, John (Jefferson)
Pudy, Benjamin (Walton)
    Robert (Walton)
Pugh, John (Jackson)
    Martin (Hall)
    Robert (Burke)
    Sampson (Jackson)
    William (Hall)
Puickard, John (Jasper)
Pulaski (John) (Putnam)
    William (Putnam)
Pullen, Elisha (Wilkes)
    John (Wilkes)
    Joseph (Wilkes)
    Major (Wilkes)
    Moses (Laurens)
    Robert (Greene)
    Samuel (Columbia)
    Sanford (Wilkes)
    Sarah (Hancock)
    Thomas (Laurens)
    Thomas, Sr. (Laurens)

    Thomas (Wilkes)
    William (Columbia)
Pulliain, Joseph (Elbert)
Pullin, (ind.) (Lincoln)
    George (Morgan)
    George (Wilkes)
    Green (Gwinnett)
    James (Wilkes)
    James, Sr. (Wilkes)
    Joseph (Wilkes)
    Levin (Hancock)
Pulling, James, Sr. (Wilkes)
    Joseph (Wilkes)
Pullom, Robert (Elbert)
Pullom, Matthew (Elbert)
Pullum, Richard (Putnam)
Purcel, John (Habersham)
Purdon, Thomas (Wayne)
Purejoy, A. (Jasper)
Purer(?), Isham (Madison)
Purify, Archibald (Putnam)
    William (Putnam)
Purken, Uriah (Wilkinson)
    Wright (Wilkinson)
Purkins, (ind.) (Laurens)
    Abraham (Greene)
    Alexander (Greene)
    Allen (Burke)
    Archibald (Greene)
    David (Burke)
    Ezekiel (Greene)
    Jessie (Greene)
    Leah (Burke)
    Newton (Burke)
    Tabitha (Burke)
    William (Burke)
Purnell, Samuel (Columbia)
Pursell, Cowel (Appling)
    John (Appling)
Purver(?), Zilpha (Appling)
Puryear, John (Clarke)
    Peter (Clarke)
Pusnal, William (Walton)
Putnam, Charles E. (McIntosh)
    Ezekiel (Hall)
    Priscella (Putnam)
    Thomas (Hall)
Pye, Henry (Putnam)
    James (Jasper)
    James (Screven)
Pyle, John (Walton)
    Samuel (Jasper)
    Theophilus (Jasper)
Pyles, Francis (Lincoln)
Pyor, Nancy (Jefferson)
Pyron, William (Greene)

Q

Quarles, Penual (Hall)
Quarterman, Elizabeth
              (Liberty)

    John S. (Liberty)
    Joseph (Liberty)
    Partrick (Walton)
Querard, Henry (Richmond)
Quesenberry, James (Columbia)
Quick, William (Washington)
    Zachariah (Washington)
Quin, William, Jr. (Lincoln)
    William, Sr. (Lincoln)
Quinn, John (Montgomery)
Quinney, John (Jefferson)
Quizinberry, T. (Richmond)
Quyly, Charles (Wilkes)

R

Rabb, William (Richmond)
Raben, Berwell (Putnam)
Rabfus(?), John (Chatham)
Rabun, Hannah R. (Greene)
    Mary (Hancock)
Raburn, Rinson (Warren)
Rachaels, William (Washington)
Rachals, Zedock (Warren)
Rachells, Burwell (Hancock)
    George (Hancock)
    Miles (Hancock)
Rachels, Ezekial (Burke)
    William (Burke)
Rachney, John (Hancock)
Radcliff, Moses (Jasper)
Raddin, Abner (Jasper)
Raddish, Samuel (Warren)
Radford, Henry (Columbia)
    John (Morgan)
    Martha (Richmond)
Radney, John (Hancock)
    Thomas (Jones)
Rads, Elijah (Jasper)
Radsford, William (Jones)
Raft, David (Hall)
Ragan, Asa (Jasper)
    Brice (Wilkinson)
    David (Oglethorpe)
    Hamilton (Oglethorpe)
    James (Elbert)
    Jeremiah (Greene)
    John (Oglethorpe)
    Mark (Oglethorpe)
    Nathaniel (Lincoln)
Ragland, Abner (Putnam)
    Benjamin (Wilkes)
    Priscilla (Jefferson)
Raglin, Ephraim (Jasper)
Ragsdale, Elijah (Walton)
    James (Wilkes)
    John W. (Gwinnett)
    Larkin (Gwinnett)
    Michal (Habersham)
    Richard (Habersham)
Rahn, Mrs. (Chatham)

Rahn, Emanuel (Effingham)
John C. (Effingham)
Jonathon, Sr. (Effingham)
Joseph (Effingham)
Matthew (Effingham)
William (Chatham)
Raiford, Alexander G.
(Jefferson)
Baldwin (Jefferson)
John S. (Jefferson)
Maurice (Jefferson)
Maurice, Sr. (Jefferson)
Raimey, M. F. (Jackson)
Raine, Allen (Wilkinson)
Rainer, John W. (Wilkes)
Raines, William negroes
(Wilkes)
Raines, Henry (Oglethorpe)
Joseph (Wilkinson)
Rainey, Frederick (Putnam)
John (Putnam)
Matthew (Oglethorpe)
William (Wilkes)
Rains, Alan (Washington)
Cadwalader (Baldwin)
Edmunds (Morgan)
John (Washington)
John G. (Montgomery)
Josiah (Wilkes)
Lila (Hall)
Nathaniel (Jones)
Sarah (Jones)
Thomas (2) (Morgan)
Washington (Washington)
Winney (Washington)
Rainus, David B. (Oglethorpe)
Rainy, Thomas (Jackson)
Woodson (Jackson)
Rakestraw, William (Gwinnett)
Ralds, James (Jefferson)
Raleigh, Abner (Warren)
Henry (Warren)
Isaac (Warren)
James (Warren)
Sally (Warren)
Ralls, Abram (Hancock)
Hector (Greene)
James (Greene)
Robenson (Putnam)
Ralston, A. A. (Richmond)
John (Habersham)
Rambart, Samuel (Elbert)
Ramey, John, Jr. (Clarke)
John, Sr. (Clarke)
Nancy (Morgan)
Rammage, Josiah (Wilkinson)
Ramney, Edward (Putnam)
Ramsey, (torn) (Laurens)
Hannah (Oglethorpe)
James (Columbia)

Randle (Columbia)
Ramsey, Benjamin (Elbert)
Edmond (Oglethorpe)
George (2) (Jasper)
Jacob (Hall)
James (Jackson)
Moses (Wilkinson)
Nancy (Walton)
Noah (Jasper)
Thomas (Jasper)
Thomas (Walton)
Thomas (Wilkinson)
Ramsy, Randolph (Lincoln)
Randal, Rosannah (Hancock)
Randall, Newton (Jasper)
Randel, James (Hall)
Randle, Edmond (Hancock)
James (Greene)
James G. (Greene)
William (Morgan)
Willis (Morgan)
Randol, Arthur (Wilkinson)
Rosannah (Hancock)
Randolph B., Overseer for
(Burke)
Beverly (Burke)
Charles (Gwinnett)
G. (Richmond)
J. (Jasper)
J. H. (Richmond)
John (Jackson)
P. (Jackson)
Richard (Wilkes)
Robert (Columbia)
Thomas P. (Columbia)
Rane, Cornelious (Camden)
Joseph (Camden)
Raney, Daniel (Oglethorpe)
Isom (Oglethorpe)
John (Telfair)
Reuben M. (Greene)
Thomas F. (Oglethorpe)
Rankin, Ezekial (Greene)
Robert C. (Morgan)
Rankle, Peter (Warren)
Ransey, William (Washington)
Ranshorn, Noel (Washington)
Ransom, Dudley (Greene)
James (Greene)
John (Greene)
Samuel (Hancock)
Ransome, (?) (Hancock)
Robert (Hancock)
Rapshear, John (Jasper)
Rasberry, Archabale
(Oglethorpe)
Daniel (Jackson)
James (2) (Oglethorpe)
Joseph (Clarke)
Reuben (2) (Jackson)
William (Jackson)

Rasor, Garrington (Putnam)
Rassel, Ignatius (Jasper)
Rathbone, W. P. (Richmond)
Ratliff, Ezekiel (Lincoln)
James (Wayne)
John (Hall)
Mark (Burke)
Polly (Washington)
Saul (Habersham)
Thomas (Lincoln)
✳ Rattry, Mrs. (Chatham)
Ravenel(?), John (Habersham)
Raver(?), Jacob (Chatham)
Ravins, James H. (Oglethorpe)
Rawles, Dempsey (Washington)
Rawlings, William (Washington)
Rawls & Cresett(?) (Pulaski)
Rawls, Elizabeth (Wayne)
Isaac (2) (Jackson)
John (Bulloch)
John (Screven)
Joseph (Screven)
Shak (Jackson)
Thomas (Bulloch)
William (Wayne)
Rawson, Elizabeth (Chatham)
Ray, Ambrose, Sr. (Washington)
Andrew, Jr. (Greene)
Andrew, Sr. (Greene)
Austin (Morgan)
Bartlett (Putnam)
David (Walton)
Duncan (Pulaski)
Elijah (Jasper)
Elizabeth (2) (Columbia)
Gabriel (Washington)
Hardy (Washington)
Howel (Walton)
Jacob (Wilkes)
Jane (Columbia)
John (Madison)
John (Morgan)
John (Wilkes)
John H. (Greene)
Jurushun (Greene)
Mark (Jasper)
Moses (Oglethorpe)
Neil (Putnam)
Peter (Elbert)
Phares (Putnam)
Thomas (Jasper)
Thomas (Richmond)
Thomas (Walton)
Ursa(Fem.) (Jones)
Thomas W. (Putnam)
William (Hancock)
William (Pulaski)
William (Screven)
William D. (Baldwin)
William H. (Greene)
Willie (Greene)

(122) ✳ Raulerson, Jacob
(Appling)

Raymonton, Robert (Greene)
Raynes, Robert (Wilkinson)
Raynolds, John (Richmond)
Rea, Andrew (Greene)
    James (Greene)
Read, Cunningham D.
           (Putnam)
    Henry (Morgan)
    Hiram (Putnam)
    J. W. (Richmond)
    James (Lincoln)
    James (Putnam)
    Jesse (Morgan)
Read(?), John (Chatham)
Read, John (Lincoln)
    Luke (Richmond)
    Samuel (Jasper)
    Thomas (Putnam)
    William (Oglethorpe)
    Zacheriah (Putnam)
Reading, James (Habersham)
Ready, Elizabeth (Camden)
Reamer, Redding (Gwinnett)
Rease, James (Richmond)
Reasin, Drury (Telfair)
Reason, Benjamin (Gwinnett)
Reavel, Green (Jasper)
Reaves, Burges (Gwinnett)
    Frederick (Gwinnett)
    George (Hancock)
    Henry (2) (Jones)
    Irvin (Greene)
    Isaac (Gwinnett)
    James (Jones)
    Jesse (Jones)
    Jessey (Wilkinson)
    John (Gwinnett)
    John (Jones)
    Jonathon (Gwinnett)
    Lofton (Gwinnett)
    Malachi (Gwinnett)
    Sally (Jones)
    Stephen (Jones)
    Thomas (Wilkinson)
    William (Jasper)
    William (Walton)
Rebellec, F. (Chatham)
Red, James (Gwinnett)
    Job (Gwinnett)
    Reuben (Gwinnett)
Redd, Charles A. (Greene)
    Reuben (Hall)
    William (Burke)
Reddak, John (Effingham)
Reddak(?), Samuel (Effingham)
Redden, John (Greene)
Reddick, Jacob (Burke)
    John (Burke)
    Peter (Screven)
    Thomas (Screven)
Reddin, James (Greene)

    John (Putnam)
    Parham (Putnam)
Redding, Anderson (Baldwin)
    Arthur (Baldwin)
    Henry H. (Screven)
    John (Bulloch)
    Nancy (Jones)
    William (Baldwin)
Reddy, Spotswood G. (Baldwin)
    Ulsey (Baldwin)
Redfield, L. J. (Richmond)
Redgen, Sarah (Washington)
Redman, Benjamin
          (Richmond)
    William (Columbia)
Redwine, John (Madison)
    William (Madison)
Reece, David A. (Elbert)
    Joseph (Jones)
    Margaret (Greene)
    William (Baldwin)
    William (Greene)
Reed, A. (Jackson)
    Anna (Madison)
    Asa (Putnam)
    Edmond (Hancock)
    Elijah (Putnam)
    Ezikiel (Columbia)
    Jacob, Est. of (Chatham)
    James (Hancock)
    James C. (Hall)
    Jane (Columbia)
    John (Chatham)
    John (Columbia)
    John (Jasper)
    John (Jones)
    John (Putnam)
    Maria (Chatham)
    Micajah (Columbia)
    Michael (Columbia)
    Murry (Effingham)
    Thomas (Columbia)
    W. (Richmond)
Reedy(?), Thomas (Chatham)
Rees, A. F. (Putnam)
    Benjamin T. (Columbia)
    Cuthbert (Jasper)
    F. B. (Putnam)
    Hugh (Columbia)
    James (Columbia)
    Jeremiah, Jr. (Columbia)
    Jeremiah, Sr. (Columbia)
    Jordin (Putnam)
    Judy (Putnam)
    Rowell (Putnam)
    Sarah (Jefferson)
    Simeon (Columbia)
    Susan (Columbia)
    William (Putnam)
Reese, Aaron (Wilkinson)
    Benjamin (Warren)

    Ebenezer, McIntosh)
    Harris (Warren)
    Henry L. (Clarke)
    Isham (Jones)
    James (Burke)
    James, Jr. (Hancock)
    James, Sr. (Hancock)
    Joel, Est. of (Burke)
    John C. (Morgan)
    Jordan (Jones)
    Joseph (Morgan)
    Nancy (Warren)
    Oneson C. (Clarke)
    Reuben (Warren)
    Richard (Warren)
    William L. (Morgan)
Reeves, (ind.) (Camden)
    Bennet (Wilkes)
    Edmond (Walton)
    Hannah (Wilkes)
    Harriet E. (Washington)
    Ichabod (Wilkes)
    Jeremiah (Clarke)
    Jesse T. (Putnam)
    Joel (Hancock)
    John (Columbia)
    Jonathan (Jasper)
    Joshua (Walton)
    Lee (Hancock)
    Lucius (Putnam)
    Malachi (Wilkes)
    Spencer (Columbia)
    Spias (Burke)
    Terry (Wilkes)
    Thomas (Emanuel)
    Thomas (Wilkes)
    William, Sr. (Hancock)
    William (Wilkes)
    Willis (Pulaski)
    Wyatt (Jasper)
Regan, Daniel (Pulaski)
    Elias (Pulaski)
    Joseph (2) (Pulaski)
Regins, James (Jasper)
Register, David (Laurens)
    Jesse (Washington)
    John (Laurens)
    John (Washington)
    Nancy (Montgomery)
    Thomas (Laurens)
    William (Bulloch)
    William (Washington)
Reid, (ind.) (Telfair)
    Alexander (Putnam)
    Asa (Gwinnett)
    Elisha (Putnam)
    George, Jr. (Gwinnett)
    George, Sr. (Gwinnett)
    Isaac (2) (Hall)
    James (Putnam)
    John (Jasper)

Reid, John B. (Jefferson)
  Joseph (Gwinnett)
  Joseph (Hall)
  O. (Richmond)
  R. R. (Richmond)
  Rhosa (Gwinnett)
  Samuel (2) (Gwinnett)
  Samuel (Putnam)
  Samuel D. (Hancock)
  Stephen (Hall)
  William (Hall)
Reiley, John (Chatham)
Reilly, T. (Chatham)
Reis, David (Putnam)
Reiser, David (Effingham)
  Matthew (Effingham)
Reives, John (Jasper)
Rembert, Alexander (Putnam)
Remonde, P. (Chatham)
Remshart, Daniel (Chatham)
Render, Christopher (Wilkes)
  James (Wilkes)
  Joshua (Wilkes)
Renfro, Joel (Jones)
  Nancy (Jones)
  Nathan, Jr. (Jones)
  Stephen (Jones)
Renfroe, Avent (Washington)
  Elisha (Washington)
  Enoch (2) (Washington)
  John (Washington)
  Nathan (Washington)
  Peter (Washington)
  Stephen (Morgan)
  William (Washington)
Renney, Jesse (Greene)
Rentfro, Ashel (Telfair)
  Ephraim (Warren)
Rentz, George (McIntosh)
Reshard, Sarian (Camden)
Resow, Avery (Jasper)
Respass, Richard (Gwinnett)
  Richard (Putnam)
  Thomas (Putnam)
Revel, Matthew (Columbia)
Revels, Edmund (2) (Appling)
  Harvey(?) (Appling)
  Hermery (Appling)
  Jeremiah (Tattnall)
Revere, B. Est. (Wilkes)
  Drury (Wilkes)
  John K. (Warren)
  Robert Est. (Wilkes)
Revil, Claiborn (Columbia)
Reylands, David (Hancock)
Reynolds, Mrs. (2) (Lincoln)
  (ind.) (Walton)
  (ind.) (Wilkes)
  A. (Richmond)
  Bartemus (Hall)
Reynolds(?), Benjamin (Jones)

Reynolds, Charles (Elbert)
  Elizy B. (Wilkes)
  Gallant (Gwinnett)
  George (Putnam)
  Grinsberry (Clarke)
  Hugh (Wilkes)
  James (Elbert)
  James (Lincoln)
  James (2) (Putnam)
  James (Warren)
  James M. (Wilkes)
  Jemima (Gwinnett)
  John (Burke)
  John (Columbia)
  John (Warren)
  John W. (Burke)
  Mary (Columbia)
  Reuben (Columbia)
  Richard (Putnam)
  Richard (Warren)
  Robert (Lincoln)
  Silas (Wilkes)
  Spence (Wilkes)
  Thomas (Putnam)
  Thomas (Walton)
  Thomas (Richmond)
  William (Baldwin)
  William (Burke)
  William (Putnam)
Reynolds, Mrs. (Hancock)
  David (Hancock)
  George (Hancock)
  James (Hancock)
  John (Hancock)
Rheiny, Charles (Burke)
  John (Burke)
Rhen, William (Jasper)
Rheney, Samuel (Camden)
Rhoads, Benjamin (Warren)
  Lionel (Warren)
  Richard (Oglethorpe)
Rhocelander, Peter (Elbert)
Rhodes, A. (Richmond)
  Andrew (Liberty)
  Eslinda (Wilkes)
  Eustace (Lincoln)
  Henry (Hancock)
  Henry (Wilkes)
  Isaac (Oglethorpe)
  James (Madison)
  John (Warren)
  John (Wilkes)
  John W. (Wilkes)
  Joseph (Wilkes)
  Lewis (Burke)
  N. H. (Liberty)
  Samuel (Wilkes)
  Thomas (Wilkes)
  William G. (Richmond)
Rhymes, William (Greene)
  Willis (Warren)

Rials, J. (Richmond)
Rice, (ind.) (Wilkes)
  Allen P. (Lincoln)
  Anderson (Jones)
  Arthur (Morgan)
  Demsey (Hall)
  Ebenezer (Hall)
  Elizabeth (Chatham)
  Jesse (Elbert)
  John (Habersham)
  John (Screven)
  Leonard (Elbert)
  Richmond (Bryan)
  Robert (Jackson)
  Samuel (Columbia)
  Samuel (Wilkes)
  Susan (Baldwin)
  William (Elbert)
  William (Morgan)
Ricer, John (Jasper)
Rich, Archibald (Walton)
  Charles (Habersham)
  Daniel E. (Emanuel)
  Edward (Emanuel)
  Leah (Chatham)
  Martin (Emanuel)
  Mary (Elbert)
  Stephen (Appling)
  Stephen (Emanuel)
  Washington (Emanuel)
  William (Elbert)
  William (Habersham)
Richard, Rebecca (Elbert)
  Reuben (Hall)
  Sterling (Morgan)
  William (Morgan)
Richards, Burwell (Columbia)
  Elizabeth (Madison)
  George (Greene)
  Jedidiah (Greene)
  John (Greene)
  Matthew C. (Morgan)
  Robert (Early)
  Tery (Greene)
  Thomas (Early)
  Thomas (Madison)
  Thomas S. (Putnam)
  William (Jasper)
  William (Putnam)
  Willis (Columbia)
Richardson(?), (ind.) (Putnam)
Richardson & Hancock
                  (Madison)
Richardson, Abm. (Bulloch)
  Allen (Oglethorpe)
  Amos (Elbert)
  Armstid (Putnam)
  Benjamin (Hancock)
  David (Gwinnett)
  Edmon (Camden)
  Gabriel (Putnam)

Richardson, George (Jasper)
Green H. (Putnam)
Henry (Wilkes)
Isaac (Bulloch)
Jacob (Putnam)
James (Hancock)
Jane (Hancock)
John (Oglethorpe)
John (Wilkinson)
Lawrence (Columbia)
Moses (Putnam)
Newman (Hancock)
Richard (Chatham)
Richard (Elbert)
S. (Chatham)
Samuel (Chatham)
Samuel (Morgan)
Thomas (Jasper)
Walker (Elbert)
William, Sr. (Chatham)
William (Columbia)
William (Elbert)
William (Hancock)
William (Oglethorpe)
William B., Jr. (Chatham)
William H. (Elbert)
Riche, Elijah (Hall)
Richerson, John (Jones)
Livy (Walton)
Rickerson, Abraham (Hancock)
William(?) (Hancock)
Ricketson, Benjamin (Warren)
James (Warren)
Jesse (Warren)
Rickett, Prucilla (Jones)
Robert (Jones)
Thomas (Jones)
Ricks, Eleanor (Jasper)
John (Emanuel)
Richard (Emanuel)
Riddell, William (Jasper)
Riddle, Anderson (Washington)
Anderson (Wilkes)
Archibald (Wilkes)
Cato (Washington)
Wiley (Baldwin)
Riddoch, David (Baldwin)
Ridgeway, Burrel (Elbert)
Drury (Clarke)
James (Elbert)
Ridley, John, Jr. (Wilkes)
John, Sr. (Wilkes)
Robert (Wilkinson)
Ridling(?), John (Jackson)
Rieves, Robert (Jackson)
Thomas (Jackson)
Thomas (Putnam)
Rigby, Jesse (Warren)
William (Warren)
Rigdon, Daniel (Bulloch)
Riggs. Rachel (Bulloch)

Right, Eleat (Jones)
Elisha (Jones)
Eve (Camden)
Jesse (Jones)
Sarah (Oglethorpe)
Rightonan(?), John (Burke)
Rigie, Michael (Jones)
Riggs, Amos (Gwinnett)
Riggins, Johnny (Hall)
Martha (Laurens)
Rigons, James (Jasper)
Rigsby, Allen (Walton)
Riley, Charles (Wilkinson)
David F. (Columbia)
Jacob (Greene)
James (Elbert)
James (Greene)
James (Hall)
James (Jones)
John (Hall)
John (Greene)
Joseph (Greene)
Lemuel (Hall)
Lensey (Wilkinson)
Michel (Greene)
Morris (Richard)
Peter Greene
Sarah (Jones)
Thomas (Greene)
William (2) (Morgan)
Rimson, Rem(?) (Lincoln)
Riner, Elizabeth (Emanuel)
Ring, James (Camden)
Ringard(?), Mary (Chatham)
Ringold, J. (Richmond)
Rion, Jacob (Morgan)
Ripley, Robert (Camden)
Ritter, Catherine (Chatham)
William (Laurens)
Rivers. Betsy (Columbia)
James (Jasper)
John (Jasper)
Jones (Putnam)
Thomas (Jasper)
Thomas (Warren)
Thomas (Washington)
Roach, (ind.) (Hancock)
James (Habersham)
James (Pulaski)
Jesse (Emanuel)
Johnathan (Hancock)
William (Hancock)
William (Laurens)
Roads, Allen (Greene)
William (Screven)
Roan. Jesse J. (Morgan)
Mary (Morgan)
Willis J. (Morgan)
Roary. John (Wilkes)
Rob, Amelia (Habersham)
Robarts, David (Wilkinson)

Eliza G. (Liberty)
Thomas (Morgan)
Robartson, William (Wilkes)
Robason, Alexander (Wilkinson)
Robbins, Arthur (Screven)
Elijah (Screven)
George (Screven)
William (Hall)
Roberson, Aaron (Jones)
Adam (2) (Jones)
Ellick (Wilkinson)
J. J. (Richmond)
James (Walton)
John (Walton)
John (2) (Wilkinson)
Margarett (Wilkinson)
Nancey (Wilkinson)
Thomas (Pulaski)
William (Walton)
Robert, Elias E. (Chatham)
Henry (Richmond)
James (Putnam)
John (Chatham)
Rea (Greene)
Roberts, (torn) (Laurens)
Est. of (Bryan)
(ind.) (Laurens)
Abraham (Putnam)
Allen (Hancock)
Amey (Clarke)
Arthur (Lincoln)
Awbry (Jackson)
Bartholmew (Morgan)
Benjamin (Hancock)
D. (Jasper)
Daniel W. (Morgan)
David P. (Columbia)
Delia (Burke)
Demps (Putnam)
Eli (Emanuel)
Elias (Bulloch)
Elijah (Hall)
Elijah (Screven)
Elizabeth (Liberty)
Elizabeth (Morgan)
Ensley (Hall)
George (2) (Columbia)
George (Jackson)
Graystock, Jr. (Burke)
Graystock, Sr. (Burke)
Green (Burke)
Greystock (Montgomery)
Harwood (Columbia)
Hugh (Wilkes)
Isaac (Greene)
Isom (Emanuel)
Jacob (Laurens)
James (Burke)
James (Chatham)
James (Screven)
Jeremiah (Columbia)

Roberts, Jesse (Columbia)
Jesse (Elbert)
Jesse (Morgan)
John (Appling)
John (Columbia)
John (2) (Elbert)
John (Emanuel)
John (Morgan)
John A. (Burke)
John A. (Walton)
John B. (Screven)
John G. (Greene)
John H. (Warren)
John M. (Screven)
Joseph (Hancock)
Josiah (Columbia)
Lewis (Wayne)
Luke (Jones)
M. (Jackson)
Mark (Laurens)
Mary (Burke)
Mary (Richmond)
Mary (Warren)
Nathaniel (Screven)
Osburn A. (Hall)
Ranson J. (Screven)
Reuben (2) (Jones)
Robbin (Telfair)
Robert (Jackson)
Roland (Screven)
Sherod (Warren)
Simeon (Burke)
Step (Gwinnett)
Thmoas (Wilkes)
Urby (Putnam)
Willard (Burke)
William (Clarke)
William (2) (Jones)
William (Liberty)
William (Montgomery)
William (Pulaski)
William, Jr. (Screven)
William (2) (Wilkinson)
Willis (Columbia)
Wilson (Elbert)
Zachariah (Columbia)
Zake (Camden)
Robertson, Mrs. (Chatham)
Abel L. (Jasper)
Allen (Putnam)
Ann B. (Hancock)
Benjamon (Putnam)
David (Oglethorpe)
Elberry (Putnam)
Eli (Oglethorpe)
Elizabeth (Hancock)
Fansina (Putnam)
Francis (Wilkes)
Frederick (Warren)
Henry (Morgan)
Ignatious (Warren)

Isaac (Washington)
James (Jasper)
James (Oglethorpe)
James (Tattnall)
Jeffery (Warren)
Jesse M. (Greene)
John (3) (Jackson)
John (Morgan)
John (3) (Putnam)
John (Warren)
John A. (Putnam)
John R. (Baldwin)
Joseph (Columbia)
Joseph W. (Wilkes)
Joshua (Warren)
Josiah (Telfair)
Littleberry (Morgan)
Lydia (Jasper)
Martha (Clarke)
Matthew (Jefferson)
Obedience (Warren)
Osborn (Putnam)
Pleasant (Oglethorpe)
Randle (Putnam)
Robert (Oglethorpe)
Solomon (Baldwin)
Thomas (Jasper)
Thomas (Morgan)
Thomas (Putnam)
W. T. G. (Jasper)
William (2) (Baldwin)
Wililam (Elbert)
William (2) (Putnam)
William (Washington)
William (2) (Wilkes)
Zacheriah (Putnam)
Robeson, Jacob (Appling)
Robey, Elijah (Hall)
Robert (Jasper)
Robinett, Allen (Jasper)
Jesse (Jasper)
Robins, B. (Richmond)
Sarah (Greene)
Robinson, Alexander N.
(Clarke)
Corns. (Jasper)
Daniel (Greene)
David (Burke)
Epaphroditus (Greene)
Fryer (Clarke)
Henry (Baldwin)
Henry (Burke)
Henry (Wilkinson)
Isaac (Laurens)
Jacob (Laurens)
James (Greene)
James (Jones)
James B. (Richmond)
James T. (Greene)
Jane (Jasper)
Jemima (Habersham)

Jesse (Jefferson)
John (Appling)
John (Habersham)
John (Jasper)
John (Putnam)
Jonathan(?) (Bulloch)
Jonathon (Jefferson)
Luke (Baldwin)
Luke (Gwinnett)
Machael (Jones)
Miller (Greene)
Nancy (Jones)
Patrick (Gwinnett)
Patrick L. (Greene)
Philip (Burke)
R. (Jasper)
Robert (Bryan)
Samuel (Pulaski)
Samuel (Washington)
William (Chatham)
William (Greene)
William (Jones)
William (Laurens)
Willis (McIntosh)
Robison, John (Washington)
John S. (Washington)
Lenellen M. (Washington)
Moses (Washington)
Thomas (2) (Washington)
Robson, Frederick (Wayne)
James (Wayne)
Sabery (Wayne)
Wiley (Wayne)
Robuck, Benjamin (McIntosh)
James (Pulaski)
Roby, Archelaus (Wilkes)
Mathew (Putnam)
Timothy (Putnam)
Williamson (Putnam)
Rochfort, George (Clarke)
Rockhill, Isaac A. (Chatham)
Rockmore, James (Jones)
Rockwall, Samuel (Baldwin)
Rockwell, Riley (Putnam)
Roddenberry, William (Bulloch)
Rodes, Heflen S. (Greene)
Thomas (Wilkinson)
Rodger, John (Wilkinson)
Rodgers, Benjamin (Jasper)
Cannon R. (Baldwin)
David (Jasper)
David (Wilkinson)
James (Gwinnett)
James A. (Hancock)
John (Bryan)
John (Warren)
John C. (Jasper)
John P. (Montgomery)
Joseph (Warren)
Joseph (Wilkinson)
Micajah (Warren)

Rodgers, Polly (Baldwin)
    Reuben, Jr. (Warren)
    Reuben, Sr. (Warren)
    Simion (Hancock)
    Stephen (Jefferson)
    Thomas (Jasper)
    Thomas (Pulaski)
    Thomas (Warren)
    William (Pulaski)
    Winifred (Clarke)
Roe, Asa (Putnam)
    Churchwell (Warren)
    David (Warren)
    James (Warren)
    John (Early)
    John (2) (Hancock)
    Joseph (Burke)
    Joshua, Jr. (Warren)
    Joshua, Sr. (Warren)
    Michael (Warren)
    Shadwick (Putnam)
Roebuck, Robert (Elbert)
    William (Elbert)
Rogan, Martha B. (Oglethorpe)
Roger, John (Wilkes)
Rogers, Anon (Putnam)
    Britian (Hancock)
    Burwell (Putnam)
    Charles (Washington)
    Charles W. (Putnam)
    D. (Jasper)
    Daniel (Washington)
    David (Jackson)
    David (Putnam)
    Dempsey (Jackson)
    Drury (Jasper)
    Edward (Burke)
    Edmond (Liberty)
    Elisha (Putnam)
    Eliza (Washington)
    Enoch (2) (Jackson)
    Eph'm (Jasper)
    Ephaaim (Putnam)
    George W. (Baldwin)
    Harvey (Washington)
    Henry (Greene)
    Henry (Putnam)
    J. (Burke)
    James (2) (Jefferson)
    James (Putnam)
    James, (Jr. (Warren)
    James, Sr. (Warren)
    Jacob (Jackson)
    John (Bulloh)
    John (2) (Burke)
    John (Gwinnett)
    John (2) (Jackson)
    John (Jefferson)
    John (Morgan)
    John (Putnam)
    John (Tattnall)

    John (Warren)
    Josiah (Jones)
    Josiah (Putnam)
    Meshach (Washington)
    Nathan (Screven)
    Nathan (Washington)
    Osboun (Hancock)
    Peter (Screven)
    Pleasant H. (Putnam)
    Reuben (Putnam)
    Rhoda (Jackson)
    Richard (Burke)
    Richard (Screven)
    Robert (Morgan)
    Sally (Jackson)
    Stephen (Washington)
    Susannah (Chatham)
    Wiley (Putnam)
    William (Burke)
    William (Putnam)
    William (Tattnall)
    William, Sr. (Tattnall)
    William (Washington)
    Zacheriah (Washington)
Roggers, Sarah (Baldwin)
Roi, Joseph (Chatham)
Roland, James (Pulaski)
    Richard (Oglethorpe)
    William (Lincoln)
    Williamson (Columbia)
Rolandson, Robert (Washington)
Rolens, L. (Jasper)
Roler, Michael (Lincoln)
Roley, Robert (Chatham)
Roling, Benjamin (Richmond)
    Merit (Columbia)
Rolling, William (Tattnall)
Rollins, Davis (Gwinnett)
    Elizabeth (Burke)
    John (Burke)
    John (Pulaski)
    Raleigh (Burke)
    Samuel (Burke)
    William (Burke)
Rollison, Nimrod (Wayne)
Rolls, Caleb (Wilkes)
    William (Emanuel)
Rolston, John (Bryan)
Roman, Robert (Richmond)
Rona, Joseph (Baldwin)
Rone, Benjamin (Chatham)
    Hugh (Walton)
Roney, Thomas (Columbia)
Rooks, Daniel (Jackson)
    Hardiman (Jackson)
    Isaac (Screven)
    John (Jackson)
    John (Putnam)
    John (Wayne)
    Virdaman (Telfair)
    William (Jackson)

Rooney, Lawrence (Chatham)
Rooper, John M. (Baldwin)
Root, George (Putnam)
Roper, M. (Jasper)
Ropier, John (Hall)
Roquemon, John (Putnam)
    Thomas (Putnam)
Roquimon, Peter (Putnam)
Rose, Amos (Elbert)
    Grantum (Elbert)
    Henry (Wilkes)
    Hudson (Emanuel)
    John (Jones)
    Sunnah (Jones)
    Washington (Putnam)
    William (Jones)
    William (Lincoln)
Roseboro, Alexander (Putnam)
Rosetto, Georgia (Chatham)
Rosier, Alexander (Greene)
    Samuel (McIntosh)
Rosignal, Louis (Chatham)
Ross, Mrs. (Chatham)
    Abram (Bulloch)
    Daniel (Elbert)
    David (Hancock)
    Duke (Jones)
    Edward (Columbia)
    Ethelred (Lincoln)
    Frances (Liberty)
    George (Chatham)
    George (Jones)
    Isom (Emanuel)
    James (2) (Columbia)
    James (Emanuel)
    James (Hall)
    James (Wilkinson)
    Jeanny (Chatham)
    Jesse (Jones)
    John (Jackson)
    John (2) (Putnam)
    John (Wilkinson)
    Jonathon (Jefferson)
    Josiah (Chatham)
    Margaret (Chatham)
    Mary (Hancock)
    Roland (Jones)
    Silas (Chatham)
    William (Emanuel)
    William (2) (Wilkinson)
    Wyly (Jackson)
Rosser, Aaron (Hancock)
    Benjamon (Putnam)
    Daniel (Jones)
    David (Putnam)
    Elizabeth (Putnam)
    James (Putnam)
    John (Hancock)
    Lurna(?) (Hancock)
Rosseter, Appleton (Baldwin)
Rossier, Elizabeth (Wilkinson)

Rossignol, Paul (Richmond)
Rossin, Thomas (Jackson)
Rossiter, Timothy (Hancock)
　White (Clarke)
　William (Jones)
Roswell, William (Jones)
Rouark, Lemuel (Columbia)
Roughton, Elizabeth (Greene)
　Enoch (Washington)
　Jacob (Wayne)
　Martha (Washington)
　Matthew (Greene)
Roundtree, Cader (2) (Morgan)
　Francis (Morgan)
　George (Emanuel)
　Joshua (Emanuel)
　John (Emanuel)
　Roby (Morgan)
Rountree, Arthur (Jefferson)
　Francis (Bulloch)
　James (Pulaski)
　John (Screven)
　Moses (Telfair)
Rourke, Thomas (Chatham)
Rousarall(?), David (Clarke)
Rouse, James (Walton)
　Joseph (Pulaski)
　Martin (Emanuel)
Roush, Joshua (Appling)
Rousseau, Hiram (Morgan)
　James (Baldwin)
Routon, John (McIntosh)
Roux, John (Camden)
Rowden, H. A. (Jasper)
Rowdon, John (2) (Jasper)
Rowe, Edward (Screven)
　Frederick (McIntosh)
　George (Pulaski)
　Samuel (Wilkes)
　William (Bulloch)
Rowel, James (Camden)
　James (Wilkinson)
　Joab (Burke)
Rowell, Humphrey
　　　　　(Washington)
　Ned (Richmond)
Rowery, Winslow (Elbert)
Rowland, Daniel (Warren)
　Hiram (Greene)
　James (Burke)
　James (Warren)
　John (Laurens)
　John, Jr. (Laurens)
　Jordon (Greene)
　Nathan (Emanuel)
　Richard (Emanuel)
　Robert (Warren)
　Thomas (Warren)
　William (Emanuel)
　William (Greene)
　Willis (Gwinnett)

Rowles, Thomas (Greene)
Rowling, Charles (Screven)
Rowsey, Edmond (Elbert)
　Foster (Elbert)
　Stephen (Elbert)
Rowzer, James (Elbert)
Royal, Asa (Burke)
　John (Burke)
　John (Jackson)
　John S. (Burke)
　Mary (Burke)
　Sam (Burke)
　Seaborn L. (Burke)
Royals, James (Gwinnett)
Royston, Richard C. (Greene)
Rozar, Aaron (Wayne)
Rozen, John (Chatham)
Rozier, Charles (Bryan)
　John, Jr. (Pulaski)
　John, Sr. (Pulaski)
　Oliver (McIntosh)
　Robert, Jr. (Wilkinson)
　Robert, Sr. (Wilkinson)
　Wiley (Glynn)
Ruaker, Nancy (Jones)
Ruark, Babtha (Warren)
Rucker, Gideon (Wilkes)
　James (2) (Elbert)
　Joseph (Elbert)
　Mary (Hancock)
　William (Elbert)
　Willis (Lincoln)
Rucks, James F. (Gwinnett)
　William (Gwinnett)
Rud, Jacob (McIntosh)
Ruddle, Andrew (Wilkes)
Rudisil, John (Hancock)
Rudolph, Christopher (Camden)
　Elizabeth (Camden)
Ruell, Green (Putnam)
Ruff. Moses (Richmond)
　Stephen (Elbert)
　William (Walton)
Ruffin, James (Jones)
　Robert R. (Jones)
Rufus, C. McHarty (Baldwin)
Ruke, Dennis (Morgan)
Rumph, Jacob (Glynn)
　Joseph (Glynn)
Rumsey, James (Wilkes)
　Richard (Wilkes)
　Thomas (Wilkes)
Runnalds, William (Clarke)
Runnels, Betsy (Burke)
　George (Oglethorpe)
　James (Greene)
　John (Greene)
　John (Jackson)
　Levi (Morgan)
Runnelson, Andrew (Burke)
Runnitz, Reuben (Jones)

William (Jones)
Rupert, John (Oglethorpe)
Rush, Betsy (Habersham)
　James (Hancock)
　Lewis B. (Elbert)
Rushin, Joel (Jones)
　William (Jones)
Rushing, Eli (Washington)
　Sarah (Washington)
　William (Bulloch)
　William (Tattnall)
Rushton, Mary (Gwinnett)
Rusler, T____ (Chatham)
Russ, Thomas (Oglethorpe)
Russan, Travis (Putnam)
　William, Jr. (Putnam)
Russeau, George (Putnam)
　John (Putnam)
　William (Putnam)
Russel, Mrs. (Wayne)
　Abel (Jefferson)
　Isaac (Chatham)
　James G. (Baldwin)
　James (Burke)
　James (Hall)
　Jane (Oglethorpe)
　John (Baldwin)
　John M. (Chatham)
　Martin (Baldwin)
　Rebecca (Chatham)
　Robert (Hall)
　Samuel (Chatham)
　Stephen (Habersham)
　William R. (Oglethorpe)
Russell, Benjamin (Wilkes)
　Burwell (Morgan)
　Clary Ann (Lincoln)
　David (Habersham)
　David (Jasper)
　George (Madison)
　Henry (Jones)
　Henry W. (Chatham)
　James (Glynn)
　James (Habersham)
　Jesse (Wilkes)
　John (Madison)
　John B. (Jasper)
　Joseph D. (Wilkinson)
　Mark (Wilkes)
　Capt. S. (Richmond)
　William (Jones)
　William C. (Lincoln)
　William R. (Jasper)
Rutherford, Abner M.
　　　　　(Washington)
　Benjamin H. (Washington)
　David (Gwinnett)
　Franklin (Washington)
　Isaiah (Oglethorpe)
　Israel (Oglethorpe)
　James (Irwin)

Rutherford, John (Baldwin)
  Nathaniel I. (Washington)
  Robert (Baldwin)
  Samuel (Warren)
  Thomas (Hall)
  Thomas B. (Washington)
  William (Baldwin)
Rutkins, John (Jones)
Rutland, Willie (Greene)
Rutledge, James (2)
      (Oglethorpe)
  John (Burke)
  John (Gwinnett)
  John (Morgan)
  Joseph (Oglethorpe)
  Joseph (Putnam)
  Kiah (Morgan)
  Rebecca (Putnam)
  Samuel (Morgan)
  Thomas (Clarke)
  William O. (Wilkes)
Rutt, Dianah (Oglethorpe)
Ryalds, Joshua (Wilkinson)
Ryall, Charles (Effingham)
Ryals, David (Laurens)
  Henry (McIntosh)
  Herbert (McIntosh)
  Isaac (Wilkinson)
  John (McIntosh)
  Jordon (McIntosh)
  William (Montgomery)
Ryan, Mrs. (Chatham)
  Dennis L. (Warren)
  Edward (Tattnall)
  Hiram (Jasper)
  John (Columbia)
  Philip (Jackson)
  Richard (Wilkinson)
  William L. (Chatham)
Ryce, William (Putnam)
Ryding, Benjamin (Jackson)
Rye, (ind.) (Laurens)
  Dunn (Wilkinson)
  John W. (Wilkinson)
  Jonathon (Wilkinson)
  Joseph (Hancock)
Ryland, Alan (Washington)
  Benone (Washington)
  John (Washington)
Rylander, Elizabeth (Effingham)
Ryle, John (Wilkinsono)
  Isaac (Putnam)
  William (Wilkinson)
Ryly, John (Lincoln)
Rymes, John (Bulloch)
  William (Bulloch)
Rysor, John (Habersham)

S

Sacrer, Thomas (Pulaski)
Sadler, H. R. (Camden)
  Henry (Camden)
  James (Putnam)
  Nathaniel (Putnam)
  William (Elbert)
  William T. (Putnam)
Saffold, Adam G. (Morgan)
  Bird (Wilkes)
  D. (Jasper)
  Elizabeth (Wilkes)
  Rhoda (Wilkes)
  Sarah (Wilkes)
  Sebourn S. (Greene)
  William (Wilkes)
Safold, Isham H. (Washington)
Sager, Ann (Greene)
  John D. (Greene)
Sagus, John (Wilkes)
Sailon, Christopher (Jackson)
  David (Jackson)
  John (Jackson)
Sailors, James (Madison)
St. George, (torn) (Laurens)
  James (Emanuel)
  John (Jasper)
  L. (ind.) (Emanuel)
  Lewis (Emanuel)
Sale, Giddeon (Baldwin)
Sales, Leroy (Wilkes)
  Richard (Wilkes)
Salisbury, James G. (Burke)
Sallet, Robert (McIntosh)
Sally, Larkin (Richmond)
  Michael (Lincoln)
Salmonds, Ephraim (Gwinnett)
  Groves (Gwinnett)
  H. (Richmond)
Salter, Benjamin (Wilkinson)
  Charles (Washington)
  John (Washington)
  Peter (Warren)
  Robert (Wilkinson)
  Simon (Washington)
  Zadock (Washington)
Salton, (ind.) (Pulaski)
Saltus, Jacob (Effingham)
Samford, Thomas (Wilkinson)
Sammonds, Howel (Gwinnett)
Sammons, Benjamin (Jefferson)
  Foster(?) (Warren)
  Lewis (Jefferson)
  Richard (Morgan)
Sample, John (Putnam)
  Nathaniel (Jefferson)
  Sally (Oglethorpe)
  Usiah (Putnam)
  William (Putnam)
Sampler, Jerimiah (Columbia)

Sampson, B. (Richmond)
  Isham (Richmond)
Sampson(?), Mary (Chatham)
Sams, Edward (McIntosh)
  Francis (McIntosh)
  John (Oglethorpe)
  Joseph (Oglethorpe)
Samuel, Benjamin (Lincoln)
  Edward (Lincoln)
Sandefur, John (Jefferson)
  John L. (Jefferson)
  Judith (Jefferson)
Sanderling, Benjamin (Bryan)
Sanders, Alexander (Burke)
  Aesay (2) (Jones)
  Arden (Wilkinson)
  Billinstone (Columbia)
  Burril (Washington)
  Burton (Putnam)
  Charlotte (Hancock)
  Coalson (Wilkinson)
  D. (Jasper)
  Daniel (Putnam)
  David (Putnam)
  Eliza (Lincoln)
  Elizabeth (Washington)
  Ephraim (Jones)
  George (Morgan)
  Henry (Wilkinson)
  Isaac (Hall)
  Isaac (Jones)
  J. (Jasper)
  Jacob (Hall)
  James (Columbia)
  James (Madison)
  James (Morgan)
  James (Wilkinson)
  Jesse (Walton)
  Jessey (Wilkinson)
  John (2) (Jones)
  John (2) (Lincoln)
  John (Madison)
  John (Screven)
  John (2) (Wilkinson)
  John L. (Putnam)
  John M. (Hancock)
  Jonathon (Madison)
  Joseph (Madison)
  Lewis (Laurens)
  Micajah (Jones)
  Malaki (Wilkinson)
  Mary (Hancock)
  Nancy (2) (Hancock)
  Nathan (Hancock)
  Nathaniel (Jones)
  Nelly (Putnam)
  Peter (Jones)
  Reuben (Columbia)
  Richard (Morgan)
  Robert (Laurens)
  Samuel (Putnam)

Sanders, Samuel (Wilkinson)
   Sarah (Putnam)
   Stephen (Baldwin)
   Thomas (Elbert)
   Thomas (Jones)
   Thomas (Putnam)
   William (Hancock)
   William (Madison)
   William (2) (Putnam)
   William (Screven)
   William (Washington)
   Zach (Greene)
Sandford, Benjamin (Emanuel)
   Benjamin (Hancock)
   Burkley (Putnam)
   Jeremiah (Hancock)
   William (Wilkes)
Sandifer, Harris (Wilkes)
   James (Putnam)
   John (Morgan)
   Patrick (Morgan)
Sandiford, Abner (Emanuel)
   Benjamin (Warren)
   James (Liberty)
   John (Columbia)
   John (Warren)
   Sarah (Columbia)
Sandil, John (Glynn)
Sandling, John (Glynn)
Sandrage, Clabon (Elbert)
Sands, John (Tattnall)
   Rae (Camden)
Sandwich, Margaret
    (Richmond)
   Thomas H. (Lincoln)
Sandyford, N. T. (Burke)
   William (Burke)
Sanford, Frederick (Baldwin)
   Henry (Greene)
   Joshua (Liberty)
   Judith (Warren)
   Thornton (Putnam)
   Vincent (Greene)
   William (Baldwin)
   William (Greene)
Sanges, John (Richmond)
Sangford, James (Jones)
Sansom, Elizabeth (Wilkes)
   James (Jasper)
   Micajah (2) (Walton)
   Robert (Jasper)
   Sarry (Walton)
Santes, Henery (Camden)
Sap, Elisha (Appling)
Sappenton, Caleb (Wilkes)
Sappington, John (Wilkes)
Sapp, Abraham (Wilkinson)
   Addison (Burke)
   Benjamin (Tattnall)
   Darling (Liberty)
   Elizabeth (Burke)
   Elisha (Appling)

Everet (Burke)
   Hardy C. (Burke)
   Henry (Liberty)
   Henry (Tattnall)
   Isaiah (Burke)
   James (Burke)
   James (Wayne)
   John (Bryan)
   John (2) (Burke)
   John (Liberty)
   Levy (Emanuel)
   Luke, Jr. (Burke)
   Luke, Sr. (Burke)
   Luke (Tattnall)
   Margaret (Jefferson)
   P. S. (Tattnall)
   Riley (Wilkinson)
   Shadrack, Jr. (Liberty)
   Shadrack, Sr. (Liberty)
   Wiley (Burke)
   Wiliam (2) (Burke)
   William, Jr. (Burke)
   William, Sr. (Burke)
Sarrow, Elijah (Elbert)
Sartain, Elisha (Madison)
   John (Madison)
Sasnett, Joseph R. (Hancock)
Sasser, Britton (Putnam)
   Bryant (Screven)
   William (Jones)
Saterwhite, Milly (Columbia)
   William (Columbia)
Satherland, John (Columbia)
Satterwhite, Elijah (Jones)
   James (Elbert)
   James (Jones)
   Obed (Jones)
   Stephen (Jones)
   Wavid (Jones)
Saturwhite, Francis (Elbert)
Saul, Meredith (Bryan)
Sauls, Abraham (Jefferson)
   Allen (Telfair)
   Daniel (Washington)
   Isaac (Liberty)
Saunders, James (Warren)
   Mary (Warren)
Savage, Allen (Hall)
   Benjamin (Chatham)
   Charles (Pulaski)
   D. (Richmond)
   Danl., Overseer for
    (Burke)
   Elizabeth (Richmond)
   Mary (Bryan)
   Nathaniel (Pulaski)
   William (2) (Bryan)
   William (Richmond)
   Zebulon (Hall)
Savat(?), Nathan, Jr.
    (Bulloch)

Savier, Phillis (Chatham)
Savoir, Made. (Chatham)
Sawls, Daniel (Jasper)
Sawyer, Charles (Hancock)
   Johnson (Putnam)
   Jonathon (McIntosh)
   Robert (Habersham)
Sawyers, John (Putnam)
Saxon, Benjamin (Jasper)
   Elizabeth (Habersham)
   John (Burke)
   Samuel (Burke)
   William (Burke)
Saxton, John (Hall)
   Wiley (Wilkes)
Say, James (Jackson)
Saye, Margaret (Madison)
Saylers, William (Madison)
Sayres, David (Morgan)
Scaggs, Charles (Putnam)
   Henry M. (Putnam)
   James (Putnam)
   John R. (Putnam)
   Lemuel B. (Putnam)
   Richard (Putnam)
Scal, Richard I. (Elbert)
Scales, Aaron (Elbert)
   John (Elbert)
   Thomas (Elbert)
Scarboro, Reddic (Bulloch)
Scarborough, Aaron (Pulaski)
   Adam (Pulaski)
   Elizabeth (Emanuel)
   Hardy (Screven)
   James (Emanuel)
   Joel (Burke)
   Mily (Jones)
   Samuel (Burke)
   Silas (Burke)
   Thomas (Burke)
   William (Burke)
   William (Chatham)
Scarbourgh, Frederick
    (Madison)
Scarbrough, (ind.) (Laurens)
   Aaron (Pulaski)
   Eliza (Laurens)
   James (Laurens)
   John (Laurens)
   Joshua (Jefferson)
   Nancy (Pulaski)
   Nicholas (Wilkinson)
   Turner (Jefferson)
Schaffin, Andrew (Chatham)
Schetton, Charles I. (Telfair)
Schiry, Isaiah (Washington)
Schley, George (Chatham)
   John J. (Jefferson)
Schneider, H. (Chatham)
Schuman, James (Effingham)

Schweighoffen, Margaret)
 (Chatham)
Scoggin, Henry (Jackson)
 Seaborn T. (Jackson)
Scoggins, Benjamin (Jackson)
 Gillium (Jasper)
 James (Jones)
 Josiah (Washington)
 Seaborn (Jackson)
 Wiley (Oglethorpe)
Scoggings, Wright (Greene)
Scogin, Franky (Walton)
 Gresham (Putnam)
 Joshus (Morgan)
Scolds, Rachel (Wilkes)
 Robert (Wilkes)
Sconyers, William
 (Montgomery)
Scotes, Thomas (Walton)
 Zedikiah (Walton)
Scott, (ind.) (Hancock)
 Mrs. (Chatham)
 Abram (Jackson)
 Absalom (Warren)
 Adam (Columbia)
 Andrew (Burke)
 Ann (Jasper)
 Archibald H. (Greene)
 Benjamin (Hancock)
 Benjamin (Morgan)
 Britton (Emanuel)
 Charles (Burke)
 Daniel (Jasper)
 Daniel (Wilkes)
 David (Wilkinson)
 Frances (Putnam)
 Francis (Warren)
 Henry (Columbia)
 Henry F. (Greene)
 Jacob (Morgan)
 James (Clarke)
 James (Hall)
 James, Sr. (Liberty)
 James (Madison)
 James (Screven)
 James, Jr. (Screven)
 James (Washington)
 James E. (Liberty)
 James M. (Wilkinson)
 John (Jones)
 John (Madison)
 John (Oglethorpe)
 John (Richmond)
 John (Warren)
 John C. (Bryan)
 John P. (Greene)
 John R. (Baldwin)
 Joseph (Chatham)
 Joseph (Jackson)
 Mary (Jefferson)
Scot, Nathan (Screven)

Patrick (Madison)
Reuben (Wilkes)
Samuel (Liberty)
Samuel (Morgan)
Samuel (Warren)
Stephen P. (Putnam)
Susan (Glynn)
Thomas (Jasper)
Thomas B. (Greene)
Thomas B. (Emanuel)
William (Chatham)
William (Columbia)
William, Jr. (Columbia)
William (Gwinnett)
William (Jasper)
William (Jones)
William (Liberty)
William (Madison)
William F. (Hancock)
William R. (Chatham)
Word H. (Hancock)
Screven, Major (Chatham)
Screws, Jesse (Jefferson)
Scriven, Rev. C. O. (Liberty)
Scroggin, Thomas E. (col)
 (Oglethorpe)
 King H. (Jones)
 Smith (Baldwin)
Scrogin, Thomas (Oglethorpe)
Scruggs, Abishai (Burke)
 Alethea (Effingham)
 Groce, Sr. (Effingham)
 Nelly (Columbia)
 Richard (Screven)
Scrutchens, Josiah (Burke)
Seabert, Charles (Pulaski)
Seaborn, Bailey (Jones)
 Richard (Jones)
Seagars, John (Gwinnett)
 Mary (Gwinnett)
Seagler, Joseph (Walton)
Seagrove, Ann (Camden)
Seal, Anthony (Putnam)
 John (Elbert)
Seale, Redman G. (Lincoln)
Sealer, George (Elbert)
Seales, R. G. (Lincoln)
 Joel (Elbert)
Seals, Archabald (Warren)
 Arnold (Jones)
 Eli (Jones)
 John (Jackson)
 Spencer (Hancock)
 William (Camden)
 William (Hancock)
Searl, E. (Richmond)
Searcy, Aaron (Baldwin)
 William (Baldwin)
Sears, David (Montgomery)
 Elizabeth (Greene)
 James (Greene)
Harrison (Appling)

Timothy (Wilkinson)
William R. (Jones)
Searsey, Elizabeth (Wilkinson)
Seath, Mary (Wilkinson)
Seay, John (Jackson)
 Phebe (Columbia)
 Thomas (Columbia)
Seckinger, (ind.) (Effingham)
 Benjamin (Effingham)
 John C. (Effingham)
 John G. (Effingham)
 Jonathon (Effingham)
Sedan, Isaac (Jasper)
Seeley, Edward (Laurens)
Segar, Benjamin (Burke)
 Charles T. (Burke)
 Joab (Burke)
 John (Jackson)
 Samuel (Burke)
Segars, John (Gwinnett)
 Southard (Gwinnett)
Segroves, Burrel (Madison)
Sekes, Joseph (Jones)
Self. (torn) (Laurens)
 Ezekiel (Bulloch)
 Vincent (Hall)
Sellars, James (Jackson)
Seller, James (Richmond)
Sellers, John (Appling)
 Judy (Hall)
 Samuel (Appling)
 Soloman (Emanuel)
Selman, Benjamin (Morgan)
 John (Clarke)
Selp, Thomas (Telfair)
Semmes, Andrew G. (Wilkes)
Sempler, William (Warren)
Sentell, Nathan (Walton)
 Samuel (Walton)
Senter, Abner (Habersham)
 Dawson (Habersham)
 Levi (Habersham)
Senterfrit, Henry (Pulaski)
 Jesse (Pulaski)
Sentis, John (Jones)
Senton, Elizabeth M. (Elbert)
 Leovid (Elbert)
Seppard, John (Wilkinson)
Sermon, Abner (Emanuel)
Sermons, Benjamin (Emanuel)
Sesogzing, George (Jones)
Sessions, Asa (Morgan)
 Benjamin (Washington)
 George (Washington)
 F. (Jasper)
 John (Jasper)
 Joseph (2) (Washington)
 Lewis (Washington)
 Richard (Morgan)
 Robert F. (Jasper)

Sessoms, Nicholas
(Montgomery)
Setze, John P. (Chatham)
Seurlock, William (Baldwin)
Seutel, Joseph (Jasper)
Sevan, William (Jefferson)
Sever, William (Emanuel)
Sevier, John (Burke)
Sewther(?), Charles (Bulloch)
Sexton, M. (Jasper)
Solomon (Jackson)
Seward, William (Laurens)
Sewell, John (Morgan)
Seymour, Edward (McIntosh)
Shabney(?), Henry (Wilkinson)
Shackleford, Edmond (2)
(Elbert)
Edmond (Putnam)
Edmund (Baldwin)
John (Wilkes)
Mildy (Jackson)
Philip (Jackson)
Richard (Columbia)
Shadde, Solomon (Chatham)
Shaderick, Nancy (Putnam)
Shadok, Mary (Jackson)
Shadral, Anthony (Glynn)
Shadwick, Elizabeth
(Richmond)
Shafer, James L. (Richmond)
Shaffer, D. (Richmond)
Frederick (Chatham)
Jacob (Chatham)
M. (Chatham)
Mary (Chatham)
Shakleford, Henry (Elbert)
Shamlen, Nancy (Warren)
Shanaday, Thomas (Camden)
Shank, John (Wilkes)
Valentine (col.) (Wilkes)
Shanks, Henry (Wilkes)
Shanley, William (Wilkes)
Shannon, Evans (Morgan)
Mary (Glynn)
Thomas (Pulaski)
William (Richmond)
Sharber(?), Richard (Screven)
Shark. J. (Richmond)
Basdil (Burke)
Cade (Burke)
Sharp, Clemy (Burke)
Francis (Morgan)
Givies (Montgomery)
Henry (Jackson)
Henry (2) (Morgan)
Hiram (Morgan)
Howel (Laurens)
Ibbirella (Jackson)
James (Greene)
John (Baldwin)
John (Lincoln)

John (Tattnall)
Joshua (Appling)
Louisa (Jasper)
Marshal (Greene)
Parkes (Tattnall)
Polly (Burke)
Robert (Jasper)
William (Baldwin)
William (Chatham)
Sharpe, James (Wilkes)
Mattan (Washington)
Shanklin, Robert (Columbia)
Shave, Jeremiah, Sr. (Liberty)
Shaver(?), Daniel (Pulaski)
Shaves, John (Liberty)
William (Liberty)
Shaw, Mrs. (Camden)
Alexander (Chatham)
Shaw(?), Alexander
(Habersham)
Shaw, Amos (Oglethorpe)
Daniel (Montgomery)
Daniel (Warren)
Elijah (Jackson)
Elizabeth (Clarke)
George (Morgan)
George (Warren)
Gilbert (Jasper)
Jacob W. (Oglethorpe)
James (Columbia)
John, Jr. (Greene)
John (Sr. (Greene)
John (2) (Jasper)
John H. (Morgan)
Jane (Clarke)
Joseph (2) (Jackson)
Josias W. (Jackson)
Margaret (Columbia)
Margaret (Morgan)
Martha (Clarke)
Nancy (Jones)
Neel (Jones)
Norman (Telfair)
Rebecca (Gwinnett)
Robert (Columbia)
Thomas (Jasper)
William, Sr. (Clarke)
William (Jones)
William W. (Greene)
Shawn, Martin (McIntosh)
Shay, David (Clarke)
Shealy, Henry G. (Screven)
Shearer, (ind.) (Wilkes)
Elijah (Wilkes)
William (Wilkes)
Shearman, Clement (Wilkes)
Edward (Camden)
John (Wilkes)
Godlieb (Effingham)
Sheats, Charles (Walton)
Nicholas (Clarke)

Shebert, Warner (Putnam)
Sheets, Archer (Wilkes)
Reuben (Wilkes)
Tarlton (Wilkes)
Shefield, Bryant (Camden)
Sheffield, Isham (Bulloch)
John (Bulloch)
John (Bulloch)
Pliny (Wayne)
Sherard (Wayne)
West (Wayne)
William, Sr. (Bulloch)
William, Jr. (Bulloch)
Zachariah (Morgan)
Sheftall, Adam, Jr. (Chatham)
Adam, Sr. (Chatham)
Abraham (Chatham)
Benjamin (Chatham)
Isaac (Chatham)
Moses (Chatham)
Shehee, A. B. (Washington)
Allafair (Washington)
Shehe, John (Washington)
Thomas (Washington)
Sheley, Moses (Washington)
Shell, Byron (Hancock)
Green (Hancock)
Shelly, Lewsy (Wilkinson)
S. D. (Richmond)
Shelman, Michael (Jefferson)
Shelton, Abel (Morgan)
Allen (Greene)
Baley W. (Gwinnett)
Henry (Warren)
Himan(?) (Habersham)
John (Elbert)
Joseph (Hancock)
Shepard, John (Clarke)
Shepherd, Andrew (Wilkes)
Bazil (Burke)
Benjamon (Putnam)
Edward (Laurens)
Francis (Columbia)
Jacob (Jefferson)
James (Burke)
James (Morgan)
John, Jr. (Liberty)
John, Sr. (Liberty)
John (Walton)
John M. (Putnam)
Joseph (Wilkes)
Joshua (Jefferson)
Nathan (Liberty)
Orlando (Columbia)
Peter (Elbert)
Rebecca (Liberty)
Samuel (Elbert)
Talman (Morgan)
Thomas (Clarke)
Thomas (Jones)
Thompson (Wilkes)

Shepherd, William (Putnam)
Shepherdson, Elizabeth (Burke)
Sheppard, Charles (Washington)
David (Baldwin)
David (Washington)
Henry (Washington)
James (Washington)
John (Putnam)
John (Washington)
Mermin(?) (Screven)
Nimrod (Clarke)
Simon G. (Screven)
Thomas (Washington)
Wiley (Wilkinson)
William, Sr. (Screven)
William (2) (Wilkinson)
Shepperd, John (Jefferson)
William (Jefferson)
Sheptrine, Daniel (Wilkes)
Sherburn, Charles F. (Wilkes)
Sheridon, Dene (Greene)
George (Habersham)
Sherlin, James (Washington)
Sherlock, Edward (Chatham)
Michael (Chatham)
Sherlong, Richard (Greene)
Sherly, Aaron (Jones)
Edward (Jones)
Elizabeth (Jones)
Sherman, James (Jasper)
James (Putnam)
Robert (Jasper)
Sherod, Benjamin (Wilkes)
James (Jefferson)
Sherrard, Benjamin (Emanuel)
Sherrill, Benjamin (Screven)
Elizabeth (Greene)
Sherrow, Francis (Wilkinson)
James (Wilkinson)
Thomas (Wilkinson)
Shick, John (Chatham)
Shield, George (Jackson)
Shields, James (Columbia)
James (Jackson)
Mary (Columbia)
Samuel (Morgan)
William (2) (Morgan)
Shiflet, Powell (Elbert)
Shiflett, Picket (Elbert)
Shinatt, Nelson (Elbert)
Shinholster, George (Wilkinson)
John U. (Wilkinson)
Ship, Mrs. Francis (Hancock)
James (Columbia)
Shipp, John C. (Morgan)
Lemuel (Columbia)
Mark (Columbia)
Ship, Richard (Morgan)
Thomas (Lincoln)
William (Jackson)
William (Pulaski)

Shipley, William (Habersham)
Shira, Lona (Madison)
Shirdevant, Joel (Walton)
Shiresan(?) Thomas (Chatham)
Shirley, Benjamin (Habersham)
James (Washington)
Moses (Habersham)
Shirling, Richmond (Wilkes)
Shirley, Robert (Jackson)
William (Jackson)
William (Warren)
Shisk, Peter (Chatham)
Shiver, (torn) (2) (Laurens)
Abram (Laurens)
Byers (2) (Wilkinson)
Jacob, Jr. (Wilkinson)
Jacob, Sr. (Wilkinson)
Shivers, Barnaby (Hancock)
John M. (Hancock)
Jonas (Warren)
Thomas W. (Warren)
William (Hancock)
Shley, John (Jefferson)
William (Jefferson)
Shoalders, Bryan (Early)
Shoar, Isaac (Jefferson)
Shoars, Elijah (Putnam)
Shockley, Benjamin (Greene)
John (Greene)
Jonathan (Greene)
Leonard (Hancock)
Thomas (Greene)
Thomas (Hall)
Shockly, Gideon (Jackson)
Shoemaker, Talton (Elbert)
Shook, Solomon (Habersham)
Shop, Daniel (Wilkes)
Shops, Luis (Wilkes)
Shores, Plana (Putnam)
Short, Amelia (Columbia)
Barber (Wilkes)
David (Putnam)
Edward (Columbia)
John (Hall)
Labrum (Oglethorpe)
Minny (Jones)
Peter B. (Columbia)
William T. (Jasper)
Young W. (Oglethorpe)
Shorter, Eli S. (Putnam)
Henry (Greene)
R. C. (Jasper)
Shotwell, Nathanl (Jackson)
Shoud, John D. (Wilkes)
Shrimp, Ann C. (Effingham)
Shropsheer, I. W. (Jasper)
Shropshire, Walter (Greene)
Shroshers, William (Jones)
Shruptrine, Israel (Effingham)
Shuffied, Isom (Early)
Shuffield, John C. (Washington)

Reuben (Warren)
Robert (Warren)
Wes (Early)
William (Hancock)
William, Sr. (Pulaski)
William (Pulaski)
Wright (Laurens)
Shuffle, Everitt (Habersham)
Sarah (Bryan)
Shuirley, William S. (Jefferson)
Shults, Henry (Richmond)
Shumake, Joseph (Burke)
Shuman, George H. (Bryan)
Godlip (Effingham)
Martin (Bryan)
Shumate, William (Wilkes)
Shumatt, Elizabeth W. (Liberty)
Shurdivant, Elizabeth (Walton)
Shurley, Edward (Jones)
Nathan (Warren)
Nathaniel (Jones)
Shurman, John F. (Hancock)
Shute, Giles (Pulaski)
Shy, James (Hancock)
Samuel (Jasper)
Simeon (Warren)
Sibley, J. (Camden)
R. (Richmond)
Sid, Joseph (Jones)
Sieler(?), Jese (Appling)
Siers, Jane (Putnam)
Siery(?), Herman(?) (Appling)
Sikes, Arthur (Appling)
(ind.) (Laurens)
Barnard (Putnam)
Edward (Bryan)
Jacob (Bryan)
James (Richmond)
John (Telfair)
William (Gwinnett)
Siland, James (Jefferson)
Silas. David (Warren)
Fatha (Warren)
James (Warren)
John (Warren)
Sillavant, Martha (Jefferson)
Mary (Montgomery)
Sillivan, Dennis (Burke)
Sillivant, William (Montgomery)
Sills, Edward (Wilkinson)
Jonathon (Warren)
Macklin (Columbia)
Nancy (Burke)
Silver, Anto (Chatham)
Emanuel(?) (Chatham)
Loxianne (Chatham)
Sylvister (Camden)
Silvy, Drury (Gwinnett)
Stephens (Oglethorpe)
Simeson, Asea (Hancock)
Simmons, (ind.) (Lincoln)

(133)

Simmons, Abram (Madison)
Alford M. (Putnam)
Allen (Jasper)
Asa (Putnam)
Beverly A. (Pulaski)
Benjamin (Hancock)
Benjamon (Putnam)
Caleb (Wilkes)
Charity (Jones)
Charles (Oglethorpe)
Daniel (Liberty)
David (Oglethorpe)
Elizabeth (Oglethorpe)
George (Jasper)
Hannah (Chatham)
Henry (Jones)
Henry (Putnam)
Henry (Tattnall)
Isaac (Madison)
Isaac H. (Baldwin)
Jacob (Lincoln)
James (Hancock)
James (Walton)
James H. L. (Hancock)
James T. (Jasper)
Jesse (Gwinnett)
Jesse (2) (Hancock)
Jesse (Putnam)
Simmons(?), Jesse (Wilkes)
Simmons, John (Baldwin)
John (Clarke)
John (Elbert)
John (Habersham)
John (Hancock)
John (Jones)
John, Sr. (Lincoln)
John B. (2) (Hancock)
John F. (Wilkinson)
John R. (Jasper)
Joseph (Columbia)
Joshua (Hall)
Margery (Bulloch)
Martin (Hancock)
Pheriby (Burke)
R. H. (Jasper)
Samuel (Emanuel)
Samuel (Screven)
Samuel (Wilkes)
Sollomon (Oglethorpe)
Stephen, Sr. (Chatham)
Stephen (Putnam)
Thomas (Lincoln)
Thomas (Madison)
Thomas (Morgan)
Thomas (Putnam)
Valentine (Warren)
Vincent (Ogethorpe)
William (Jones)
William (Morgan)
Wiliams (Putnam)
William (Warren)

William B. (Jasper)
Zadock (Wilkinson)
Simmonton, Joel (Greene)
Ezekiel (Greene)
Simms, Benjamin (Jackson)
Horatio (Columbia)
Ignatius (Wilkes)
Jacob (Effingham)
James (2) (Hancock)
James (McIntosh)
John (Warren)
Larkin (Putnam)
Mann (Columbia)
Mary (Wilkes)
Reuben B. (Morgan)
Richard (Hancock)
Robert (Jackson)
Robert (Putnam)
Thomas (Wilkes)
Williams (Putnam)
Simon, John (Pulaski)
Abraham (Wilkes)
Simons, Billy (Chatham)
Christian M. (Columbia)
Elizabeth (Wilkes)
Isaac (Jasper)
James (Warren)
John, Jr. (Lincoln)
Robert (Jasper)
Silas (Telfair)
Simonton, Abner (Greene)
Felex (Greene)
Simpson, Alexander (Pulaski)
Christopher (Pulaski)
David (Pulaski)
David (Wilkes)
Frederick (Pulaski)
George (Baldwin)
Hardy ,Jefferson)
Hester (Wilkes)
Jacob (Pulaski)
James (Chatham)
James (2) (Hancock)
John (2) (Wilkinson)
John N. (Wilkes)
Joseph (Wilkes)
Joseph J. (Baldwin)
Leah (Chatham)
Mary (Elbert)
Mathew (Chatham)
Robert (Wilkes)
Soffy (Chatham)
Thomas (Pulaski)
William (Baldwin)
William (Camden)
William (Chatham)
William (Wilkes)
Sims, A. S. (Jasper)
Allen (Oglethorpe)
Benjamin (Richmond)
Britian (2) (Hancock)

Burkley (Madison)
Charles (Madison)
Edmund (Jones)
Fanny (Oglethorpe)
Federick (Baldwin)
Frederick (Jones)
George (Putnam)
Isham (Madison)
Jacob (Liberty)
James (Clarke)
John (Bulloch)
John (Jones)
John (Oglethorpe)
John (Pulaski)
John M. (Oglethorpe)
Leonard (Lincoln)
Leonard (Walton)
Lewis (Oglethorpe)
Mortan (Oglethorpe)
Nathan (Morgan)
Parker (Clarke)
Richard (Oglethorpe)
Sarah (Hancock)
Wiley (Oglethorpe)
William (Chatham)
William (Jasper)
William (Jones)
William (Richmond)
Zachariah (Clarke)
Simson, Cain (Putnam)
Singer, John (Hancock)
Singfield, L. (Richmond)
Singletary, John (Wilkinson)
Thomas W. (Telfair)
Singleterry, Michael R.
(Pulaski)
Singleton, Bigers (Pulaski)
George (Effingham)
Hansel (Washington)
Henry (Putnam)
Hezekiah (Putnam)
James (Washington)
James (Putnam)
Joseph (Jackson)
Richard (Morgan)
Thomas C. (Putnam)
William (Jones)
Wyatt (Jones)
Singo, Elizah (Baldwin)
Sinquefield, Moses
(Washington)
William (Washington)
Sintell, William (Baldwin)
Sirmons(?), Allis (Telfair)
Josiah (Appling)
Sisson, Charles (Habersham)
James (Jackson)
John (Jackson)
Sistrunk, John (Lincoln)
Skelly, Samuel (Warren)
Shelton, Elijah (Elbert)

(134)

Skener, Michael (Washington)
Skidmore, Samuel (Morgan)
Skinner, (ind.) (Elbert)
  Charles (Burke)
  Clary (Elbert)
  Florah (Baldwin)
  George M. (Elbert)
  John (2) (Burke)
  John (Hancock)
  John (Jackson)
  John (Putnam)
  John (Richmond)
  Jonas (Burke)
  Langston (Richmond)
  Mary (Hancock)
  Robert (Burke)
  Robert (Jasper)
  Sarah (Burke)
  Seth (Hancock)
  Thomas (Putnam)
  Uriah (Burke)
  William (Richmond)
Skipper, Barney B. (Wilkinson)
  Benjamin (Wilkinson)
  Daniel (Wilkinson)
  James (Chatham)
Skonyers, Celia (Burke)
  Richd. (Burke)
Skrine, Sarah (Hall)
  Sarah (Washington)
Skye, Ann (Chatham)
Slack, Benjamin (Wilkes)
  Jacob (Wilkes)
  Jesse (Wilkes)
  John (2) (Wilkes)
Slade, Jeremiah (Tattnall)
  William (Telfair)
Slain, Matthew (Burke)
Slappy, Aren (Jasper)
Slater, Burrel (Bulloch)
  James (Screven)
  Jesse (Screven)
  Samuel (Bulloch)
  Samuel (Jefferson)
  William (Bulloch)
Slaton. Arthur (Columbia)
  Zachriah (Oglethorpe)
Slatter, Nancy (Jones)
Slatter(?), Thomas F. (Hanock)
Slaughter, A. (Richmond)
  Aaron (Telfair)
  Beverley (Putnam)
  Francis (Jasper)
  H. G. (Greene)
  John (Baldwin)
  John (2) (Greene)
  John (Jones)
  Martin (Greene)
  Moses (Montgomery)
  Rebecca (Putnam)
  Reuben (Jones)

Samuel (Baldwin)
Thomas (Greene)
William (Jones)
William A. (Putnam)
Slay, Frederick (Richmond)
Slayton, Arthur (Morgan)
Sledge, Alexander (Baldwin)
  Amos (Jones)
  Manus (Hancock)
  Shurley (Putnam)
  Whitfield (Hancock)
Slocum, Fitch J. (Irwin)
  John C. (Jones)
Slone, Sally (Burke)
  William (Irwin)
Slotin, William (Wilkes)
Small, William (Jefferson)
Smalley, James (Columbia)
Smally, Michael, Jr. (Columbia)
  Michael, Sr. (Columbia)
Smallwood, Elijah (Hall)
  Isaac (Hall)
  John (2) (Habersham)
  Mark (Elbert)
  Mary (Wilkes)
  William (2) (Habersham)
  William (Wilkes)
Smart, Elisa (Jasper)
  Elisha (Jones)
  Elija (Jasper)
  Henry T. (Jasper)
  Littleberry (Jasper)
  Loanza (Liberty)
  Nathan (Liberty)
Smathers, G. (Richmond)
Smead, Elijah (Hancock)
Smedley, James (Putnam)
  Thomas (Putnam)
  Thomas, Sr. (Putnam)
Smiles, Robert H. (Wilkes)
Smith, Mrs. (Chatham)
  (torn) (2) (Laurens)
  A. R. (Chatham)
  Aaron (Hancock)
  Aaron (Jasper)
  Abraham (Appling)
  Agnes (Wilkinson)
  Alan (Washington)
  Albington F. (Hancock)
  Alexander (Jefferson)
  Alexander (Lincoln)
  Allen (Wilkinson)
  Ambrose (Clarke)
  Ambros (Telfair)
  Mr., The Anchorite
              (Chatham)
  Andrew (McIntosh)
  Andrew O. (Tattnall)
  Ann (Jackson)
  Anthony G. (Oglethorpe)
  Archibold (Chatham)

Absalom (Appling) — handwritten annotation

Archibald (Emanuel)
Archibald (Greene)
Archibald (Montgomery
Archibald (Morgan)
Archibald (Tattnall)
Archibald (2) (Telfair)
Arthur (Jasper)
Arthur (Richmond)
Arthur (Walton)
Asail (Hall)
B. G. (Jasper)
B. W. (Chatham)
Banister (Putnam)
Barnett (Putnam)
Battle L. (Morgan)
Baxter (Liberty)
Benjamin (Burke)
Benjamin (Elbert)
Benjamin (Hancock)
Benjamin (Jasper)
Benjamin (Jones)
Benjamin (Oglethorpe)
Benjamin (Pulaski)
Benjamin (Walton)
Benjamin (Wilkes)
Benjamin (Wilkinson)
Benjamin P. (McIntosh)
Benjamin S. (Gwinnett)
Berwell (Putnam)
Beunet (Jefferson)
Bird (Morgan)
Brinkley (Oglethorpe)
Brittain (Walton)
Calab (Wilkinson)
Caty (Washington)
Charles (Appling)
Charles (Baldwin)
Charles (Elbert)
Charles (Habersham)
Charles (Hall)
Charles, Sr. (Hall)
Charles (Morgan)
Charles (2) (Oglethorpe)
Charles (Richmond)
Charles (Walton)
Charles (Wilkes)
Charles L. (Oglethorpe)
Charles W. (Jones)
Claborn (Jackson)
Colesby (Washington)
Cooper John (Washington)
Cresard, Sr. (Pulaski)
D. (Jasper)
D., Jr. (Jasper)
Daniel (Columbia)
David (Appling)
David (Bryan)
David (Burke)
David (Elbert)
David (Greene)
David (2) (Hall)

Smith, David (Jackson)
David (Jasper)
David (Laurens)
David (Madison)
David (Morgan)
David (Pulaski)
David (2) (Putnam)
David (Richmond)
David (2) (Walton)
David D. (Putnam)
David T. (Jefferson)
Davis (Laurens)
Dred (Jefferson)
Eady (Warren)
Ebenezer (Greene)
Ebenezer (2) (Wilkes)
Edmund (2) (Morgan)
Edward (Pulaski)
Edy (Jones)
Elbert (Wilkes)
Eli (Greene)
Elihu (Walton)
Elijah (Glynn)
Elijah (Walton)
Elizabeth (Chatham)
Elizabeth (Greene)
Elizabeth (Jones)
Elizabeth (Lincoln)
Elizabeth (Madison)
Elizabeth (Warren)
English (Washington)
Ezekiel (Hancock)
Ezekiel (Jones)
Ezekiel (Montgomery)
Francis (Baldwin)
Francis (Jasper)
Francis B. (Walton)
Frederick (Oglethorpe)
George (Bulloch)
George (2) (Hancock)
George (2) (Morgan)
George (Washington)
George (Wilkes)
George G. (Columbia)
Gideon W. (Morgan)
Gillam (Warren)
Guy (Morgan)
Guy (Wilkes)
H. (Jackson)
Hardy (Jones)
Hardy (2) (Washington)
Harrison K. (Jones)
Harrison (Oglethorpe)
Henry (Elbert)
Henry (Jones)
Henry (Lincoln)
Henry (Madison)
Henry (Pulaski)
Henry (Wilkes)
Henry T. (Jasper)
Herbard (Jefferson)

Hill (Oglethorpe)
Hugh (Tattnall)
Hugh B. (Columbia)
Isaac (2) (Morgan)
Isaac (Telfair)
Isham (Laurens)
Isham (Oglethorpe)
Isham (Putnam)
Ivy (Tattnall)
J. (Richmond)
J.____(?) (Screven)
J. B. (Jasper)
J. R. (Chatham)
Jacob (2) (Laurens)
Jacob (Lincoln)
Jacob (Telfair)
Jacob (Warren)
James (Appling)
James (Chatham)
James (2) (Clarke)
James (Gwinnett)
James (Habersham)
James (Hancock)
James (3) (Jackson)
James (Jasper)
James (2) (Jones)
James (Jefferson)
James (Laurens)
James (Lincoln)
James (McIntosh)
James (Oglethorpe)
James (Putnam)
James (2) (Screven)
James (Tattnall)
James (2) (Warren)
James (Washington)
James (Wilkes)
James (2) (Wilkinson)
James C. Roy (Oglethorpe)
James D. (Clarke)
James D. (Morgan)
James H. (Oglethorpe)
James and I. (Liberty)
James J. (Burke)
James M. (Hall)
Jarvis P. (McIntosh)
Jesse (Elbert)
Jesse (Hall)
Jesse (Jones)
Jesse (Tattnall)
Jesse (Walton)
Jesse (Washington)
Jesse (Wilkinson)
Jessie (Greene)
Jeremiah (Jefferson)
Jeremiah (Jones)
Job (Washington)
Job (Walton)
Joel (Jones)
Joel T. (Wilkes)
John (3) (Appling)

John (Burke)
John (2) (Chatham)
John (2) (Columbia)
John, Sr. (Columbia)
John (Early)
John (Elbert)
John (Greene)
John (Hall)
John (2) (Jackson)
John, Jr. (Jackson)
John, Sr. (Jackson)
John (2) (Jasper)
John (2) (Jones)
John, Sr. (Jones)
John (Montgomery)
John (Morgan)
John (2) (Oglethorpe)
John (3) (Pulaski)
John (2) (Putnam)
John (Richmond)
John (Screven)
John, Sr. (Screven)
John (Telfair)
John (Warren)
John (Washington)
John (Wilkes)
John (2) (Wilkinson)
John B. (Oglethorpe)
John B. (Walton)
John C. (Jones)
John C. (Warren)
John G. (Hancock)
John G. (Jasper)
John G. (Putnam)
John H. (Baldwin)
John H. (Screven)
John I. (Jasper)
John M. (Wilkinson)
John N. (Morgan)
John P. (Jones)
Jonathon (Emanuel)
Jordon (Jefferson)
Jordon (Washington)
Joseph (Clarke)
Joseph (Elbert)
Joseph (Jasper)
Joseph (Morgan)
Joseph (Wilkes)
Joseph A. (Burke)
Joshua (Bryan)
Joshua (Habersham)
Joshua (Jasper)
Joshua (Telfair)
Josiah (Morgan)
Jotham (Jasper)
L. H. (Jasper)
Ladden (Washington)
Larkin (Oglethorpe)
Lawrence (Appling)
Lemuel (Hancock)
Lemuel (Jones)

Smith, Leonard (Elbert)
Leonard B. (Columbia)
Levi (Early)
Levin (Morgan)
Lewis (Appling)
Lewis (Hall)
Lewis (Washington)
Littleton (Screven)
Lor (Jasper)
Luke (Oglethorpe)
Luke H. (Screven)
Lurany (Hancock)
Lyman (Jasper)
Margaret (2) (Hall)
Margaret (Telfair)
Margaret (Liberty)
Mark (Oglethorpe)
Martin (Clarke)
Mary (Camden)
Mary (Chatham)
Mary (Emanuel)
Mary (Hall)
Mary (Pulaski)
Mary (2) (Richmond)
Mary (Walton)
Mary (Washington)
Mathew (Laurens)
Micajah (Washington)
Michal (Habersham)
Milenton (Bulloch)
Miles (Jackson)
Morris (Screven)
Moses (Gwinnett)
Moses (Jasper)
Moses (Jones)
Moses (Oglethorpe)
N. H. (Oglethorpe)
Nancy (Emanuel)
Nancy (Greene)
Nancy (Habersham)
Nancy (Hall)
Nancy (Tattnall)
Nathan (Appling)
Nathan (Greene)
Nathan (Wilkes)
Nathaniel (Oglethorpe)
Nathaniel C. (Lincoln)
Needham (Washington)
Nicholas (Morgan)
Nimrod (Walton)
Noah (Burke)
Noah (Jasper)
Parish (Elbert)
Paskell (Oglethorpe)
Patey (Jackson)
Penny (Columbia)
Peter (Jones)
Peter (Madison)
Peter (Putnam)
Peter (Walton)
Peterson (Oglethorpe)

Philo (Clarke)
Phiraby (Jones)
Polly (Habersham)
Rachel (Wilkinson)
Radford (Clarke)
Ralph (Habersham)
Ralph (Putnam)
Randolph (Clarke)
Ransom G. (Jasper)
Redick (Greene)
Redick (Gwinnett)
Reuben (Greene)
Reuben (Morgan)
Richard (Baldwin)
Richard (Greene)
Richard (Hancock)
Richard (Morgan)
Richard (Warren)
Richard (Washington)
Robert (Chatham)
Robert (Elbert)
Robert (2) (Hall)
Robert, Jr. (Hall)
Robert (Laurens)
Robert (Madison)
Robert (Oglethorpe)
Robert F. (Clarke)
Robert Lee (Oglethorpe)
Robert S. (Oglethorpe)
Rolen (Jasper)
Rollins (Morgan)
S. (Richmond)
Sally (Morgan)
Samuel (Chatham)
Samuel (2) (Hall)
Samuel (Jackson)
Samuel (Jasper)
Samuel (Madison)
Samuel (Montgomery)
Samuel (2) (Putnam)
Samuel (Warren)
Samuel (Wilkinson)
Samuel M. (Wilkes)
Samuel R. (Washington)
Samuel T. (Baldwin)
Samuel T. (Washington)
Sarah (Baldwin)
Sarah (Jasper)
Sarah (Jefferson)
Shadrack (Madison)
Shedrack (Oglethorpe)
Silas (Jackson)
Simon (Screven)
Sion (Oglethorpe)
Sollomon (Montgomery)
Soloman (Bryan)
Spencer (Lincoln)
Stephen (Habersham)
Stephen (Madison)
Stephen (Tattnall)
Stephen (Warren)

Susannah (Chatham)
Thomas (Baldwin)
Thomas (2) (Clarke)
Thomas (Gwinnett)
Thomas (Habersham)
Thomas (Hancock)
Thomas (2) (Jasper)
Thomas (Pulaski)
Thomas (2) (Putnam)
Thomas (Warren)
Thomas (2) (Washington)
Thomas (Wilkinson)
Thomas A. (Gwinnett)
Thomas K. (Putnam)
Timothy T. (Lincoln)
Valentine (Elbert)
W. G. (Jasper)
Wiley (Putnam)
William (Appling)
William (Burke)
William (Chatham)
William (Elbert)
William (Emanuel)
William (2) (Greene)
William (Gwinnett)
William (Habersham)
William (Jones)
William (Laurens)
William, Jr. (Liberty)
William (Lincoln)
William, Jr. (Madison)
William, Sr. (Madison)
William (Morgan)
William (2) (Oglethorpe)
William (Pulaski)
William (2) (Putnam)
William (Screven)
William (2) (Telfair)
William, Sr. (Telfair)
William (3) (Walton)
William (Warren)
William (2) (Washington)
William (Wilkes)
William (2) (Wilkinson)
William C. (Hancock)
William D. (Jackson)
William F. (Washington)
William H. (Putnam)
William H. (Wilkinson)
William T. (Wilkinson)
William W. (Putnam)
Williamson (Jones)
Williamson (Telfair)
Williford (Liberty)
Willis (Hall)
Willis (Screven)
Withers (Columbia)
Zachriah (Elbert)
Zadock (Wilkes)
Zekiel (Richmond)
Smithbaden, James (Jones)

Smithson, Hannah (Columbia)
Smithwick, Robert (Jackson)
Smithwood, Edmond (Madison)
Smithy, Isaac (Elbert)
Smylie, James, Jr. (Liberty)
    James, Sr. (Liberty)
Snead, Dudley (Burke)
    Elijah (Elbert)
    Leaston (Burke)
    Nancy (Richmond)
    Philip (Burke) *Zoucks*
    Samuel (Burke)
Sneed, Ansel (Washington)
    Archibald (Wilkes)
    John (Jones)
    Philip (Jones)
    Sarah (Washington)
Snell, Christopher (Emanuel)
    Isaac (Emanuel)
    William (Emanuel)
Snellgrove, (ind.) (Laurens)
    Edward (Laurens)
Snelling, Alexander (Morgan)
    Hannah (Pulaski)
    Rebecca (Elbert)
    Samuel (Elbert)
Snellings, John (Elbert)
    John (Morgan)
    William (Jones)
Snelson, John (Wilkes)
    William (Wilkes)
Snide, Christian (Wilkes)
Snider, Barnett (Warren)
    Jacob (Washington)
Snow, Fountain (Jackson)
    Hannah (Lincoln)
    John P. (Greene)
    Mark (Gwinnett)
    Richard (Wilkinson)
    Samuel G. (Greene)
    Sarah (Baldwin)
    Thomas (Greene)
Snowdew, Rhody (Jones)
Snyder, (ind.) (Effingham)
    John (Chatham)
    Jonathon (Effingham)
    Samuel (Effingham)
Sockwell, Levin (Jones)
Sockwill, Thomas (Jackson)
Sogin, Umphrey (Oglethorpe)
Solly, John W. (Warren)
    William (Putnam)
Solmon, William P. (Lincoln)
Solomon, James (Laurens)
Somarsell, John (Liberty)
    Stafford (Liberty)
Somersell, Thomas (Tattnall)
Sommoline, John (Glynn)
Sorews(?), James (Columbia)
Sorrel, Ethelred (Oglethorpe)
    Green (Gwinnett)

Nathan (Pulaski)
Thomas (Morgan)
William (Madison)
Sorrels, Bennet (Madison)
    Charles (Madison)
Sorrow, George P. (Oglethorpe)
    James (Oglethorpe)
    Jesse M. (Oglethorpe) *see* Spaulding
    Joshua (Madison) *Spalding*
    Randolph (Oglethorpe)
    William (Oglethorpe)
Soucks, Henry (Liberty)
Soudder, Isaiah (Wilkes)
Souder (Suter) James (Jones)
Soundcoster, S. (Jasper)
Soursby, Thomas (Burke)
Southard, John (Jackson)
Souther, John (Jones)
    Samuel (Jones)
Southerland, John (Greene)
Southerlin, Eli (Hall)
Southside, Edmond
               (Oglethorpe)
Southwell, (ind.) (Bulloch)
    Edward (Appling)
    William (Appling)
Southwick, William (Madison)
Sowel, Peggy (Tattnall)
Sowell. William (Screven)
    Zadock (Wilkes)
Spain, John (Jasper)
    Levi (Burke)
    Luellen (Burke)
    Matthew (Burke)
    Ruffin (Emanuel)
    Thomas (Jasper)
    William (Jasper)
Spalding, Henry (Columbia) *see*
    Isham (Camden) *also*
    Isham, Jr. (Camden) *Spaulding*
Span, Lany (Jefferson)
    Richard (Early)
Spann, James (Richmond)
    James B. (Burke)
    Michael (Chatham)
Sparkman, John (Camden)
    John (Chatham)
    Mary (Camden)
    Stephen (Camden)
Sparks, (ind.) (Gwinnett)
    Abel (Walton)
    Benjamin (Jasper)
    David (Morgan)
    Elwen (Jasper)
    Jeremiah (Morgan)
    John (Jasper)
    John, Sr. (Jasper)
    John (2) (Morgan)
    John (Washington)
    Martin P. (Morgan)
    Mary (Laurens)

Robert (Putnam)
Sarah (Washington)
Thomas (Putnam)
William (Habersham)
Sparrow, Andrew(?) (Jackson)
    John (Pulaski)
Sparrow(?), Christian (Pulaski)
    Thomas (McIntosh)
Speaks, Hesikiah (Wilkinson)
Spear, Ann (Elbert)
    Jane (Jasper)
    John, Jr. (Jasper)
    John, Sr. (Jasper)
    John (McIntosh)
    John (Washington)
    Lewis (Jasper)
    William (Jasper)
Spearman, John (Wilkes)
Spears, John (Burke)
    Mercer (Elbert)
    Nathaniel (Wilkinson)
    Polly (Chatham)
Speblan, Samuel (Hancock)
Speed, Mary (Richmond)
Speight, Jonathon (Washington)
    Levi (Laurens)
    Thomas (Laurens)
Spell, George (Laurens)
    Nancy (Laurens)
Spellers, Samuel (Hancock)
Spence, Alexander (Hall)
    David (Gwinnett)
    George (Morgan)
    Harris (Burke)
    Ingel (Screven)
    Isaac (Emanuel)
    John (Jasper)
    John (Morgan)
    Mary (Burke)
    Nancy (Burke)
    Nathan (Morgan)
    William (Jasper)
Spencer, A. (Richmond)
    Amy (Effingham)
    George (Oglethorpe)
    Griffith (Elbert)
    Mary (Chatham)
    Munroe (Effingham)
    Octavious (Elbert)
    Thomas (Jones)
    William (Elbert)
    William (Gwinnett)
    William (Liberty)
    William I. (Effingham)
    Zachariah (Wilkinson)
Spense, Thomas (Wilkinson)
Sperling, William (Jasper)
Spheres, Talitha (Hall)
Sphires, Rebeccah (Walton)
Spicer, John (Laurens)

Spickard(?), Jacob (Pulaski)
Spier, (ind.) (Effingham)
John (Jones)
John P. (Jones)
Molly (Effingham)
Moses (Morgan)
William (Effingham)
Spiers(?), John (Pulaski)
Thomas (Pulaski)
Spikes, Jinny (Burke)
John (Appling)
John (Jones)
Levi (Baldwin)
Mary (Lincoln)
Unity (Montgomery)
Spillars, Amos (Gwinnett)
Spillows, Elizabeth (Baldwin)
Spinholster, John (Liberty)
Spinks, Enoch (Morgan)
Enoch (Walton)
Garrett (Clarke)
Isaac (Lincoln)
Rolley, (Jones)
Rolley (Morgan)
William (Clarke)
Spires, Hezekiah (Lincoln)
Hezekiah, Jr. (Lincoln)
William (2) (Jefferson)
Zachariah (Lincoln)
Spivey, (ind.) (Laurens)
(torn) (Laurens)
Beverly (Columbia)
Caleb (Putnam)
Henry (Putnam)
Jethro B. (Laurens)
John (Columbia)
John (Putnam)
Mary (Putnam)
Moses (Putnam)
Moses (Tattnall)
William (Putnam)
Spivy, James (Warren)
Job (Warren)
Littleton (Burke)
Sussannah (Jefferson)
William (Telfair)
Willie (Warren)
Sponca, Blueford (Emanuel)
Sponell, Michael (Glynn)
Spooner, Tory (Screven)
Spradlin, Joshua (Putnam)
Spradling, Amos (Jasper)
William (Jasper)
Spraggins, Orsamus (Jackson)
Sprague, Samuel (Putnam)
Spratlin, Irwin (Putnam)
John (Wilkes)
Henry (Wilkes)
Jesse (Wilkes)
Thomas (Oglethorpe)
Spriggs, George (Camden)

Spring, Bartholmew
(Jefferson)
David (Irwin)
James (Jones)
Springer, John (Wilkes)
Jonathon (Wilkes)
Thomas (Warren)
William Q. (Hancock)
Springfield, Aaron (Jackson)
H. (Jackson)
Spruce, William (Jackson)
Spruel, Stephen (Jackson)
Spurlen, John (Jones)
Spurling, Levi (Warren)
Spurlock, James (Jackson)
John (Jackson)
Jane (Laurens)
Owen (Clarke)
Squires, Charlotte (Chatham)
Stackile, B. (Richmond)
Stackpole, Thomas (Baldwin)
Stacy, (Effingham)
John & I. (Liberty)
Stafford, Ezekiel (Tattnall)
John (Camden)
Robert (Camden)
Robert (Wayne)
Stephen (Jones)
Stagnen, Daniel (Jasper)
Stalion(?), Noah (Hancock)
Stalker, Daniel (Wilkes)
Stalling, Jesse (Jones)
Stallings, Edy (Columbia)
Elisha (Morgan)
James (Columbia)
James (Jones)
John, Jr. (Burke)
Mrs. Lidda (Greene)
Pallasiah (Morgan)
Sanders (Jasper)
Simon (Jasper)
William (Columbia)
William (Morgan)
Stallins, Moses (Oglethorpe)
Stamer, Daniel (Telfair)
Stamper, Martin W. (Putnam)
Polly (Wilkes)
Spencer (Putnam)
Susan (Morgan)
Stamps, Britton (Oglethorpe)
Eson (Jackson)
James, Sr. (Oglethorpe)
Moses (Gwinnett)
Nancy (Putnam)
Thomas (Jasper)
Thomas I. (Oglethorpe)
Stan, Samuel (Wilkes)
Stanarp, A. (Jasper)
Standaford, Benjamin (Elbert)
Standard, John (Lincoln)
Kimbro (Lincoln)

Standfield, Rebecca (Tattnall)
Standifer, John (Morgan)
Standland, Boax (Bulloch)
Demsy(?) (Bulloch)
Robert (Bulloch)
Standley, James (Gwinnett)
Standly, Jesse (Tattnall)
Robert (Tattnall)
Shad ick (Tattnall)
Stansall, Jessey (Wilkinson)
Joel (Wilkinson)
Stansel, John, Jr. (Habersham)
John, Sr. (Habersham)
Standsell, Richard (Tattnall)
Stanfield, Elizabeth
(Oglethorpe)
John (Montgomery)
John (Walton)
Richard (Walton)
Stanford, Benjamin (Warren)
David (Columbia)
J. D. (Richmond)
James (Baldwin)
Jesse (Warren)
John (Bulloch)
Jonathan (Columbia)
Jonathan (Warren)
Joseph (2) (Warren)
Joshua (Columbia)
Joshua (Warren)
Leven (Putnam)
Levi (Warren)
Nancy (Columbia)
Reubin (Warren)
Robert (Warren)
Thomas (Bulloch)
Thomas (Hancock)
William (Columbia)
William (Warren)
Stanley, Any (Jasper)
Caleb (Jasper)
Ezekiel (Clarke)
Ezekiel (Greene)
Francis (Wilkinson)
John (McIntosh)
Lewis (Greene)
Mary (Wilkinson)
Sands (Tattnall)
Sherwood (Greene)
William (Camden)
Starp, W. (Jasper)
Stanton, Batt (Putnam)
Easter (Richmond)
Henry (Columbia)
Nancy (Richmond)
Naomi (Chatham)
Thomas (Appling)
William (Hancock)
Stapeton, Job (Putnam)
Stapler, A. (Jackson)
James (Columbia)

Stapler, Thomas (Jackson)
Thomas, Jr. (Jackson)
Thomas (Wilkes)
William (Columbia)
Staples, (torn) (Laurens)
A. (Laurens)
Elizabeth (Wilkes)
Stapleton, Alexandet (Glynn)
Alford (Wilkinson)
George (Jefferson)
George, Sr. (Jefferson)
Salley (Wilkinson)
Thomas (Jefferson)
Star, D. (Richmond)
Silas (Wilkes)
Starett, Alexander (Oglethorpe)
Stark, Bowling (Warren)
Elizabeth (Warren)
Turner (Washington)
William (Morgan)
Starke, Jesse (Oglethorpe)
William, Jr. (Columbia)
William, Sr. (Columbia)
Starling, John (Wilkinson)
William J. (Jasper)
William (Appling)
Starnes, Elizabeth (Jones)
Frederick (Habersham)
John (Richmond)
Titus (Jones)
Starr, Mr. (Chatham)
Benjamin (Wilkes)
Elijah (Greene)
Henry (Morgan)
Joshua (Wilkes)
Statam, William (Wilkinson)
Stateman, Barzilla (Appling)
* Statham, Mrs. (Lincoln)
Jesse (Elbert)
John (Elbert)
Staton, Berry (Jackson)
Flemin (Jackson)
Headon (Jackson)
Joseph (Jones)
Statum, Nathaniel (Irwin)
Pleasant M. (Putnam)
Pleasant (Irwin)
Thomas M. (Irwin)
Staughter, George (Greene)
Staugher, L. S. (Richmond)
Staunton, Jonathon (Clarke)
Stave, Neill (Jasper)
Stead, Marbury (Wilkes)
Steagall, Samuel (Jasper)
Stealey, Hascal(?) (Wilkinson)
Steam Boat Company (Richmond)
Stebbins, Cath ...... (Chatham)
Steed, Green (Jackson)
Leonard (Columbia)
Phillip (Columbia)
Steedly, William (Habersham)

Steedman, Francis (Jasper)
Steel, Elizabeth (Baldwin)
Henry (Jasper)
John (Walton)
Steele, John (Gwinnett)
John (Jasper)
Steely, James (Baldwin)
Steen, George (Hall)
Steene, James (Gwinnett)
Stegall, Benjamin (Pulaski)
Stembridge, John (Putnam)
Thomas (2) (Hancock)
William (2) (Hancock)
Stephen, Alexander W. (Bryan)
H. (Jasper)
Hannah (Walton)
Isaac (Wilkinson)
John (Appling)
Levi (Chatham)
Stephens, Andrew B. (Wilkes)
Balam (Jones)
Benjamin (3) (Laurens)
Charles (Chatham)
David (Clarke)
David (Laurens)
Edward(?) (Wilkes)
Ezekiel (Madison)
Fany (Oglethorpe)
George (Jasper)
George (Wilkinson)
Hailey (Madison)
Herbert (Jones)
Hugh (Tattnall)
Isaac (Baldwin)
Isaac (Emanuel)
Jacob (Washington)
James (Clarke)
James (Jones)
James (Laurens)
James (Madison)
James (Morgan)
James (Tattnall)
James W. (Wilkes)
Jesse (Laurens)
John (Baldwin)
John (Clarke)
John (Columbia)
John (2) (Madison)
John (Oglethorpe)
John (Walton)
John (Washington)
John (Wilkinson)
Joseph (Oglethorpe)
Joseph, Jr. (2) (Wilkinson)
Josiah (Wilkinson)
Joshua (Madison)
Joshua (Wilkinson)
Leobeia(?) (Pulaski)
Mary (Jasper)
Needham (Pulaski)
Oren (Pulaski)

Pating (Madison)
Pearce (Jasper)
Robert (Bulloch)
Samuel (Pulaski)
Sarah (Madison)
Silas (Jones)
Simeon (Baldwin)
Stephen B. (Madison)
Thomas (Hall)
Thomas (Jones)
Thomas (Oglethorpe)
William (Clarke)
William (Jasper)
William (Madison)
William I. (Putnam)
William (2) (Screven)
Hardy(?) (Greene)
Stephenson, Henry (Wilkinson)
John (Greene)
Thomas (Clarke)
William M. (Clarke)
Stepp, John (Greene)
Soloman (Morgan)
Steptoe, William (Pulaski)
Sterdervant, John (Hancock)
Sterling, James (Madison)
John (Washington)
Josiah (Madison)
William (Appling)
William (Jasper)
Stetson, David (Liberty)
Steven, Edmond (Greene)
Stevens, Absalom (Habersham)
Allen (Putnam)
Burrill (Jefferson)
Corbet (Putnam)
David (Putnam)
Elijah (Putnam)
Henry (Burke)
Hezekiah (Habersham)
James (Burke)
Joel (Habersham)
John (Greene)
John (2) (Habersham)
John (Jasper)
John (Liberty)
John W. (Oglethorpe)
Jones (Jefferson)
Josiah (Jefferson)
Joshua (Habersham)
Joshua (Emanuel)
Larkin (Habersham)
Manoah (Habersham)
Martha (Greene)
Micaja (Richmond)
Moor (Putnam)
Oliver (Liberty)
Reuben (Clarke)
Robert (Jefferson)
Samuel (Liberty)
Sarah (Habersham)

* Staten, Penny (Appling)

Stevens, Shadrack (Jefferson)
Theophelus (Putnam)
Thomas (Baldwin)
William (Emanuel)
William (Putnam)
Willis (Liberty)
Stevenson, John (Jefferson)
Steward, Alex (Putnam)
Allen (Telfair)
David B. (Putnam)
Floid (Oglethorpe)
James (Putnam)
John (Oglethorpe)
John, Sr. (Oglethorpe)
John M. (Oglethorpe)
Joseph L. (Jasper)
Thomas (Oglethorpe)
William (Oglethorpe)
Stewart, Absalom (Gwinnett)
Alexander (Liberty)
Amos (Wilkes)
Andrew (Warren)
Bailey (Putnam)
Benjamin (Jones)
Charles (Jones)
David (Bulloch)
David (Warren)
Edmund (Warren)
Elias (Jones)
Elizabeth (Jasper)
Esther (Chatham)
George (Jones)
Gershom (Walton)
Gordon (Bulloch)
James (Camden)
James (Clarke)
James (Greene)
James (Hall)
James (Jackson)
James (McIntosh)
James B. (Wayne)
John (Bulloch)
John (Emanuel)
John (3) (Jones)
John (Oglethorpe)
John (Warren)
John (Wayne)
John K. (Jasper)
John P. (Jasper)
John S. (Baldwin)
Josiah (Hall)
Lanoria (Chatham)
Matthew (Greene)
Nathaniel (Washington)
Owen (Wilkes)
Reuben (Clarke)
Robert (Clarke)
Robert (Walton)
Sabitha (Wilkes)
Sarah (Camden)
Susannah (Clarke)

Thomas (Jones)
Walter (Effingham)
William (Gwinnett)
William (Jones)
S. William (McIntosh)
Genl. Daniel (Liberty)
Daniel M. (Liberty)
John (Liberty)
Stiles, Joseph (2) (Chatham)
Nicholas (Jackson)
Stillwell, Green (Jones)
Jane (Chatham)
John (Jones)
Joseph (Jones)
Reuben (Jones)
Shadrach (Jones)
Stincomb, Absolem (Elbert)
Stinson, Archibald (Jones)
Dudley (Wilkes)
Isaac (Wilkinson)
John (Baldwin)
John (Putnam)
Joseph (Lincoln)
Michael (Putnam)
Michael, Sr. (Putnam)
Phebe (Wilkes)
Porter L. (Putnam)
William (Baldwin)
Stirk, J. W. (Chatham)
Stith, John (Warren)
Stobo, Nancy (Burke)
Stockdale, John (Burke)
Stocks, John (Walton)
Thomas (Greene)
William (Morgan)
Stockton, Benjamin (Jackson)
Stodghill, Durratt (Elbert)
Stokes, (torn) (Laurens)
Archibald (Elbert)
Armstead E. (Wilkes)
Henry (Oglethorpe)
Ignatious (Jasper)
Joel (Washington)
John (Walton)
Joseph (Wilkinson)
Mark (Burke)
Martha (Burke)
Matthew (Lincoln)
Matthew (Walton)
Nancy (Washington)
Sarah (Hancock)
Susanna (Clarke)
Tellitha (Jones)
William (Hall)
William (Lincoln)
William (Washington)
William (Wilkinson)
William C. (Lincoln)
William H. (Oglethorpe)
Young (Morgan)
Young (Wilkinson)

Stokum, William (Jones)
Stone, Mrs. (Chatham)
(ind.) (Pulaski)
F. M. (Chatham)
Catherine (Clarke)
Edmond (Wilkes)
Hardy (Warren)
Henry (Bryan)
James (Gwinnett)
James (Jefferson)
John (Jackson)
John B. (Liberty)
John H.(Columbia)
John R. (Appling)
John R. (Washington)
Joseph (Walton)
Mary (Warren)
Nancy (Jones)
Osburn (Wilkes)
Rene (Columbia)
Solomon (Telfair)
Thomas (Putnam)
Thomas M. (Liberty)
Washington W. (Columbia)
William (Appling)
William (Elbert)
William (2) (Putnam)
William (Richmond)
William (Washington)
William M., Jr. (Putnam)
Stoneham, Jean (Jackson)
John (Clarke)
Stonely, Robert (Washington)
Stoner, John (Habersham)
Stonestreet, Benjamin (Wilkes)
Richard (Warren)
Storer, John (Effingham)
Storie, Michael (Putnam)
Story, Bazdel (Warren)
Benjamin (Warren)
Christianna (Jackson)
Edward (Jackson)
Jesse (Warren)
John (Jasper)
John T. (Jackson)
Lucy (Elbert)
Richard (Laurens)
Samuel (Irwin)
Solomon (Warren)
Stephen (Laurens)
Stotesbury, Emily (Chatham)
Stotsbing John(?) (Camden)
Stoutenburg(?), Peter B.
(Baldwin)
Stouttenmier, Newell (Greene)
Stovall, Bartholmew
(Oglethorpe)
Benjamin (Lincoln)
Benjamin (Oglethorpe)
Drury (Wilkes)
George (Jasper)

Stovall, John (Jackson)
   Joseph (Baldwin)
   Lewis (Lincoln)
   Polly (Greene)
   S. B. (Greene)
   Samuel (Morgan)
   Thomas (Wilkes)
Stover, Jacob (Habersham)
Stow, Warren (Hall)
Stowers, Benjamin (Elbert)
   Lewis, Jr. (Elbert)
   Lewis, Sr. (Elbert)
   Priscilla (Habersham)
   Thomas (Elbert)
Strain(?), Sarah (Hancock)
Strange, Benjamin (Morgan)
   Edmond (Gwinnett)
   Gideon (Washington)
   Samuel (Emanuel)
Straton, Acie (Hancock)
Straught, Nancy (Jones)
Straun, David (Hall)
   James (Walton)
Strawn, Amos (Elbert)
   Jane (Gwinnett)
Strawther, Aaron (Morgan)
   Francis (Lincoln)
Street, George (McIntosh)
   George S. (Clarke)
   James (Habersham)
   Samuel (Jackson)
   Thomas (Clarke)
   Thomas (Jefferson)
Streeter, Wiley (Morgan)
Streetling, Henry (Hancock)
   Jeptha (Hancock)
Streetman, Martin (Madison)
Strutman, William (Jefferson)
Stregal, Nicholas (Screven)
Stribbling, Anthony (Lincoln)
Stricklan, Eli (Jasper)
   Harmon (Morgan)
   Wiley (Jasper)
Strickland, (ind.) (Hall)
   Aaron (Tattnall)
   Aaron (Wayne)
   Archibald (Tattnall)
   B. (Jackson)
   Burgess (Madison)
   C. (Jackson)
   David (Tattnall)
   Drury (Gwinnett)
   Drury (Hall)
   Elisha (Morgan)
   Ephraim (Madison)
   Ezekiel (Morgan)
   Gabriel (Tattnall)
   Gadi (Tattnall)
   Hardy (Jackson)
   Hardy (Madison)
   Hardy, Sr. (Madison)

   Henry (Tattnall)
   Irwin (2) (Hall)
   Isaac (Madison)
   Jacob (Madison)
   James (Wayne)
   Joel (Tattnall)
   John (Columbia)
   John (Laurens)
   John (Tattnall)
   Joseph (Hall)
   Kinchen (Madison)
   Lewis (Tattnall)
   Mibza (Madison)
   Nancy (Jackson)
   Neil (Tattnall)
   Rewbin (Tattnall)
   Richard (Jackson)
   Richard (Liberty)
   Simeon (Gwinnett)
   Simon (Hall)
   Sion (Hall)
   Solomon (Madison)
   Stephen (Appling)
   Thompson C. (Madison)
   William, Jr. (Liberty)
   Wilson (Gwinnett)
Strickle, Harmon (Morgan)
Stricklen, Allen (Jones)
   Isaac (Jasper)
Strickling, Thomas (Clarke)
Strictling, Henry (Hancock)
   Jeptha (Hancock)
Strickun, Solomon (Jasper)
Stringer, Abner (Burke)
   Daniel (Emanuel)
   James (Burke)
   John (Hall)
   Reddin (Telfair)
   Ruth (Hall)
   Smith (Burke)
   Willis (Putnam)
Stringfellow, Amy (Greene)
   Benjamin (Greene)
   G. (Jasper)
   Robert (Greene)
Striplen, John (Jones)
Striplin, Arthur (Jones)
   Benjamin (Jones)
   Benjamin, Jr. (Jones)
   Mary (Jones)
   Moses (Jones)
Stripling, Benjamin (Tattnall)
   J. B. (Tattnall)
   Moses (Jones)
Strom, Marie (2) (Jones)
Strong, C. B. (Putnam)
   Charles (Oglethorpe)
   Elijah (Clarke)
   Elisha (Oglethorpe)
   Samuel (Oglethorpe)
Strother, Heskiah(?) (Hancock)

   John (Madison)
Strothers, David (Hancock)
Stroud, Isaac (Walton)
   James (Jones)
   James (Walton)
   John (Walton)
   Levi (Clarke)
   P. (Jasper)
   Thomas (Jefferson)
   William (Clarke)
   William (2) (Jasper)
   Yearly (Jasper)
   Sherwood (Oglethorpe)
Strozer, John (Morgan)
Strozier, Charles (Wilkes)
   Peter (Wilkes)
   William (Wilkes)
Strum, Henry (Laurens)
Struttin, Solo (Jackson)
Stuart, Anna (Burke)
   C. D. (Richmond)
   James (2) (Burke)
   James (Lincoln)
   James (Pulaski)
   John (Pulaski)
   Isaac (Burke)
   Williiam (Lincoln)
   William (Tattnall)
   Y. (Richmond)
Stubberfields, Colvin
            (Oglethorpe)
   Elizabeth (Wilkes)
   Peter (Wilkes)
   Seth (Oglethorpe)
   Theodrick (Wilkes)
   William S. (Burke)
Stubbs, Abner (Bulloch)
   Ann (Chatham)
   Francis (2) (Putnam)
   John (Jones)
   John (2) (Putnam)
   John (Washington)
   Peter (Baldwin)
   Peter (Putnam)
   Thomas (Wilkinson)
   Thomas B. (Baldwin)
   William (Jones)
Stuckey, Mary (Laurens)
Stucky, Hester (Richmond)
   Nancy (Wilkinson)
Studdard, Abraham (Walton)
   Margaret (Walton)
Studins, James (Jones)
Studivant, Martha (Pulaski)
Studsell, Ustus (Emanuel)
Studsill, Thomas (Tattnall)
Stuff, Isadore (Chatham)
Stull, Thomas (Jones)
Sturd, Charles (Wilkinson)
   David (Wilkinson)

Sturdevant, E. (Jasper)
Joel (Jasper)
John (Jasper)
John (Putnam)
Sturdivant, Charles (Warren)
Sturges, Daniel (Baldwin)
Henry (Lincoln)
Joseph (Lincoln)
Sturgess, N. (Richmond)
Samuel (Richmond)
Sturgis, Andrew (Columbia)
John (Columbia)
Oliver (Chatham)
Samuel (Burke)
Styson(?), William (Hancock)
Subb, Sarah (Wilkinson)
Subbs, William (Wilkinson)
Suddart, James (Morgan)
Suddath, James (Oglethorpe)
Sudduth, Anna(?) (Lincoln)
Henry (Lincoln)
James (Lincoln)
John (Lincoln)
Laurens (Lincoln)
Spencer (Lincoln)
William (Lincoln)
Willis (Lincoln)
Suggs, John (Burke)
Moses (Liberty)
Sugo, J. (Richmond)
Sulivan, S. (Richmond)
William (Emanuel)
Sullivan, Cornelius (Columbia)
John (Emanuel)
Mark (Columbia)
Spencer (Putnam)
Zachariah (Putnam)
Sumerlain, Thomas (Morgan)
Summerall, David (Bulloch)
Henry(?) (Bulloch)
Summerford, Abraham
(Wilkinson)
Henry (Wilkinson)
Jerusha (Wilkinson)
Summerland, Henry (Wayne)
Summerlin, Joseph (Clarke)
Lazarus (Clarke)
Summers. David (Clarke)
Durel (Clarke)
James (Jones)
John (Clarke)
Nicholas (Jones)
Ruarh (Early)
Summersell, Anne (Liberty)
Summervill, Sally (Washington)
Summoline, Luke (Glynn)
Sumner, Alexander (Emanuel)
Chestnut (Emanuel)
Jesse (Emanuel)
John (Jones)
Joseph, Jr. (Emanuel)

Joseph, Sr. (Emanuel)
Richard (Emanuel)
Sumner (Burke)
Sumners, Thomas (Jones)
Sunday, Francis (Richmond)
John (Wilkinson)
Surles, Robert (Lincoln)
Surrency, Jacob & I. (Liberty)
Elizabeth (Liberty)
Samuel (Tattnall)
Thomas (Liberty)
Sutherland, Daniel (Chatham)
Sutliff, John (Chatham)
Sutton, Aaron (Putnam)
Abel (Washington)
Abner (Emanuel)
Absalum (Wilkinson)
Amos (Irwin)
Anthony (Warren)
Booker (Columbia)
Catherine (Habersham)
David (Irwin)
Dozier (Habersham)
Ebemlick (Emanuel)
Elijah (Jefferson)
Elizabeth (Pulaski)
Jacob (Jefferson)
James (Habersham)
Jesse (Laurens)
Jesse (Pulaski)
John (2) (Irwin)
Jordon (Emanuel)
Margaret (McIntosh)
Martha (Jefferson)
Sarah (Putnam)
Shadrack (Irwin)
Shadrach (Pulaski)
Theophilus (Jefferson)
Theophilus (Pulaski)
Wyley (Jefferson)
Zachriah (Wilkinson)
Swain, (ind.) (Wilkes)
Cannis (Emanuel)
Etheldred (Emanuel)
Jeremiah (Columbia)
John T. (Jasper)
Josiah (Warren)
Richard (Warren)
Sterling (Emanuel)
Steven (Emanuel)
Sussannah (Warren)
Swan, Elijah (Lincoln)
Henry (Emanuel)
James (Wilkes)
Jonathan (Columbia)
Joseph B. (Putnam)
Richard (Putnam)
Thomas P. (Putnam)
William (Morgan)
William (Wilkes)
Swann, Archibald (Greene)

George (Greene)
Henry (Jackson)
John (Greene)
Joseph (Greene)
Swanson, Graves (Greene)
James (Oglethorpe)
John (Morgan)
John (Oglethorpe)
Swapshir(?), Spencer
(Oglethorpe)
Sway, George (Jackson)
Swearingen, Bolin (Pulaski)
John (Pulaski)
Samuel (Camden)
Swearingens, Baley (Laurens)
Swearington, (ind.) (Laurens)
Sweat, Mrs. (Chatham)
Rev. Mr. (Chatham)
A. W. (Tattnall)
John (Emanuel)
Nathan, Sr. (Bulloch)
William (Bulloch)
Sweatman, John I. (Jackson)
Sweet, Allen (Chatham)
Swenney, Ransom (Putnam)
Sarah (Laurens)
Swett, Richard (Chatham)
Swicard, David (Screven)
Swift. Erastus (Chatham)
Lucy (,Morgan)
Thomas (Morgan)
Swilley, Reason (Appling)
Samuel (Appling)
Swilly, Elijah (Washington)
Senas (Washington)
Swindle, Henry (Greene)
Swiney, Henry (Madison)
Swinney, Edward (Emanuel)
Elis (Walton)
James (Walton)
Joel (Walton)
Samuel (Greene)
William (Greene)
William A. (Greene)
Willie (Greene)
Swint. Edward (Washington)
Frederick (Hancock)
James (Hancock)
John (Columbia)
William (Hancock)
Switzer, Bird (Putnam)
Edward (Putnam)
Leonard (Putnam)
Williamson (Putnam)
Swords, Farmer (Gwinnett)
James (Lincoln)
Sybert, John (Lincoln)
Sykes. Arthur (Burke)
Dire (Tattnall)
John (Burke)
Josiah (Tattnall)

(143)

Sykes, Martha (Tattnall)
    Sarah (Burke)
    Thomas (Burke)
    William (Putnam)
Sylvester, Mary (Pulaski)
Synder(?), James (Chatham)

T

Tabb, Davis (Burke)
    Edward (Burke)
Taber, H. (Richmond)
Tabor, P. A. (Elbert)
Tachwell, Benjamin
          (Oglethorpe)
Taff, William (Putnam)
Taft, Elizabeth (Wilkinson)
Tait, David (Elbert)
    Elishaha (Elbert)
    Enos (Elbert)
    Enos, Sr. (Elbert)
    James (Elbert)
    James (Jackson)
    James M. (Elbert)
    John (Elbert)
    Permelia (Elbert)
    Robert L. (Madison)
    Sally (Washington)
    Sarah (Elbert)
    Sarah (Hancock)
    William (Putnam)
    Zimvi (Elbert)
Taite, Caleb (Elbert)
    Thomas B. (Putnam)
    William H. (Elbert)
Tak, Thomas (Jasper)
Talbore, Wally(?) (Jackson)
Talbot, Agnes (Wilkes)
    Edward (Jones)
    John (Jones)
    Joseph (Wilkes)
    Mathew (Wilkes)
    Mathew, Jr. (Wilkes)
    Thomas (Wilkes)
Talbott, William (Madison)
Talent, David (Hall)
Taliaferro, Benjamin (Wilkes)
Taliafero, Thornton (Wilkes)
Tall, John J. (Morgan)
Tallant, Mary (Bulloch)
Talley, John (Morgan)
    Nathan (Greene)
    Russell (Greene)
    Thomas (Morgan)
    William C. (Greene)
    William S. (Greene)
Talmage, John (Hall)
Talmons, Lewis (Elbert)
Tamblin, William (Gwinnett)
Tamplin, Frances (Jones)
    Polly (Jones)

Taner, John (Liberty)
Taney(?), William (Habersham)
Tankersly, Abner (Lincoln)
    Bennet (Hall)
    Carter (Morgan)
    Charles (Habersham)
    Fountain (Habersham)
    Fountain, (Morgan)
    Henry (Habersham)
    Henry (Madison)
    John (Habersham)
    John (Lincoln)
    Joseph, Jr. (Columbia)
    Joseph, Sr. (Columbia)
    Letty (Morgan)
    Littleton (Jackson)
    Richard (Habersham)
    William B. (Columbia)
Tanner, A. C. (Tattnall)
    Archibald (Walton)
    Becky (Washington)
    Burwell (Jones)
    Eli (Hall)
    Elijah (Jones)
    Frances (Clarke)
    Gideon(?) (Gwinnett)
    Gray (Emanuel)
    Henry (Morgan)
    Hezekiah (Gwinnett)
    Jesse (Greene)
    Joseph (Greene)
    Joseph (Washington)
    Lewis (Jones)
Tanner(?), Matthew (Hall)
Tanner, William (Liberty)
    Wilson (Emanuel)
Tans, Thomas B. (Jones)
Tant, E. (Richmond)
    T. (Richmond)
Tanton, Henry (Washington)
    Nathan (Wilkinson)
    Newsom (Washington)
Tapley, Adam (Baldwin)
    Archibald (Greene)
    Gratman (Warren)
    James (Emanuel)
    Joel (Baldwin)
    Sarah (Emanuel)
Tarboro(?), Henry (Elbert)
Tardy, E. (Richmond)
    L. C. (Jasper)
Tarnall, R. B. (Tattnall)
Tarpley, Ann (Oglethorpe)
    Joel (Oglethorpe)
    John (Oglethorpe)
    Joseph (Clarke)
Tarrentine, James (Jones)
    William (Jones)
Tarrington, William (Richmond)
Tarver, Absalem (Hancock)
Tarver(?), Andries (Wilkes)

Tarver, Benjamon (Putnam)
    Benjamin (Wilkes)
    Elisha (Jones)
    Etheldred (Richmond)
    Frederick (Washington)
    Hartwell H. (Wilkes)
    J. M. (Richmond)
    Jacob (Wilkes)
    John (Wilkes)
    Mary (Jefferson)
    Mary (Warren)
    Richard (Wilkes)
    Robert (Washington)
    S. (Richmond)
    Samuel B. (Burke)
    Sterling (Washington)
    William M. (Wilkes)
Tarvin, Churchwell (Columbia)
Tatam, Peter (Early)
Tate, John (col.) (Greene)
    John (Habersham)
    William (Greene)
    William (Wilkinson)
Tatem, Wiley G. (Lincoln)
Tatnall, Col. E. (Chatham)
    Edward F. (Chatham)
Tatom, John (Appling)
    Silas (Lincoln)
    William (Hancock)
Tatum, James (Putnam)
    Jesse (Elbert)
    John (Lincoln)
    Peter (Putnam)
    Thomas (Elbert)
Taunt, Irwin (Putnam)
Tayler, ____ph (Effingham)
Taylor (torn) (Laurens)
Taylor & Kelly (Chatham)
Taylor, Abner (Jones)
    Absolem (Greene)
    Alexander (Greene)
    Ann (Richmond)
    Benjamin (Screven)
    Burwell (Wilkinson)
    Caleb (Burke)
    Catherine (Burke)
    Catharine (Morgan)
    Charles (Oglethorpe)
    Daniel (Madison)
    Davenport (Wilkes)
    David (Burke)
    Dempsey (Telfair)
    Dimsy (Emanuel)
    Drury (Washington)
    Edmond W. (Madison)
    Edmund (Warren)
    Elias (Jones)
    Elijah (Hall)
    Evan (Wilkinson)
    Everrett (Wilkinson)
    Ezekiel (Pulaski)

Taylor, Francis S. (Lincoln)
George (Habersham)
George (Jones)
George (Wilkes)
George (Wilkinson)
George H. (Jasper)
George L. (Jones)
Grant R. (Madison)
Harbert (Pulaski)
Henry (Emanuel)
Henry (Washington)
Hodge (Putnam)
Hugh (Hancock)
Isaac (Washington)
Isiah (Emanuel)
Jacob (Pulaski)
James (Emanuel)
James (2) (Jones)
James (Walton)
James M. (Pulaski)
Jeremiah (Emanuel)
Jerimiah (Habersham)
Jesse (Putnam)
Job (Jones)
John (Clarke)
John (Elbert)
John (Emanuel)
John (Greene)
John (Gwinnett)
John (Liberty)
John (Putnam)
John (Screven)
John (Telfair)
John (Wilkinson)
John M. (Putnam)
Jordan (Wilkes)
Joseph M. (Jones)
Kenchen (Washington)
Labnun(?) (Camden)
Lemuel (Jefferson)
Littleton (Greene)
Louis (Putnam)
Mary (Laurens)
Mary (Pulaski)
Moses, Sr. (Jones)
Ozias (Jones)
Peter (Walton)
R. D. (Lincoln)
Reuben G. (Chatham)
Richard (Laurens)
Richard (Putnam)
Richard L. (Emanuel)
Robert (Chatham)
Robert (Morgan)
Robert (Warren)
Roland (Clarke)
Sarah (Wilkes)
Silas (Putnam)
Solomon (Habersham)
Stephen (Putnam)
Susanna (Jackson)

Swepson (Oglethorpe)
Sylvanus (Gwinnett)
T. C. (Richmond)
Theophilus (Habersham)
Thomas (Greene)
Thomas (Jasper)
Thomas (Washington)
W. (Jasper)
Walter (Morgan)
William (Appling)
William (Burke)
William (Chatham)
William (Elbert)
William (Habersham)
William (Irwin)
William (Liberty)
William (Morgan)
William (Oglethorpe)
William (Washington)
William (Wilkes)
William (Wilkinson)
William F. (Wilkes)
William S. (Wilkes)
Willis (Screven)
Winny (Elbert)
Teal, Calvin (Jasper)
Ledwick (Jasper)
Teasley, Isham (Elbert)
James (Elbert)
Joshua (Elbert)
Levi (Elbert)
Robert (Elbert)
Silas (Elbert)
Thomas (Elbert)
Teat, Henry D. (Walton)
Teaver, Jacob (Madison)
Tebbott, William (Washington)
Tebeau, Catherine (Chatham)
Tebow, Peter C. (Hall)
Tedby, William (Jackson)
Tedder, James (Burke)
Sion (Wilkinson)
Solomon (Clarke)
Teekle, John (Clarke)
Telfair, Alex (2) (Chatham)
Margaret (Wilkes)
Temple, Ann (Hancock)
Temples, Andrew (Emanuel)
Frederick (Emanuel)
John (Emanuel)
Templeton, Greenberry
(Morgan)
William (Richmond)
Zepheniah (Morgan)
Tendall, Jacob (Washington)
Joshua (Washington)
Tennelle, John P. (Washington)
Mary (Washington)
Tennille, William A.
(Washington)
Terel, Thomas D. (Jefferson)

Terrel, Simeon (Habersham)
Timothy (Hall)
William (Habersham)
William C. (McIntosh)
Terrell, David S. (Greene)
Henry (Wilkes)
James T. (Elbert)
Joel H. (Wilkes)
John (Wilkes)
John (col.) (Wilkes)
John B. (Jefferson)
Joseph (Elbert)
Peter (Wilkes)
Richard (Liberty)
Richmond (Jefferson)
Thomas (Baldwin)
Thomas, Sr. (Greene)
Thomas (Wilkes)
Timothy (Elbert)
William (Elbert)
Terrill, Catherine (Putnam)
Terry, Champion (Jasper)
John (Lincoln)
John (Morgan)
Joseph (Elbert)
Richard (Baldwin)
Susan (Putnam)
Thomas (Elbert)
Thomas (Gwinnett)
Thomas (Warren)
William (Gwinnett)
William (Walton)
William (Warren)
Tessie(?), Made. (Chatham)
Test, John L. (Jasper)
Tevau(?), Frederick E.
(Chatham)
Thacker, Echo (Hall)
William (Hall)
Thagen, Osburn (Wilkinson)
Tharp, E. (Richmond)
Tharpe, George A. (Pulaski)
Presley (Pulaski)
Thaxton, Yelvington
(Oglethorpe)
Theiss, Thomas (Chatham)
Thereatt, Paterson (Hancock)
Therlkeld, John (Elbert)
Thermon, F. M. (Jasper)
John (Jackson)
Phil (Jasper)
Thermond, William (Jackson)
Thewer, Clement (McIntosh)
Thiess, Peter (Jones)
Thigpen, Claoborn (Warren)
James (Washington)
Job (Warren)
Laseur (Emanuel)
Malangton (Emanuel)
Melas (Warren)
Nathan (Warren)

Thigpen, Randle (Warren)
Thigpin, Charles (Early)
Thirabell, Jessey (Wilkinson)
Thomas, (torn) A. (Laurens)
Abraham (Appling)
Absolom (Burke)
Alexander (Oglethorpe)
Andrew (Putnam)
Banner (McIntosh)
Barnett G. (Pulaski)
Benjamin (Jefferson)
Benjamin (Tattnall)
Birdkade (Effingham)
Blassingame (Jefferson)
Bradly, (Jackson)
C. L. (Tattnall)
Charles (Chatham)
Christiana (Hall)
Claborn (Emanuel)
Daniel (Warren)
Daniel (Wilkinson)
Darius (Washington)
David (Baldwin)
David (Jackson)
Edward (Wilkes)
Edward L. (Clarke)
Elijah M. (Putnam)
Elisha (Putnam)
Elizabeth (Gwinnett)
Elliot (Wilkinson)
Ethelred (Burke)
Ethelred (Laurens)
Evan (Habersham)
Frederick G. (Hancock)
Harrison (Jones)
Isaac (Jefferson)
James (Baldwin)
James & R. (Liberty)
James (2) (Oglethorpe)
James D. (Pulaski)
James L. (Clarke)
James T. (Pulaski)
Jeremiah (Lincoln)
Jesse (Hall)
Jesse (Morgan)
John (Bulloch)
John, Jr. (Bulloch)
John (Hall)
John (Jones)
John (Laurens)
John (Oglethorpe)
John (Putnam)
John (Tattnall)
John G. (Morgan)
John L. (Baldwin)
John W. (Jackson)
Jonathan (McIntosh)
Jonathan (Putnam)
Joseph (Gwinnett)
Joseph (Putnam)
Joseph D. (Burke)

Joshua (Pulaski)
Kinchen (Lincoln)
Levin (Morgan)
Lewis (McIntosh)
Lewis (Pulaski)
Lewis (Wilkinson)
Lydia (Emanuel)
Mark S. (Hancock)
Martin (Baldwin)
Martin (Hall)
Mary (Habersham)
Meril (Clarke)
Micajah (Hancock)
Mossa (Putnam)
Peter (Wilkinson)
Philip (Jefferson)
Philip (Wilkes)
Rachel (Pulaski)
Richard (Burke)
Richard (Jones)
Richard (Morgan)
Richard (Oglethorpe)
Richard (Telfair)
Richard H. (Pulaski)
Robert (Wilkes)
Roberts (Burke)
Stephens (Clarke)
Tabitha (Lincoln)
Thomas (Lincoln)
Thompson (Morgan)
William (2) (Bulloch)
William (Jasper)
William (2) (Oglethorpe)
William (Putnam)
William (Warren)
William (3) (Wilkes)
William C. (Putnam)
William I. (Chatham)
William L. (Wilkinson)
William W. (Putnam)
Willis (Hancock)
Zemri (Hall)
Thomason, Bartlett (Walton)
John (Hall)
Susanne (Oglethorpe)
Thomas (Jasper)
William (Hall)
William (Walton)
Thomasson, David (Jackson)
Paul (Chatham)
Thomison, John (Elbert)
John (Greene)
Thompkin, Susannah
(Oglethorpe)
Thompkins, Jane (Baldwin)
John (Jefferson)
Thompsom, Benjamin (Bryan)
Thompson, (ind.) (Gwinnett)
Miss (Chatham)
Aaron (Burke)
Aaron (Wilkinson)

Alford (Laurens)
Allen (Clarke)
Andrew (Hall)
Ann (Oglethorpe)
Archabald (Wilkinson)
Archibald (Bryan)
Artemus (Burke)
Asa (Elbert)
Assa (Emanuel)
Benjamin (Burke)
Benjamin (Hancock)
Benjamin (Warren)
Betrex (Hancock)
Burkett D. (Jefferson)
Charity (Burke)
Charles (Morgan)
Christina (Madison)
Daniel (Burke)
David (Putnam)
David (Walton)
David H. (Chatham)
Eady (Burke)
Elbert (Tattnall)
Elijah (Jackson)
Elizabeth (Warren)
Elizabeth (Wilkes)
Esther (Gwinnett)
Federick (Walton)
Gaines (Elbert)
George (Jasper)
Henry (Jones)
Henry (2) (Warren)
J. (Jackson)
James (Baldwin)
James (2) (Greene)
James (Hall)
James (Hancock)
James (2) (Jasper)
James (Jones)
James (Laurens)
James (Madison)
James (Walton)
James (Warren)
James (Wilkes)
Jane (Burke)
Jeremiah (Jackson)
Jeremiah (Jasper)
Jesse (Jackson)
Jinnesy (Jones)
Joel (Madison)
John (Bulloch)
John (Burke)
John (Clarke)
John (Greene)
John (Gwinnett)
John (Hancock)
John (Jackson)
John (Jasper)
John (Jefferson)
John (Jones)
John (Madison)

Thompson, John (Oglethorpe)
John (Wilkes)
John (Wilkinson)
Joseph (Baldwin)
Joseph (Gwinnett)
Joseph (Hall)
Joseph(?) (Hall)
Joseph (Jackson)
Joseph (Jasper)
Leonard (Columbia)
Leslie (Chatham)
Lidda (Greene)
Lydia (Warren)
Margaret (Jefferson)
Martha (Burke)
Martha (Gwinnett)
Mary (Warren)
Mary (Wilkes)
Mathew (Putnam)
* Melander (Warren)
Moses (Warren)
Nancy (Morgan)
Nathaniel, Jr. (Warren)
Nathaniel (Warren)
Oliver (Jackson)
P. P. (Chatham)
Rebecca (Jefferson)
Rebekah (Warren)
Richard (Hall)
Richard (Jackson)
Robert (2) (Jackson)
Robert (Morgan)
Robert (Pulaski)
Robert (Washington)
Robert (Wilkes)
Samuel (Greene)
Samuel (Jackson)
Samuel (Jasper)
Samuel (Oglethorpe)
Samuel, Sr. (Oglethorpe)
Sarah (Hall)
Sarah (Wilkes)
Shadrack (Jefferson)
Sherod (Jackson)
Silas (Hall)
Solomon (Bryan)
Solomon (Burke)
Solomon (Warren)
Thomas (Clarke)
Thomas B. (Bryan)
Thomas M. (Wilkinson)
Wells (Elbert)
Wiley (Elbert)
Wiley (Richmond)
William (Baldwin)
William (2) (Bryan)
William (Burke)
William (Elbert)
William (Greene)
William (Jasper)
William (2) (Jefferson)

William (Laurens)
William (2) (Madison)
William (Oglethorpe)
William (Pulaski)
William (Tattnall)
William (2) (Warren)
William G. (Jasper)
Williiam H. (Richmond)
Winny (Madison)
Zachariah (Gwinnett)
Thomson, Eliza (Lincoln)
Jeremiah (Jasper)
Mary (Lincoln)
Reubin (Emanuel)
Richard (Tattnall)
Samuel (Lincoln)
William (Habersham)
Thorn, Maddleton (Screven)
Thornbridge, Henry R.
(Hancock)
Thornton, (ind.) (Wilkes)
Benjamin (Elbert)
Benjamin, Jr. (Elbert)
Ceila (Jasper)
Daniel (Elbert)
Dozier (2) (Elbert)
Elizabeth (Elbert)
Evans (Elbert)
Ezekel (Liberty)
H. (Baldwin)
Henry (Jasper)
Herod (Oglethorpe)
Isham (Hancock)
James (Hancock)
James (2) (Jones)
Jeremiah (Elbert)
John (Chatham)
John (Hancock)
John (Oglethorpe)
John (Wilkes)
Jonathon (Elbert)
L. (Jasper)
Linsley (Jones)
Lindsey, Jr. (Jones)
Lucy K. (Elbert)
Mark (Morgan)
Nathaniel (Greene)
Penelope (Jackson)
Phillip T. (Wilkes)
Prior (?) (Jackson)
Rebecca (Jones)
Reddick (Bulloch)
Redman (Greene)
Reuben (Elbert)
Reubin (Greene)
Samuel (Tattnall)
Sandford (Elbert)
Thomas (Hall)
Thomas (Jasper)
Thomas (Oglethorpe)
Thomas (Walton)

William (3) (Jasper)
Wyley (Oglethorpe)
Young (Jasper)
Thorp, Charles W. (McIntosh)
Randle (Warren)
Thorpe, David (Chatham)
Ralph (Hall)
Thralkeh(?), William
(Oglethorpe)
Thrash, Andrew (Putnam)
Christopher (Putnam)
David (Putnam)
Isaac (Putnam)
Jacob, Jr. (Putnam)
Martin (Jasper)
Valentine (Putnam)
Thrasher, Barton (Clarke)
David (Morgan)
Isaac (Clarke)
John (Clarke)
Thratch, Jacob (Walton)
Threadcraft, S. G. (Chatham)
Seth G. (Effingham)
Thresher, Thomas (Habersham)
Thrift, Robert (Washington)
Througher, Willis (Screven)
Thrower, Jesse (Wilkinson)
Margaret (Putnam)
Sarah (Wilkinson)
Thomas (Gwinnett)
Thruwitt, Sarah (Jefferson)
Thuman, Polly (Oglethorpe)
Thunderbark, D. (Morgan)
Thurlkill, Thomas (Elbert)
Thurman, Philip (Early)
Stephen (Hancock)
Willis (Hall)
Thurmon, John (Morgan)
Micajar (Walton)
Thurmond, (ind.) (Wilkes)
Charles (Wilkes)
Hm. (Jackson)
John (Wilkes)
Mary (Jackson)
Nancy (Jackson)
Powaton B. (Wilkes)
Robert (Jackson)
Sarah (Gwinnett)
William (Gwinnett)
William (Wilkes)
Thurston, Jurdon (Jasper)
Thweat, Susannah (Jones)
Thweatt, James (Jones)
John (Hancock)
Kinchew (Jones)
Thomas (Hancock)
Williamson (Hancock)
Tibits, Thomas (Elbert)
Tice, David (2) (Jones)
Ticknor, Orry (Jones)
Tidwell, Calendar (Hall)

* Moses (Appling)

(147)

Tidwell, Elizabeth (Gwinnett)
  Henry (Hall)
  Job (Hall)
  John (Morgan)
  John (Putnam)
  Mathew (Wilkinson)
  Minor (Jones)
  Polly (Hall)
  Wilie (Jones)
  William (2) (Putnam)
  William (Wilkinson)
Tieran, Hugh (Screven)
  James (Screven)
  Mathew (Screven)
Tignier, Hope H. (Clarke)
Tignor, John (Jones)
Tilghman, Aaron (Clarke)
Tiller, Burwell (Oglethorpe)
  John (Oglethorpe)
  Randal (Oglethorpe)
  William (Oglethorpe)
Tillery, John (Putnam)
  Ruth (Putnam)
Tilley, George (Wilkes)
Tillinghast, Steeley (Burke)
Tillman, Asa (Putnam) *Stukely or Stucky*
  Henry (Effingham)
  James (Putnam)
  James (Tattnall)
  John L. (Putnam)
  Joseph (Chatham)
  Penny (Jones)
  Richard (Chatham)
Tillory, William (Jones)
Tillus, Joseph (Camden)
  Tapley (Camden)
Tilly, Betsy (Burke)
  George (Burke)
  Isaac (Burke)
  John (Early)
  Joseph (Burke)
  William (Burke)
Tilman, Aaron (Jackson)
  Green (McIntosh)
  Isaac (Liberty)
  James (Appling)
  James (Hancock)
  John (Bulloch)
  Joseph (Bulloch)
  William (Madison)
Tilory, John (Jones)
Timmons, Abijah (Morgan)
  Elizabeth (Appling)
  Zachariah (Glynn)
Timms, John (Jackson)
Timons, Richard (Hancock)
Tims, Amos (Jones)
  Walter (Madison)
Tinbrook, Emily (Richmond)
Tindal, James (Montgomery)
Tindale, Samuel (Morgan)

Tindall, James, Jr. (Burke)
  Samuel (Morgan)
Tindel, Elizabeth (Columbia)
  Pleasant (Columbia)
Tindell, Bird B. (Columbia)
Tindle, William (Columbia)
Tindley, (ind.) (Richmond)
  D. (Richmond)
  John (Richmond)
  Nancy (Richmond)
  Phillip (Richmond)
  William (Richmond)
Tiner, Gordon (Effingham)
  Jackson (Putnam)
  John G. (Effingham)
  William (Wilkinson)
Tingle, John (Jefferson)
  Solomon (Hancock)
Tinney, Rebecca (Wilkinson)
  William (Wilkinson)
Tinnon, John (Walton)
Tinny, Isaac (Washington)
Tinsley, Abraham (Columbia)
  James (Richmond)
  John (Putnam)
  John (Washington)
  Samuel (Baldwin)
  Williaim (Putnam)
Tinsley, Lucy (Columbia)
  Phillip (Columbia)
Tippery, Wiley (Oglethorpe)
Tippet, Susannah (Greene)
Tippin, John L. (Gwinnett)
Tippins, G. W. (Tattnall)
  J. A. (Tattnall)
  Josiah (Chatham)
  Lemuel (Tattnall)
  Philip (Tattnall)
  William (Tattnall)
Tipton, Amy (Burke)
  Johnathan (Burke)
  Reuben (Burke)
Tirbirrlle, Taply (Jackson)
Tire, Louis (Appling)
  M. (ind.) (Appling)
Tisdel, John (Camden)
Tisdol, Rhenderson(?) H.
    (Putnam)
Tison, Aaron (Laurens)
  Aaron P. (Putnam)
  Cammul (Effingham)
  Edmund (Effingham)
  Luther (Effingham)
  Mary (Chatham)
  Mephen (Washington)
  Thomas (Warren)
Tisworth, Isaac (Jackson)
Tobin, Thomas (Chatham)
Todd, Ann W. (Greene)
  Gabriel (col.) (Wilkes)
  Hardy (Washington)

  James (Jackson)
  James (Warren)
  James (Wilkinson)
  James E. (Lincoln)
  Jessy (Wilkinson)
  Job (Warren)
  John (Jackson)
  John (McIntosh)
  John (Morgan)
  John (Putnam)
  Joseph (Wilkes)
  Joseph W. (Jackson)
  Patience (col.) (Wilkes)
  Sally (Warren)
  William (Jackson)
  William (Putnam)
  William (Tattnall)
  William (Wilkes)
Toedwell(?), F. S. (Burke)
Toland, Michael (Jones)
Tolard, Edward A. (Hancock)
Tolbert, George W. (Wilkinson)
  Green (Morgan)
  James (Clarke)
  William (Morgan)
Toler, Arin (Jasper)
  Daniel (Burke)
Toles, Coonrod (Morgan)
  Mrs. Delany (Bryan)
  James (Wilkes)
  John (Bryan)
  Suddeth (Wilkes)
Toller, Martha (Morgan)
  Susannah (Warren)
  William (Warren)
Tollerson, Jesse (Morgan)
Tolson, Rebeccah (Jackson)
Tomason, John (Hancock)
  Richard (Hancock)
  William (Hancock)
Tombarland, John (Wilkinson)
Tomberlin, William (Appling)
Tombs, Catherine (Wilkes)
Tomison, Susannah (Hancock)
Tomkins, Burrel (Washington)
  Reekin (Washington)
  Samuel (Warren)
  Samuel (Washington)
Tomlin, Harris (Burke)
  Jacob (Morgan)
  James (Putnam)
  John (Burke)
  Owen (Putnam)
Tomlinson, Daniel (Morgan)
  Elizabeth (Putnam)
  George (Wilkes)
  John (Lincoln)
  John (Putnam)
  Mary (Baldwin)
  Nathan (Putnam)
Tomlison, Aaron (Jefferson)

Tomlison, Jared (Jefferson)
William (Jefferson)
Tommas, Elly (Glynn)
Sarah (Glynn)
Tomme, Joseph (Morgan)
Tommy, John W. (Putnam)
Tompkins, Jiles (Putnam)
John (Camden)
John (Putnam)
Nicholas (Putnam)
Polly (Washington)
Templin, Charles (Hancock)
Rhowden (Hancock)
Tompson, James (Richmond)
Moses (Appling)
Samuel (Putnam)
Tondee, Charles (Effingham)
Tonkins(?), Ulah(?)
(Habersham)
Toodle, Milley (Appling)
Tooke, Benjamin (Jones)
Isom (Greene)
Starling (Pulaski)
Tool, Bolden (Jones)
George W. (Columbia)
James (Jones)
James (Richmond)
Polly (Columbia)
Toole, Charles (Jasper)
James (Columbia)
Tooley, William (Jones)
Tooten, Sarah (Washington)
Tootle, Richard (Tattnall)
Robert (Burke)
Torbut, James (Oglethorpe)
Torrance, Amelius (Baldwin)
Torrence, Easter (Baldwin)
Ebenezer (Greene)
James (Burke)
John (Gwinnett)
John W. (Greene)
Joseph (Warren)
Samuel (Warren)
Tosey(?), Willis (Burke)
Totmon, Benjamin (Elbert)
Totty, William (Greene)
Touchstone, Christopher
(Effingham)
James (Effingham)
Levinia (Putnam)
Stephen (Tattnall)
Toussaint (ind.) (Chatham)
Towas, Benjamin (Greene)
Tower, David (Warren)
William (Hancock)
Towers, Mrs. (Chatham)
Isaac (Gwinnett)
William (Gwinnett)
Towler, Louis (Putnam)
Towns, Drury (Greene)
Gideon (Lincoln)

James (Madison)
James (Wilkes)
John (Jasper)
John G. (Jasper)
Rebecca(?) (Wilkes)
Soloman (Wilkes)
Townsan, Benjamin (Screven)
Townsand, Andrew (Clarke)
Townsend, Absalom (McIntosh)
Edward (Habersham)
Frances (McIntosh)
Jesse (Walton)
Jessie (Liberty)
John (Jones)
John (Oglethorpe)
John (Walton)
Light (Liberty)
Solomon (Gwinnett)
Thomas (2) (Habersham)
Thomas (McIntosh)
Townshend, Henry
(Washington)
Townsley, Job (Washington)
Victor Sikes (Washington)
Townson, Mr. (Chatham)
Tracy, Elezer (Wilkes)
Trailor, Edward (Oglethorpe)
Trainum, Reuben (Morgan)
Tramel, John (Lincoln)
Peter (Wilkes)
William (Lincoln)
Trammel, Dennis, Sr. (Lincoln)
Elisha(?) (Wilkes)
James (Hall)
John (Clarke)
John (Habersham)
John, Sr. (Lincoln)
Peter (Lincoln)
Thomas (Clarke)
William (Elbert)
Trammell, Farr H. (Walton)
John (Walton)
Thomas (Wilkes)
Thomas W. (Lincoln)
Woodard (Wilkes)
Trammuel, Amos (Montgomery)
Trantham, Nasellor (Madison)
Trapp, Benjamin (Jones)
Rachel (Baldwin)
Timothy (Baldwin)
Travias, Amos (Warren)
Travis, John (Morgan)
Whitmel (Warren)
William (Morgan)
Trawick, Elizabeth
(Washington)
Martha (Clarke)
Moses (Washington)
Traylor, Edward (Putnam)
James (Putnam)
John (Jasper)

John S. (Putnam)
M. B. (Jasper)
Richard (Greene)
William (Jasper)
William (Putnam)
Traywick, Elizabeth (Hancock)
George (Hancock)
Henry (Hancock)
Martha (Hancock)
Robert (Hancock)
Treadaway, Ellis (Hall)
Treadwell, Isaac (Clarke)
John (Gwinnett)
Stephen (Clarke)
Tredaway, Thomas (Hall)
Tredwell, A. (Richmond)
D. (Jasper)
Isaac (Walton)
Jacob (Walton)
James (Walton)
Tremble, James (Jefferson)
John H. (Jasper)
Moses (Jasper)
P. L. (Jasper)
Trent, James (Jones)
Trespar, Christian (Chatham)
Tresvan, Daniel (Chatham)
Treutlan, Christian (Effingham)
Trewett, Pernal (Morgan)
Tribble, Benjamin (2)
(Oglethorpe)
Trible, Benjamin (Madison)
Thomas (Madison)
Tribling, Thomas (Richmond)
Trice, Benjamin (Baldwin)
Charley, (Jones)
Elisha (Jones)
Elizabeth (Jones)
William (Jones)
Willis (Jones)
Trimble, John (Burke)
John (Morgan)
Joseph (Gwinnett)
Moses (Morgan)
Robert (Morgan)
Trimblin(?), James (Camden)
Trip, James (Pulaski)
Triplet, William (Oglethorpe)
Triplette, James (Richmond)
Triplitt, William (Tattnall)
Tripp, John (Putnam)
Robert (Jasper)
Truney(?) (Pulaski)
William (Jasper)
Trippe, Henry, Jr. (Hancock)
Trot, Charles (Effingham)
Trothers, George (Jones)
Trotman, Blount (Washington)
Troup, (ind.) (Laurens)
James (McIntosh)
(Ind.) M. (Laurens)

Troup, Robert L. (Montgomery)
Troupe, George (Chatham)
Trout, George (Hall)
    Sarah (Jackson)
Troutman, D. Hiram (Baldwin)
Trowel, James (Burke)
Truchelet (?), Mrs. (Chatham)
Truchelet John B. (Chatham)
Truchet, Mrs. (Chatham)
Truett, Nathan (Wilkes)
    Purnel (2) (Wilkes)
Truit, Thomas (Wilkes)
Truitt, John (2) (Columbia)
Trulock, Joseph (Jefferson)
Truman, Basil (Richmond)
Trumel, Barsheba (Putnam)
Trussel, John (Screven)
Truvant, Daniel (Bryan)
Truvit, Brite W. (Wilkinson)
Tubman, R. (Columbia)
    R. (Richmond)
Tuck, Josiah (Oglethorpe)
Tucker, (torn) (Laurens)
    Allen (Greene)
    Andrews (Camden)
    Ann (Washington)
    Crabtree (Jones)
    Daniel (Jasper)
    Elijah (Camden)
    Eppes (Elbert)
    Francis (Elbert)
    G. (Richmond)
    Gabriel (Appling)
    Henry C. (Montgomery)
    Isaiah (Warren)
    Jacob (Baldwin)
    Jesse (Jasper)
    John (Elbert)
    John (Morgan)
    John C. (Putnam)
    Joseph (Baldwin)
    Joseph (Wilkes)
    Littleberry (Hancock)
    Mrs. M. (Hancock)
    Moses (Morgan)
    Reuben (Clarke)
    Robert (Columbia)
    Robert (Elbert)
    Robert (Greene)
    Ruthy (Wayne)
    Sarah (Morgan)
    Shem (Elbert)
    Tarpley (Oglethorpe)
    Thomas (Camden)
    Thomas R. (Camden)
    Whitefield (Morgan)
    William (Greene)
    William (Jasper)
    William (Washington)
Tucks, James (Jones)
Tuder, John (Morgan)
    John (Walton)
Tudor, Ann (Columbia)
Tufts, Francis (Chatham)
Tufts(?), Gardner (Chatham)
Tugle, Charles (Madison)
    George (Greene)
    John (Hall)
    L. (Jasper)
    Robin (Jasper)
    William (Greene)
Tullace, Richard (Tatttnall)
Tulles, Stephen (Chatham)
Tumbline, Susannah (Effingham)
Tunell, Anthony (Putnam)
    Robert (Putnam)
Tunnell, John (Madison)
Tunney, Martin (Washington)
Turbwille, Nathaniel (Jones)
Turk, Theodocius (Baldwin)
    Thomas (Baldwin)
Turkenit, G. A. (Richmond)
Turlington, Thomas (Washington)
Turlow, John (Putnam)
Turman, Edmond (Jones)
    George (Elbert)
    John (Richmond)
Turman(?) Martin B. (Oglethorpe)
Turmon, George (Elbert)
Turnbull, N. (Chatham)
Turner, A. C. A. (Baldwin)
    Abisha (Bulloch)
    Absolom (Burke)
    Alexander (Jefferson)
    Alexander (Laurens)
    Andrew (Oglethorpe)
    Anne (Emanuel)
    Archibald (Greene)
    Benjamin (Oglethorpe)
    Berry (Habersham)
    David (Tattnall)
    Eason (Morgan)
    Edward (Gwinnett)
    Elenor (Hancock)
    Elisha P. (Hancock)
    Elizabeth (Hancock)
    Elizabeth (Wilkinson)
    Francis(?) (Appling)
    George (Hancock)
    George (Putnam)
    George (Warren)
    Henry (Baldwin)
    Henry (Burke)
    Henry (Hancock)
    Henry (Putnam)
    Hezekiah (Putnam)
    Isham (Wilkinson)
    J. D. (Washington)
    Jacob (Putnam)
    Jacob P. (Hancock)
    James (Columbia)
    James (2) (Jasper)
    James (Jones)
    James (Morgan)
    James (Tattnall)
    James (Warren)
    James (Washington)
    James B. (Lincoln)
    John (Burke)
    John (Columbia)
    John (Greene)
    John (2) (Hancock)
    John (Jefferson)
    John (Madison)
    John (Pulaski)
    John (2) (Putnam)
    John (Tattnall)
    John (Warren)
    John, Jr. (Warren)
    John C. (Warren)
    John D. (Madison)
    John G. (Jasper)
    John H. (Gwinnett)
    John W. (Glynn)
    John W. (Putnam)
    Johnathan (Hancock)
    Joseph (Putnam)
    L. (Jasper)
    Lewis (Chatham)
    Lewis (Hancock)
    Mary (Chatham)
    Mary (Jefferson)
    Matthias (Hall)
    Meshack (Lincoln)
    Micajah (Habersham)
    Monson (Jasper)
    Moses (Wayne)
    Noah (Jefferson)
    Obednego (Lincoln)
    Pas.... (Oglethorpe)
    Phillip (Hancock)
    Pleasant (Jackson)
    Reuben (Burke)
    Reuben (Wayne)
    Richard (Jasper)
    Sam'l., Jr. (Hancock)
    Samuel, Sr. (Hancock)
    Samuel P. (Putnam)
    Sarah (Elbert)
    Sharack, Jr. (Lincoln)
    Shadrack, Sr. (Lincoln)
    Stephen C. (Warren)
    Thomas (Emanuel)
    Thomas (Hancock)
    Thomas (Jones)
    Thomas B. (Gwinnett)
    William (Hancock)
    William (Lincoln)
    William (Putnam)
    William (2) (Washington)

Turner, William (Wilkes)
  Wilson (Baldwin)
Turnham, Thomas (Jones)
Turpin, C. P. (Richmond)
  William H. (Richmond)
Turving, Lucius (Burke)
Futon, Ridgon (Glynn)
Tutt, William (Richmond)
Tuttle, Isaac S. (Richmond)
  Peterson (Oglethorpe)
Tweddell, Jeremiah (Clarke)
  Sarah (Clarke)
Twiggs, Abraham (Richmond)
  Asy (Richmond)
Twilley, James (Jasper)
Twitty George (Walton)
Tye, Samuel (Oglethorpe)
Tyler, Misses (Morgan)
  Elisha (Washington)
  Henry (Elbert)
  Reuben S. (Elbert)
  William (Jasper)
Tylor, Willis (Greene)
Tyner, Elijah (Effingham)
  Ephraim (Effingham)
  Harris (Elbert)
  Richard (Elbert)
  Tolison (Elbert)
Tynor, Mary (Jackson)
✳ Tyre, John (Liberty)
Tyres, Lewis (Hancock)
Tyson, Frederick (Washington)
  Frederick, Jr. (Washington)
  James T. (Jones)
  Job (Glynn)
  John (Washington)
  Noah (Washington)
Tyus, Mary R. (Hancock)

U

Ubanks, Daniel (Washington)
  James (Jackson)
  Mary (Washington)
Ulm, Henry (Columbia)
Ulman, John Est. of (Liberty)
Ulmer, Charles (Chatham)
  Phil (Chatham)
  Philip (Effingham)
Umphres, Joseph (Screven)
Umphries, Hez. (Screven)
  William C. (Morgan)
Underhill, Joseph (Bulloch)
Underwood, Aaron (Gwinnett)
  Archibald (Putnam)
  Benjamin (Wilkinson)
  Daniel (Greene)
  Enoch (Baldwin)
  Isaac (Putnam)
  Isham (Wilkinson)
  James (Bulloch)

James (Laurens)
Jarrett (Elbert)
Joseph (Elbert)
Joshua (Elbert)
Josiah(?) (Warren)
Lemuel (Elbert)
Reuben (Washington)
Sarah (Wilkinson)
Thomas (Tattnall)
Thomas (Wilkinson)
William (Tattnall)
William (Wilkinson)
Williaim H. (Elbert)
William S. (Gwinnett)
Unival(?), Mrs. (Chatham)
Unphtel, Asa (Warren)
Unter, Stephen (Telfair)
Upchurch, Benjamin
              (Washington)
  Charles (Putnam)
  Eaton (Greene)
  Keyton (Putnam)
Upshaw, Forrester (Madison)
  Hastern (Madison)
  John, Sr. (Elbert)
  Leroy (Elbert)
  Rebecca (Elbert)
  Richard (Elbert)
  William (Wilkes)
Upson, John (Wilkinson)
  Stephen (Oglethorpe)
Uptain, George (Walton)
Upton, Benjamin (Warren)
  Tobin (Warren)
  William (Columbia)
Urquhart, Alex (Jasper)
  D. (Richmond)
  N. (Jasper)
  Neill (Jasper)
  William (Burke)
Usery, Levy (Wilkinson)
Usher(?), D. (Richmond)
Usher(?), H. (Richmond)
Usra, Carroll (Warren)
  John (Warren)
  William (Warren)
Ussery, Abner (Jefferson)
  Daniel (Laurens)
  John (Hall)
  Thomas (Laurens)
Utley, Elisha H. (Burke)
  Henry (Burke)

V

Vacon(?), John (Greene)
Valentine, Thomas (Wilkinson)
Vallean, Henry I. (Chatham)
Vallentine, Levy (Wilkinson)
Vallois(?), Charles (Chatham)
Vallotton, Francis S. (Burke)

Jeremiah (Chatham)
Rachel (Burke)
Value, Henry J. (Chatham)
Van, Thomas (Richmond)
Vanbrackle, John (Bryan)
Vance, John (Jones)
Vandavier, Lamkin (Baldwin)
Vanderford, John (Walton)
  Richard (Clarke)
  Thomas (Walton)
Vandever, Adam (Habersham)
Vandiver, Mathew W. (Greene)
VanLandingham, Benjamin
              (Wilkinson)
  Betsy (Oglethorpe)
  John (Morgan)
  Peter (Wilkinson)
VanLeonard, Van D. (Morgan)
Vann, Abraham (Washington)
  Benjamin (Montgomery)
  Henry (Washington)
  Henry, Jr. (Washington)
  Josiah (Burke)
  Milly (Hall)
  Samuel (Washington)
  Sanders (Jasper)
  Sarah (Hall)
  Susan (Hall)
  Thomas (Wilkinson)
Vanoy, Daniel (Hall)
VanWaggoner, Benjamon
              (Putnam)
  John (Putnam)
Vardeman, Joseph (Morgan)
  Thomas (Putnam)
Varnedoe, Nathaniel (Liberty)
Varnedore, Henry (Laurens)
  John (Laurens)
Varner, Edward (Putnam)
  Frederick (Oglethorpe)
  George (Oglethorpe)
  George (Putnam)
  Henley (Putnam)
  Marcus (Putnam)
  William (Putnam)
Varns, Isaac (Camden)
Varnum, John (Oglethorpe)
Varren, John (Putnam)
Vason, Joseph (Morgan)
  William (Morgan)
Vass, Elizabeth (Pulaski)
  John W. (Jefferson)
Vasser, John (Hancock)
  John (Lincoln)
  Micajah (Washington)
Vasy, James (Jasper)
Vaughan, Alexander (Warren)
  Benjamin (Habersham)
  James (Warren)
  William (Chatham)
  William (Jasper)

✳ Lewis (Appling)
  Major (Appling)

(151)

Vaughan, William (2)
  (Oglethorpe)
Vaughn, Daniel (Columbia)
  Frederick (Walton)
  Howel (Morgan)
  James (Burke)
  James (Telfair)
  John (Morgan)
  Sterling (Walton)
  William (Burke)
Vuwn, Alexander (Elbert)
  Jessey (Wilkinson)
  John (Wilkinson)
Vawter, Lounnia (Elbert)
Veal, Anderson (Putnam)
  George (Washington)
  James (Madison)
  John (2) (Putnam)
  Joseph (Putnam)
  Nathan, Jr. (Washington)
  Nathan, Sr. (Washington)
  Thomas (Washington)
  William, Jr. (Putnam)
Veall, Edward (Washington)
Veassy, Abner (Putnam)
  Calep (Greene)
  Ezekeel (Greene)
  Ezekiel (Morgan)
  John (Greene)
  John H. (Greene)
  Timothe (Greene)
Veasy, James (Hancock)
  Jesse (Hancock)
  John (Hancock)
  Nancy (Hancock)
  Stephen (Hancock)
  Thomas (Baldwin)
  Zebulon (Hancock)
Veazey, Ezekiel (Wilkinson)
Venable, Abraham (Oglethorpe)
  Charles (Jackson)
  John (Jackson)
  Nathanl (Jackson)
  Robert (Hall)
  Thomas (Jackson)
  William (Walton)
Venset, Alert (Bryan)
Verdane, B. F. (Richmond)
Verdary, Mrs. (Richmond)
Verdell, John A. (Elbert)
Verden, William (Warren)
Vernon, Asa (Jackson)
  Frederick (Oglethorpe)
Vero, J. (Richmond)
Vessels, Thomas (Effingham)
Vest, Valentine (Jasper)
Vesta, Tabitha (Pulaski)
Vial, Louis D. (Putnam)
Vicars, Drewry (Irwin)
  Elijah (Jasper)
  Hatcher (Irwin)

Wiley (Irwin)
  Young (Irwin)
Vick, (torn) (Laurens)
  David (Montgomery)
  Elisha (Elbert)
  Moses (Appling)
Vickars, John (Clarke)
Vicker, Jarrell (Greene)
Vickers, Abraham (Jefferson)
  Abram (Pulaski)
  Bryant (Washington)
  Drury (Montgomery)
  Elijah (Washington)
  Frederich (Burke)
  Hart(?) (Pulaski)
  James (2) (Laurens)
  Joel (Montgomery)
  Nathan (Burke)
  Oren (Bulloch)
  Penelope (Burke)
  Salaz (Walton)
  Thomas (Hancock)
  Thomas (Wilkinson)
  Vinson T. (Baldwin)
  William (Walton)
  William (Washington)
Vickers, Abraham (Jefferson)
  Polly (Jackson)
Vickey, James (Clarke)
Vickory, James (Elbert)
  Joseph, Sr. (Elbert)
Victory, Thomas (Greene)
Vigul, George (Lincoln)
Villa(?), Eliza (Chatham)
Vincen, Nathan (Washington)
Vincent, Alsey (Washington)
  Garrett (Jones)
  George (Washington)
  John (Jones)
  John (Lincoln)
  Josias (Washington)
  Pleasant (Walton)
  Richard (Burke)
Vines, Elizabeth (Jones)
  Hyrum (Jones)
  Hugh (Warren)
  Sarah (Elbert)
Vineyard, James (Madison)
  Joseph (Madison)
Vining, Abraham (Jefferson)
  Ann (Jefferson)
  Benjamin (Morgan)
  John (Gwinnett)
  John (2) (Jefferson)
  Pheriby (Putnam)
  Reuben (Putnam)
  S. (Jasper)
  Samuel (Putnam)
  Simeon (Putnam)
Vinson, Benjamin (Baldwin)
  Elija (Wilkinson)

Elisha (Putnam)
  Isaac (Madison)
  Isaac (Putnam)
  John (Hancock)
  Mason (Jackson)
  Nimrod (Putnam)
  Obediah (Clarke)
  Selby (Putnam)
  Virgil N. (McIntosh)
  West (Hancock)
  William (2) (Putnam)
Vinter, Stephen (Jones)
Vinton, Eaterten, (Jones)
Vinzant, William (Tattnall)
Vitrey, Thomas (Glynn)
Vocell, John (Camden)
Voicle, Lewis (Hancock)
Voss, Alexander (Putnam)
Vowel, David (Gwinnett)
  Rachel (Gwinnett)

W

Waddel, Moses (Clarke)
Wade, Asa (Gwinnett)
  Charles (Columbia)
  Edward, Sr. (Gwinnett)
  Edward (Gwinnett)
  Hezekiah (Pulaski)
  Hudson T. (Morgan)
  James (Gwinnett)
  James (2) (Morgan)
  John (Columbia)
  John (Gwinnett)
  John (Morgan)
  Joshua (Greene)
  Mary (Habersham)
  Peyton (Morgan)
  Richard (Morgan)
  Robert (Columbia)
  Samuel (Warren)
  William L. (Hancock)
Wadel, Henry (Habersham)
Wadkins, Benjamin (Jackson)
  David (Jackson)
  H. B. (Jackson)
  Henry (Jackson)
  John (Elbert)
  John (Jackson)
  William (Jackson)
Wadsworth, Daniel (Jones)
  Ignatious (Putnam)
  James (Jones)
  James (Lincoln)
  John (Washington)
  Nancy (Lincoln)
  Thomas (Hancock)
  Thomas (Lincoln)
  William (Jackson)
  William (Jones)
Wafer, James T. (Jackson)
Wafford, Absalom (Jackson)

Wafford, Abm. (Jackson)
Daniel (Jackson)
Joseph (Habersham)
Polly (Habersham)
Sol (Jackson)
Wagen, Mary (Richmond)
William (Richmond)
Waggoner, Amos (Putnam)
George B. (Warren)
John (Hall)
Nicholas (Jones)
Simeon (Putnam)
William (Greene)
William, Sr. (Greene)
Wagnon, Daniel (Greene)
Richard (Greene)
Thomas (Greene)
Thomas P. (Walton)
William O. (Walton)
Waid, James H. (Screven)
Zachariah (Wilkinson)
Wain, William C. (Screven)
Wair, William C. (Richmond)
Waites, William (Hall)
Waits, Benj'n (Jasper)
Hanophrey (Hall)
Jeremiah (Hall)
John (Hall)
Jonathan (Jackson)
Mark (Jasper)
Sarah (Jackson)
William (Hall)
Wakefield, John (Morgan)
Walburger, Jacob (Chatham)
Waldburg, Jacob (Chatham)
Walden, Alexander (Clarke)
Edward (Jefferson)
Eli (Jefferson)
Henry (Jackson)
Henry (Warren)
James (Jasper)
Oliver (Bryan)
Reuben (Pulaski)
Richard (Warren)
Sally (Jones)
Samuel (Jefferson)
Samuel (Pulaski)
Tanner (Morgan)
William (Jones)
Waldhour, John, Jr. (Effingham)
John, Sr. (Effingham)
Waldon, Henry (Jasper)
John (Jefferson)
Waldripe, David (Putnam)
James (Putnam)
Mathew (Putnam)
Waldron, Martha (Chatham)
Waldrop, Benjamin (Jones)
George (Jones)
Waldrope, John (Warren)
Walea, James (Emanuel)

Wales, Isaac M. (Hancock)
James (Gwinnett)
John F. (Oglethorpe)
Sarah B. (Madison)
Waley, William (Burke)
Walker, A. (Burke)
Alfred wid. (Wayne)
Arthur (Habersham)
Arthur (Putnam)
Bathia (Burke)
Benjamon (Putnam)
Benjamin (Wilkinson)
Charity (Warren)
Church (Jasper)
Daniel (Lincoln)
David (Appling)
David (Columbia)
David (Putnam)
Dorset (Washington)
E. (Jasper)
E. (Richmond)
Edmund (Morgan)
Eli (Putnam)
Elijah (Burke)
Elisha (McIntosh)
Elizabeth (Jackson)
Elizabeth (Jefferson)
F., Overseer for (Burke)
Freeman (Richmond)
G. M. (Richmond)
George (Columbia)
George (Jones)
George (Pulaski)
George (Wilkes)
H. (Jasper)
Henery (Jefferson)
Henry (Jefferson)
Henry (Warren)
Henry G. (Lincoln)
Holliberry (Warren)
I. (Putnam)
Isaac (Morgan)
Isaih (Lincoln)
Isham (Camden)
J. F. (Putnam)
James (Jasper)
James (Oglethorpe)
James (Putnam)
James C. (Columbia)
James W. (Morgan)
James Y. (Putnam)
Jane (Warren)
Jeptha (Putnam)
Jeremiah (Lincoln)
Jeremiah (Morgan)
Jesse (Lincoln)
Joel (Pulaski)
Joel (Putnam)
John (Camden)
John (Columbia)
John (Greene)

John (Laurens)
John (Morgan)
John (Walton)
John (Warren)
John (Washington)
John (Wilkes)
John H. (Lincoln)
John H., Sr. (Putnam)
John S. (Columbia)
John S. (Putnam)
John S. (Wilkes)
Johnson (Greene)
Jonathon (Walton)
Joseph (2) (Putnam)
Joseph (Walton)
L. (Jasper)
Levi (Putnam)
Lewis (Greene)
Littlebury (Appling)
Loudy (Gwinnett)
Mary (Pulaski)
Mason (Oglethorpe)
Moses (Burke)
Moses (Jones)
Moses P. (Morgan)
N. (Jasper)
Nancy (Richmond)
Naomi (Columbia)
Nathaniel (Putnam)
Nathaniel F. (Putnam)
Parsons (Warren)
R. (Richmond)
Rachel (Lincoln)
Rebecca (Habersham)
Richard (Appling)
Mjr. GenL Robert
(Richmond)
Robert (Richmond)
Samuel (Greene)
Samuel (Jasper)
Sanders (Richmond)
Simeon (Morgan)
Soloman (Washington)
Solomon (Wayne)
Thomas (Jackson)
Thomas (Jefferson)
Thomas (Putnam)
Thomas G. (Jasper)
V. Overseer for (Burke)
Virgil H. (Putnam)
Walter (Screven)
West (Habersham)
William, Jr. (Greene)
William, Sr. (Greene)
William (Hancock)
Williaim (2) (Jasper)
William (Lincoln)
William (Oglethorpe)
William (Putnam)
William (Wayne)
William (Wilkes)

(153)

Walker, William F. (Putnam)
Williaim L. (Putnam)
William W. (Putnam)
Willis J. (Warren)
Wall, Mrs. (Chatham)
Mrs. B. (Chatham)
Benj., Jr. (Chatham)
Billy (Chatham)
Burgess (Putnam)
Clairborn (Warren)
Clary (Baldwin)
Conrad (Columbia)
Delia (Chatham)
Ezekiel (Washington)
Jesse (Washington)
John (Putnam)
Mary (Washington)
Mrs. Rd. (Chatham)
Samuel (Morgan)
Thomas (Burke)
Wiley (Elbert)
William D. (Montgomery)
Willis (Elbert)
Wallace, Mrs. (Chatham)
Charles (Madison)
Charnal (Bryan)
Elizabeth (Putnam)
Enoch (Baldwin)
Fanny (Morgan)
James (Chatham)
James (Clarke)
James (Hall)
James (Lincoln)
James A. (Lincoln)
John (Burke)
John (2) (Putnam)
Josiah (Burke)
Levi (Jackson)
Mary (Glynn)
Mary (2) (Hancock)
Michael G. (Putnam)
Norman (Chatham)
Pheriby (Burke)
R. D. (Chatham)
Rachel (Jackson)
Richard W. (Hall)
Robert (Lincoln)
Samuel (Morgan)
Stirling (Burke)
Susan (Lincoln)
William (Burke)
William (Lincoln)
William (Morgan)
William (Putnam)
Walladay, Henry (Jones)
Wallan, John (McIntosh)
William (McIntosh)
Waller, Arch'd (Jasper)
Charles R. (Putnam)
Daniel R. (Putnam)
Elijah (Greene)

Elizabeth (Hancock)
Ellis M. (Hancock)
Handy (Putnam)
Hurbele (Hancock)
Isaac (Putnam)
James (Warren)
James B. (Wilkes)
Job (Hancock)
John (Chatham)
John T. (Putnam)
Losa (Jones)
Nimrod (Wilkes)
Sally (Washington)
Smith (2) (Hancock)
William (Jones)
William, Sr. (Washington)
Zephaneah (Hancock)
Walley, Michael (Jones)
William (2) (Jones)
Wallingham, F. (Jasper)
Wallings, Michel (Jackson)
Wallis, Benjamin (Wilkes)
Daniel (Jackson)
Elijah (Jackson)
G. (Richmond)
James (Irwin)
Jesse (Jackson)
John (Greene)
John (Jackson)
Luther (Walton)
Nicholas (Walton)
Peter (Gwinnett)
Rhody (Elbert)
Thomas (Elbert)
Thomas (Jackson)
W. C. (Jasper)
William (2) (Jackson)
William (Jasper)
Wallmaker, John (Wilkes)
Walls, Adam (Gwinnett)
Arthur (Gwinnett)
Charles (Gwinnett)
Elizabeth (Jones)
John, Sr. (Jackson)
John (Jackson)
John (Wilkes)
Mary (McIntosh)
William (Jones)
Williamson (Jackson)
Walraven, Archibald (Hall)
Isaac (Hall)
William (Hall)
Walsingham, Catherine
(Effingham)
E. (Richmond)
Walston, James (Montgomery)
Walter(?), John C. (Effingham)
Walter, Tedford (Morgan)
Walters, (ind.) (Hall)
Clement (Habersham)
Eleanor (Habersham)

John E. (Baldwin)
Nancy (Habersham)
Philip (Lincoln)
Walthall, E. (Jasper)
Walthour, Andrew (Liberty)
Walton, Benjamin (Chatham)
Daniel (Burke)
Everet (Burke)
Hiram (Morgan)
Isaac R. (Morgan)
Jesse (Burke)
John (Lincoln)
John (Oglethorpe)
John (Putnam)
John H. (Lincoln)
Josiah (Wilkes)
Newell, Sr. (Lincoln)
Newell (Lincoln)
Noah (Lincoln)
Overton (Putnam)
Peter (Morgan)
Pleasant (Lincoln)
R. (Richmond)
Robert (Lincoln)
Robert (Warren)
Sarah (Columbia)
Timothy (Lincoln)
Thomas J. (Richmond)
Wamic, Josiah (Putnam)
Wammack, Benjamin (Screven)
Wammock, Abraham (Jones)
Charles (Jones)
Wammuck, Thomas (Putnam)
Wand, Emanuel (Chatham)
Wanks, Thomas (Jones)
Wanslow, Reuben (Elbert)
Wanston, Thomas (Elbert)
Ward, _____ (Chatham)
Abner (Elbert)
Alberton (Putnam)
Amos (Putnam)
Ann (Jones)
Benjamin (Bryan)
Benjamin (Walton)
C. (Richmond)
Charity, Sr. (Madison)
David (Burke)
David (Emanuel)
Edward (Camden)
Elain(?) (Clarke)
Elias (Emanuel)
Frederick (Putnam)
Francis (Burke)
Francis (Putnam)
Hannah (Gwinnett)
Ivy (Gwinnett)
James (Appling)
James (2) (Burke)
James (3) (Wilkinson)
James S. (Greene)
Jane(?) (Burke)

Ward, Jesse (Warren)
John (Burke)
John (Oglethorpe)
John (Putnam)
John (Richmond)
John (Warren)
John (Wilkinson)
Jonathon (Greene)
Leonard (Clarke)
M. B. (Burke)
Mary (Chatham)
Obadiah (Walton)
Richard (Elbert)
Richard G. (Putnam)
Ridley (Fem.) (Jones)
Robert, Sr. (Lincoln)
Samuel (Oglethorpe)
Samuel (Wilkinson)
Sarah (Laurens)
Seth (Oglethorpe)
Solomon (Wilkinson)
Stephen (Putnam)
Thomas (Burke)
Thomas (Oglethorpe)
Thomas E. (Emanuel)
Wiley (Clarke)
Wiley (Morgan)
William (Elbert)
William (Jackson)
William (Liberty)
William (Morgan)
William (Oglethorpe)
William (Pulaski)
Warden, Anderson (Putnam)
Wardlaw, James (Gwinnett)
William (Gwinnett)
Wardsworth, John (Jones)
Ware, Edward, Sr. (Madison)
Elisha (Madison)
Henry (Jasper)
Hudson T. (Morgan)
Isaac (Jackson)
James, Jr. (Madison)
James, Sr. (Madison)
James (Morgan)
James, Jr. (Morgan)
John (Greene)
John (Lincoln)
John (Morgan)
Nicholas (Morgan)
Nicholas (Richmond)
Philip (Madison)
Robert (Wilkes)
Thomas (Greene)
William (Appling)
Warner, Benjamin (Jefferson)
Ellijah (Jefferson)
J. D. (Tattnall)
John R. (Chatham)
Solomon (Hancock)
William (Wayne)

(margin, sideways:) William (Appling)

Warnock, Bazil (Burke)
Benjn. (Burke)
Jane (Jefferson)
John (Habersham)
Warnold, Asa (Liberty)
Jacob (Liberty)
William (Liberty)
Warpool, John (Wilkinson)
Thomas (Wilkinson)
Warrell, Simon S. (Greene)
Warren, (ind.) (Richmond)
Doct. (Chatham)
Amos (Emanuel)
Benjamin (Emanuel)
Benjamin H. (Richmond)
Carlos (Burke)
Dread (2) (Jasper)
Easter (Putnam)
Edman (Jasper)
Edmund (Bulloch)
Fanny (Putnam)
George (McIntosh)
Harrison (Elbert)
Henry (Morgan)
James, Jr. (Emanuel)
James, Sr. (Emanuel)
James (2) (Hancock)
James (Jasper)
James (Laurens)
Jeremiah (2) (Hancock)
Jeremiah (Jones)
Jesse, Sr. (Hancock)
Jesse (Wilkinson)
Joseph (2) (Jasper)
Josiah (Emanuel)
Josiah (Wilkinson)
Lott (Laurens)
Mary (Chatham)
Mary (Tattnall)
Moss (Jackson)
R. (Jackson)
Reuben (Laurens)
Reuben (Pulaski)
Robert (Baldwin)
Robert (Hall)
Sampson (Hancock)
Slady (Greene)
Stephen (Morgan)
Valentine (Hall)
William (Gwinnett)
William (2) (Hancock)
William (2) (Jackson)
William (Putnam)
Warrendon, George (Wilkinson)
Wasbon, John (Jasper)
Wasden, Philip U. (Jefferson)
Wasdon, Thomas (Jefferson)
Washburn, Arby (Richmond)
Washington, George H. (Wilkes)
James (Chatham)
James (Columbia)

Richard (Wilkes)
Robt. B. (Baldwin)
Wasman(?), Samuel (Jasper)
Wasthall, E. (Jasper)
Wm. P. (Jasper)
Wateau, Major (Richmond)
Waterman, A. (Richmond)
Waters, George (Chatham)
George (Screven)
George M. (2) (Bryan)
Isaac (Screven)
J. (Camden)
James (Wilkinson)
Jane (E.) (Wilkes)
John (Bulloch)
John (Chatham)
John (2) (Wilkinson)
John, Sr. (Wilkinson)
Joseph (Oglethorpe)
Lency (Elbert)
Littlebery (Pulaski)
Martha (Washington)
Michal (Screven)
Richard (Washington)
Thomas (Bulloch)
William (Chatham)
William (Effingham)
William H. (Screven)
Waterson, John (Jackson)
Watkins, (ind.) (Oglethorpe)
A. (Richmond)
Ansel L. (Washington)
Arthur (Jefferson)
Barnet (Hall)
George (Greene)
Griffin (Hall)
Hartwell (Jefferson)
J. (2) (Richmond)
Jacob (Walton)
James, Jr. (Elbert)
James (Hall)
Job (Habersham)
John (Habersham)
John (Hall)
John (Jefferson)
John (Putnam)
Joseph (Elbert)
Josiah (Greene)
Leonidas (Richmond)
Matthew (Hall)
Mills (Jefferson)
Mitchell (Washington)
Moses (Clarke)
Moses (Jasper)
Philip (Oglethorpe)
Rhoda (Burke)
Robert (Richmond)
Samuel (Elbert)
Sarah (Wilkinson)
Theophiles (Wilkes)
Thomas (Richmond)

(155)

Watkins, Thompson (Wilkes)
  Zachariah T. (Wilkes)
Watley, Daniel (Jones)
  Robert (Greene)
  Solomon (Jones)
  Tilmon (Jones)
Watson, (ind.) (Laurens)
  Alexander (2) (Telfair)
  Allen (Baldwin)
  Andrew (Habersham)
  Arthur (Walton)
  Asa (Wilkinson)
  Benjamin (Columbia)
  D. (Jasper)
  David (Columbia)
  David (Gwinnett)
  Douglas (Morgan)
  Duglas (Greene)
  Elijah (Washington)
  Elisha (Laurens)
  Elisha (Oglethorpe)
  Ezekiel (Washington)
  Fereby (Washington)
  Frederick (Irwin)
  George (Columbia)
  Isaac (Columbia)
  Israel (Emanuel)
  Jacob (Jones)
  Jacob (Pulaski)
  James (2) (Chatham)
  James (2) (Columbia)
  James (Jones)
  James (Tattnall)
  James C. (Baldwin)
  Jane (Oglethorpe)
  John, Sr. (Baldwin)
  John, Jr. (Columbia)
  John, Sr. (Columbia)
  John (2) (Elbert)
  John (2) (Jackson)
  John (Madison)
  John (Oglethorpe)
  John (Tattnall)
  John (Walton)
  Jonathon (Liberty)
  Joseph (Greene)
  Joseph (Gwinnett)
  Joshua (Jackson)
  Joshua (Jefferson)
  Margaret (Wilkes)
  Martha (Emanuel)
  Maryann (Wilkes)
  Michael (Jefferson)
  Milly (Columbia)
  Nathaniel (Hall)
  Nehemiah (Greene)
  Obidiah (Jackson)
  Park I. (Greene)
  Peter (Columbia)
  Rebeca (Columbia)
  Reuben (Putnam)

Richard S. (Wilkinson)
Richmon R. (Pulaski)
Robert (Laurens)
Robert (Morgan)
Robert T. (Baldwin)
Samuel H. (Morgan)
Seth G. (Pulaski)
Silas (Laurens)
Siley (Irwin)
Soloman (Emanuel)
Solomon (Wilkes)
Thomas (Columbia)
Thomas (Elbert)
Thomas (Gwinnett)
Valentine (Hall)
William (Columbia)
William (Greene)
William (Morgan)
Watsons, (torn) (Laurens)
Watt, Anne (Habersham)
Watt (Wall), Elizabeth
          (Chatham)
Watt, Hugh (Jones)
Watters, William (Tattnall)
Wattley, Green (Wilkinson)
Watts, Edmond (Putnam)
  Hery (Jackson)
  Jabel E. (Morgan)
  Jacobus (Morgan)
  Jeremiah (Putnam)
  John (Morgan)
  Josiah (Greene)
  Leadwell (Jasper)
  Littleberry (Clarke)
  Mary (Jones)
  Mary (Morgan)
  Pleasant (Morgan)
  Pope H. (Gwinnett)
  Richard J. (Gwinnett)
  Samuel (2) (Hancock)
  Thomas (Morgan)
  Thomas (Walton)
  Thomas B. (Morgan)
  William (Jackson)
  William (Laurens)
  William (Madison)
  William H. (Greene)
Watty, Solomon (Jones)
Waugh, Robert (Habersham)
Way, estate of (Liberty)
  Edward (Liberty)
  John (Jefferson)
  John 3 (probably third)
          (Liberty)
  John, Sr. (Liberty)
  John, Jr. (Liberty)
  Joseph (Liberty)
  Moses (Liberty)
  William (Jefferson)
  William G. (Liberty)
  William N. (Liberty)

Wayne, George (Wilkinson)
  James M. (Chatham)
  John (2) (Hancock)
  John (Wilkinson)
  Richard (Chatham)
  Thomas (2) (Hancock)
Weak, Harry P. (Telfair)
Weatherford, Charity (Walton)
Weatherill, Benjamin
          (Chatham)
Weatherington, John
          (Montgomery)
  William (Montgomery)
Weatherinton, Richard (Elbert)
Weatherly, Benjamin (Jones)
  George N. (Jones)
  John (Wilkes)
  Septemus (Jones)
  Septemus, Sr. (Jones)
  William (Clarke)
Weathers, Benjamin (Liberty)
  Isom (Greene)
  Jessie (Greene)
  John (Greene)
Weatherson, Thomas
          (Richmond)
Weatherspoon, James (Jackson)
Weathey, Samuel (Lincoln)
Weathington, Leven (Greene)
  Thomas (Walton)
Weatt, John (Jasper)
Weaver, (torn) (Warren)
  Andrew (Oglethorpe)
  Aron (Richmond)
  Drury A. (Warren)
  Edward (Jones)
  Elizabeth (Wilkinson)
  Frederic (Habersham)
  Janet (Wilkes)
  Jethro (Laurens)
  John (Jones)
  John P. (2) (Oglethorpe)
  Jonathon (Early)
  Julius (Early)
  Martha (Jefferson)
  Othnial (Early)
  Peter (Habersham)
  Reuben (Walton)
  Samuel (Wilkes)
  Solomon (Pulaski)
  Stephen (Emanuel)
  Susan (Morgan)
  William (Morgan)
  William B. (Oglethorpe)
Webb, (ind.) (Wilkinson)
  Auguston (Elbert)
  Benjamin (Emanuel)
  Benj'n (Jasper)
  Burrel (Elbert)
  Clinton (Gwinnett)
  Dawson (Wilkinson)

Webb, Edward (Jasper)
Elias (Jefferson)
Ethelred (Wilkinson)
Giles (Washington)
Hocket (Walton)
Homer (Hancock)
James (Elbert)
James (Jasper)
James (Jones)
Jesse (Laurens)
John (Elbert)
John (Jasper)
John (Putnam)
John (Washington)
John (E.) (Wilkes)
John W. (Wilkinson)
Levy (Emanuel)
Lewis (Emanuel)
Margaret (Elbert)
Mary (Greene)
Perry (Wilkinson)
Pleasant (Oglethorpe)
Rice (Jefferson)
Samuel (Washington)
Stephen (Walton)
Thomas (Liberty)
Wiley (Elbert)
Wiley (Jefferson)
William (Elbert)
William (Oglethorpe)
Webbington, E. (Jasper)
Webster, Elizabeth (Wilkes)
G. B. (Richmond)
Laban (Wilkes)
Martin (Wilkes)
Samuel (Lincoln)
William (Hall)
William (Wilkes)
Wedington, Zeno (Putnam)
Weeks, (ind.) (Laurens)
B. (Richmond)
Charles (Morgan)
Francis (Clarke)
Jas. S. (Jasper)
John (Morgan)
Nancy (Warren)
T. (Richmond)
Thomas (Burke)
William (Jefferson)
William (Putnam)
Weeler, Michell (Emanuel)
William (Emanuel)
Weems, B. (Jasper)
John (Jasper)
Samuel (Jasper)
Weever, David (Putnam)
John C. (Pulaski)
Samuel (Putnam)
Weissinger, Winifred
(Columbia)
Welbourn, Jack (Greene)

Thomas (Greene)
William (Greene)
Welburn, Robert (Wilkinson)
Welch, Asa (Washington)
Caleb (Jefferson)
Elizabeth (Columbia)
James (Burke)
James (Jasper)
James (Madison)
James (Wilkinson)
Jesse (Columbia)
John (Morgan)
Juda (Jackson)
Nicholas (Habersham)
William (Baldwin)
William (Washington)
Welcher, Jeremiah (Warren)
Welden, Larkin (Jasper)
Weldon, Andrews (Jasper)
Isaac (Jasper)
Moses (Jasper)
Samuel (Hancock)
Wellborn, Abner (Wilkes)
Amos (2) (Morgan)
Burkett (Morgan)
Carlton (Wilkes)
Coial (Wilkes)
David (Morgan)
Elias (Columbia)
Jeremiah (Wilkes)
Sanders (Morgan)
Shadale (Wilkes)
Starnes (Wilkes)
Thomas (Putnam)
William (Wilkes)
Wellingham, T. (Jasper)
William (Jasper)
Wellman, F. (Chatham)
Wells, (torn) (Laurens)
Abner (Putnam)
Elijah (Wilkinson)
Elijah (Putnam)
Francis (Washington)
George (Putnam)
Hettie (Wilkes)
Isaac (Bryan)
James (Effingham)
John (Bryan)
John (Elbert)
John (2) (Hancock)
John (Putnam)
John (Wilkes)
Joshua G. (Putnam)
Josiah (Jefferson)
Martin (Jefferson)
Mathew (Greene)
Tabna (Jones)
Thomas (Clarke)
Thomas B. (Jefferson)
Thomas F. (Richmond)
William (Bryan)

William (Jones)
William (Putnam)
William H. (Jasper)
Wellson, George (2) (Jasper)
Josh (Jasper)
Thomas (2) (Jasper)
Welsh, Edmond (Walton)
Michael (Warren)
Nicholas (Walton)
Wereman, Charles (Warren)
Werter, Edward (Gwinnett)
Wesdom, Frank (Jasper)
West, Andrew (Elbert)
Arthur (Burke)
Dr. C. (McIntosh)
Charles (Washington)
Crafford (Putnam)
Davy (Richmond)
Elizabeth (2) (Hancock)
Ephraim (Morgan)
Frances (Greene)
Gibson (Burke)
James (Jones)
James (Oglethorpe)
James (Walton)
Jeremiah (Jasper)
Jesse (Jones)
John (Columbia)
John (Greene)
John (Jasper)
John (Washington)
John W. (Chatham)
Jonathon (Walton)
Richard (Chatham)
Sion (Putnam)
Warren (Putnam)
William (2) (Burke)
William (Morgan)
William (Wilkinson)
Westberry, Moses (Liberty)
Westbrooks, Allen (Greene)
Thomas (Greene)
William (Greene)
Westby, Thomas (Columbia)
Wester, Benjamin (Morgan)
Emund P. (Appling)
John (Gwinnett)
Richard (Tattnall)
Westley, Thomas (Hancock)
Westmoreland, John (Jasper)
R. (Jasper)
Weston, Job (Elbert)
S. & Co. (Putnam)
Wetherby, Caroline (Burke)
Septimus (Putnam)
Wetherley, Calvin (Telfair)
Wethers, Elisha (Lincoln)
Valentine (Lincoln)
Wever, Gilberd (Irwin)
Whaley, Charles (Jasper)
Eli (Walton)

Whaley, William (Morgan)
James (Putnam)
Samuel (Walton)
Wharton, Benjamin (Hall)
Joseph (Jackson)
Whatley, Abner (Putnam)
Archy (Gwinnett)
Clary (wid.) (Morgan)
David H. (Wilkes)
Elizabeth (Walton)
Green (Jones)
John (2) (Jasper)
John B. (Morgan)
Michael (2) (Morgan)
Orwon (Morgan)
Polly (Morgan)
Samuel (Wilkes)
Weson (Walton)
Wilinsth T. (Jones)
Willis (Clarke)
Wyatt (Putnam)
Wheat, Harvy (Lincoln)
Wesley (Hall)
Wheatley, Joseph (Wilkes)
Wheatly, Abel (Wilkes)
Wheaton, William H.
(Richmond)
Wheeler, Amos (Pulaski)
Amos (Putnam)
Anney (Wilkinson)
Asberry (Baldwin)
Benjamin (Elbert)
Charles (Columbia)
Charles (Elbert)
George (Elbert)
George (Oglethorpe)
George W. (Columbia)
Isaac (Warren)
Isham (Warren)
James (2) (Jackson)
James (Warren)
Jesse (Baldwin)
Jesse (Effingham)
John (Jefferson)
Joseph (Elbert)
Joseph (Morgan)
Lott (Burke)
Merit (Putnam)
Rebecca (Baldwin)
Robert I. (Liberty)
Sabra (Effingham)
William A. (Wilkes)
Wheeless, Abner (Greene)
Wheelis, Edmond (Jones)
Elijah (Morgan)
Hardy (2) (Jones)
Lewis (Morgan)
Lyon (Jones)
Mathew (Jones)
Wheelor, Mourni (Jackson)
Wheler, Lucy (Elbert)

Whickard, Philip (Pulaski)
Whid, Elisha (Screven)
Whidby, John (Jones)
Whiddon, David (Tattnall)
Elias (Tattnall)
William (Tattnall)
William (Washington)
Whigham, Alexander (Jefferson)
John (2) (Jefferson)
Joseph (Jefferson)
Thomas (Jefferson)
William (Jefferson)
William (Pulaski)
Whilley, William (Jones)
Whipple, (ind.) (Richmond)
Whisonant, Adam (Habersham)
Whitacre, John (Columbia)
Polly (Columbia)
Samuel (2) (Columbia)
Thomas (Columbia)
William (Columbia)
Whitaker, (ind.) (Richmond)
Abel (Warren)
Abraham (Wilkes)
Benjamin (Jefferson)
Daniel (Morgan)
Henry (Putnam)
J. B. (Jasper)
John (Morgan)
John (Walton)
Joseph I. (or J.) (Putnam)
Joshua (Richmond)
Mary (Putnam)
Oran (Washington)
Richard (Pulaski)
Samuel (Washington)
Simon (Baldwin)
William (Washington)
Willis (Washington)
Whitby, Susan(?) (Wilkes)
White, Abel (Habersham)
Abel, Sr. (Habersham)
Abram (Hancock)
Alexander (Gwinnett)
Allen (Emanuel)
Allen (Jackson)
Anderson (Elbert)
Ann (Jasper)
Arthur (Burke)
Benedict (Baldwin)
Benjamin (Baldwin)
Benjamin (Jones)
Benjamin (Morgan)
Briant (Jones)
Constant (Burke)
Cyrus (Jasper)
Daniel (Hancock)
Daniel (Putnam)
David (Elbert)
David L. (Putnam)
Dudley (Putnam)

Elisha (Warren)
Elisha (Washington)
Elizabeth (Elbert)
Espy (Elbert)
Ezekial (Burke)
Gayne (Glynn)
George (McIntosh)
George (Morgan)
Henry (Burke)
Henry (Effingham)
Henry (Elbert)
Henry P., Jr. (Madison)
Henry P., Sr. (Madison)
James (Chatham)
James (2) (Greene)
James (2) (Gwinnett)
James (Morgan)
James (Wilkes)
James E. (Elbert)
James M. (Wayne)
James T. (Wilkinson)
Jeptha (Habersham)
Jesse (Burke)
Jesse (Putnam)
John, Sr. (Elbert)
John (4) (Elbert)
John (2) (Greene)
John (2) (Hancock)
John (Jackson)
John (Jones)
John (Putnam)
John (Screven)
John E. (Baldwin)
John M. (Elbert)
John W. (Elbert)
Jonah (Morgan)
Jonathon (Oglethorpe)
Joseph (Jasper)
Joseph (Jones)
Joshua E. (Chatham)
Levi (Greene)
Levi (Putnam)
Luke (Elbert)
Macajah (Putnam)
Martin (Elbert)
Mary (Bryan)
Moses D. (Jasper)
Nicholas (Jones)
Pleasant (Jasper)
Reuben (Greene)
Richard (Habersham)
Robart (Wilkinson)
Robert (Burke)
Robert (Tattnall)
Robert (Warren)
Sally (Morgan)
Samuel (Wilkinson)
Sarah (Greene)
Sarah (Montgomery)
Shelton (Elbert)
Simeon (Hall)

(158)

White, Solomon (Jones)
  Stan(?) (Chatham)
  Stephen (Elbert)
  Stephen (Wilkes)
  Sterling (Jackson)
  Steven (Madison)
  T. S. (Richmond)
  Thomas (Columbia)
  Thomas (Jones)
  Thomas M.(?) (Columbia)
  Vincent (Hall)
  Wade (Clarke)
  Wiley (2) (Morgan)
  William (Baldwin)
  William (Burke)
  William (2) (Elbert)
  William, Sr. (Greene)
  William (Greene)
  William (Gwinnett)
  William (Jasper)
  William & Mother (Jasper)
  William (Montgomery)
  William (Putnam)
  William (2) (Richmond)
  William (Wilkinson)
  Winny (Warren)
  Zachariah (Effingham)
  Zacharich (Jasper)
Whitehead, Amos P. (Burke)
  Benjamin (Gwinnett)
  Bird (Hancock)
  Eliza (Laurens)
  Henery (Jefferson)
  James (Burke)
  James (Clarke)
  Joel (Oglethorpe)
  John, Sr. (Burke)
  John (Burke)
  Rachel (Clarke)
  Reason (Clarke)
  Richard (Clarke)
  Samuel (2) (Oglethorpe)
  Thomas (Hall)
  Thomas (Putnam)
  William (Jackson)
  William (Putnam)
Whitehurst, David (Appling)
  Hillory (Appling)
  John (Montgomery)
  Levi (Montgomery)
  Simon (Montgomery)
Whiteman, Hannah (Effingham)
  Lewis (Effingham)
  Matthew (Effingham)
Whiten, William (Appling)
Whitfield, Alexander (Clarke)
  Benjamon (Putnam)
  Bryan (Burke)
  Bryan (Washington)
  Darky (Jackson)
  G. (Richmond)

Horatho (Putnam)
  James (Jefferson)
  James (Putnam)
  Jemime (Washington)
  John S. (Bryan)
  Lewis (Burke)
  Reuben (Washington)
  Robert (Washington)
  Tucker (Jackson)
  William (Chatham)
  William (Putnam)
  William (Washington)
Whithead, Jacob (Habersham)
  Joseph (Habersham)
Whitich, Ernest C. (Morgan)
Whitier(?), John (Wilkinson)
Whiting, John (Washington)
Whitington, Burrel G., Sr.
                        (Liberty)
  Sherod (Columbia)
Whitley, Nathan, Jr. (Walton)
  Nathan, Sr. (Walton)
  John (Walton)
  Mary (Pulaski)
  Wiley (Morgan)
Whitlie, (torn) (Wilkes)
Whitlock, (ind.) (Hall)
  Beasley (Morgan)
  Mary (Greene)
  Nathaniel (Hall)
  Thomas (Hall)
Whitly, Ditus (Walton)
  Micajah (Walton)
Whitman, Israel (Effingham)
  John (Jackson)
  William (Elbert)
Whitmire, Mary (Jackson)
Whitmoore, Elizabeth (Jasper)
Whitmore, Parly (Camden)
  William (Camden)
Whitney, Josiah (Emanuel)
Whitress, Bartlett (Wilkinson)
  Charles (Wilkinson)
  Sandfour (Wilkinson)
Whitrock, Jourdain P.
                    (Wilkinson)
Whitsett, George (Oglethorpe)
Whitson, John (Chatham)
Whitten, Dempsey (Washington)
Whittingham, Ephraim
                    (Hancock)
Whittington, Burrel G. (Bryan)
  Gady (Jasper)
  Irwin (Warren)
  Jock (Hancock)
  John (Hancock)
  William (Bryan)
Whittle, Ambrose (Washington)
  Burrel (Washington)
  John (Washington)
Whitton(?), Boling (Clarke)

Whitton, George (Lincoln)
  James (Camden)
Whitton(?), James (Richmond)
Whitwell, F. R. (Liberty)
Whitworth, Richard (Madison)
  Thomas (Hall)
Wholey, James (Jasper)
Wholsing, Mathew (Richmond)
Whorton, Bartlet (Walton)
  Elijah (Walton)
  William (Walton)
Whyman, W. (Liberty)
Wicker, Nathaniel (Washington)
  William (Washington)
Widdon, Eli (Emanuel)
Wide, Samuel (Jasper)
Wideman, William (Hall)
Wier, John (Clarke)
  Samuel (Clarke)
Wigan, Daniel (Irwin)
Wiggans, William (Warren)
Wiggingbothom, R. (Jasper)
Wiggins, Amos (Burke)
  Daniel (Irwin)
  Elias (Emanuel)
  James (Jefferson)
  Jesse (Burke)
  Jesse (Emanuel)
  John (Emanuel)
  John (Greene)
  John (Richmond)
  Michael (Burke)
  Orren (Greene)
  Peter (Liberty)
  Peter (Warren)
  Richard (Irwin)
  Richard (Warren)
  Whitendon (Putnam)
  William (Burke)
  William (Washington)
  William (Wilkinson)
Wigins, Stephen (Irwin)
Wigley, Allen (Hall)
  Joseph (Hall)
Wigs(?), Joseph (Hancock)
Wilay, Thomas (Baldwin)
Wilborn, James (Jackson)
Wilbourn, James (Greene)
Wilcher, Charles (Walton)
  Jeremiah (Jefferson)
  Jordon (Jefferson)
  Mary (Warren)
  William (Warren)
Wilcox, Abijah (Liberty)
  James (Montgomery)
  Thomas (2) (Telfair)
  Uriah (Liberty)
Wilcoxson(?), Elijah (Appling)
Wilcoxson, John (Appling)
Wild, John (Richmond)
Wilder, Edmond (Jones)

(159)

Wilder(?), Elizabeth (Screven)
Green (Jones)
Hanson (Screven)
James (Morgan)
Levy (Oglethorpe)
Mary (Jones)
Rachel (Hancock)
Sampson (Walton)
Sampson (Warren)
Simeon (Walton)
Solomon (Warren)
Ward (Jones)
William (Jasper)
William (Jones)
William (Tattnall)
Wiley, Aldrege (McIntosh)
Ann (Baldwin)
Enoch (McIntosh)
George (Madison)
James (Madison)
John (McIntosh)
Nicholas (Wilkes)
Peter (Bulloch)
Taylor (Columbia)
Thomas (Morgan)
William (Columbia)
William C. (Jefferson)

see also Wylly

Wilford, John (Montgomery)
Lewis (Montgomery)
Wilhight, John R. (Elbert)
Lewis (Elbert)
Wilhite, John (Madison)
Meschack T. (Madison)
Montfort (Putnam)
Philmon R. (Elbert)
Wilie, Washington (Hall)
Wilinot, John (Jones)
Wilke, Osburn (Oglethorpe)
Wilkens, Elizabeth (Liberty)
Wilkenson, Easter (Wilkinson)
John (Putnam)
William (Putnam)
Wilkerson, Abel (Jasper)
Adam (Hancock)
Ann (Wilkes)
Francis (Wilkes)
H. (Jasper)
(torn) H. (Laurens)
Isaac (Walton)
Jane (Columbia)
Jemmima (Wilkes)
John (Wilkes)
L. (Jasper)
R. (Jasper)
Sary (Walton)
Thomas (Wilkes)
Moses (Oglethorpe)
Wilkey, Samuel (Oglethorpe)
Wilkie, Betsy (Washington)
Wilkins, A. (Jasper)
Abadon (Jasper)
Agnes (Wilkes)
Betsey (Clarke)
Catherine (Hancock)
Gilas (Columbia)
Henry (Columbia)
James (Clarke)
James (Gwinnett)
Job (Clarke)
John (Columbia)
John (Elbert)
Paul H. (Liberty)
Samuel (Columbia)
Samuel (Liberty)
Thomas (Gwinnett)
William (Columbia)
William (Gwinnett)
William (Putnam)
William A. (Columbia)
Wilkinson, (torn) (Laurens)
Archibald (Baldwin)
Carter (Lincoln)
D. D. (Elbert)
Duncan (Putnam)
Hugh (Jefferson)
J. (Jasper)
John (Burke)
John (Telfair)
Lemuel (Putnam)
Malcolm G. (Baldwin)
Polly (Warren)
Roland (Clarke)
Thomas (Morgan)
William (Telfair)
Zere (Putnam)
Wilkison, Abner (Greene)
John (Walton)
Mathew (Walton)
Robert (Greene)
Sherwood (Greene)
Wilks, Aaron (Oglethorpe)
Elisha (Emanuel)
James (Putnam)
Willaby, Aaron (Wilkinson)
William (Wilkinson)
Willaford, John (Oglethorpe)
Willard, Elijah (Morgan)
Willcox, John (2) (Richmond)
John (Telfair)
Martin (Richmond)
Willey, Francis C. (Richmond)
James (Emanuel)
Willhite, Rex (Putnam)
William, Cornelius (M. C.) (McIntosh)
Elizabeth (Richmond)
Nathan (Telfair)
Williams, (ind.) (Laurens)
Aaron (Burke)
Abraham (Hancock)
Mrs. Abygale (Greene)
Amos (Habersham)
Anderson, Jr. (Effingham)
Anderson, Sr. (Effingham)
Arthur (Burke)
Avington (Walton)
Benjamon (Putnam)
Benjamin (Wilkes)
Benjamin (Wilkinson)
Bird (Madison)
Britten (Greene)
Bryant (Walton)
Buckner (Putnam)
Charles (Chatham)
Charles (Walton)
Charlotte (Burke)
Chrischany (Hancock)
Daniel (Chatham)
Daniel (2) (Washington)
Daniel (Wilkes)
David (Clarke)
David (Irwin)
David (Washington)
David (Wilkinson)
Davis (Jackson)
Dawson (Madison)
Del---- (Bulloch)
Dennis (Jefferson)
Dennis (Washington)
Denton (Hall)
Drewry (Wilkinson)
Duke (Greene)
E. B. (Elbert)
Ealer (Habersham)
Ebenezer T. (Columbia)
Edward (Camden)
Edward (Jasper)
Edward (Morgan)
Elijah (Madison)
Elisah (Hall)
Elisha (Putnam)
Elizabeth (Bulloch)
Elizabeth (Camden)
(ind.) (Bulloch)
Frances (Putnam)
Francis (Wilkinson)
Frederick (Telfair)
Frederick H. (Greene)
Garret(?) (Bulloch)
Green (Walton)
H. (Richmond)
Harriet (Chatham)
Miss Helener (Bryan)
Henry (Oglethorpe)
Henry (Warren)
Henry (Washington)
Henry J. (Morgan)
Hester (Burke)
Hezekiah (2) (Putnam)
Isaac (Hall)
Isaac (Jefferson)
Isaac (Wilkinson)
Isham (Gwinnett)

Williams, J. (Richmond)
Jacob (Morgan)
Jas. (Bryan)
James (Chatham)
James (Effingham)
James (Habersham)
James (Jefferson)
James (Madison)
James (Oglethorpe)
James (Pulaski)
James (Putnam)
James (Tattnall)
James (Telfair)
James (Wilkinson)
Jane (Burke)
Jane (Wilkes)
Jaudon (Effingham)
Jeremiah (Columbia)
Jeremiah M. (Putnam)
Jesse (Early)
Jesse (Gwinnett)
Jesse (Hancock)
Jesse (Montgomery)
Jesse (Wilkes)
Joel (Laurens)
John (Bulloch)
John (Burke)
John (Clarke)
John (Glynn)
John (Greene)
John (Habersham)
John (Hall)
John (2) (Hancock)
John (Jasper)
John (Jefferson)
John (Jones)
John (Liberty)
John (Madison)
John (3) (Morgan)
John (Putnam)
John (2) (Warren)
John (4) (Washington)
John (2) (Wilkes)
John F. (Liberty)
John L. (Putnam)
John M. (Jones)
Johnson (Wilkes)
Jonas (Morgan)
Jordan (Wilkinson)
Joseph (Greene)
Joseph (Warren)
Kezziah (Warren)
Kirby (Bryan)
Lamant (Chatham)
Lewis (Tattnall)
Lott, (Jefferson)
Lucy (Oglethorpe)
Luke (Jasper)
Martha (Bulloch)
Martin (Hall)
Mary (Baldwin)

Mary (Wilkinson)
Mathews (Oglethorpe)
Mathew (Putnam)
Matthew L. (Elbert)
Micaja (Wilkinson)
Micajah (Hall)
Moses (Jasper)
N. (Jasper)
Nathaniel (Walton)
Nicholas (Warren)
Osborn T. (Putnam)
Paul (Washington)
Perminas (Madison)
Peter I. (Greene)
Priscilla (Chatham)
Priscilla (Hall)
Putnam T. (Putnam)
Rachael (Richmond)
Rachal (Wilkinson)
Rebeca (Habersham)
Reuben (Clarke)
Richard (Washington)
Rich'd F. (Chatham)
Robert, Jr. (Madison)
Robert, Sr. (Madison)
Robert (Screven)
Robert (Washington)
Robert (Wilkes)
Robert O. (Oglethorpe)
Roland (Wilkinson)
Rowland (Wilkes)
Samuel (Bulloch)
Samuel, Jr. (Bulloch)
Samuel (Burke)
Samuel (Camden)
Samuel (Effingham)
Samuel (Wilkinson)
Sarah (Jones)
Shepherd (Bulloch)
Silas (Pulaski)
Sinai (Hall)
Stafford (Jones)
Stephen (Chatham)
Stephen (Early)
Stephen (Emanuel)
Stephen (Putnam)
Stephen (Washington)
Stephen W. (Wilkinson)
Sugas (Greene)
Susannah (Warren)
Syllatus (Washington)
Thiesphilus (Screven)
Thomas (Bryan)
Thomas (Burke)
Thomas (Chatham)
Thomas (Hancock)
Thomas (Oglethorpe)
Thomas (Putnam)
Thomas (Walton)
Thomas (Washington)
Thomas, Jr. (Washington)

Thomas M. (Washington)
Thomas S. (Hancock)
Timothy (Clarke)
W. (Jasper)
W. (ind.) (Pulaski)
Wiley (Putnam)
William (Bryan)
William (2) (Bulloch)
William (Chatham)
Willia.n (Early)
William (Gwinnett)
William (Jackson)
William (Jasper)
William (Jones)
William (Morgan)
William (2) (Putnam)
William (Screven)
William (Telfair)
William (Walton)
William (Warren)
William (Washington)
William (3) (Wilkes)
William (Wilkinson)
William B. (Warren)
William F. (Chatham)
William R. (Morgan)
Willis (Jackson)
Willson (Putnam)
Wilson (Greene)
Wilson (Jones)
Wilson (Wilkinson)
Winifred (Telfair)
Wright (Burke)
Wyatt (Oglethorpe)
Zachariah (Columbia)
Williamson, A. (Jackson)
Adam (Jackson)
Ann (Clarke)
Benjamon (Putnam)
Benjamin (Screven)
Benjamin (Washington)
C. (Baldwin)
Charles (Washington)
Clabrook (Wilkes)
David (Appling)
George (Jackson)
George (Oglethorpe)
Green (Jones)
Henry (Putnam)
I. (Jasper)
Isaac (Putnam)
Isaac (Wilkes)
J. P. (Chatham)
James (Jasper)
John (3) (Jackson)
John Sr. (Jackson)
John (Montgomery)
John (Screven)
John P. (Chatham)
John P. (Gwinnett)
Jonathan (Jones)

Williamson, Joseph (Hancock)
Lethe (Jones)
Lidum(?) (Jones)
Littleton (Putnam)
Lydia (Emanuel)
Malechi (Washington)
Mason (Fem.) (Jones)
Nathan (Montgomery)
Pleasant (Jasper)
Reuben (Putnam)
Reuben J. (Putnam)
Robert M. (2) (Screven)
Ruth (Lincoln)
Sarah (Burke)
Thomas (Putnam)
W. (Jasper)
Walker W. (Elbert)
William (Gwinnett)
William (2) (Jackson)
William (Jasper)
William (Jones)
William (Laurens)
William (Tattnall)
William (Washington)
Zachariah (Putnam)
Willie, (? Wylly) Solomon
          (Jefferson)
Williford, Benjamin (Warren)
Hardy (Warren)
Jephtha (Madison)
Joel (Warren)
Judah (Madison)
Nathan (Madison)
Samuel (Madison)
William (Madison)
William W. (Madison)
Winney (Warren)
Willingham, A____ (Oglethorpe)
Abner (Columbia)
Betsy (Columbia)
Calib (Jones)
Cash (Columbia)
Charles (Madison)
Foy (Oglethorpe)
George (Columbia)
George (Morgan)
Isaac (2) (Columbia)
James (Baldwin)
Jesse (Madison)
Jessee (Oglethorpe)
John (3) (Columbia)
John C. (Columbia)
John G. (Columbia)
Molly (Columbia)
Reuben (Columbia)
Robason (Jackson)
Samuel (Jackson)
Thomas (Columbia)
Thomas (Morgan)
William (Lincoln)
William (Morgan)

William B. (Columbia)
Willink, Fred'k (Chatham)
Willis, Benjamin (Laurens)
Brittian (Baldwin)
D. H. (Jasper)
Dempsey (Jones)
Edny (Wilkes)
Ephraim (Emanuel)
George (Liberty)
George (Wilkes)
George E. (Wilkes)
Gideon (Effingham)
Henry (Effingham)
Henry (Greene)
Isaac (Liberty)
James (Warren)
James Est. (Wilkes)
Jesse, Jr. (Jones)
Jesse (Lincoln)
Joel, Sr. (Jones)
John (Elbert)
John C. (Jasper)
John M. (Wilkes)
Jonathon (Liberty)
Joseph (Jones)
Joshua (Wilkes)
Loudon (Greene)
Martin (Lincoln)
Miller M. (Wilkes)
Moses P. (Wilkes)
Paul S. (Wilkes)
Phillip (Oglethorpe)
Price (Baldwin)
Redding (Wilkinson)
Richard I. (Wilkes)
Robert (Jasper)
Robert (Jefferson)
Thomas (Jones)
W. E. (Chatham)
William (Greene)
William, Jr. (Jones)
Zachariah (Pulaski)
Willisons, George (Putnam)
Willowby, Sarah (Camden)
Wills, Benjamin (Telfair)
Wills, (Wells), Bullock (Jones)
Wills, (or Mills), Jeremiah
          (Telfair)
Wills, Samuel (Wilkinson)
Thomas (Putnam)
William (Clarke)
Willson, A. (Jasper)
Barber (Washington)
Benj'm H. (Jasper)
Daniel (Washington)
Hugh (Jasper)
Isaac (Putnam)
James (Jasper)
Est. of James dec'd.
          (Liberty)
Jenkins (Jasper)

Jos. (3) (Jasper)
Joseph (Putnam)
Josiah (Liberty)
N. (Jasper)
Richard (Jasper)
Sally (Oglethorpe)
Wilson, Barbery (Appling)
Benjamin (Hancock)
Daniel (Greene)
David (Warren)
Mrs. E. (Chatham)
E. (Jackson)
Eleas (Warren)
Elizabeth (Chatham)
Elizabeth (Hancock)
Fennel (Jackson)
George (Clarke)
George (Hall)
George W. (Jackson)
Henry (Warren)
Hugh (Hall)
James (Baldwin)
James (Burke)
James (Chatham)
James (Clarke)
James, Jr. (Effingham)
James, Sr. (Effingham)
James, Jr. (Elbert)
James, Sr. (Elbert)
James (Hancock)
James (4) (Jackson)
James (Screven)
Jeremiah (Effingham)
John (2) (Baldwin)
John (Chatham)
John (Greene)
John, Sr. (Greene)
John (Hall)
John (Jackson)
John (Richmond)
John (2) (Warren)
John (Wilkes)
Joseph (Hall)
Laton (Glynn)
Lucrecy (Telfair)
Luke (Effingham)
Matthew (Hall)
Mary (Columbia)
Moses (Jackson)
Moses (Pulaski)
Penelope (Oglethorpe)
R. William (Emanuel)
Robert (Hall)
Robert (Hancock)
Robert (Jackson)
S. (Richmond)
Samuel (Bulloch)
Samuel (Greene)
Samuel (Jackson)
Samuel (Jefferson)
Samuel (Jones)

Wilson, Samuel (Screven)
Samuel (Warren)
Solomon (Burke)
Solomon (Early)
Susan (Chatham)
Tabitha (Clarke)
Thomas (Elbert)
Thomas (Greene)
Thomas (2) (Hall)
Thomas (Jackson)
William (Effingham)
William (Greene)
William (Hall)
William (3) (Jackson)
William, Jr. (Jackson)
William (Liberty)
William (Madison)
William (Morgan)
Wimberly, Abner (Jones)
David (Washington)
Henry (Jones)
John (Burke)
John (Jones)
Lewis (Burke)
Lewis (Jones)
Lucretia (Burke)
Needham (Burke)
Titus (Jones)
Wiley (Burke)
William (Burke)
Zach (Burke)
Wimbern, Priscilla (Warren)
Wimbush, Anna (Jones)
Wimms, George (2) (Jackson)
Wimpey, John (Oglethorpe)
Mathew (Walton)
Wimpy, John (Burke)
Winans, Josiah (McIntosh)
Winborn, William (Pulaski)
Winchester, William
(Richmond)
Windham, Benjamin
(Washington)
Edward (Warren)
Windsor, Jesse (Jackson)
Windum, John (Baldwin)
Winfield, James (Greene)
John (Elbert)
John, Jr. (Greene)
John, Sr. (Greene)
Nathan (Greene)
William (Greene)
Winfrey, Benjamin E.
(Columbia)
George (Jackson)
John (Morgan)
Reuben (Morgan)
William (Oglethorpe)
Winfry, Samuel (Jones)
Sarah (Columbia)
Wing, Christina (Chatham)

Edward (Lincoln)
George F. (McIntosh)
John (Lincoln)
William (Hall)
Wingate, Amos (Baldwin)
Michael (Baldwin)
Richard M. (Pulaski)
Wingfield, Garland (2) (Wilkes)
James (Wilkes)
John (Morgan)
John (Wilkes)
John L. (Wilkes)
Mary (Wilkes)
Peggy (W. C.) (Wilkes)
Robert C. (Jackson)
Samuel (Wilkes)
Thomas (Greene)
Thomas (Wilkes)
Winfred, Mrs. (Columbia)
Winkler, Strobar (Chatham)
Winman, John (Lincoln)
Winn, (ind.) (Gwinnett)
Est. of Mjr. dec'd (Liberty)
Abn (Jackson)
Benjamin (Elbert)
Elisha (Gwinnett)
George (Wilkes)
Hamilton (Habersham)
Hamlin (Putnam)
Hinchey (Clarke)
Jane (Wilkes)
John (Gwinnett)
John (Jackson)
John (Lincoln)
John (Putnam)
Jones (Putnam)
Joseph (Putnam)
Joseph I. (McIntosh)
Lemuel (Jackson)
Littleton (Putnam)
Peter & W. (Liberty)
Richard (Hall)
Ruby (Jackson)
Thomas (Glynn)
Thomas (Hall)
Thomas (Putnam)
Winnett, Avery (Wilkinson)
Winslett, Jonathan (Greene)
Mary (Greene)
Peggy (Greene)
Richard (Greene)
Samuel, Jr. (Greene)
Samuel, Sr. (Greene)
Winter, F. (Richmond)
Henry (?) (Chatham)
J. C. (Richmond)
James (Richmond)
Jeremiah (Richmond)
John (Chatham)
Winters, Albert (Jackson)
Geo. W. (Jackson)

John (2) (Jackson)
Winton, Henrietta (Wilkes)
Wiot, Margaret (Burke)
Wird, R. H. (Richmond)
Wisdom, Jesse (Greene)
Wise, Burwell (Warren)
David (Wilkinson)
Henry (Jasper)
Herren (Wilkinson)
Jacob (Oglethorpe)
James (Jasper)
Joel (Jasper)
John (Bulloch)
John (Jasper)
John (Oglethorpe)
John (Washington)
John (Wilkes)
Joseph (Wilkinson)
Margaret (Oglethorpe)
Mary (Wilkes)
Patterson (Clarke)
Preston (Bulloch)
Sarah (Wilkes)
William (Burke)
Wiseman, Margaret (Richmond)
Robert (Columbia)
William (Chatham)
Wisenbaker, Christian
(Effingham)
Wisinbach, Mary (Effingham)
Witcher, Benjamin (Madison)
James (2) (Morgan)
John (Morgan)
Withers, Daniel (Lincoln)
Joel (Lincoln)
Samuel (Lincoln)
Witt, David (Jackson)
Wofford, Isaiah (Hancock)
James (Hancock)
William (Habersham)
William B. (Habersham)
Wolcott, Robert S. (Putnam)
Wolcox, Cyprian (Hancock)
Woldroup, A. (Jasper)
Woler, Josh (Jasper)
Wolf. Andrew, Sr. (Wilkes)
Andrew, Jr. (Wilkes)
Frederick (Pulaski)
John (Emanuel)
Stephen (Laurens)
Wolfe, George (Effingham)
John (Effingham)
Stephen (Chatham)
Stephen (Effingham)
Wolloburgh, Jacob & G.
(Liberty)
Womack, Bird (Greene)
Frederick (Effingham)
John (2) (Chatham)
Mne(?) (Hancock)
Thomas (Chatham)

Womack, William (Effingham)
William (Hancock)
Wyly (Hancock)
Womble, Allen (Warren)
Daniel (Pulaski)
Edmond (Warren)
Egbert (Washington)
Elisha (Washington)
Henery (Jefferson)
Luis (Richmond)
Nathaniel (Pulaski)
Wommack, Jacob (Wilkinson)
Wonston, Thomas (Greene)
Wood, Abram (Pulaski)
Allen (Jasper)
Allen (Warren)
Augustus (Columbia)
Aves (Jasper)
Ballenger (Jefferson)
Catherine (Chatham)
Charles (Putnam)
David (Jefferson)
Eldredge (Putnam)
Eli (Greene)
Elisha (Baldwin)
Eliza (Jackson)
Ellit (Morgan)
Frederick (Pulaski)
George (Washington)
Green (Greene)
Green (Jackson)
Henry (Morgan)
J. B. (Chatham)
Jacob (McIntosh)
Jacob (Pulaski)
James, Sr. (Columbia)
James (Elbert)
James (Jackson)
James (Jasper)
James (Putnam)
Jario (Washington)
Jethro (Greene)
John (Baldwin)
John (Camden)
John (Effingham)
John (Hall)
John (Richmond)
John (Wilkes)
John C. (Morgan)
John L. (Oglethorpe)
Jonathan (Columbia)
Jonathon (Laurens)
Joseph (Putnam)
Joseph (Warren)
Martin (Pulaski)
Misael (Washington)
Peter (Washington)
Richard (Lincoln)
Richard W. (Jackson)
Samuel (Habersham)
Tabitha (Walton)

Thomas (Gwinnett)
Thomas (Morgan)
Thomas (Richmond)
Whitmell (Wilkinson)
William (Elbert)
William (Hall)
William (2) (Jackson)
William (Morgan)
William (Richmond)
William (Warren)
Willis (Baldwin)
Willis (Laurens)
Woodall, Abner (Wilkinson)
Archibald (Jones)
James (Jasper)
James (Jones)
John (Gwinnett)
John (Jasper)
John (Jones)
Martin (Greene)
William (Gwinnett)
William (Wilkes)
Woodard, John (Putnam)
Joshua (Burke)
Lemuel (Burke)
Oren (Hancock)
Thomas (Laurens)
Woodbroon, William (Baldwin)
Woodbridge, Mrs. (Chatham)
Woodbury, Margaret (Chatham)
Woodcock, John (Bryan)
William (Bulloch)
Woodham, Edward (Greene)
Edward (Washington)
James (Greene)
Wooding, Edward (Columbia)
Woodley, Andrew (Elbert)
Caleb (Jasper)
Woodliff, J. C. (Richmond)
Woodman, John (Bulloch)
Woodroff Benjamin
(Oglethorpe)
Woodrough, James (Greene)
Woodruff, Clifford (Jasper)
Clifford (Oglethorpe)
Elish (Oglethorpe)
George (Camden)
Isaac (Richmond)
James (Jasper)
James (2) (Wilkes)
Philo D. (Putnam)
Reuben (Oglethorpe)
Richard (2) (Wilkes)
Woods, Catherine (Gwinnett)
Cyrus (Greene)
Demsey, Jr. (Montgomery)
Demsey, Sr. (Montgomery)
Isaac (Jefferson)
Isabela (Gwinnett)
James (Greene)
James (Morgan)

John (Jefferson)
John (Madison)
John (Putnam)
John (Tattnall)
John W. (Clarke)
Matthew M. (Jefferson)
Robert (Bulloch)
Robert, Jr. (Madison)
Robert, Sr. (Madison)
Samuel (Hall)
Samuel (Madison)
Samuel (Oglethorpe)
Thomas (Burke)
Thomas (Tattnall)
Timothy C. (Walton)
William (Elbert)
William (Lincoln)
Woodson, Jonathan (Jones)
Jonathan C. Jr. (Jones)
Woodward, Aron (Walton)
Benjamin S. (Warren)
Isham (Putnam)
Jesse (2) (Morgan)
Mills (Emanuel)
Tabitha (Warren)
Woody, George (Wilkes)
Henry (Jackson)
Jesse (Jackson)
William (Appling)
Woodyard, Paschal (Morgan)
Robert (Morgan)
Woolbright, Barnaby (Greene)
Daniel (Wilkes)
Jacob (Wilkes)
Woolcot, George M. (Putnam)
Woolcott, Isaac (Putnam)
Wooldridge, Abselom (Putnam)
Wooldrop, Sol. (Jasper)
Wooldroup, William (Jasper)
Woolfolk, Austin (Richmond)
Thomas (Jones)
Woolhoptor, Mrs. (Chatham)
Woolly, Bazil (Hall)
Woolsey, Benjamin (Baldwin)
Woolsy, John M. (Putnam)
Seth (Putnam)
Wooten, Branson D. (Greene)
Collen (Greene)
Counsel (Pulaski)
James (Greene)
James, Jr. (Hancock)
James A. (Greene)
Jerusa (Burke)
John (Jasper)
Joseph (Walton)
Mournin (Burke)
Nevel (Hall)
Readen (Telfair)
Richard (Telfair)
William (Habersham)
Wooton, Jesse (Walton)

Wootten, John (Baldwin)
James (Wilkes)
Lemuel (Wilkes)
Richard (Wilkes)
Thomas (Wilkes)
Worall, Jacob (Baldwin)
Word, Joshua (Habersham)
Worley, I. (Camden)
Obadiah (Habersham)
Worling(?), E. (Richmond)
Wormek, John P. (Oglethorpe)
Wormmick, P. (Jasper)
Wornam, William (Putnam)
Worrall, B. (Chatham)
Worrel, Alexander (Jefferson)
Worrell, Ranson (Elbert)
Stephen (Jefferson)
William (Greene)
Worrill, Solomon (Wilkinson)
Worsham, Archer (Baldwin)
Archy (Baldwin)
Daniel B. (Baldwin)
David G. (Baldwin)
Joseph (Wilkes)
Thomas (Hancock)
William H. (Walton)
Worshey, John (Jones)
Worsley, Sampson (Warren)
Simon (Emanuel)
Wortham, John (Wilkes)
Susanna (Clarke)
Thomas, Jr. (Wilkes)
William (Morgan)
William (Wilkes)
Worthen, Elijah, Sr.
(Washington)
Elijah, Jr. (Washington)
William (Washington)
Worthinson Nathan (Jones)
Worthy, Anderson (Putnam)
Elison (Washington)
Leo'd (Jasper)
Peggy (Washington)
Thomas (Gwinnett)
William (Gwinnett)
Wosham, Appleton (Putnam)
William (Putnam)
William, Sr. (Putnam)
Wratchford, (Ratchford), Joseph
(Jackson)
Wray, John (Oglethorpe)
Jonathan (Oglethorpe)
Phillip (Oglethorpe)
William (Jasper)
William (Oglethorpe)
Wren, Francis (Jefferson)
John (Jefferson)
William (Jefferson)
Wright, (ind.) (Putnam)
(torn) (Warren)
Abednigo (Hancock)

Abraham (Jones)
Alexander (Gwinnett)
Ambrose (Jefferson)
Amos (Warren)
Ann (Chatham)
Asa (Oglethorpe)
Asa (Putnam)
Caleb (Jefferson)
Catherine (Richmond)
Charles (Wilkinson)
David (Columbia)
David (Elbert)
David (Morgan)
Eleat (Jones)
Elisha (Jones)
Ezekiel (Jefferson)
Flewellen (Warren)
Garred (Emanuel)
George (Jefferson)
George (Wilkinson)
Hagar (Chatham)
Henry (Oglethorpe)
Henry (Wilkinson)
Isaac (Elbert)
Isaac (Lincoln)
James, Esq. (Columbia)
James (Columbia)
James (2) (Morgan)
James (Putnam)
James (Warren)
James B. (Glynn)
James S. (Jackson)
James W. (Putnam)
Jarret (Greene)
Jesse (Hall)
Jesse (Jones)
John (Columbia)
John (Greene)
John (Gwinnett)
John (Jackson)
John (Jasper)
John (Lincoln)
John (Putnam)
John (2) (Wilkes)
John (Wilkinson)
John H. (Baldwin)
John M. (Washington)
Johnson (Oglethorpe)
Joseph (Greene)
Joseph (Tattnall)
Joseph (Warren)
Josh (Jasper)
Laban (Effingham)
Louis (Putnam)
Marshal (Walton)
Milly (Warren)
Nathan (Lincoln)
Pleasant (Putnam)
Pryor (Baldwin)
Randol (Putnam)
Reuben, Jr. (Putnam)

Reuben, Sr. (Putnam)
Robert (Greene)
Robert (Hancock)
Robert (2) (Putnam)
Samuel (Lincoln)
Samuel (Putnam)
Sarah (Morgan)
Sarah (Wilkes)
Shohn(?) S. (Putnam) *John*
Solomon (Wilkinson)
Spenser (Wilkinson)
Stephen (Greene)
Stephen S. (Putnam)
Susannah (Columbia)
Temperance (Warren)
Thomas (Chatham)
Thomas (2) (Putnam)
Thomas (2) (Washington)
Wiley (Chatham)
William (Bulloch)
William (Clarke)
William (Columbia)
William (Greene)
William (Jasper)
William (Laurens)
William, Sr. (Lincoln)
William, Jr. (Lincoln)
William (Oglethorpe)
William (Putnam)
William (Wilkinson)
William D. (Baldwin)
William S. (Jones)
Winfield (Laurens)
Zebulon (Greene)
Write, Samuel (Wilkinson)
Wyatt, Hardy (Laurens)
John (Morgan)
Thomas (Morgan)
William (Bulloch)
Wyche, George (Elbert)
George (Montgomery)
Henry (Jones)
Litleton (Montgomery)
Peter (Jones)
Wyley, Edwin (Hancock)
William (Hancock)
William (Jackson)
Wylie (William (Hall)
Wylley, Leonidas (Chatham)
Wylly, Alexr. C. (Glynn) *see also*
Thomas (Effingham) *Wiley*
Wyly, James A. (Habersham)
Wynn, Anne (Emanuel)
Benjamin (Warren)
Clement (Warren)
Clemmons (Warren)
Hannah (Jones)
James (Warren)
John (2) (Emanuel)
John, Jr. (Madison)
John, Sr. (Madison)

(165)

Wynn, John (Oglethorpe)
John P. (Montgomery)
Lemuel (Jasper)
Lewis (Jones)
Peter (Warren)
Robert (Baldwin)
Thomas (2) (Warren)
Thomas C. (Greene)
Thomas P. (Burke)
William (Burke)
William (Warren)
Wynne, Burwell I. (Hancock)
Emily (Burke)
John (Columbia)
John W. (Pulaski)
Robert (Columbia)
William (Warren)
William (Wilkinson)
Wynnes, John (Jones)

Y

Yalbery, C. (Camden)
Yancey, Caroline (Hancock)
Ezekial (Gwinnett)
Means (Hall)
Richard (Hall)
Thomas (Oglethorpe)
Wesley (Gwinnett)
William (Hall)
Yancy, Charles (Gwinnett)
James (Jackson)
James (Jasper)
Louis (Jasper)
William (Jackson)
Yarboro, Ambrose (Jackson)
Joseph (Jackson)
Yarborough, Benjamin
(Washington)
Isaac (Hancock)
Jerry (Morgan)
John (Hall)
Nancy (Hancock)
Peter (Morgan)
Thomas (Columbia)
Thomas (Morgan)
Yarborrough, I. (Jasper)
Yarbraugh, John (Oglethorpe)
Yarbrough, Geptha (Walton)
James (Columbia)
James (Putnam)
James (Walton)
Joshua (Walton)
Lewis (Pulaski)
Lewis (2) (Walton)
Moses (Warren)
Nimrod (Warren)
Randol (Pulaski)
Rebecca (Columbia)
Samuel (Warren)
William (Columbia)

William (Pulaski)
William (Putnam)
William (Walton)
Yarbur, William (Appling)
Yarnold, Benjamin (Richmond)
Yates, (torn) (Laurens)
Abraham (Greene)
Burrel (Emanuel)
Eli (Emanuel)
Elijah (Walton)
Hezekiah (Oglethorpe)
Jacob (Pulaski)
James (Clarke)
James (Washington)
John (Clarke)
Peter (Clarke)
Thomas (Bulloch)
William (Clarke)
Yaun, Simon (Telfair)
Yawn, (torn) (Laurens)
Benjamin (Laurens)
David (Appling)
Nicholas (Columbia)
Yeager, Abner (Hall)
Yeamans, Frederick (Glynn)
Yearly, Henry (Montgomery)
Yeats, Barnett (Warren)
Yeomans, John (Emanuel)
Redding (Emanuel)
Solomon (Emanuel)
Yinpoles, Frederick (Jones)
Yipper, James (Oglethorpe)
Yoes, Catherine (Elbert)
Yoats, Ervin (Walton)
Yopp, Samuel (Laurens)
York, Archibald (Hall)
David (Columbia)
Elizabeth (Jackson)
Henry (Jackson)
Isaac (Jackson)
James (Lincoln)
John (Lincoln)
John, Jr. (Lincoln)
Mary (Jackson)
Singleton (Lincoln)
Thomas (Jackson)
Youmans, S. P. (Tattnall)
Young, (ind.) (Oglethorpe)
Doctor (Chatham)
Mrs. (Chatham)
Alexander (Burke)
Amos (Baldwin)
Augustine (Gwinnett)
Benjamin (Appling)
Benjamin (Jefferson)
Benjamin (Jones)
Bernard (Hancock)
Charles (Wilkinson)
Charlotte (Madison)
Daniel (Warren)
David (Walton)

Elam (Jefferson)
Elijah (Jefferson)
Elizabeth (Jefferson)
Elizabeth (Washington)
Fedrick (Oglethorpe)
Ganet (Chatham)
George (Oglethorpe)
H. (Chatham)
Henery (Jefferson)
Henry (Oglethorpe)
Isaac (Effingham)
Jacob, Jr. (Jefferson)
Jacob, Sr. (Jefferson)
James (Bulloch)
James (Jefferson)
James (Wilkinson)
Jane (Chatham)
Jesse (Washington)
John (Appling)
John (Bryan)
John (Camden)
John (Hall)
John (Jackson)
John (Jones)
Jones, Jr. (Oglethorpe)
Joseph (Greene)
Joseph (Richmond)
Lenard (Oglethorpe)
Leonard (Oglethorpe)
Martain (Wilkinson)
Michal (Bulloch)
Moses (McIntosh)
Mrs. P. (Chatham)
Pierson (Washington)
Rebecca (Clarke)
Rebecca (Jefferson)
Robert (Hall)
Robert (Putnam)
Samuel (Wilkes)
Sarah (Columbia)
Thomas (Baldwin)
Thomas (2) (Chatham)
Thomas (McIntosh)
W. T. (Richmond)
Warren (Gwinnett)
Ways (Oglethorpe)
William (Columbia)
William (Hancock)
William (McIntosh)
William (Washington)
William (Wilkinson)
William A. (Washington)
William C. (Putnam)
Willis (Screven)
Zilphay (Burke)
Youngblood, Abraham (Burke)
Abraham (Columbia)
B. (Richmond)
Francis (Columbia)
Isaac (Hancock)
Isaac (Washington)

Youngblood, Jacob (Hancock)
    James, Jr. (Hancock)
    James, Sr. (Hancock)
    John (Columbia)
    John (Jones)
    Nathan (Hancock)
    Peter (Gwinnett)
    Polly (Columbia)
    Rebecca (Hancock)
    Thomas (Hancock)
    William L. (Hancock)

Z

Zachary, John (Jones)
    Lewis (Warren)

Zachry, Abner (Morgan)
    Clemntius R. (Morgan)
    James (Putnam)
    Jesse (Putnam)
    Sarah (Putnam)
Zackry, John L. (Columbia)
    William (Columbia)
Zallar, Jacob (Lincoln)
Zeigler, Emanuel (Effingham)
Zelanoi, Mrs. (Chatham)
Zenotte, J. (Richmond)
Zeolner, Andrew (Lincoln)
    John (Lincoln)
Zeolour, George (Lincoln)
Zettrour, Godlief (Effingham)
    Gotlieb (Effingham)

    Solomon (Effingham)
Ziegle(r), David (Effingham)
Zimmerman, Bernard (Wilkes)
Zinn, E. (Richmond)
    H. (Richmond)
    Valentine (Richmond)
Ziperer, John (Chatham)
Zipperer, Christian (Effingham)
    Emanuel (Effingham)
    Jonothon (Effingham)
* ___Phoebe (Effingham)
Zuber, Daniel (Oglethorpe)
    Emanuel (Oglethorpe)

*Zoucks see Soucks

(167)

www.ingramcontent.com/pod-product-compliance
Lightning Source LLC
Chambersburg PA
CBHW061740270326
41928CB00011B/2320